Yacht Design Explained

A SAILOR'S GUIDE TO THE PRINCIPLES
AND PRACTICE OF DESIGN

Yacht Design Explained

A SAILOR'S GUIDE TO THE PRINCIPLES AND PRACTICE OF DESIGN

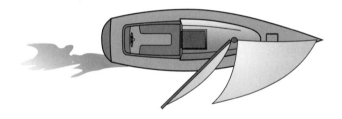

STEVE KILLING
DOUGLAS HUNTER

W·W·NORTON

NEW YORK · LONDON

For information about permission to reproduce selections from this book, write to
Permissions, W. W. Norton & Company, Inc., 500 Fifth Avenue, New York, N.Y. 10110

Book design by Douglas Hunter
Cover photograph by Sharon Green

Library of Congress Cataloging-in-Publication Data

Killing, Steve.
    Yacht design explained : a sailor's guide to the principles and practice of
design / Steve Killing and Douglas Hunter.
            p.   cm.
    Includes bibliographical references and index.
    ISBN 0-393-04646–X
    1. Yachts—Design and construction.   I. Hunter, Doug, 1959–
II. Title.
VM331.K555   1998
623.8'1223–DC21   97-47120
                                              CIP
                                              Rev

W. W. Norton & Company, Inc., 500 Fifth Avenue, New York, N.Y. 10110
                http://www.wwnorton.com

W. W. Norton & Company Ltd., 10 Coptic Street, London WC1A 1PU

2 3 4 5 6 7 8 9 0

To my grandfather, Forrest, an architect who knew how to blend beauty with engineering.
To my parents, Beth and Vic, for their enthusiastic support of my chosen vocation.
To my own family, Margaret, Jonathan, and David, for sharing my passion for things that float.
—*S.K.*

acknowledgments

Thanks to:

George Cuthbertson, for providing the "summer job" that kindled my career in 1972.

George Hazen, for his continuing friendship and advice on all matters technical and marine.

Rob Mazza, Simon Slater, and **George Cuthbertson,** for allowing me to redraw their boats for this book.

Sharon Green, for her superb photos.

Bruce Parsons, Institute for Marine Dynamics, for his insight into the world of tank testing.

Bruce Hays and the staff at Proteus Engineering, for their support in modifying FastShip software to meet and exceed my needs.

Garth Wilson, of the National Museum of Science and Technology in Ottawa, for his insight into the *Vasa*.

—*S.K.*

Words of appreciation are in order for:

Our editor, **John Barstow,** who patiently (I think) waited for nearly three years as Steve and I tinkered and fiddled with this one-year project.

Pamela Benner, for her ruthless and efficient copyediting job.

Robin Brass of Robin Brass Studio, who continues to field my technical questions and never fails to steer me on a proper course.

My wife, **Debbie Christmas,** for continually saying, "Are you *still* working on that book?" without once implying there was something better I should be doing.

—*D.H.*

contents

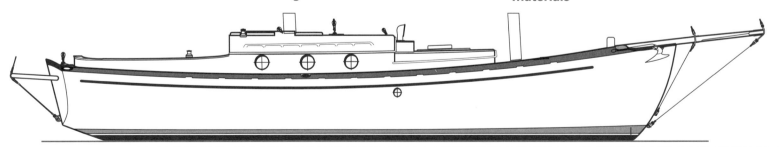

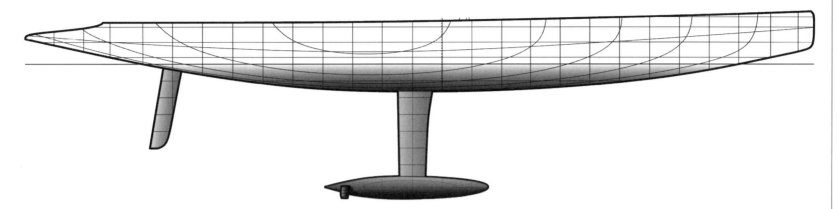

A guide to hull terminology

Many of the general terms employed in this book are shown on these views of a 40-foot sloop. More detailed terminology is explained within each chapter. See also the Glossary on page 247.

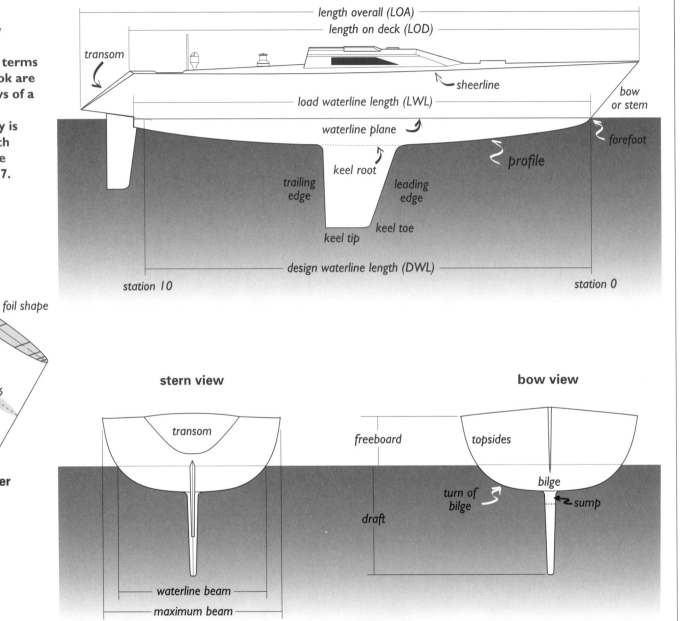

length overall (LOA)

length on deck (LOD)

transom

sheerline

bow or stem

load waterline length (LWL)

waterline plane

forefoot

keel root

profile

trailing edge

leading edge

keel tip

keel toe

design waterline length (DWL)

station 10

station 0

foil shape

span

chord length

keel and rudder

stern view

transom

bow view

freeboard

topsides

bilge

turn of bilge

sump

draft

waterline beam

maximum beam

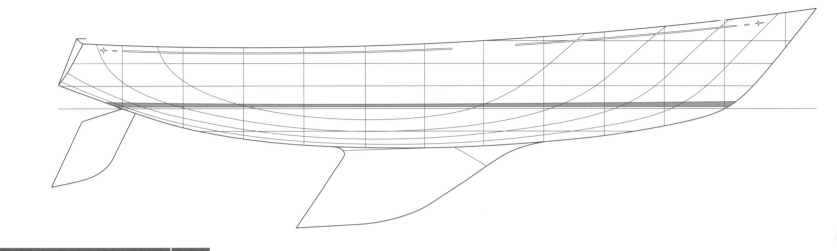

introduction

A modest mission statement:

to explain the science behind

the art of yacht design.

a practical response to a beautiful question

We set to work writing, designing, and illustrating *Yacht Design Explained* because there was a genuine need for a book that would inform the layperson, in an easily understandable way, of the principles and practices of yacht design. There is something magical about the way a sailboat works, but it shouldn't be *that* magical. Nor should it be impenetrably encased in jargon, half-truths, misconceptions, and wishful thinking. Sailboats behave the way they do for often elegantly simple reasons, but they often look the way they do for reasons that are not simple or elegant or sometimes even advisable.

A walk through any marina or yacht club in the off-season provokes an array of design questions. Why, for example, do these keelboats have such different rudders? Is one design really better than the rest?

More than two hundred years ago, renowned Swedish ship designer and builder Fredrik Chapman cast his gaze upon the seagoing world. "If we were to take a view of the immense number of ships that have been built since mankind first began to navigate upon the ocean," he proposed in 1775, "and note all the different steps which have been taken in improving their construction, we should at first sight be inclined to believe that the art of ship-building had, at length, been brought to the utmost perfection." Chapman more wisely believed that this was anything but the case, given the sheer diversity of design, construction, and rigging methods he had encountered. As a pioneer in tank testing and the mathematical analysis of hull forms, Chapman hoped that a perfect shape could be determined for each class of vessel afloat that would produce standardized configurations. Everything would be the same because nothing could be made any better, and certainly should not be made any worse.

Today, Chapman would surely be impressed by the progress made in the science of ship design, yet he would have to be struck by the plethora of hull shapes and rigs in sailing craft, even be forced to conclude that the search he had helped launch for an ideal form was, thus far, a complete failure. The evidence is in your yacht club or marina, each boat a living museum of design trends. Sailboats whose christenings span decades provide a wealth of contrasts and contradictions, and never more so than in the off-season, when yachts have been hauled out and stored in their cradles, immodestly exposing all their appendages. Far from yielding an ideal form, two centuries of inquisitiveness have brought forth still greater diversity. Even experienced sailors can be forgiven for their Chapman-like puzzlement. Why is the rudder hung below the waterline on this boat, and yet mounted on the transom on that boat? Why does this boat have a keel with lots of aft sweep, and that one a keel with no sweep at all? Why does that boat have a bow with a vertical stem, and this one a graceful curve and pronounced overhang? Why does the cross section of this boat's hull appear to be like a wine glass, and that boat's hull like a cereal bowl?

The overriding questions that come to mind are: among all the differences on display, is one approach better than the other? Or are we just seeing a crazy-quilt collection of yacht design's idiosyncratic moments, each with its own story to tell?

Some ideas do work better than others, but you must define "better at what" before choosing a winner. Features that work fantastically on one boat would be disastrous on another, because boats are designed for different purposes. And yes, there is a crazy-quilt to ponder, underscoring the lesson that the history of yacht design is not a steady march of progress, but a tangle of competing, overlapping, and often contrary avenues of theory and practice. We will try to provide as many answers as we can to the questions posed above.

A bit of cultural anthropology is required in answering these questions—we have to address the practices of sometimes isolated populations, incompatible belief systems, and technologies that reach from the space age back to the Stone Age. Anthropologists take pains not to be judgmental, not to label ideas or practices right or wrong, but rather "different." In writing about yacht design, though, it is often prudent and even imperative to say that one idea is better than another. But there is still plenty about the nature of boats that is neither right nor wrong but rather, as our field ethnologist studying the headhunters of the Amazon would conclude, different.

You can use science to explain why a design feature is wrong, or less than ideal, but you must also realize that, while modern yacht design employs science, this does not necessarily make it absolutely scientific, and it is all the richer for this. Rare, if not nonexistent, are craft that spring fully formed from a stream of calculations. Yacht design is definitely an art or craft, for few boats are launched without the designer making some effort to please the eye. Certain elements like sheerline and transom shape obey some underlying practical criteria, but to a large degree aesthetics are in charge—these elements look the way they do because we want them to. Why we want them to is another matter, for yacht design can be a tail-chasing exercise. Is beauty the child of function—if we set out to make something that works well, will it end up looking handsome? If we believe that, then we might also believe that things we find beautiful, even if we don't understand them, are a particular shape because practicality made them that way.

If you cannot agree wholeheartedly, then you will likely agree instead that sometimes we impose on ourselves things that are beautiful but not entirely practical. This is not necessarily a bad thing, but we are not always honest with ourselves about the trade-off we are making. A cutter rig might not make much practical sense on a small boat, but people do not go pleasure-boating for purely practical reasons—although they are wont to argue that they are doing just that when they make a rig selection that has more to do with conjuring a picturesque image of the traditional than satisfying sail management criteria.

The performance of a design cannot always be measured with a knotmeter alone. It is the designer's job sometimes to ensure the client gets the boat he wants in as sound a package as possible. At the end of the day, though, the designer can only hope to make the client understand the consequences of certain aesthetic decisions, and even make him understand that those decisions are purely aesthetic ones, have no underlying performance benefit, and indeed might even compromise performance. Designers must make

Notes on style

Who's talking now?
We have written this book for the most part with a collective viewpoint. However, there are points in the text—in particular Chapters 10 and 11—that demand a first-person narrative, as they draw on Steve Killing's personal design experience. Whenever you encounter the word "I," Steve is speaking.

Gender alert
Although sailing is a sport enjoyed by men and women alike, its language is not gender-neutral. As a result, we have resigned ourselves to using traditional terms such as *helmsman,* and masculine pronouns, rather than resorting to clumsy alternatives.

Measure for measure
The default measurement system in this book is imperial. Metric is used only when appropriate to a particular design rule. Conversion factors and values can be found on page 251.

extremely practical yachts at least a little beautiful, and extremely beautiful yachts at least sensibly practical.

Having distinguished beautiful from practical, we must also distinguish theoretical from practical. The science underlying yacht design can lead one to attempt all kinds of things that are terrific from a theoretical perspective, but which are nightmarish from a practical one. The theoretical can invite solutions that are too complex and/or too expensive to build, too difficult to manage, and even too dangerous to leave the dock with. The most efficient keel would have near-infinite draft (and have ballast of spent uranium), but try sailing it anywhere. A rig can similarly be highly efficient in generating horsepower, but be so complex to manage that a rival boat with a simpler, so-called less efficient rig can outperform it because its crew can keep theirs operating at peak efficiency while the high-tech wizards are overwhelmed by fine-tuning demands. In yacht design, the ideal is always answerable to the attainable and the manageable. Not to mention the beautiful.

The process of understanding yacht design occurs at two levels. The first is the underlying science that governs essential elements, such as the foil shape of a keel and the stability role of the centers of buoyancy and gravity. This science is hard at work no matter how good or bad a job the designer has done of creating a particular craft, and was hard at a work centuries before designers even knew what this science was. One of the fascinating and enlightening aspects of yacht design is applying this underlying science to ships of ages past, to understand—in a way the original designers and builders never could have—how their vessels were destined to behave. Sometimes, in the case of maritime disasters, the lessons can be sobering, as we bring to bear hindsight to grasp why a catastrophe occurred.

The second level is the culture of the particular boat being examined. The science can tell you how the boat performs, but it cannot tell you why the boat looks the way it does. The designer may have been studiously applying science as he drew the lines, or he might not have been applying much science at all. The intended use of the boat provoked a myriad choices in general shape and individual elements. A rating rule may have been forcing or compelling decisions that had nothing to do with what was truly fast, but rather with what a rule would think was slow—and therefore cheat the rule into assigning a rating lower than the boat deserved. If the boat were a custom commission for a particular owner, unique elements, or combinations of elements, would be expected. If the boat was intended to be mass-produced, then the builder was likely after a design that could appeal to as many people as possible, thereby encouraging compromises to avoid extremes.

When people look at yachts, they tend to divide them automatically into racers and cruisers. Yacht design has become unnecessarily polarized by the perception of two distinct camps. Racing boats should not tolerate speed or ratings contrivances over basic safety; cruising designs should not sacrifice attainable performance criteria through misinformed ideas about old ways being better ways. Both camps can benefit greatly from an understanding of design principles, and that is what we have set out to deliver here.

This book is not intended to allow readers to design their own boats, although a careful read will give you a fair idea of the issues involved. Nor does it tackle such burning design issues as how long a V-berth should be, or how many drawers can be stuffed into the galley of a 35-footer. Our hope is that you will gain a practical knowledge of yacht design in both theory and practice. Then perhaps you can decide if what is functional is also beautiful. And if what is beautiful is also functional.

—*Steve Killing and Douglas Hunter*

CHAPTER 1 hulls

The focal point of the design process, the hull is where all considerations of performance, practicality, and style begin and end.

in the beginning:
yacht designers log in

The earliest hull shapes fashioned by prehistoric naval architects are a matter of speculation, but I would envision as a likely prototype a fallen tree trunk offering a free ride downstream. It was a humble beginning with much opportunity for refinement. The stability of a cylindrical log is low, as neither its center of gravity nor its immersed shape changes as it rotates. A few kayak-like rolls would have enticed some damp and clever craftsman to reshape some trees in pursuit of a more seaworthy vessel.

The development from log to raft to canoe to ship saw design and construction knowledge progress in fitful jumps. Certainly over the centuries many vessels large and small have had to go to the bottom for ship design to make necessary advances. Progress could have come quicker were it not for a seriously compromising factor: the hard evidence for what went wrong ended up far from reach, on the bottom of some ocean, and many if not all witnesses had gone down with it. Perhaps it was this frustrating lack of data and firsthand reports that compelled scientists to tackle the essential mysteries of ship stability with mathematics rather than waiting for the forensic evidence to wash up on shore.

In any event, Sir Isaac Newton's *Principia* of 1687 compelled researchers in the Age of Enlightenment to seek out an ideal hull form based on his concept of a "solid of least resistance." This purely mathematical construct promised a perfect hull shape from the perspective of drag. Investigating this shape would keep theorists busy for the next two hundred years. (See Fig. 1.1.)

It proved to be a fruitless search, as William Froude's correct division of drag into frictional and wavemaking components in the late nineteenth century finally ruled out an ideal seagoing Newtonian form. But if Newton's perfect solution eventually proved not to exist for ship hulls, the pursuit of it helped drive the quest for knowledge that did prove practical.

Before the sixteenth century, little was known of ship design science; it was experience rather than theory that taught the shipbuilder (who was often the designer) what was fast and what was seaworthy. Experimentation was the only way to make a new ship better than the last, and sometimes progress wasn't progress at all. In 1697, Paul Hoste, a French Jesuit priest and professor of mathematics who was beginning to explore the new science that Newton's example inspired, wrote: "It cannot be denied that the art of constructing ships…is the least perfect of all the arts….The best constructors build the two principal parts of the ship viz., the bow and the stern, almost entirely by eye, whence it happens that the same constructor, building at the same time two ships after the same model, most frequently makes them so unequal, that they have quite opposite qualities."

Progress in the early days was at best a slow row against the current and at worst a fast tumble over a metaphoric Niagara Falls. One would hope that today's designers and builders have a clear view of the course of progress, and that learning moves in a more predictable, and less catastrophic, way. Unfortunately, the sinking, due to structural failure (thankfully with

The Dutch Republic was a maritime colossus in the seventeenth century. The powerful little trading nation combined its seaward focus with an affluent population to create some of the world's first pleasure yachts. The Dutch have handed down to us the very word "yacht," which derives from jaght, the term for the fast craft used to pursue pirates. Whether built for pleasure or commerce, the designs of Dutch vessels were no more scientific than those of craft anywhere else. Science did not take firm hold in ship design until the late nineteenth century.

DETAIL: *SHIPS IN THE ROADS* BY WILLEM VAN DE VELDE THE YOUNGER. COLLECTION: MAURITSHIUS MUSEUM, THE HAGUE no loss of life), of *OneAustralia* during the 1995 America's Cup challengers' series showed that, even with the latest scientific know-how on hand, we're still learning things the hard way.

Mishaps aside, there is no question that yacht design has made tremendous progress—not only since Newton's time, but over the last few decades. While some of the basic science in yacht design is centuries old, a large body of knowledge has emerged only in recent years, and is still emerging. There are aspects of yacht performance we cannot completely explain, especially in the realm of laminar and turbulent flow.

Navies and commercial traders who valued the design research inspired by Newton did so because they wanted warships and cargo vessels that operated at peak efficiency. With sail having given way to power in war and commerce, much of the impetus for ongoing research has come from high-tech racing events, in which individual campaign budgets have financed the investigations of hulls, foils, and rigs that have benefited sailors near and far, on and off the racecourse.

h ull length: is bigger really better?

Hull length has such an impact on the cost, usefulness, and speed of a boat that it should be one of the first decisions made by the designer and prospective owner. Certainly length permeates the mind-set of the purchaser and the production builder, infinitely more so than displacement or sail area. The length/price ratio of production boats can encourage absurd marketing strategies, with models given names that do not reflect their actual size. The boat advertised as a Blue Ocean 42 may actually be only 40 feet overall, but the name creates visions of safe and comfortable ocean passages at a reasonable price; 22 ▶

FIG 1.1
Newton's solid of least resistance

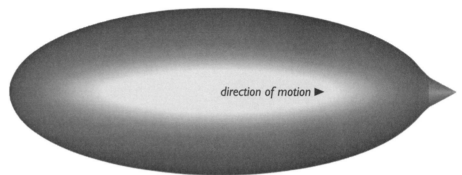

direction of motion ▶

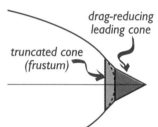

drag-reducing leading cone

truncated cone (frustum)

In his *Principia* of 1687, Sir Isaac Newton provided a mathematical blueprint for creating a shape he called the *solid of least resistance*. An ellipse with a circular cross section was capped by a *frustum* (a flat-topped cone), which was in turn capped by a cone. The diameter/length (d/L) ratio of the body could vary; we have shown it above at 2.75. Newton believed such a form would produce the least amount of drag when moving point-first through water. Wrote Newton: "This proposition I conceive may be of use in the building of ships." His "proposition" became a focal point of ship design research, but the idea of a perfect form ultimately proved imperfect. Current research into submerged objects like keel bulbs has produced a far different, blunt-nosed low-drag shape, as shown below at the same d/L ratio.

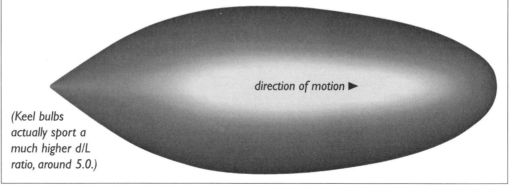

direction of motion ▶

(Keel bulbs actually sport a much higher d/L ratio, around 5.0.)

Reading the lines

A hull's shape is described with an illustration known as a *lines drawing*. The drawing shows the boat from three views: from the side (the *profile drawing*), the bottom (the *plan view*), and split fore and aft (the *body plan*). The three-dimensional hull is translated into two-dimensional measurements by slicing it in three directions. These slices are called *waterlines*, *buttock lines*, and *stations*.

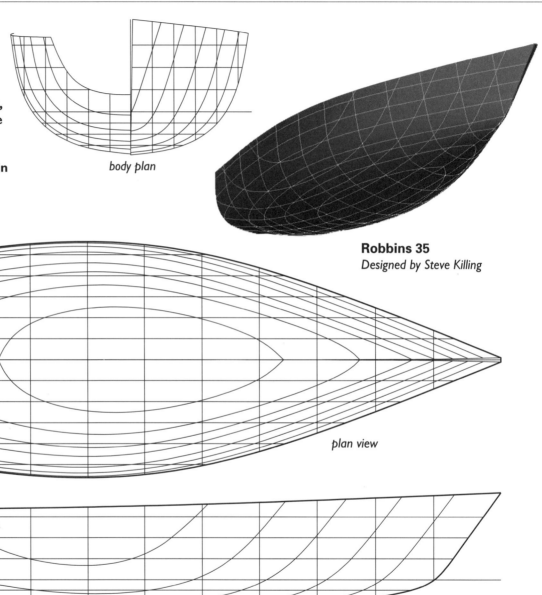

body plan

Robbins 35
Designed by Steve Killing

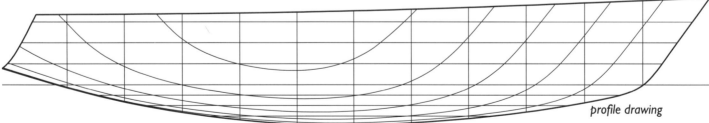

plan view

profile drawing

Stations

Stations describe the sectional shape of the hull at evenly spaced points along its length. They generally begin and end at the extremes of the waterline, although additional stations can be positioned beyond the waterline, to help describe bow and stern overhangs. They are numbered from bow to stern.

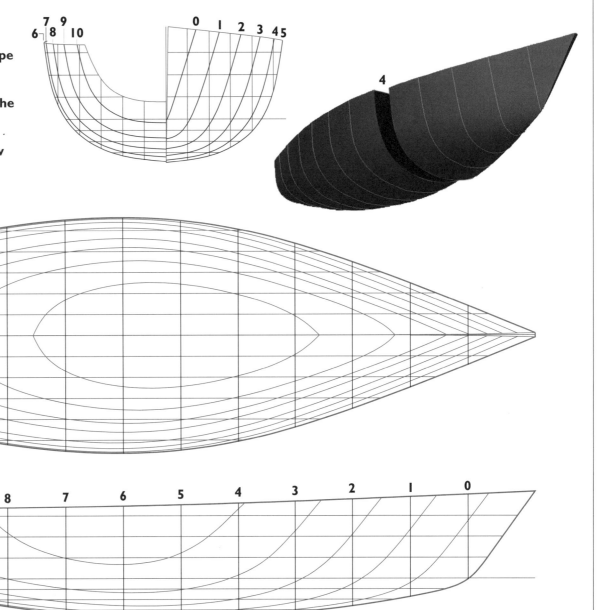

Waterlines

Waterlines slice the hull from top to bottom parallel to the *design waterline (DWL),* the plane on which the designer intends the boat to float. As the primary fairing lines, they are spaced above and below DWL at convenient intervals —in this case at 12 inches above DWL, 6 inches below DWL. They are labeled according to their distance from DWL.

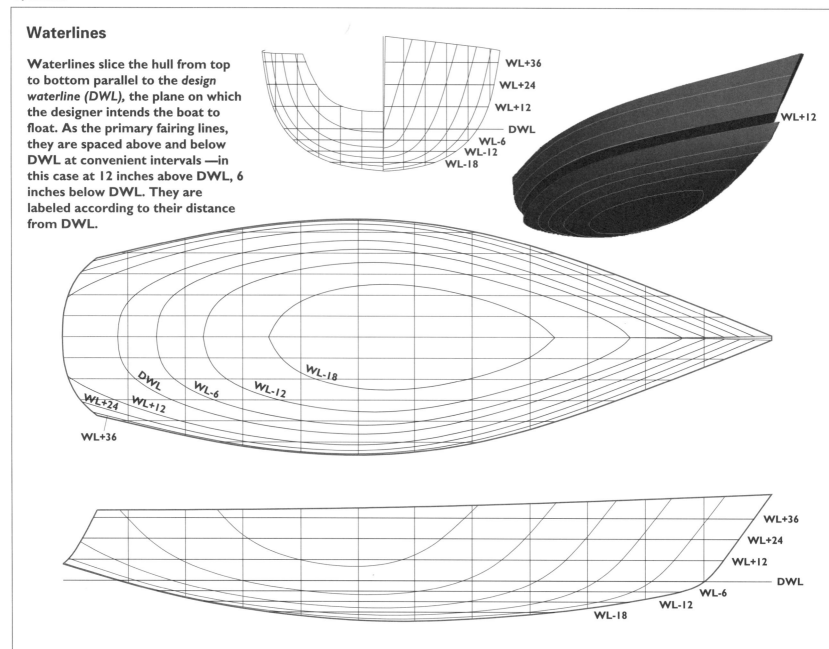

Buttock lines

Buttock lines slice the hull from bow to stern, parallel to the *centerline (C/L)*. They are spaced to either side of the centerline at intervals that ensure the fairness of the hull (particularly below the waterline)—in this case at 12 inches. They are labeled according to their distance from C/L.

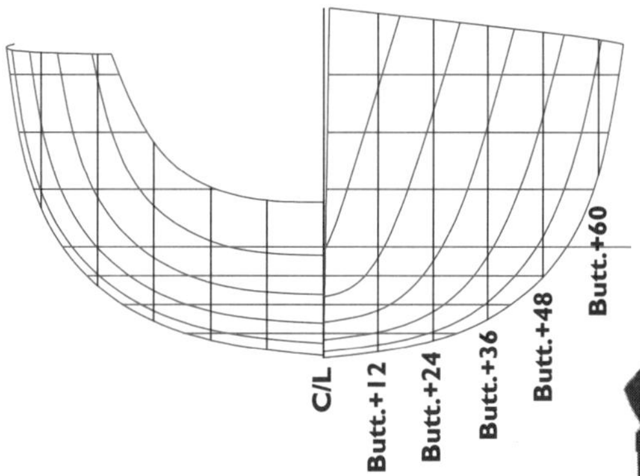

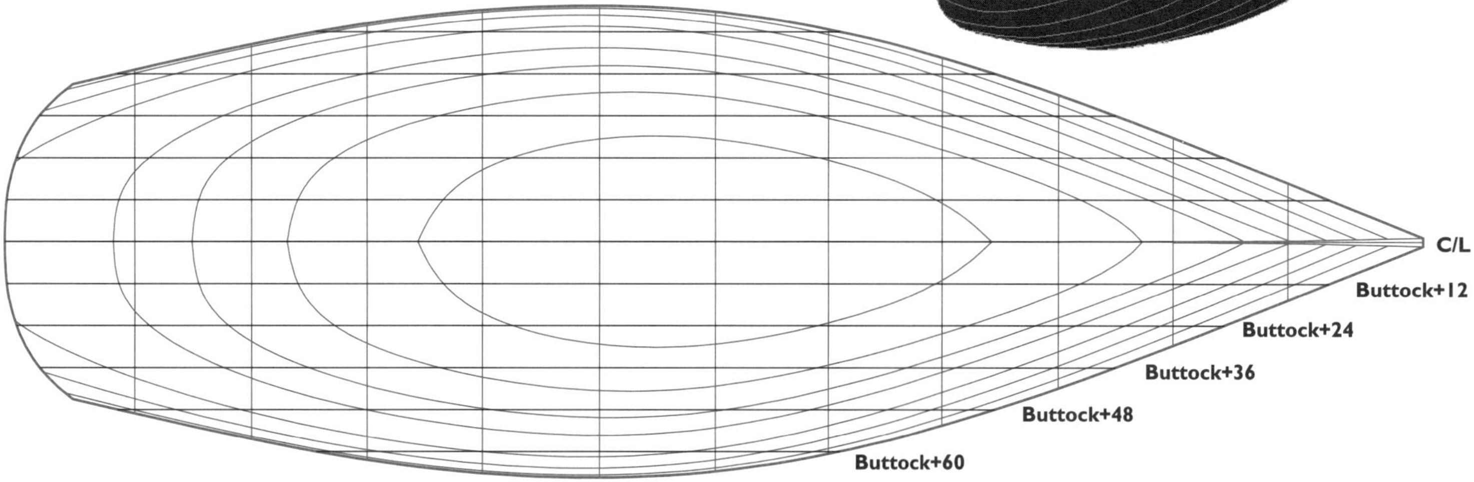

Butt.+48

C/L
Butt.+12
Butt.+24
Butt.+36
Butt.+48
Butt.+60

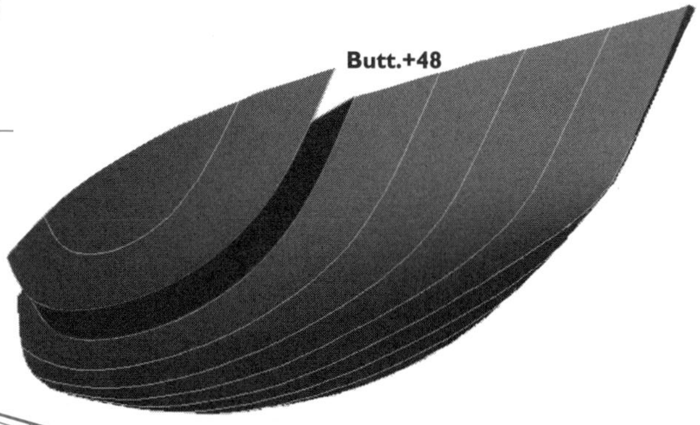

C/L
Buttock+12
Buttock+24
Buttock+36
Buttock+48
Buttock+60

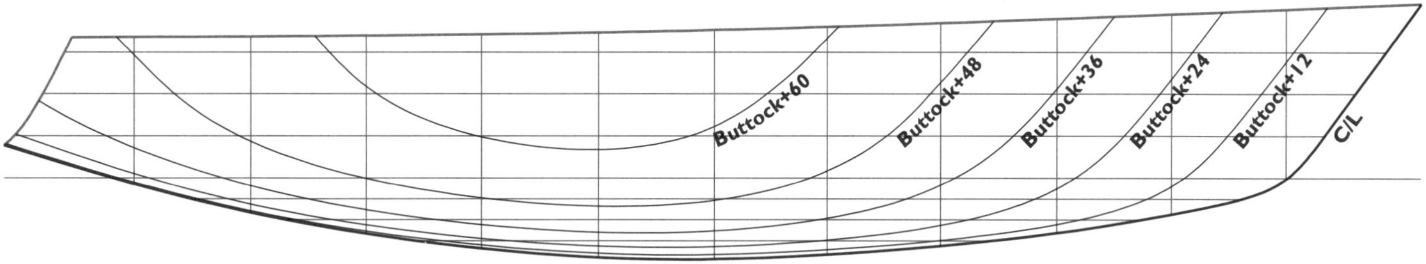

Buttock+60
Buttock+48
Buttock+36
Buttock+24
Buttock+12
C/L

There is no ideal size for a racing yacht. Factors such as competitive forums, crew availability, and campaign budgets mean bigger is not necessarily better.

◄ **17** conversely, the Zippy 38, actually 40 feet over-all, is promoted as a "fast boat for its length." Of course, it's easy to be faster than all the 38-footers when your boat is 2 feet longer.

The marketing-wizard reasoning behind this tape-measure tomfoolery is sometimes too convoluted to comprehend. The important thing is that the length of a boat—real or imagined—is critical to a buyer's per-ception of its value. But the initial purchase cost is only the first of many expenditures related to the length of the boat. Still to be considered are the expense of transporting it, covering it for the winter, renting space for it (by the foot) at the marina, caring for its sails, and feeding its guests.

The obvious benefit of a large boat is the space it contains. It is just like a large house: there is more room for comfortable living, more space in which occupants can be alone (often an important factor one week into a close-quarters cruise), and more room for food and supplies. There are instances, though, when longer doesn't mean better. A 40-foot sailboat can be much more difficult to handle than a 30-footer. The area and weight of the sails increase, which means that not only are they more difficult to carry up on the deck and hoist, but sheeting them in also requires greater force. Jobs like moving the traveler to windward, which can be done by hand on a small boat, require a winch on a larger boat. A retired couple might appreciate the below-deck amenities of a larger boat, but could find sailing it overwhelming or at least tiring and inconve-nient. And with a larger boat, even the cruising ground is surprisingly altered. The larger boat often will expand the territory, since longer voyages are now possible on larger bodies of water. But what happens when the boat arrives at its destination? A 45-foot cruiser, while spa-cious and fast, won't be able to enter many fine little anchorages due to the increased depth of its keel.

For every sailor there is an ideal boat length. Many cruisers find that a boat in the range of 35 to 39 feet offers the best trade-off: small enough to be ably handled by one or two, but large enough that a family of four may cruise with some comfort.

For racers, the decision on size is complicated by seemingly infinite considerations of the kind of racing they find attractive. Invariably, the bigger the boat, the bigger the budget that is required to keep campaign-ing. Sometimes competitive sailors tire of the hassles and expense of major keelboat campaigns and decide to focus on the quality of racing, which leads them to downsize into used J/24s or Etchells-22s. Saving money is not the only impetus here: sometimes the difficulty of maintaining a large, cohesive, and trained crew drives them into a boat that requires only three or four people to race. This is no solution for sailors hooked on long-distance ocean racing, and many competitors aren't looking for a solution at all. In handicap racing, there will always be a certain charisma to having the "scratch" boat—the largest or fastest yacht in the fleet, and some racers will only ever be satisfied knowing they have the boat that will be first to finish, regardless how its final position works out on corrected time. Essentially, boat size for racing sailors is a matter of personal preference of racing format, the ability to shoulder a campaign budget, and the ability or desire to manage a standing crew.

making waves: length and performance

No matter how clever the designer or how competent the sailor, there is no more significant way of raising the ultimate speed of a displacement sailboat than increasing the length, as the two are directly related. One rule of thumb suggests that the maximum speed of a boat (or "hull speed," as many call it) is equal to 1.34 times the square root of the waterline length. The term "hull speed" is rather deceiving, as it implies that for each boat there is a fixed speed that cannot be exceeded. Anyone who has sailed through a summer squall knows this is not the case—a boat on a broad reach will always go a little faster if the wind speed increases. And any designer with some level of confidence will assert that he can create a boat faster "for its length" than any other. Other factors—the keel, the shape and fairness of the hull, the sail area, and the weight—influence the boat's performance and render the 1.34 factor an estimate only. That said, there is something to be learned from the simple approximation. If not irrevocably bound by it, speed is definitely

proportional to the square root of the waterline length. If a designer takes one of his designs and increases its length, an increase in speed does follow.

It seems rather mysterious that a number as unintuitive as 1.34 somehow ties the length of a boat to its potential speed. The mystery ends when one examines the behavior of water, for the physics of wave generation has a profound influence on the ultimate speed of a boat. (See Fig. 1.2.)

Before analyzing waves generated by a hull, it is important to observe natural waves on lakes or oceans. Small waves created by light winds move along at a slow but predictable pace. (It's worth noting that the waves, not the actual water, do the moving, much like a wave can move along an outstretched rope.) 26 ▶

Above: the Express 35, designed by author Steve Killing. Many couples find that a yacht in the 35- to 39-foot range best suits their cruising needs: large enough to provide the desired accommodations, but not too large for two adults to handle.

FIG. 1.2
Hull speed and the length of waves

Why do all displacement sailboats have a theoretical maximum hull speed governed by the number 1.34? The answer lies in the property of waves.

The speed of travel of a wave is determined by the distance between its crests (or any other two points in the same position of the wave cycle), which is known as a *wavelength*. The square root of the wavelength (in feet) multiplied by 1.34 gives the wave speed (in knots).

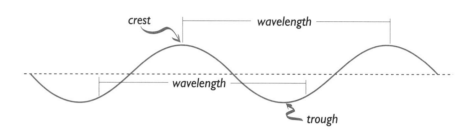

This custom 38-foot schooner, designed by author Steve Killing, shows how wave speed determines boat speed.

As a boat moves, it generates its own waves, at the bow and stern. The bow wave is the main indicator of speed. Below, the boat is generating a bow wave with a wavelength of 17.5 feet. The square root of this distance, multiplied by 1.34, gives a wave speed of 5.6 knots. Because the wave is being generated by the boat's forward motion, this is also the speed of the boat itself.

$$S = \sqrt{WL} \times 1.34$$

S: speed of wave (in knots)
WL: wavelength (in feet)

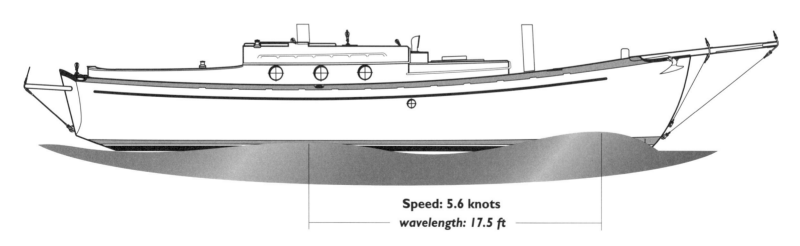

Speed: 5.6 knots
wavelength: 17.5 ft

As a boat's speed increases, the bow wave correspondingly lengthens until it forms one wave cycle with the stern wave. The wavelength is now 32 feet, the same as the boat's waterline length. With no more room for expansion of the bow/stern wavelength, maximum theoretical hull speed has been reached. The square root of 32 feet, multiplied by 1.34, yields a speed of 7.6 knots.

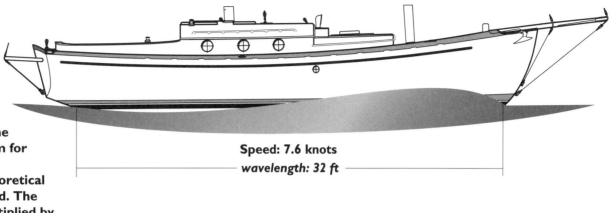

Speed: 7.6 knots
wavelength: 32 ft

Why does waterline length limit hull speed? If the boat goes any faster, the bow wave stretches back beyond the waterline measurement (in this scenario to a wavelength of 40 feet) so that its trough is near the stern. The lack of buoyant support causes the stern to drop and the boat to take on an "uphill" stance. More power than the average displacement sailboat's rig can generate is required for it to climb the bow wave and go any faster. Substantial engine power is needed to push this boat to 8.5 knots—0.9 knot more than its theoretical maximum hull speed.

While the waterline length calculation is a good indicator of potential hull speed, boats can be designed to surpass their theoretical hull speed without having to resort to auxiliary power. Hull fullness aft provides extra buoyancy, preventing the stern from squatting as the bow-wave trough moves back, thereby extending the boat's speed range.

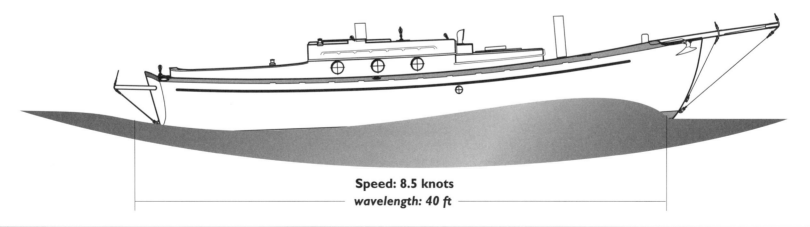

Speed: 8.5 knots
wavelength: 40 ft

FIG. 1.3
Hull volume and sailing length

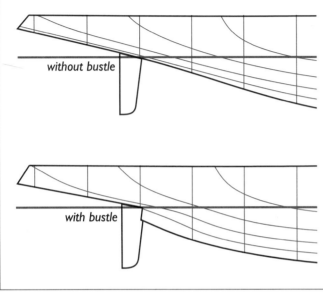

without bustle

with bustle

A 12-Meter hull shows how a "bustle," a swelling of the hull forward of the rudder, increases effective sailing length. The additional volume gives buoyant support to the stern as the yacht approaches hull speed, and the trough of the bow wave moves aft. This volume prevents the hull from "squatting" and allows the boat to exceed its theoretical hull speed.

◄ **23** Wave motion is the result of energy transferred from the wind.) After the wind has had a chance to build the waves to a greater height and longer length, they are no longer traveling at a sedate pace. Moreover, their speed is directly related to the spacing of the crests. The speed of a wave (in knots) equals 1.34 times the square root of the distance (in feet) between the crests. So, the speed-length relationship of hulls somehow is directly related to one of the properties of water. But why does wave speed and its numerical governor of 1.34 influence the speed of a boat?

Close observation of the waves along the side of a boat tells the tale. A boat creates waves of its own, at both ends. As the bow cuts through the water, the volume of the forward part of the boat pushes a wave out to the side. The troughs and crests of this bow wave travel aft along the side of the boat until they meet up

with the stern wave, which has been created by the water rising up from under the hull. At low speeds, there may be several cycles to the bow wave before it reaches the stern. However, as the speed of the boat increases, the size and length of the bow wave also increase, until the critical point is reached at which the bow-wave length (the distance between crests) equals the waterline length.

Now the boat is in an awkward situation. If the boat's speed increases further, then the bow wave, as it continues to lengthen, leaves a trough exactly where the stern of the boat needs support. The stern drops into this trough and the entire boat takes on an uphill stance. For many boaters, this is not a revelation—they have felt this bow-up attitude when under auxiliary power, with no sail forces influencing the trim. If the boat is a displacement design (more on planing boats later) and the engine is pressed to its upper limit, the boat will gain little speed as the transom begins to bury in the water. A hull is going just about as fast as it can when the waterline length is in sync with the crest-to-crest length of the bow wave. In other words, the bow wave and stern wave have become one wave cycle, with a single trough separating the crests at the bow and stern. The beginning of the "squat" happens when the crest-to-crest length of the waves exceeds the waterline length and the trough moves into the territory of the stern. Therein lies the reason to estimate maximum boat speed as equal to the speed of a wave whose length is equal to the waterline.

Designers are always trying to improve both the top-end and the light-air speed of their boats. Maximum speed, while governed roughly by the length of the waterline, can be influenced to a great extent by hull shape. In particular, the amount of volume placed just forward of the rudder has a big influence on the "effective length" of the hull. *Effective length*, a term now used in many velocity prediction programs, establishes the potential speed of the boat. It takes into account the volume of the boat at each station along its length. A boat with a larger aft end will have a longer effective length. Our discussion of waves along the side of the boat makes the obvious link—a deeper afterbody will supply more buoyancy and therefore the stern will drop less into the trough of the bow wave when moving at hull speed.

Olin Stephens of Sparkman & Stephens was one of the first designers to put this knowledge to good use by adding a "bustle," as it came to be known, just forward of the rudder of the America's Cup 12-Meter *Intrepid* in 1967. (See Fig. 1.3.) With a racing rule that limited the waterline length, it was particularly important to increase the effective length without altering the actual waterline length. (See Chapter 10 on the America's Cup for more on this.)

level and heeled: symmetry's deception

Sailboats surely are unique among objects created by humankind in that they are perceived and even created in one configuration but employed in another. Like a powerboat, a sailboat is designed and viewed "at rest"—perfectly level, sitting obediently on its waterline, its volume distributed symmetrically to port and starboard. A sailboat takes on an entirely different attitude when it is actually sailing. Except when running downwind, a sailboat is heeled, and asymmetry comes into play. The symmetrical lozenge of the waterline plane becomes distorted as areas of the hull that were below the water when the boat was at rest rise above it, and vice versa. Total wetted surface changes dramatically, and it changes further as fore-and-aft trim is adjusted while underway. (See Fig. 1.4.) Designers must work these changes to their advantage—and help the

sailor capitalize on the ability to make such changes as the boat sails in different conditions. A sailboat is a dynamic entity, and it is the designer's task to anticipate those dynamics and wherever possible to optimize them when creating the "at rest" version.

The changes in a design's characteristics are not always for the better once the boat starts sailing. In particular, hulls that are very wide aft and narrow forward above the waterline lift the stern and drop the bow as they heel. (Such a configuration would be found in a design with a fine entry for cutting through flat water, and enhanced beam aft at the deck level to move crew weight outboard.) Because the bow drops, the forefoot gets a better bite on the water, and the hull's center of lift moves forward. These side effects of heeling increase weather helm just when the sailor doesn't want it. Another detrimental effect of raising the aft end is loss of rudder control. A rudder that is lifted partially out of the water has a direct loss in area, but it also loses efficiency as the top of the rudder breaks the surface. (See Chapter 4 for more.) All in all, boats like this, which might make great sense from the perspective of a particular rating rule or a narrow performance window, can be nightmarish to handle.

A shape that becomes very asymmetric as it heels also affects the helm because of its curvature. Canoeists who want to increase the speed of a turn heel the boat to the outside of the turn, immersing the curved shape of the boat in the water to augment its cornering ability. Similarly, when a sailboat heels it wants to turn into the wind, following the curvature of the hull on the leeward side. (Part of the technique of *roll-tacking* a boat in light winds involves shifting crew weight to heel the boat to leeward so that the boat's shape helps the tack begin.)

Many boats exhibit a wholesale loss in sailing length as the wind presses them over. A boat with ample beam and short overhangs will lift 32 ▶

Waterline words

A yacht's waterline is defined several different ways, and these definitions can overlap and be somewhat confusing. Here's a field guide to terminology:

DWL: refers to *design waterline length*. This is the measurement on the lines plan, customarily between stations 0 and 10, and is often used for rating purposes. Additional waterlines spaced above and below it are used for lofting. (See page 20.)

LWL: refers to *load waterline length*. This is the plane along which the boat floats, measured along the centerline. This dimension depends on whether the boat is floating in fresh water or salt water. Boats float higher in salt water, due to its higher density, and therefore will exhibit a shorter LWL than when they are in fresh water. In some cases the LWL includes the skeg and even the rudder. An LWL that includes the rudder chord length does not reflect the actual speed potential of the hull; nor should it be used in calculating prismatic coefficient. (See page 55.)

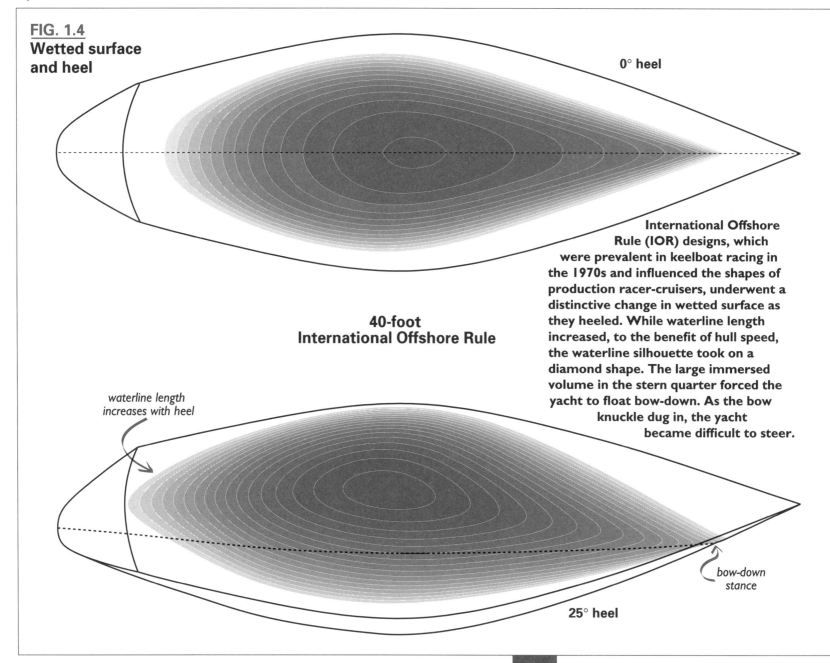

FIG. 1.4
Wetted surface and heel

0° heel

40-foot International Offshore Rule

International Offshore Rule (IOR) designs, which were prevalent in keelboat racing in the 1970s and influenced the shapes of production racer-cruisers, underwent a distinctive change in wetted surface as they heeled. While waterline length increased, to the benefit of hull speed, the waterline silhouette took on a diamond shape. The large immersed volume in the stern quarter forced the yacht to float bow-down. As the bow knuckle dug in, the yacht became difficult to steer.

waterline length increases with heel

bow-down stance

25° heel

62-foot 12-Meter
(International Rule)

0° heel

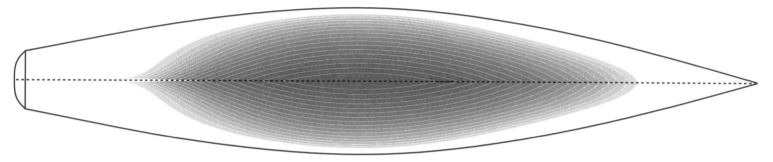

Author Steve Killing's 12-Meter design *True North I* demonstrates a Meter boat's significant redistribution of wetted surface when heeled. The long overhangs of this International Rule design greatly increase the waterline length when the boat heels, giving the boat a higher potential hull speed than would be indicated by the rated waterline, measured when the boat is level.

increased waterline length

25° heel

increased waterline length

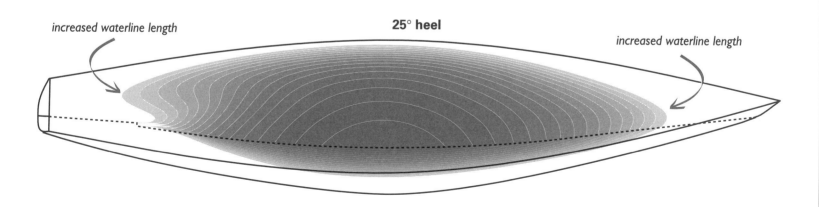

38-foot cruiser

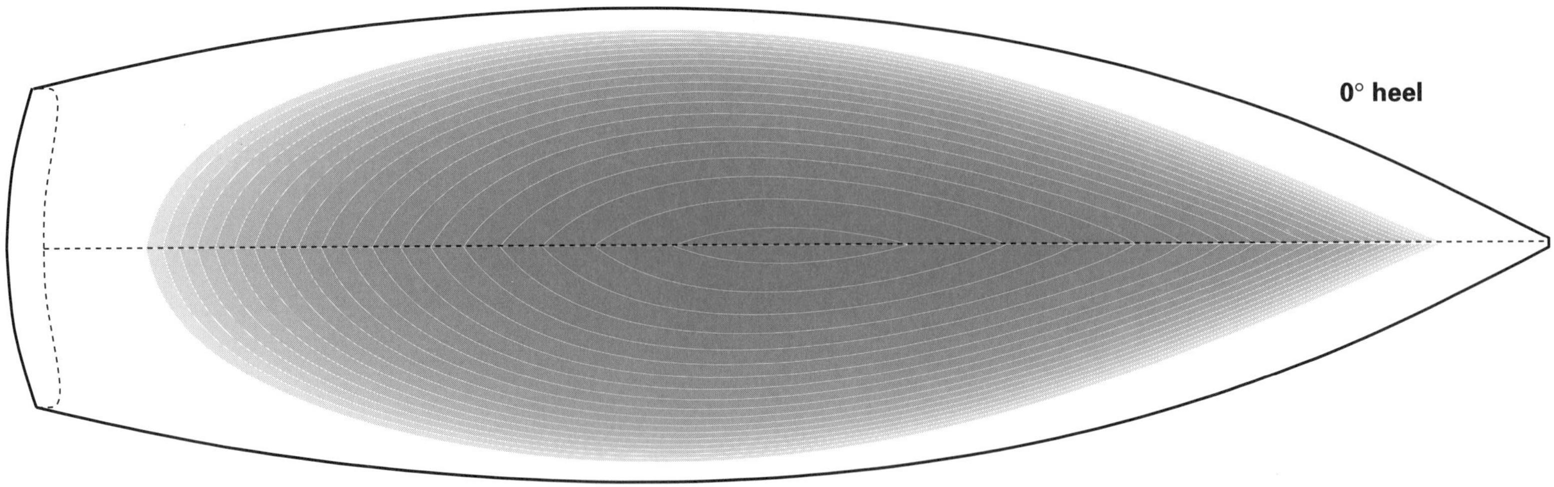

0° heel

With no rating rules to satisfy, the designer of a cruising yacht aims to create a hull shape that is seakindly while striking an acceptable balance between interior volume and all-round performance. No dramatic distortions of the immersed volume should appear as the boat heels. The waterline length of this 38-footer increases beneficially, and the wetted surface shape is free of extreme characteristics that would adversely affect handling.

waterline length increases with heel

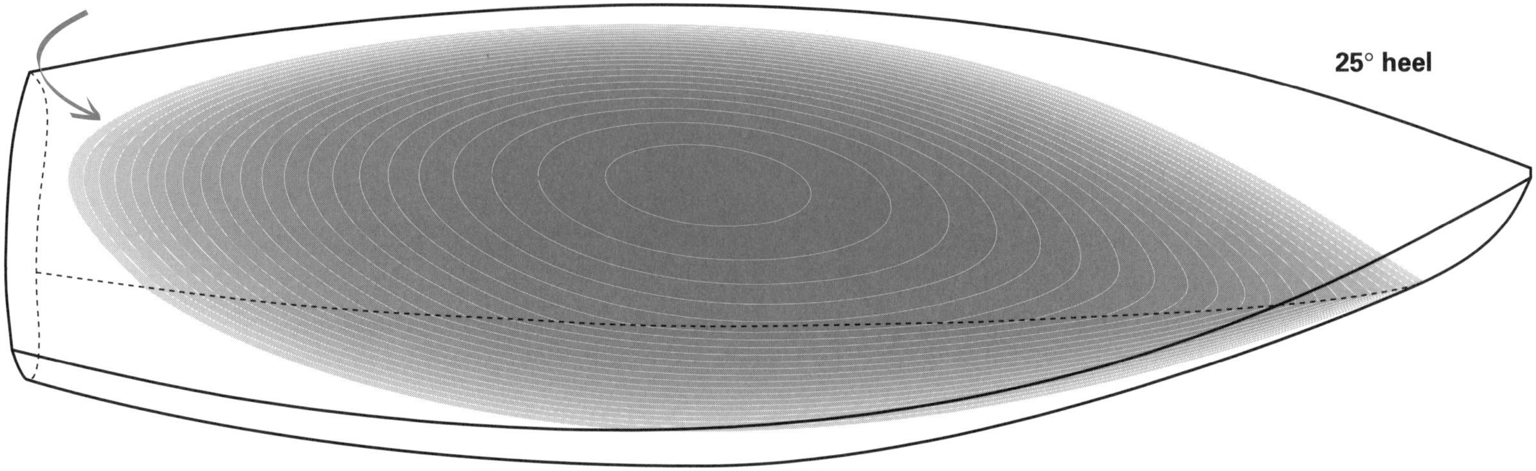

25° heel

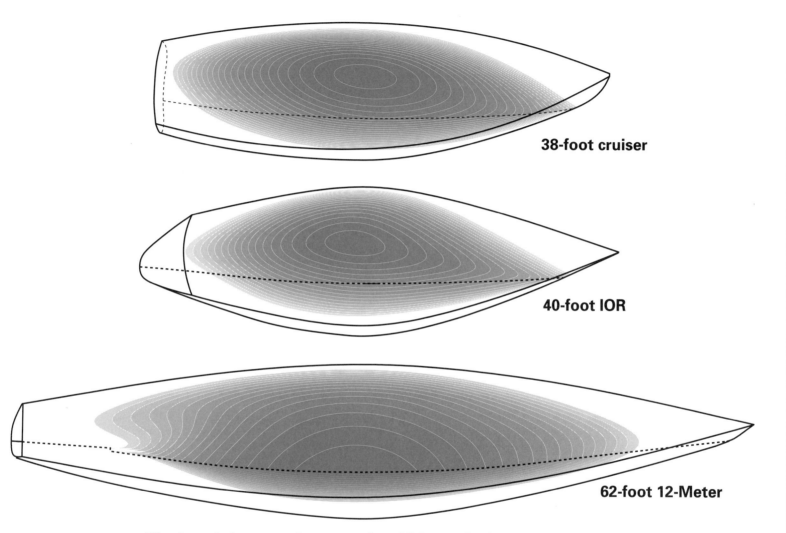

38-foot cruiser

40-foot IOR

62-foot 12-Meter

The three design types, shown to scale at 25 degrees heel, reveal the distinct characteristics of their immersed shapes when underway. The full-bodied cruiser shows the least distortion, having no rating rule to influence its shape. The IOR design displays a typical diamond-shaped waterline and bow-down stance. The 12-Meter illustrates the extreme gains in waterline length of International Rule designs.

International America's Cup Class yachts in a fleet race produce vivid wave trains on a close reach. As hull speed increases, wavemaking drag claims a higher proportion of overall resistance than frictional drag. See page 36.

◀ **27** up bodily, thereby shortening its effective length and so reducing potential speed. These boats will benefit when sailed at a conservative 20 to 25 degrees of heel rather than at the oft perceived-to-be-fast heel angle of 30 degrees.

Narrow boats with long, shallow overhangs behave in a totally different way. Whether upright or heeled, these sailboats sink lower in the water as their speed increases. As the trough of the bow wave moves toward the middle of the hull, buoyant support is lost and the entire boat sinks to further immerse the ends, increasing the effective length. The longer and shallower the overhangs are, the greater is the benefit. This length increase in turn pushes the bow and stern waves farther apart, raising the maximum potential speed beyond what one would expect based on the static waterline length.

Keeping the measured waterline short and employing long overhangs is a clever technique if the measurement of waterline length (or some length near the waterline) is used in a particular rating rule as a speed indicator. The design types in Fig. 1.4 illustrate how, even without considering the effect of sinking due to the wave trough in the center of the boat, waterline length increases with heel. But if there is no rating or racing benefit to keeping the waterline short, then extremely long overhangs are not a quality often sought in a design. It would be better to keep the overall length of the boat the same and lengthen the waterline.

the canary sings: prismatic coefficient

The sailing characteristics of a design depend in part on the "fullness" of its ends, or how volume is distributed fore and aft. One indication of relative fullness in the ends is *prismatic coefficient (Cp)*. (See Fig. 1.6.) A numerical canary in the coal mine, the "prismatic" compares the volume of the hull to the volume of an odd-shaped benchmark hull whose midsection shape extends right to the ends of the waterline.

A supertanker might have a prismatic of 0.9, indicating its shape is very close to a rectangular box. This is fine for a floating cargo carrier being shoved along by powerful diesels, whose performance is judged by how much barley it can carry in one trip, but it's not desirable for a sailboat. A very fine-ended sailboat might have a prismatic of 0.45, but it is unusual for a sailboat to have a prismatic outside the range of 0.50 to 0.60. A low value of 0.50 to 0.53 indicates a hull that would excel in light air but would be limited in its maximum speed, lacking fullness aft. The normal range for an all-round boat is 0.53 to 0.57, while 0.60 would be targeting heavy-air conditions. The effect of increasing volume aft can be seen in the 12-Meter shown in Fig. 1.3. Without a bustle, it has a prismatic of 0.525. The bustle raises the prismatic substantially, to 0.555.

There is an important relationship between a hull's prismatic and its *center of buoyancy:* the center of buoyancy is the center of the underwater volume of the hull, which by definition must be directly below the hull's *center of gravity*. If the designer creates a hull with its largest section placed well aft of the midlength of the waterline, then the center of buoyancy is well aft. A boat with its maximum beam at 60 percent of the waterline (not an uncommon spot) might have its center of buoyancy at 53 percent.

Designers have realized (with some intuition) that the combination of a center of buoyancy that is pushed aft and a high prismatic is not good. It means there is an inordinate amount of volume packed in the back end of the boat—the high prismatic indicates that there is a lot of volume in the ends of the boat, and the aft location of the center of buoyancy further indicates that much of this extra volume is in the back end. **36 ▶**

FIG. 1.5
Prismatic coefficient and center of buoyancy

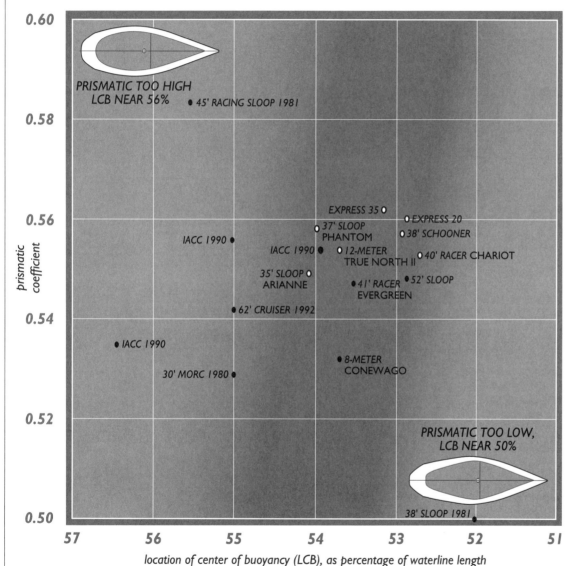

0.60

PRISMATIC TOO HIGH
LCB NEAR 56% ● 45' RACING SLOOP 1981

0.58

0.56

EXPRESS 35 ○
● 37' SLOOP   ○ EXPRESS 20
PHANTOM   ○ 38' SCHOONER
IACC 1990 ●   ○ 12-METER   ○ 40' RACER CHARIOT
TRUE NORTH II
IACC 1990 ●
35' SLOOP ○   ● 52' SLOOP
ARIANNE   ● 41' RACER
EVERGREEN

0.54

● 62' CRUISER 1992

● IACC 1990

● 8-METER
CONEWAGO
30' MORC 1980 ●

0.52

PRISMATIC TOO LOW,
LCB NEAR 50%

0.50
38' SLOOP 1981 ●

prismatic coefficient

57   56   55   54   53   52   51

location of center of buoyancy (LCB), as percentage of waterline length

Prismatic coefficient (see Fig. 1.6) is used to assess how full or how fine a hull's ends are, based on its total immersed volume and its midsection shape. However, the prismatic value cannot tell you how that volume is distributed fore and aft. Designers look at the position of the center of buoyancy to provide clues. If a design has a high prismatic value and a center of buoyancy positioned well aft along the waterline length, a large amount of the immersed volume is in the stern. Some volume aft is beneficial in increasing the effective sailing length, but too much volume will cause excessive drag. A design with a low prismatic value and a center of buoyancy close to halfway along the waterline length will suffer by having insufficient volume aft to increase the effective sailing length.

This chart plots prismatic and center of buoyancy values for a variety of designs (Steve Killing's designs are marked with a white circle). The desirable range for these values is contained within the dark blue band.

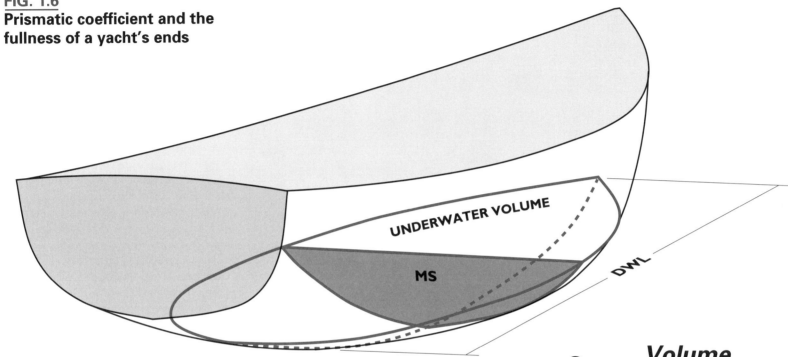

FIG. 1.6
Prismatic coefficient and the fullness of a yacht's ends

UNDERWATER VOLUME

MS

DWL

$$Cp = \frac{Volume}{MS \times DWL}$$

A signature characteristic of design types is prismatic coefficient (Cp), a tool used to assess the fullness of a yacht's ends. The calculation can serve as a mathematical warning to the designer when a potential hull shape is falling outside a desired performance envelope.

To calculate the prismatic coefficient of a particular hull, you must determine its underwater volume, as this coefficient provides a quick assessment of how that volume is distributed. Next, you need to know the maximum cross-sectional area of the underwater volume, which is usually located just aft of the middle of the boat. Finally, you need to know the waterline length. From there the math is simple. The waterline length is multiplied by the cross-sectional area, and the result is divided into the underwater volume.

Volume: hull volume under the waterline (in cubic feet)

MS: maximum cross-sectional area of underwater volume (in square feet)

DWL: length of the design waterline (in feet)

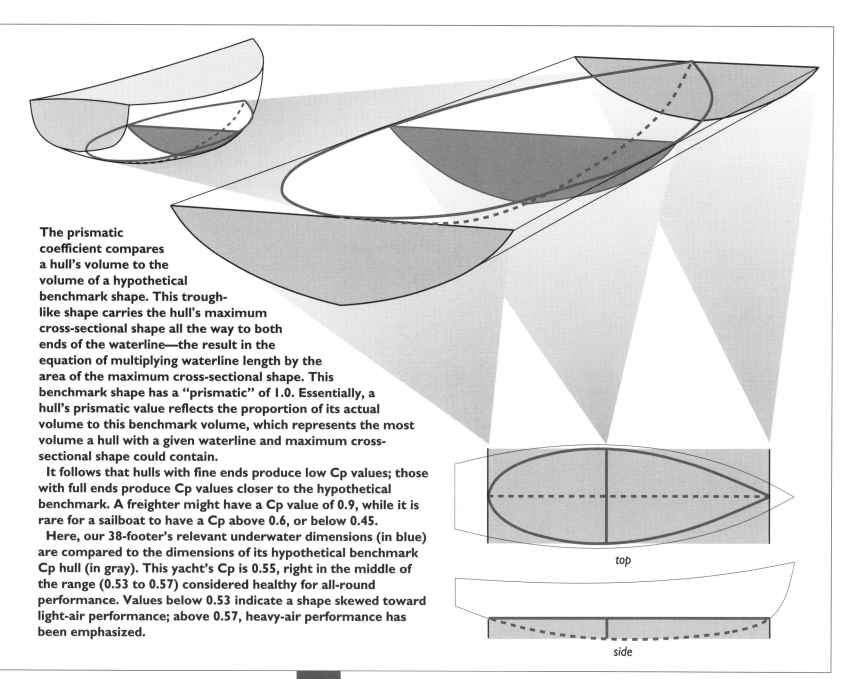

The prismatic coefficient compares a hull's volume to the volume of a hypothetical benchmark shape. This trough-like shape carries the hull's maximum cross-sectional shape all the way to both ends of the waterline—the result in the equation of multiplying waterline length by the area of the maximum cross-sectional shape. This benchmark shape has a "prismatic" of 1.0. Essentially, a hull's prismatic value reflects the proportion of its actual volume to this benchmark volume, which represents the most volume a hull with a given waterline and maximum cross-sectional shape could contain.

It follows that hulls with fine ends produce low Cp values; those with full ends produce Cp values closer to the hypothetical benchmark. A freighter might have a Cp value of 0.9, while it is rare for a sailboat to have a Cp above 0.6, or below 0.45.

Here, our 38-footer's relevant underwater dimensions (in blue) are compared to the dimensions of its hypothetical benchmark Cp hull (in gray). This yacht's Cp is 0.55, right in the middle of the range (0.53 to 0.57) considered healthy for all-round performance. Values below 0.53 indicate a shape skewed toward light-air performance; above 0.57, heavy-air performance has been emphasized.

top

side

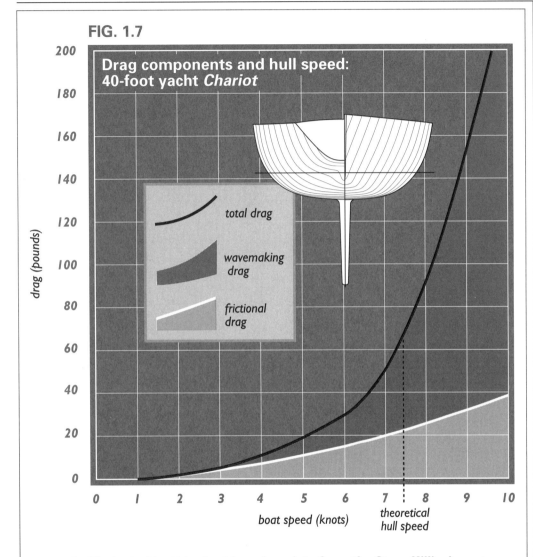

FIG. 1.7

Drag components and hull speed: 40-foot yacht *Chariot*

drag (pounds)

- total drag
- wavemaking drag
- frictional drag

boat speed (knots)

theoretical hull speed

As illustrated by this chart based on data from the Steve Killing's custom 40-foot design *Chariot*, at low hull speeds, frictional drag constitutes the largest proportion of total drag. But as a yacht approaches and exceeds its theoretical hull speed, wavemaking drag becomes more significant.

◀ **32** Fig. 1.5 shows a plot of the location of the center of buoyancy versus the prismatic coefficient, featuring some typical boats analyzed by Steve Killing. This data is fairly select, as these figures are not published by designers, and would be known only from an intimate familiarity with the boat.

frictional and wavemaking drag: resistance adds up

Much like the trade-off between frictional and induced drag that occurs when designing keels (see Chapter 2), the hull-design exercise battles with frictional and wavemaking drag. Wavemaking drag is related to waterline length as discussed above, but displacement and hull form muddy the waters.

Frictional drag is simple to deal with and to predict. Only the area of the hull in contact with the water, called the *wetted surface,* must be calculated to know the frictional drag. A wide, flat-bottomed boat will have an extreme amount of wetted surface for a given volume, while a narrow, rounded hull will have little. The conditions under which the boat is expected to sail will determine how much importance is placed on each drag component. For light-air competitions, in which boat speed is not expected to soar near the maximum set down by waterline length, wavemaking drag takes a back-seat consideration to the basic frictional drag of wetted surface. Narrow boats with small appendages will do well in these conditions. For cruising boats intended for all-round use, or racing boats expecting to see some stronger winds, frictional drag becomes less important and wavemaking drag takes the lead. The accompanying plot for a typical 40-foot sailboat (Fig. 1.7) shows how each component of drag changes with speed. At the upper speed ranges, wavemaking drag comprises more than 70 percent of total drag.

As a rough guide, wavemaking drag is proportional to the fourth power of weight, which means a boat with twice the weight will have 16 times the wavemaking drag. The relationship between weight and wavemaking drag is significant food for thought the next time you pack the cooler.

jousting at waves: the bulbous bow

Routinely seen on freighters, the bulbous bow is a cylindrical snout that projects forward of the true bow below the waterline to reduce wavemaking drag (Fig. 1.8). For reasons we will discuss shortly, despite experimentation these somewhat incongruous appendages have not met with success on sailboats.

This bow extension, not visible when the boat is at rest, serves an important function when the boat is moving, creating a wave ahead of the boat's normal bow wave. The shape of the bulbous section is so designed that the trough of its wave coincides with the peak of the bow wave; therefore, one wave partially cancels the other. The bulbous bow's effect can be dramatic, reducing the waves all along the hull to less than half of their normal size.

Since the size and position of the wave patterns from both the bulbous bow and the normal bow vary with speed, bulbous bows tend to work better at a specific speed fine-tuned by the designer. At low speeds, when wave drag is minimal, the total drag of the vessel increases due to the extra wetted surface and volume of the bulb. However, at the operating speed of the vessel to which the bulb has been tuned, overall drag can be reduced by up to 5 percent, creating significant fuel savings for a freighter.

On sailboats, the bulbous bow has not found easy acceptance. This is not because an appendage sticking

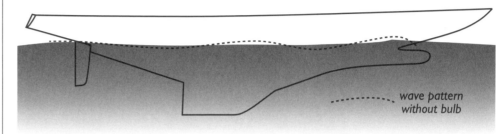

FIG. 1.8
Bulbous bows

wave pattern without bulb

The bulbous bow—a tubular extension of the hull just below the waterline—has both intrigued and frustrated sailors. The bow extension reduces drag by creating its own bow wave ahead of the hull's bow wave, and the two wave patterns cancel each other out. These extensions are commonplace on large ships, which use them to realize savings in wavemaking drag of 5 to 15 percent. (The wave reduction shown in the above illustration of an 8-Meter equipped with a bow extension is based on actual data from tank-testing bulbous-bow ships.) Cargo ships use them to burn less fuel, and racing sailors would love to use them to go much faster. But pitching effects and the inability to fine-tune a bulb's wave-reducing benefit to a particular hull speed (which is essential to their success in ship applications), among other problems, have rendered them experimental curiosities in yacht design.

forward of the waterline lacks aesthetic appeal, for history has shown that if something turns out to be fast and useful, sailors will somehow find it beautiful. The fault lies in two main drawbacks. Unlike a freighter, which spends most of its time operating at a specific speed, a sailboat must be efficient at many speeds. It is therefore significant if the boat must take a drag penalty at low speeds to gain a performance edge at higher speeds. The bulb, remember, reduces wave drag only within a narrow speed range.

And since most sailboats are shorter than freighters, their motion is affected more by sea conditions—the hull pitches up and down through waves, which in turn drives the bulbous bow in and out of

FIG. 1.9
Drawn to extremes

This drawing shows the typical shape of a circa 1880 British cutter in the 38- to 40-foot waterline range. The beam-to-waterline length ratio is a slender 1:5; most yachts today are closer to 1:3.

Yachts were forced into this peculiar—and unseaworthy shape—by the Thames Rule of 1855. This simple rule was a direct descendant of formulas devised in the late seventeenth century to rate the carrying capacity of commercial shipping—hence the calculation's result being expressed in tons.

There were only two measurements under the Thames Rule: length (L) and maximum beam (B). Initially, length was measured between the "perpendiculars," the bow stem and rudder post. The measurement made plumb bows virtually mandatory, as any forward overhang would be treated as sailing length. At the same time, the length definition encouraged exaggerated overhang aft to increase the effective (and unmeasured) sailing length. In 1878 the length measurement was changed to the load waterline, but plumb bows initially persisted.

A shortcoming of the rule was its failure to measure actual draft. It did include a measurement of half the beam, a borrowing from commercial ratings dating back to 1694 that was meant to assess the cargo-carrying capacity of the ship—as a rule of thumb, ships' holds were about half the depth of the beam. Essentially, yachts were rated according to their cargo-carrying capacity, or

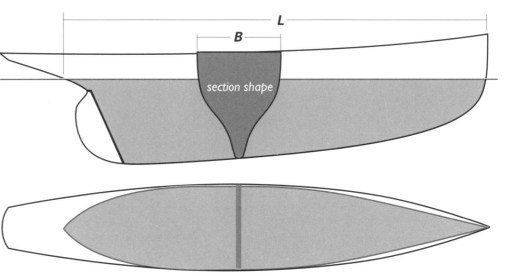

volume, with the practical load-carrying length being L–B, the width being B, and the depth being half of B.

The formula severely penalized beam. At around 8 feet of beam our sample yacht rated 10 tons. Increasing the beam 50 percent, to 12 feet, would have virtually doubled her rating. While such an increase would have provided far more form stability, it certainly would not have made her twice as fast, as the rating would have it.

Designers naturally began to minimize beam while increasing the unmeasured draft in an effort to maintain stability. Unfortunately, these "plank-on-edge" designs were far from stable. One spectacular sinking finally forced the scrapping of the Thames Rule in 1887.

Thames Rule

$$\frac{(L-B) \times B \times 0.5B}{94}$$

A typical British-style cutter from the Royal Canadian Yacht Club sails Lake Ontario in an 1884 painting by William Armstrong.

the waves. This motion is present in exactly the conditions when the bulb's benefits are needed: in the higher speed regime. Extra drag is produced by the entry and exit of the bulb from the water, while the influence of the bulb on wave formation is inconsistent.

Paul Elvstrom tried the bulbous bow on a 6-Meter design in the 1970s, but the experiment had limited success for the above reasons, and bulbous bows have not seen much experimentation since. A side effect that arose during the testing of this innovation was a tendency for the hull to want to travel in a straight line. The significant extension of the forward end of the waterline produced incredible resistance to turning. It was very difficult for the helmsman to respond to changes in wind direction and, presumably, to movements of competitors. The prospect of entire fleets of racing yachts with poor handling characteristics holing each other below the waterline like rogue narwhals probably makes it just as well that the device hasn't caught on.

on the level: hull form and stability

There has been no limit to variations in beam over centuries of yacht design. Some of the skinniest boats in history were designed to the English Thames Rule of 1855. For more than 30 years, the rule encouraged boats commonly known as "plank-on-edge," due to their deep, narrow (and unstable) shapes. (See Fig. 1.9.)

The rule's formula precipitated the increasingly extreme shapes by rewarding designs that minimized beam. Because the rule did not measure draft, the designs became deeper, to improve the position of ballast. These boats were so narrow (some with a beam less than one-sixth of the waterline length), deep, and

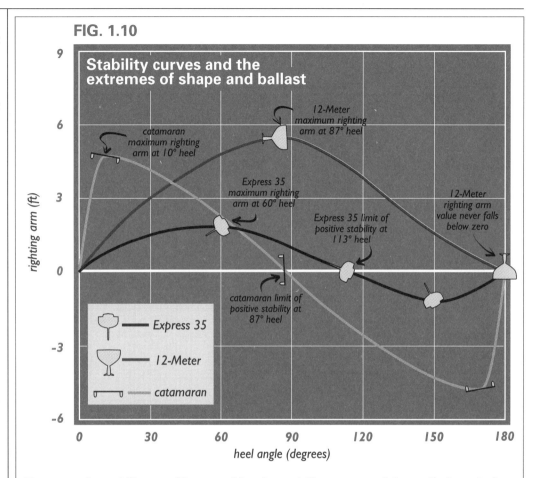

FIG. 1.10

Stability curves and the extremes of shape and ballast

catamaran maximum righting arm at 10° heel

12-Meter maximum righting arm at 87° heel

Express 35 maximum righting arm at 60° heel

Express 35 limit of positive stability at 113° heel

12-Meter righting arm value never falls below zero

catamaran limit of positive stability at 87° heel

Legend:
— Express 35
— 12-Meter
— catamaran

righting arm (ft) — vertical axis: 9, 6, 3, 0, -3, -6
heel angle (degrees) — horizontal axis: 0, 30, 60, 90, 120, 150, 180

Extremes in stability are illustrated by the stability curves of three distinct design types. The catamaran, with no ballast, relies entirely on the form stability delivered by its extreme beam. At only 10 degrees of heel, its maximum righting arm value—the distance from the center of gravity to the center of buoyancy—is reached. At near-perpendicular (87 degrees), it has expended all positive stability. The Express 35 employs both ballast and form stability to achieve a curve typical of production racer-cruisers, with positive stability still at hand more than 20 degrees past horizontal. The 12–Meter depends almost exclusively on ballast to remain upright, and is so stable that it essentially has no limit of positive stability, as its righting arm is never less than zero.

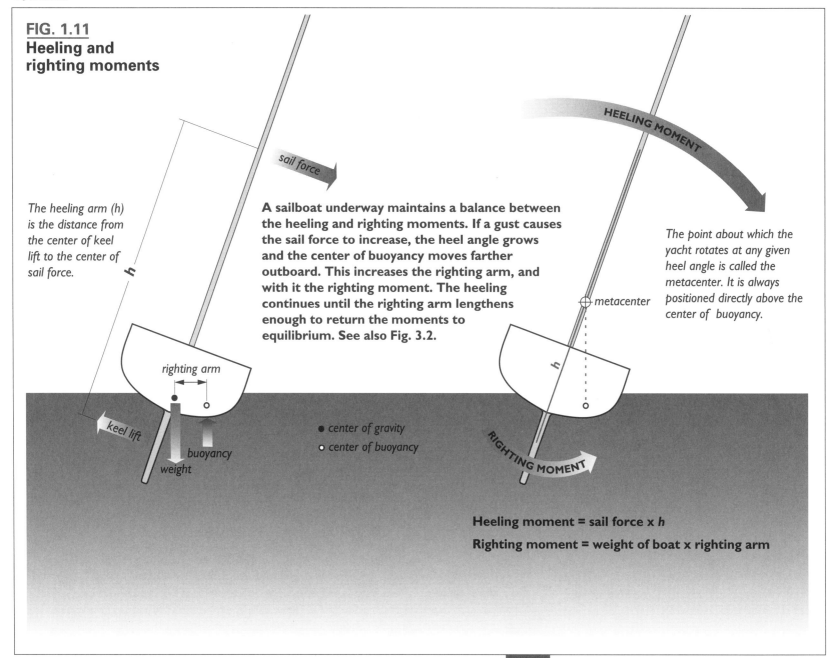

FIG. 1.11
Heeling and righting moments

The heeling arm (h) is the distance from the center of keel lift to the center of sail force.

sail force

A sailboat underway maintains a balance between the heeling and righting moments. If a gust causes the sail force to increase, the heel angle grows and the center of buoyancy moves farther outboard. This increases the righting arm, and with it the righting moment. The heeling continues until the righting arm lengthens enough to return the moments to equilibrium. See also Fig. 3.2.

HEELING MOMENT

The point about which the yacht rotates at any given heel angle is called the metacenter. It is always positioned directly above the center of buoyancy.

h

metacenter

righting arm

keel lift

buoyancy

weight

● center of gravity
○ center of buoyancy

RIGHTING MOMENT

Heeling moment = sail force x h

Righting moment = weight of boat x righting arm

heavy that many sank, leading to the abolition of the culpable handicapping rule in 1887.

Beam alone was not their problem, however. Other boats that followed them—some Meter-class designs, for example—had even higher length–beam ratios. The plank-on-edgers, however, lacked the high positive stability values of Meter boats because of poor ballast placement (designers and builders were reluctant to locate lead outside the hull). They also had a disconcerting habit of developing lee helm as they heeled in a breeze, which further compromised their seaworthiness. After sailing a plank-on-edge replica, the late, great British designer Uffa Fox related how "she carried so much lee helm that though fitted with a wishbone tiller the whole of my arm was in solid water as she ploughed her way up past the Nab…."

In contrast to the Thames Rule oddities, wide boats have been designed to meet specific cruising needs and in some cases as a response to racing rules. The International Offshore Rule (IOR), which was most prevalent in offshore keelboat competition in the 1970s, recognized—although not quite with the correct emphasis—the speed-reducing effect of beam through drag, and gave a rating credit to wide boats. This led to a decade of beamy boats as designers discovered that beam under the IOR received more credit than it should.

In the absence of artificial pressure from rating rules, the beam of a hull can be optimized for other reasons, chiefly speed, stability, and interior volume. However, the influence of beam on stability is so great that it deserves first discussion.

Stability—the ability of a boat to remain within about 30 degrees of upright even when the wind is pressing hard on the sails—is fundamental to any sailing yacht. The strength of the tendency to remain upright is indicated by the *righting moment,* which as the name implies is a moment (a force times a distance)

that tries to right the craft. The size of the righting moment, and therefore the stability of the boat, is dependent on the weight of the boat, the location of the majority of that weight (including the keel), and the shape of the hull. The effect of the ballast, its shape and material of construction, is covered in Chapter 3, while here the concern is the effect of hull shape.

Children playing on a raft in a pond have an intuitive feel for the basics of stability. Width and weight are everything. A heavy, wide raft will have the greatest stability, while a narrow platform made from lightweight material will quickly send everyone into the drink. Making the leap from intuition to science is difficult, but rest assured that intuition still holds true.

When one analyzes a hull that has flat rather than rounded sections, the calculations for stability get rather intense. In fact, before the advent of computers, many designers would make do with estimates of heeled stability because of the difficulty of calculating exact figures. Computers now make fast work of the righting moment, but an understanding of the physics behind stability is still important.

Fig. 1.11 shows a hull heeled 20 degrees and the resulting positions of the centers of gravity and buoyancy. When a boat is fully upright, these centers are aligned vertically. In our heeled example, the center of gravity is still on the centerline of the boat, somewhere near the waterline, but the center of buoyancy, which indicates the center of force supporting the hull, has moved off the centerline because of the heel. The lateral distance between these two equal and opposite forces is known as the *righting arm.* (If these opposing forces were not equal, the boat would either rise or sink until they did become equal.) The product of the righting arm and the buoyancy force is the righting moment.

Form stability describes the component of stability controlled by the cross-sectional hull shape, independent of ballasting considerations. The key to form

FIG. 1.12
Stability and volume distribution

This comparison of the waterline planes of two very different 38-footers, a cruiser and an IOR racer, shows why maximum waterline beam provides an incomplete picture of form stability. The hulls have the same displacement, waterline length, and maximum waterline beam, but the cruiser's beam is more evenly distributed fore and aft, compared with the typical diamond shape of the IOR design.

The cruiser's additional beam fore and aft adds greatly to stability. As shown in the graph, at about 15 degrees of heel the cruiser enjoys a righting arm 22 percent longer than that of the IOR racer.

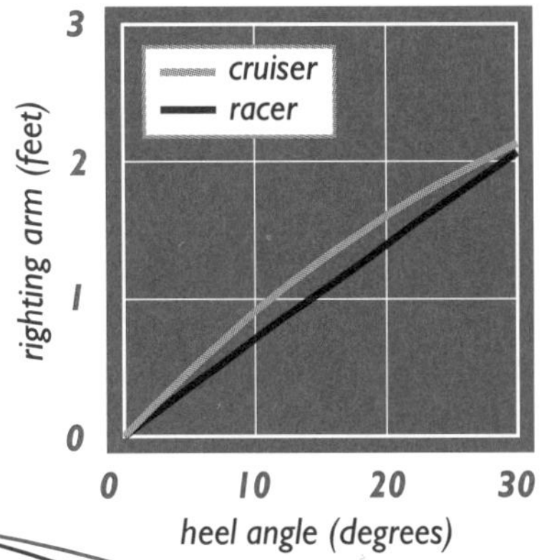

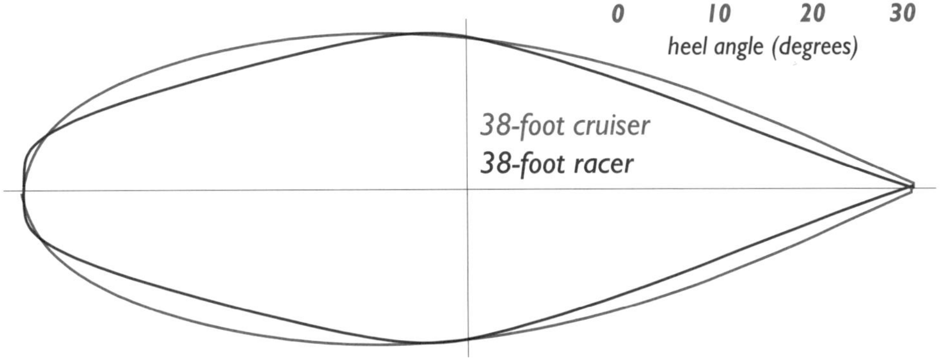

38-foot cruiser
38-foot racer

away from the centerline (and in turn away from the center of gravity), the wind pressure on the sails finds it "harder" to immerse the leeward side.

Meter-class designs have less form stability than beamier boats; the design rule demands that ballast be used almost exclusively to keep the boat upright. The less important (or less available) ballast is, the more important form stability becomes as a design tool. And the wider the boat is for a given length, the farther the center of buoyancy can be moved from the center of gravity. (See Figs. 1.10, 1.13.)

As a boat heels, the center of buoyancy continues to pull steadily away from the center of gravity, until it reaches a maximum at between 40 and 90 degrees, depending on the hull shape and the exact center of gravity location. At a heel angle of 90 degrees (with the mast parallel to the water), the center of gravity location has its greatest influence on stability. Consequently, boats that depend on form stability, not weight, are most vulnerable at this point.

A variation on the traditional form stability strategy is topside flare. The hull is typically kept quite narrow at the waterline to minimize wetted surface, then flares dramatically to the deck level. The flared topsides can provide form stability when the boat heels, but it is not particularly efficient, as the large surface area creates undesirable drag once immersed. The flare is more important for getting crew weight outboard on the opposite side, to act as ballast. The topside flare in this kind of design is usually transitional—more upright in the forward sections, then flaring in the aft sections, where the crew's weight can be put to use. This design approach, then, which initially might appear to follow the strategy of moving the center of buoyancy away from the center of gravity, is actually a scheme to get the center of gravity (through the portable ballast of crew weight) far from the center of buoyancy. As explained more fully in Chapter 10, in

stability in general is getting the center of buoyancy as far as possible from the center of gravity as the boat heels, because this distance determines the righting arm. The simplest way to do this is to increase the beam. Greater gains can be made by changing the cross-sectional shape, redistributing volume so that a larger proportion is away from the centerline. If a hull shape is perfectly circular, it has virtually no form stability. There is little about its shape to impede it from heeling over. If more volume (which by definition is buoyant) is placed

FIG. 1.13
Beam and stability

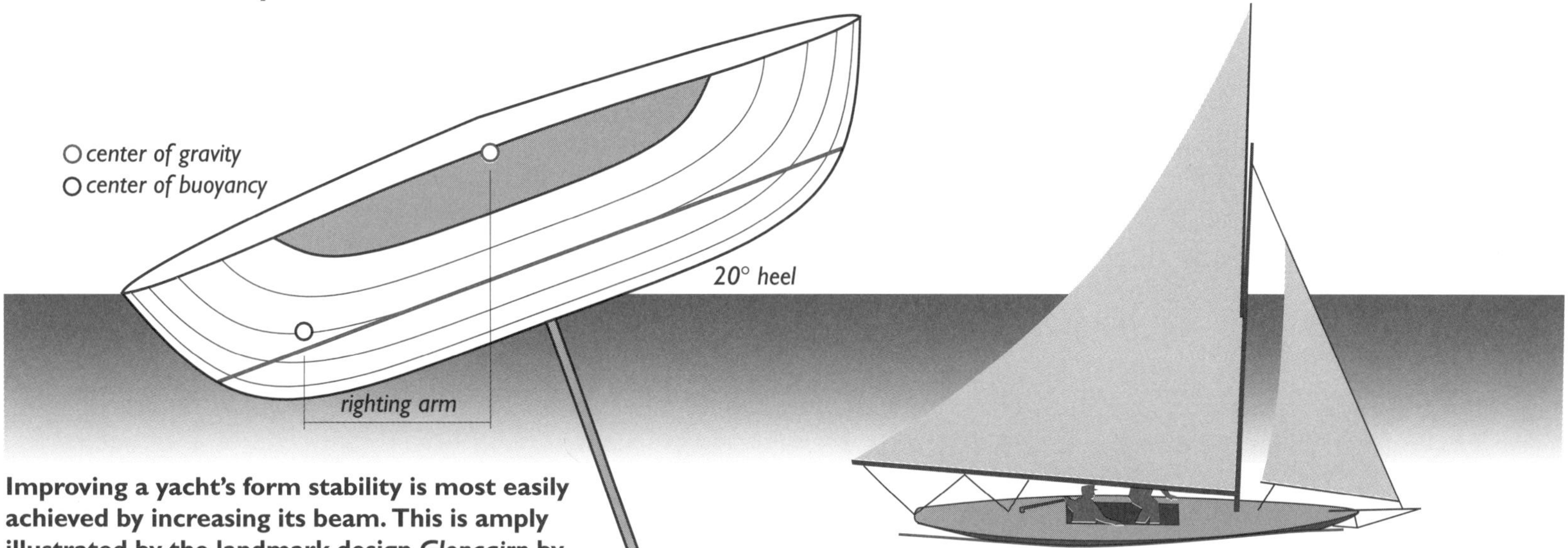

○ center of gravity
○ center of buoyancy

20° heel

righting arm

Improving a yacht's form stability is most easily achieved by increasing its beam. This is amply illustrated by the landmark design *Glencairn* by G. Herrick Duggan (below). A Canadian railway engineer, Duggan created some outstanding sailing craft in his spare time, including in 1896 the 23-foot *Glencairn,* the world's first scow. She caused a sensation as the first challenger for the Seawanhaka Cup, a match-racing series for small craft sponsored by the Seawanhaka Corinthian Yacht Club of Oyster Bay, New York. Sailing for Duggan's Royal St. Lawrence Yacht Club of Montreal, *Glencairn* won the match and stood design convention on its ear with her radical hull form. As a centerboarder, *Glencairn* could not depend on a ballasted keel for stability. While her trim could be aided by the weight of her crew, her shallow, wide hull form provided a tremendous righting arm at relatively small angles of heel.

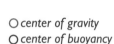

Glencairn was designed to the Seawanhaka Rule, which was devised in 1883 and spurred on more than a decade of design innovation permitted by its simple parameters. It was a pure horsepower rule, asking only that waterline length be balanced against sail area. Beam, draft, and displacement were all left unmeasured.

Seawanhaka Rule

$$\frac{LWL + \sqrt{SA}}{2}$$

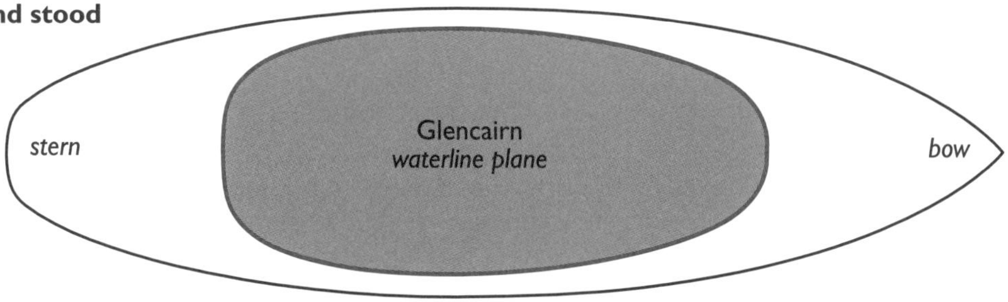

stern

Glencairn
waterline plane

bow

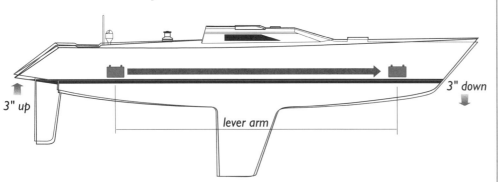

FIG. 1.14
Fore-and-aft stability

3" up

lever arm

3" down

It is common to think of a yacht's stability solely in transverse terms, but there is also a fore-and-aft component. While it adheres to the same physical principles as transverse stability, rather than describing it in terms of righting moment, inches are used—that is, the moment required to raise and lower the bow and stern a combined distance of so many inches.

In the above example, relocation of 400 pounds of batteries has produced a change in fore-and-aft trim (shown in blue) of 6 inches: 3 inches up at the stern, and 3 inches down at the bow.

than that of a cruising boat with much greater beam near the ends. (See Fig. 1.12.)

Sailors primarily think about the transverse stability of a boat—how much it heels in how much wind—but motion in the fore-and-aft direction obeys the same physical laws. As the boat puts its bow down, the length, not the beam, becomes important for pitching resistance. Although this could be referred to as a righting moment just like the transverse stability, it is usually expressed in terms of inches—that is, the moment required to lower the bow and raise the stern a combined distance of 1 inch. (See Fig. 1.14.)

When reballasting, moving crew, or shifting batteries to improve the trim of a boat, the designer or owner can use this figure to determine how much movement is required for a given trim change. For example if the bow needs to be raised 0.5 inch for the boat to float level, and the moment to trim 1 inch (0.5 inch at the bow and 0.5 at the stern) is 1,200 foot-pounds, then the strategy for moving 400 pounds of batteries can be determined. The batteries would need to move aft 3 feet (1,200/400=3). And just as the beam away from the center section has an influence on the transverse stability, so the length of the boat off the centerline (or the fineness of the waterline) influences the fore-and-aft moment required to trim.

the International America's Cup Class, initial design experimentation favored topside flare that moved crew outboard. But the additional wetted surface and increased wave drag proved detrimental.

It is important to understand that the stability of a boat is not just a function of its width at the center section. The shape of the waterline all along the length of the boat contributes to stability. The larger sections have a proportionately greater influence on the stability, but overall shape can be very influential. For example, some racing boats have been designed with very diamond-shaped waterlines as viewed from above. The beam in these designs, although great in the middle of the boat, quickly diminishes near the bow and stern. The stability of such a boat is noticeably less

racing hulls: the changing shape of handicapping

Racing hull shapes change as often as the rules, so the shapes used here to illustrate the typical racing hull may already be dated by the time this book is published. Current rules in the sailboat racing world include the Mount Gay 30 and Whitbread 60, the International Measurement System (IMS), the Performance Handicap Racing Fleet (PHRF)—which is not

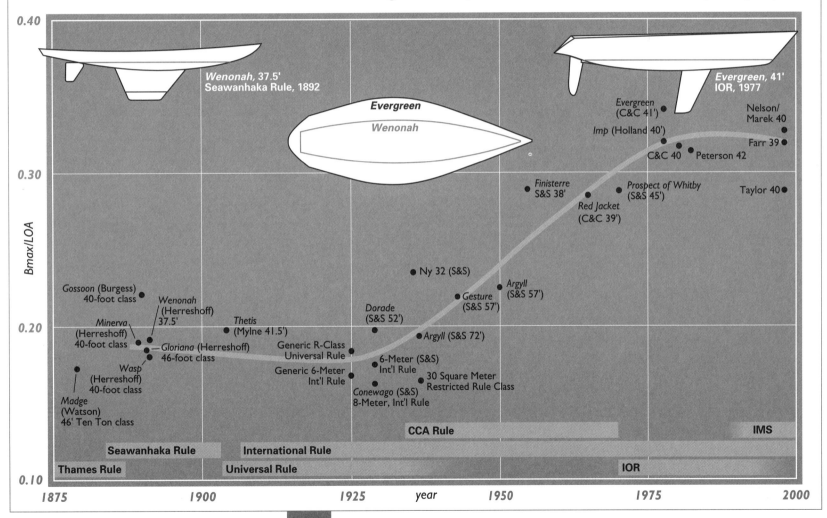

FIG. 1.15
Beam vs. LOA in racing designs

This chart shows a 125-year trend in the ratio of maximum beam (Bmax) to length overall (LOA) in racing designs, as well as the years of influence of a number of leading design rules. Yachts have not always been built to conform to a particular rule, but this chart shows the unmistakable character of certain rule types. Yachts created under the Thames, Seawanhaka, Universal, and International Rules were relatively narrow in beam. The Cruising Club of America (CCA) Rule encouraged a racing-cruising shape with the beam required for a habitable interior, while the International Offshore Rule (IOR), which succeeded it, encouraged extreme beam, as much for rating advantages as stability. The Bmax/LOA ratio has been trending downward under the International Measurement System (IMS).

Bmax/LOA

0.40

0.30

0.20

0.10

Wenonah, 37.5'
Seawanhaka Rule, 1892

Evergreen
Wenonah

Evergreen, 41'
IOR, 1977

Evergreen
(C&C 41')

Nelson/
Marek 40

Imp (Holland 40')

C&C 40   Peterson 42

Farr 39

Finisterre
S&S 38'

Prospect of Whitby
(S&S 45')

Taylor 40

Red Jacket
(C&C 39')

Ny 32 (S&S)

Argyll
(S&S 57')

Gesture
(S&S 57')

Gossoon (Burgess)
40-foot class

Wenonah
(Herreshoff)
37.5'

Dorade
(S&S 52')

Minerva
(Herreshoff)
40-foot class

Thetis
(Mylne 41.5')

Gloriana (Herreshoff)
46-foot class

Argyll (S&S 72')

Generic R-Class
Universal Rule

Wasp
(Herreshoff)
40-foot class

6-Meter (S&S)
Int'l Rule

30 Square Meter
Restricted Rule Class

Generic 6-Meter
Int'l Rule

Madge
(Watson)
46' Ten Ton class

Conewago (S&S)
8-Meter, Int'l Rule

CCA Rule   IMS

Seawanhaka Rule   International Rule

Thames Rule   Universal Rule   IOR

1875   1900   1925   year   1950   1975   2000

As shown by this Bermuda 40, cruising designs require more beam than racers to compensate for the loss in stability due to reduced draft. Interior amenities also have an important influence on beam.

a measurement rule, but a handicapping rule based on observed performance—and many one-design rules that simply dictate that all the boats must be the same.

In typical IMS hull shapes "today," bows are fairly vertical, keels are deep, and stability is high. In these boats, speed is the primary goal. The safety feature and accommodation requirements, compared with the IOR, are more rigidly enforced by the rules, although most designers take the attitude that they will create interiors that conform but will not add unenforced luxuries. Keel draft, which now commonly stretches to 10 feet in a 45-foot boat, is not compromised for cruising.

But the focus in this chapter is on the hull shape. The accompanying chart (Fig. 1.15), which compares maximum beam (Bmax) to length overall (LOA), shows how the trends in racing boats have changed over time, beginning with ultranarrow craft of the late nineteenth century and a persisting sleekness under the International and Universal Rules in this century. Beam has been greatest under the IOR in the 1970s, retreating under the IMS in the 1990s. The large beam encouraged by the IOR has given way to more wholesome shapes. These trends are important for the club racer and performance cruiser, as cutting-edge racing rules have long had such an influence on the design of production boats in general.

The most "appropriate" beam for a boat is a matter of taste for, assuming the designer has attached an appropriate amount of ballast to provide adequate stability, one of the main differences in how a boat sails is its "feel" in waves. A narrow boat like an 8-Meter will slice through waves with an exciting sensation of power, while a wide IOR boat will do more pounding and make greater course changes. The narrow boat, though, tends to be wetter, as waves make their way over the deck rather than being pushed to the side. While no rating rule is perfect, the IMS is at least homing in on the design characteristics of a yacht that will be pleasing, safe, and exciting to sail.

cruising hulls: beam me up

Even though it is convenient for the sake of design discussion to lay out the parameters for a hull separate from the keel and sail plan, this can lead to meaningless discussions. A cruising boat, for example, which requires a shorter keel to enter those fine anchorages, will require more beam to compensate for the loss in stability due to reduced draft. It is therefore pointless to champion the perfect narrower hull if it must be ruled out because it lacks stability. In general then, cruising hulls will be beamier for two reasons: stability and increased interior volume.

A pernicious school of design thinking rates the cruising boat as somehow second class to the racer, allegedly requiring less talent on the part of its creator. There is no reason for this attitude, which is fostered mostly by designers who don't have the talent to produce either type of boat. In many cases the design of a cruising boat is a more challenging exercise than that of a racing boat, although the exercises are certainly different. The racing designer must optimize the speed relative to the handicap rating, knowing that his skill will be measured in seconds per mile. While the cruising sailor seldom wields the racer's ruthless performance measuring stick, he is much more critical in his assessment of a boat's seaworthiness, stability, and interior. Bad cruising boats designed with too much weather helm or too little stability exist, but just as many inappropriate racing boats have hit the water. A well-designed cruising boat, often dubbed a "performance cruiser," will find a useful life as a safe and speedy cruiser and as a club racer.

Over time, cruising designs have been free to accept or reject trends in racing designs. In the nineteenth century, racing craft commonly lived out their retirement years as cruisers, although what made them swift racers did not necessarily make for ideal cruising. Part of the problem was rating rules that forced racers into extreme shapes that had nothing to do with pure performance or seaworthiness. In recent years, however, the arrival of "fairer" rating systems like the IMS has caused the gap between what is fast on the racecourse and what is fast, seaworthy, and comfortable to close considerably. Racing designs that are no longer considered cutting edge are undergoing retrofits by new owners, with better-appointed interiors giving them a fresh and deserving lease on life.

A one-design E-22 surfs under spinnaker. Displacement yachts can use the power of waves to accelerate beyond hull speed.

over the top: planing and surfing

Sailboats and planing powerboats differ significantly in the shape of their hulls. The powerboat has either a flat or V-shaped planing surface aft. When the boat begins to plane, it breaks free from the grip of wavemaking drag and operates in a new regime. We have seen how waterline length limits the speed of a displacement boat as the aft end flops into the trough of the bow wave. If enough power is available—and a substantial amount is actually required—the boat can be pushed up the sloping bow wave until it is riding on top of the water rather that pushing through it. **50 ▶**

How long? How heavy?

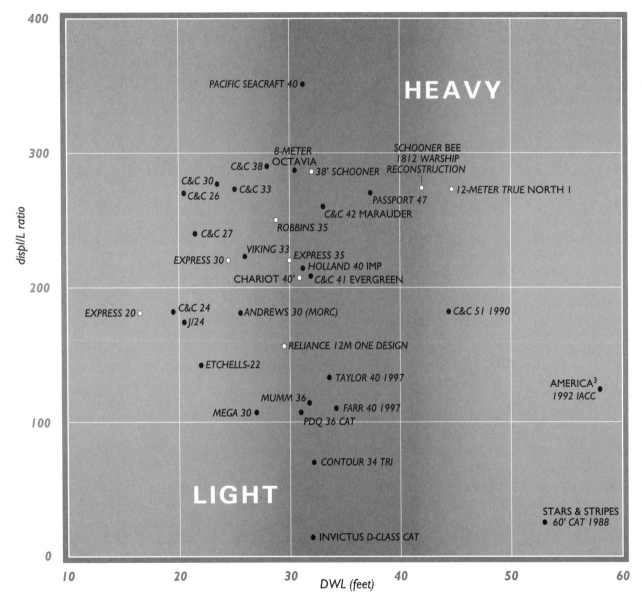

HEAVY

LIGHT

PACIFIC SEACRAFT 40

8-METER
OCTAVIA
C&C 38
C&C 30
C&C 26 C&C 33
38' SCHOONER
SCHOONER BEE
1812 WARSHIP
RECONSTRUCTION
12-METER TRUE NORTH 1
PASSPORT 47
C&C 42 MARAUDER
ROBBINS 35
C&C 27
VIKING 33
EXPRESS 30 EXPRESS 35
HOLLAND 40 IMP
CHARIOT 40' C&C 41 EVERGREEN
EXPRESS 20
C&C 24
J/24
ANDREWS 30 (MORC)
C&C 51 1990
RELIANCE 12M ONE DESIGN
ETCHELLS-22
TAYLOR 40 1997
AMERICA³
1992 IACC
MUMM 36
MEGA 30 FARR 40 1997
PDQ 36 CAT
CONTOUR 34 TRI
STARS & STRIPES
60' CAT 1988
INVICTUS D-CLASS CAT

displ/L ratio

400
300
200
100
0

DWL (feet)
10 20 30 40 50 60

The chart at left compares the displacement/length (displ/L) ratios for a variety of yachts (length being design waterline) and plots them horizontally according to their length. Steve Killing's own designs are plotted with white dots. The dark blue band marks the range of designs with moderate displ/L values.

As the chart at right reveals, heavy displacement doesn't necessarily mean a heavy hull. The preballast weight values show that a Meter-class design, while heavy according to the chart at left, employs lightweight construction techniques to reserve most of its displacement for ballast.

Displacement/length ratio formula

$$\frac{displ/2,240}{(.01 \times L)^3}$$

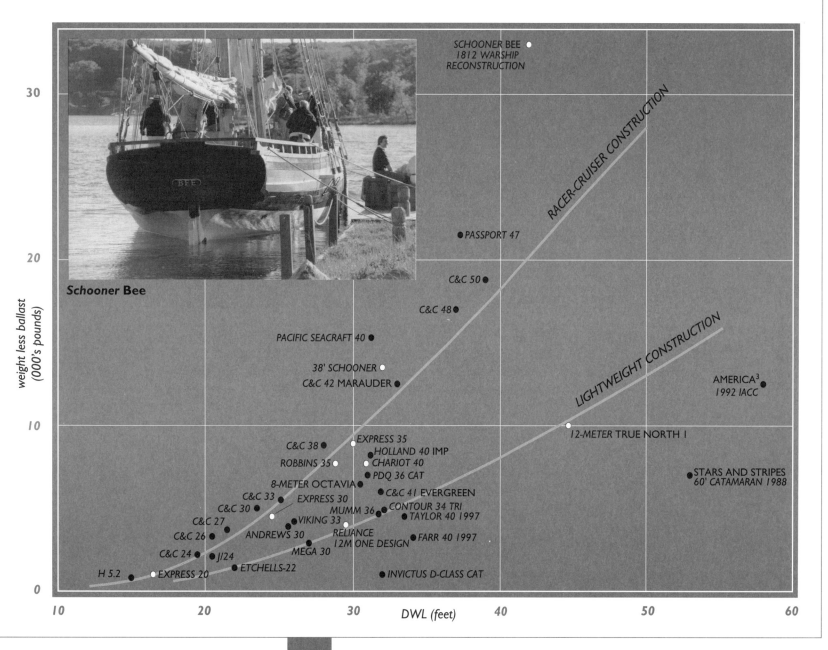

Schooner Bee

weight less ballast (000's pounds)

30

20

10

0

SCHOONER BEE
1812 WARSHIP
RECONSTRUCTION

RACER-CRUISER CONSTRUCTION

LIGHTWEIGHT CONSTRUCTION

● PASSPORT 47

C&C 50 ●

C&C 48 ●

PACIFIC SEACRAFT 40 ●

38' SCHOONER ○

C&C 42 MARAUDER ●

AMERICA[3]
1992 IACC

12-METER TRUE NORTH I

EXPRESS 35

C&C 38 ●

HOLLAND 40 IMP

ROBBINS 35 ○   ○ CHARIOT 40

● PDQ 36 CAT

STARS AND STRIPES
60' CATAMARAN 1988

8-METER OCTAVIA ●

● C&C 41 EVERGREEN

C&C 33 ●

EXPRESS 30

C&C 30 ●

MUMM 36 ●   ● CONTOUR 34 TRI

C&C 27 ●   ○   VIKING 33 ●   ● TAYLOR 40 1997

C&C 26 ●   ANDREWS 30 ●   RELIANCE   ● FARR 40 1997
                                         12M ONE DESIGN

C&C 24 ●   ● J/24   MEGA 30 ●

H 5.2 ○   ○ EXPRESS 20   ● ETCHELLS-22   ● INVICTUS D-CLASS CAT

DWL (feet)

10   20   30   40   50   60

◄ **47** In a powerboat with an appropriately flat aft running surface, all that is required for *planing* is a suitably powerful engine. On a small aluminum fishing boat, which is light and very flat, a 10-horsepower outboard can easily get the boat to plane. The same boat with four people on board, however, will revert to a displacement craft.

In the world of sailboats, the same planing phenomenon can occur, but control of horsepower is not as simple—it is not waiting to be applied with the throttle. Boats that plane typically are light and flat: the International 14 (see Chapter 7) has a crew of two, and the most recent designs are very flat aft to promote planing both upwind and on a reach. In larger boats like the Mumm 30 and Mount Gay 60, planing can be achieved off the wind, but not upwind.

A hull shape that works for planing is almost the opposite of one that is optimized for displacement sailing. To extend the upper speed range of a displacement hull, the underwater volume aft is increased by adding a bustle, and wetted surface is minimized by avoiding flat sections. The abrupt changes in shape near the back end of the boat prevent planing—there would be too much turbulence and drag at high speed. In high-performance designs, the low-speed wetted-surface configuration is often compromised in favor of high-speed planing. This usually means the planing hull is combined with a large sail plan to try to make up for the extra light-air drag. The International 14, for example, is loaded with sail area, and permits two crew on the trapeze to hold the boat flat. It can plane upwind in airs of about 8 knots.

Surfing is artificially enhanced planing; it can be

The hull form of the Whitbread Round the World Race's Whitbread 60 class (drawn here by Steve Killing) is flat and wide for excellent surfing ability and maximum effect of water ballast.

the heavy-displacement boat's chance to feel the thrill of the plane. When a boat of any size and weight is sailing in windy and wavy conditions, it can get a speed boost as it travels down the face of a wave. Because the boat is literally sailing downhill, like a toboggan running on hard-packed snow, speed can increase dramatically and planing can be initiated without the requirement of large sail forces or a specially adapted hull shape. Being able to sustain surfing is one of the many talents of a skilled helmsman. Speeds can soar from a presurfing condition of 7 knots to a full surf at 10 or 12.

corners and curves: sectional shapes

The sectional shape of the hull is the result of many decisions made by the designer and prospective owner. In the middle of the hull, the shape through the maximum section is often the first of the curves to be defined. With the weight and therefore the displacement of the boat determined, the boat can be made shallow and wide, or narrow and deep, with equal volume. The wider boat will have more stability, but less speed (assuming we are not discussing planing boats). But even then, the flat, wide boat will have more stability at low heel angles and less at the higher angles. In this way, a trade-off is made between ultimate safety and initial stability. The Whitbread 60 class of the Whitbread Round the World Race is a good example of a boat that is wide and flat for excellent surfing ability and maximum effect of water ballast, which requires expanded beam on deck for off-center water ballasting tanks.

Extreme forward shapes (primarily flat) were inadvertently promoted by the IOR, which had a forward depth measurement just off the centerline and aft of the forward end of the waterline. By enlarging this measurement, the designer could increase the rule's perception of displacement and so lower the rating. But enlarging the measurement meant severely flattening the section. These boats had a tendency to pound in large seas as the flat section struck the waves, sending a shudder through the boat. Boats not influenced by such a point-measurement rule have more rounded or veed sections forward for better slicing of the waves, less wetted surface, and better heavy-air performance.

hard edges: chines and hull efficiency

Chines, those longitudinal hard edges seen in some hulls, are generally used when the construction material calls for them. Steel and plywood (and sometimes aluminum) are easy to bend in one direction but difficult to form into a compound curve, and so are often shaped into boats with one to three chines per side. Use of such construction material is often dictated by the nature of the builder. Simple methods offer inexpensive construction, two qualities of high interest to home builders. After the Second World War, plywood manufacturers actively encouraged the creation of do-it-yourself designs. One such initiative that caught the fancy of sailors was the 26-foot Thunderbird sloop, built with two chines per side.

Chines in smaller craft predate the plywood bonanza. The 22.5-foot one-design Star class keelboat (Fig. 1.16) was created in 1908, while the 19-foot centerboard Lightning class was designed by Olin Stephens in 1938. Both have single chines; this configuration provides good form stability, as well as directional stability and wave-cutting performance when heeled and moving to windward. The chine is also tailor-made for creating large planing sections aft. And

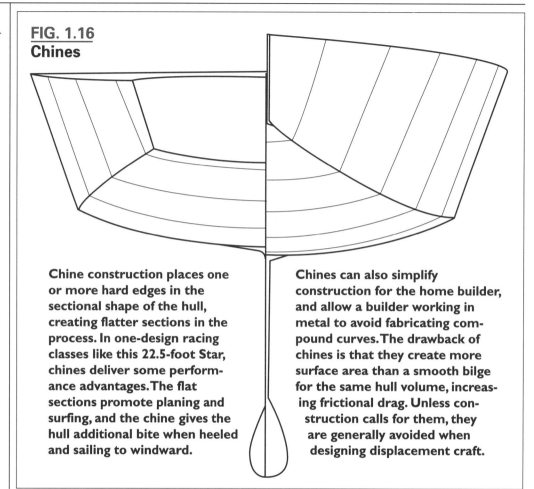

FIG. 1.16
Chines

Chine construction places one or more hard edges in the sectional shape of the hull, creating flatter sections in the process. In one-design racing classes like this 22.5-foot Star, chines deliver some performance advantages. The flat sections promote planing and surfing, and the chine gives the hull additional bite when heeled and sailing to windward.

Chines can also simplify construction for the home builder, and allow a builder working in metal to avoid fabricating compound curves. The drawback of chines is that they create more surface area than a smooth bilge for the same hull volume, increasing frictional drag. Unless construction calls for them, they are generally avoided when designing displacement craft.

chines are used in fast planing dinghies to help detach the spray from the hull. Without these chines, a round-bilge planing boat incurs extra drag by having the spray continue to adhere to the hull rather than be deflected out to the side.

In a displacement boat, chines are not desirable, for they mean greater wetted surface over a comparable smooth-bilge shape. This extra wetted surface of course means extra frictional drag, and unless the chines hap-

FIG. 1.17
Hull trim and wetted surface

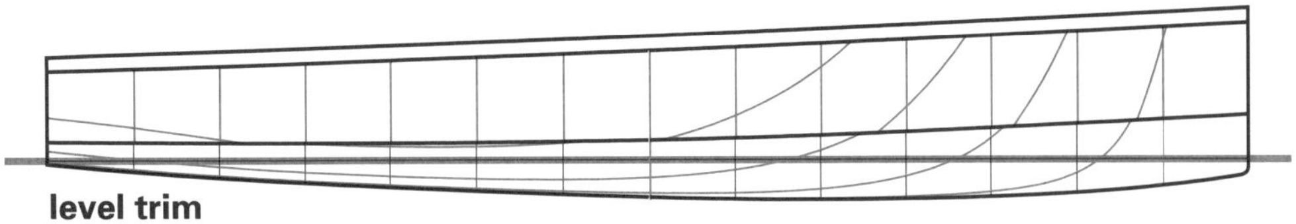

level trim
wetted surface area: 40 sq ft

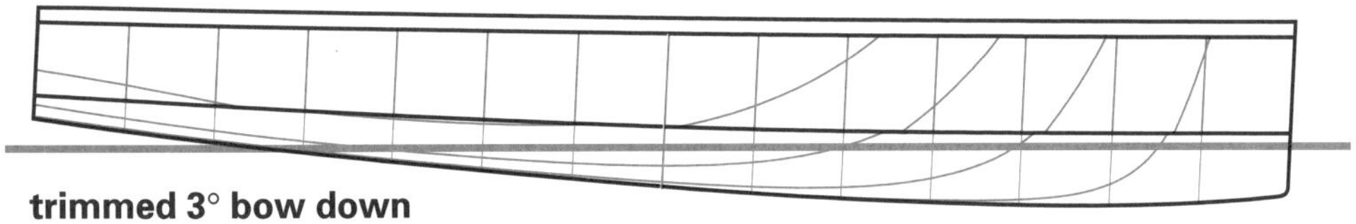

trimmed 3° bow down
wetted surface area: 34 sq ft

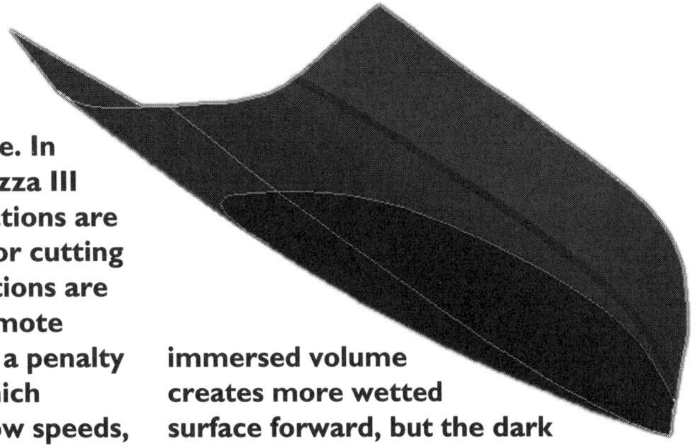

Because hull volume is distributed differently fore and aft, changes in trim can greatly reduce wetted surface. In planing dinghies, like this Mazza III International 14, forward sections are deeper and more rounded, for cutting through waves, while aft sections are shallower and flatter, to promote planing. The aft sections pay a penalty in increased surface area, which means undesirable drag at low speeds, when planing is not possible.

To reduce drag, particularly when sailing downwind in light air, the crew can shift its weight forward to trim the boat bow-down, in this case 3 degrees. This redistribution of

immersed volume creates more wetted surface forward, but the dark area in the computer-generated simulation shows that a net reduction of 15 percent in wetted surface, from 40 to 34 square feet, results, as a large portion of the aft section rises clear of the water.

pen to be aligned with the direction of water flow there is also an increase in drag due to the disturbance of this flow and the boundary layer. However, as in the case of the Thunderbird, if everyone on the racecourse has the same design, performance sacrifices can be tolerated. No one has a shape advantage in this kind of one-design competition, and, most important, everyone is able to race a boat he can afford.

trimmed for speed: managing wetted surface

Planing designs that are slowed in light wind by the large wetted surface of flat sections are sailed with particular attention paid to trim. This can be seen downwind in some outwardly unorthodox strategies. Laser sailors will move their weight forward and roll the boat dramatically to windward when running, to remove as much wetted surface from the water as possible. Racing keelboats with flatter aft sections (particularly in the rudder area) are also routinely trimmed bow-down off the wind in light air. (See Fig. 1.17.)

This trimming strategy takes advantage of the fact that volume is distributed differently at either end of the boat. Forward, the sections are deeper and rounder, containing more volume with less wetted surface, whereas aft the sections are flatter and wider.

It might help to imagine the boat's displacement as a given measure of water sloshing around in an asymmetric bowl. Tip the bowl toward the more rounded side, and the wetted surface of the flatter section is exposed; that is, less surface area is in contact with the water.

The same strategy is employed in heeling a boat to windward when running, or deliberately inducing lee-ward heel when sailing upwind in light air. Heeling the boat takes advantage of the fact that hull shape away from the centerline is usually rounder than along the bottom and so constitutes less wetted surface.

multiple choice: the physics of multihulls

Is there a more logical evolutionary result of our prehistoric floating log than the multihull? After all, you didn't have to master the art of lofting or frame construction to build the hulls of a Paleolithic catamaran. The design evolution began with the hollowing out of a tree trunk. Voilà—a canoe. To make it more stable, you didn't have to learn about form stability and righting arms. You just had to make an outrigger out of another, smaller, hollowed-out log. For ambitious ocean adventures, two equal-size hulls, widely separated, made a nice, fast, stable platform. No wonder the ancient Polynesians were able to make the leap from log rolling to spectacular passagemaking without first mastering Euclidean geometry or Newtonian physics. The speed and stability of the multihull could not be more intuitive.

Yet monohull sailors who have never sailed a multihull, and designers who have never analyzed one, have an unusual perception of the craft. Most watch as these lightweight, sometimes awkward-looking vehicles fly past, and assume that they operate under a totally different set of rules. Because their hulls are so narrow and the heel angles so low, observers conclude that multihulls disregard the displacement rules and for some reason just go fast. The stability seems magical—no lead keels and yet no heel angle to speak of.

Part of the average monohuller's bafflement is surely cultural. Multihulls developed half a world away from European shipbuilders, who were concerned with creating vessels that could transport cargo and cannons. They also had to shape craft that could handle

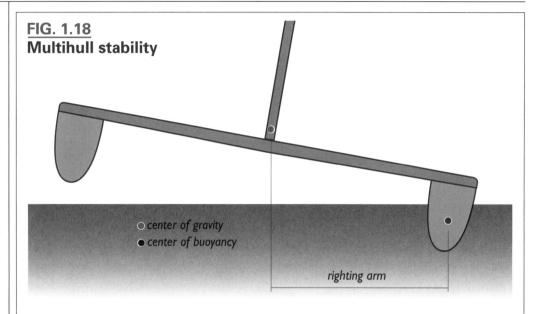

FIG. 1.18
Multihull stability

○ *center of gravity*
● *center of buoyancy*

righting arm

There is nothing mysterious about multihull stability: it adheres to the same scientific principles as the stability of a monohull. But multihull stability essentially is the antithesis of Meter-class stability. A Meter boat has almost no form stability, relying on ballast to keep it upright. A multihull, with no ballast, relies entirely on form stability. With its tremendous beam, a multihull (as demonstrated by the catamaran above) enjoys a tremendous righting arm at low angles of heel. However, because it relies on form stability to remain upright, its maximum righting arm is achieved at the low heel angle of 10 degrees, shown here. The righting arm steadily diminishes until the limit of positive stability is reached at about 87 degrees of heel. (See also Fig. 1.10.)

the cold waters of the North Atlantic; the balmier South Pacific was more tolerant of the low, exposed deck of the catamaran. The Polynesian catamaran was an unimaginable device until European explorers finally saw one in the sixteenth century, and their effect on Western design concepts was essentially nonexistent. The maritime industry of the West con-

The 1991 America's Cup defender **Stars & Stripes** flies a hull. Multihulls can be outperformed by monohulls only in very light winds, when there is insufficient sail force to lift the windward hull clear of the water and reduce drag. Diminishing this window of vulnerability was an important part of the Stars & Stripes design program.

tinued to refine the monohull and the underlying science, leaving the multihull an exotic mystery.

But none of the "unusual" features of a multihull are all that different from the standard features of a monohull. The drag on the hull still comprises frictional drag and wavemaking drag. However, the proportion of frictional to wavemaking drag differs. Because the hulls are so much narrower in a multihull, wavemaking drag is reduced. Since the wavemaking drag is lower, the resistance curve is much less steep at higher speeds than with a monohull, and the "hull speed wall" is not so pronounced.

If narrow hulls are so beneficial to multihulls, why not use them for monohulls? A multihull gains inherent stability from its arrangement of two or three hulls, while a monohull needs some beam to gain stability as it heels. As a lightweight multihull begins to heel, the total width—from the centerline of the leeward hull all the way across to the centerline of the windward hull—provides the stability. When one hull finally lifts clear of the water, the righting moment is the product of the weight of the boat pushing downward at the centerline of the craft and the buoyant force of the leeward hull lifting up. (See Fig. 1.18.)

Multihull *amas* (the Polynesian word for the outer hulls) are often semicircular in cross section, to keep the wetted surface drag to an absolute minimum, as there is no need to worry about enhancing the form stability of hull shape. The catamaran, with two hulls, often has a performance weakness in light air, since both hulls are in the water and the wetted surface is high—almost twice as high as when one hull is flying. To overcome this problem in a racing cat, crew can be sent to leeward to aid in flying the windward hull, or the sail area can be increased to enormous proportions to provide enough lift to heel the boat, even when the wind is light.

Very light winds are the only conditions in which a monohull can outperform a multihull, as there isn't enough horsepower in most rigs to get a hull flying. In preparation for the 1988 America's Cup match against the New Zealand supermonohull, Dennis Conner's 60-foot catamaran *Stars & Stripes* had her wing mast steadily enlarged. The defenders had rightly suspected that the catamaran's weakness against the large challenger would be in light air, and so continued to "up" her sail area until she could fly a hull even in 5 knots of true wind—the lightest wind in which a race would be held. The one weakness of the catamaran configuration was thus eliminated. (See page 224 for more.)

The trimaran, while most akin to a catamaran, has a larger central hull reminiscent of a monohull. Typically the center hull will house the main accommodations while the two amas provide stability. The center hull is beamier than either of a similar-size catamaran's

Weighing in:
displacement in fresh water and salt water

In describing how heavy a boat is, the terms "weight" and "displacement" are casually interchanged, but there is an important difference in their definitions, and in the implications for the vessel they describe. Part of the confusion comes from the fact that both terms are routinely expressed in pounds.

Weight is a measure of the effect of gravity on mass. You would have to take a boat to another planet to get it to weigh differently. A 35-foot yacht suspended on a hoist over Lake Michigan weighs the same 10,000 pounds that it does suspended on a hoist over the English Channel. Once that boat is lowered into Lake Michigan or the English Channel, however, it appears to weigh differently from the perspective of displacement.

The boat moved from fresh water to salt water really hasn't lost weight—it just looks like it has, because it is floating 0.375 inch higher in the water. That is because salt water is 2.5 percent more dense than fresh water. Displacement here becomes important, as the figure derives from how much water a vessel displaces when afloat. In other words, *displacement* is the weight of the total volume of water pushed aside by the hull, keel, and rudder from the waterline down—the waterline of course being the height on the hull the water reaches when the hull is floating level.

Whether a boat is in salt water or fresh water, it displaces the same total weight of water. But because salt water is more dense, a lower volume is displaced for the same weight. In the case of our 35-footer, it displaces 3.9 cubic feet less water when moved to salt water.

When a boat displaces less water, it naturally floats higher, and in yacht design seemingly small changes can be significant, particularly if a rating rule is involved. Depending on the hull shape, this change in displaced volume produces small or large changes in measured waterline length. A 55,000-pound 12-Meter, for example, floats about 0.625 inch higher in salt water than fresh water, thereby shortening its waterline about 6 inches. While this was never a great concern to 12-Meter owners, as the America's Cup must always been held in salt water, it does illustrate how significant a change in racing venue can be to a boat's measurement. And this does come up for Great Lakes racing yachts that head to events on the ocean, and vice versa. A racing yacht's different waterline length in salt water and fresh water often must be addressed with changes in total weight and sail area.

In summary, a boat displaces the same weight of water, whether salt or fresh, but the difference in the volume of water can command adjustments to the design.

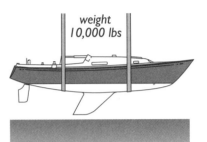

weight
10,000 lbs

Lake Michigan
hull volume:
160.2 cu ft

English Channel
hull volume:
156.3 cu ft

hulls and therefore has more wave drag. Since the trimaran's hulls are arranged so that with the smallest of heel angles the windward hull leaves the water, the seemingly large penalty of having three hulls vanishes. (Practically speaking, a *catamaran* is a two-hulled boat that usually sails on one hull, while a *trimaran* is a three-hulled boat that regularly sails on two.) Windage of the third hull is still present, however.

Cats seem to have a performance edge over tris, with less windage, potentially less wetted surface (with only one hull left in the water), and potentially less weight (since there is one less hull to build). However, I have seen greater performance differences due to the final weight of multihulls than to the inherent configuration. Heavy cruising catamarans are definitely slow, and lightweight cruising trimarans are definitely fast. The boats are weight-sensitive because their hulls are very slim. A small increase in weight or cargo inside will immerse the hulls deeper in the water (than on a comparable monohull), with a corresponding increase in wetted surface and frictional drag. Most builders of multihulls, as a result, are very weight conscious.

Some small catamarans that are expected to spend a lot of time sailing with one hull lifted clear of the water have eliminated the need for a daggerboard. By creating asymmetrical hulls with a curved inboard face and a flatter outside face, lift is generated as they move through the water. To the purist this low aspect ratio, rather inefficient lifting surface may seem laughable, but keep in mind the speeds at which these boats are traveling. If this were a slow, lumbering boat, then the leeway angles would be in the double digits, but when the boat is traveling at high speeds, very high lift can be generated at low leeway angles.

If multihulls are so fast, why don't we see more of them around? Indeed, why haven't they supplanted monohulls in racing and cruising? Multihulls have long existed on the fringe of the sailing fraternity, and for many sailors they are still "out there." While the first multihull to emerge from the drawing board of a "mainstream" designer was the catamaran *John Gilpin* by Nat Herreshoff in 1876, multis have never been part of the traditional yacht club scene. One mark against them is the practicality of beam: unless it is consigned to a mooring, a multihull needs the same berthing space as two (or more) monohulls of the same overall length. If dock space is at a premium, yacht clubs or marinas may charge prohibitive rates for multis, or forbid them altogether. Some builders have tried to address this handicap by creating clever "folding" trimaran designs that retract their amas for docking.

Multihulls are also at a disadvantage to monohulls in interior amenities. With performance requirements minimizing their beam and wetted surface, hulls as we have seen offer minimal volume. Trimarans can use the middle hull for accommodations, but cruising catamarans generally are limited to long, narrow berths, building living space into the structural area linking the hulls. A heavy-displacement multihull is a contradiction in terms, and so, even with better-appointed cruisers, amenities can be handsome but not ornate. To "accommodate" accommodations, catamarans must increase freeboard, so that a transverse-section cabin with standing headroom is well clear of the water. This, of course, increases its windage and hampers low-speed maneuverability. Cruising multihulls suffer other knocks from sailors raised on monohulls. The hull motion is far different, and some find it too bumpy when moving along at a good clip in a chop.

But there are many advantages to the multihull configuration in cruising applications. Foremost, a multi can get to a distant anchorage in half the time (or less) that it takes a mono of comparable size. During the passage, the minimal heel is a welcome novelty to monohull galley slaves used to functioning in a belowdecks world canted 20 degrees or more. At the end of the passage, a large multi can squeeze into shallow waters its ballasted cousins can only consider exploring with the yacht's dinghy. In this way, the cruising multihull overcomes the handicap of large monohull cruisers—it has both a large cruising range and the ability to exploit shallow-draft anchorages. Deck space, augmented by netted areas between the hulls, is incredible, and the cabin of a catamaran, suspended between the hulls, has novel transverse dimensions monohull sailors can attain only in hulls at least twice as long. (See Chapter 7 for more.)

In ocean racing circles, multihulls were pushing the extremes of performance long before monohullers joined in. Mainstream designers had little or no interest in them, and it was left to more intuitive enthusiasts to create the pioneering high-speed craft. Naturally, in a field that had to learn from its mistakes, mistakes were made. There were plenty of capsizes, creating the (not unfounded) perception that these innovations were low on seaworthiness. Further exacerbating this reputation, many bluewater cruising multis were the work of home builders, among whom quality control and the appreciation of the effect of materials upon performance and structural integrity is always unpredictable.

Even today, leading round-the-world races like the Whitbread, the Around Alone, and the Vendée Globe forbid multihull entries. This is because of the Achilles' heel of high-performance multihulls in the southern oceans, where towering waves can exploit the multihull's vulnerability—stability at 90 degrees of heel. (These ocean races are essentially a circumnavigation of Antarctica.) Once a multihull is pressed past 90 degrees, with no ballast to increase the righting arm it essentially falls over, upside down in the water. An upside-down multihull is exceptionally stable. Indeed, some capsized sailors have been able to live inside the overturned hulls while awaiting rescue.

The argument that monohulls are inherently more stable than multihulls is becoming less and less certain. Singlehanded round-the-world competitors have experienced multiple knockdowns, including 360-degree rolls, and kept on sailing. Monohulls have traditionally been "self-rescuing"—they usually return to an upright position and carry on, even if under jury rig. However, as monohulls become more radical, with wider beams, lighter displacement, and at least some ballasting pro-

The 1992 International America's Cup Class yacht Il Moro di Venezia *sports a weight-saving destroyer bow.*

FIG 1.19
Sheerlines and hull character

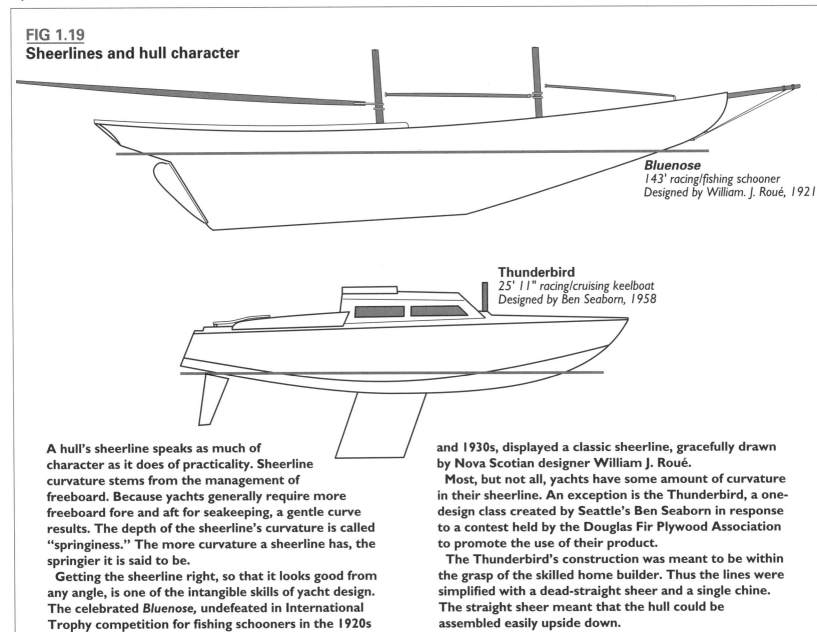

Bluenose
143' racing/fishing schooner
Designed by William. J. Roué, 1921

Thunderbird
25' 11" racing/cruising keelboat
Designed by Ben Seaborn, 1958

A hull's sheerline speaks as much of character as it does of practicality. Sheerline curvature stems from the management of freeboard. Because yachts generally require more freeboard fore and aft for seakeeping, a gentle curve results. The depth of the sheerline's curvature is called "springiness." The more curvature a sheerline has, the springier it is said to be.

Getting the sheerline right, so that it looks good from any angle, is one of the intangible skills of yacht design. The celebrated *Bluenose,* undefeated in International Trophy competition for fishing schooners in the 1920s and 1930s, displayed a classic sheerline, gracefully drawn by Nova Scotian designer William J. Roué.

Most, but not all, yachts have some amount of curvature in their sheerline. An exception is the Thunderbird, a one-design class created by Seattle's Ben Seaborn in response to a contest held by the Douglas Fir Plywood Association to promote the use of their product.

The Thunderbird's construction was meant to be within the grasp of the skilled home builder. Thus the lines were simplified with a dead-straight sheer and a single chine. The straight sheer meant that the hull could be assembled easily upside down.

vided by water, their characteristics become more those of multihulls. In particular their stability is more dependent on form rather than weight, and returning them to an upright condition after a capsize is becoming increasingly more difficult. It remains to be seen whether such "multihull-like" behavior in high-performance keelboats is considered tolerable—part of the death-defying nature of the contest—or is addressed with restrictive measures designed to make these monohulls more "monohull-like."

character traits: transoms, freeboard, and sheerline

The main defining hull characteristics are sheerline and transom styles. Cruising boat aesthetics generally dictate that the sheer have noticeable curvature (sometimes called *springiness*) when viewed from the side (Fig. 1.19), and that the transom be raked aft and up.

Transom rake generally does illustrate the boat's raison d'être. In a cruising boat the designer often finds that to maximize the useful space in the cockpit (and in turn allow as much cabin space as possible) the deck needs to be long, with a reasonable amount of overhang aft. This leads to either vertical or raked-aft transoms. A springy sheer, apart from its aesthetic quality, does serve some practical ends. Raising the sheer as it moves fore and aft provides for a drier boat, and if it is sufficiently curved toward the bow, headroom in the forward berth is increased. In small cruising boats, this curvature can be dramatic as the designer attempts to shoehorn every last inch of headroom into the forward berth.

The sheerline invokes decisions about freeboard. A springy sheer allows the designer to maximize and minimize freeboard according to where it is needed or not. It keeps freeboard relatively low in the middle of the boat, which reduces windage. High freeboard overall means lots of room inside the boat and continued form stability at high heel angles, but it pays a price in additional windage, which hurts upwind sailing and hampers control while anchoring and docking. High freeboard also is a prime consideration in the aesthetics of a boat. For many people, an accommodations-conscious design with towering freeboard is just plain ugly. At the other extreme, low freeboard overall is wet, as any ride on a Meter boat in a stiff breeze will demonstrate.

In a racing boat the emphasis is on speed and less (if at all) on the sailor's comfort. Racers are weight-conscious, and once displacement is set for a particular design, all hull volume and materials above the waterline that are not absolutely necessary to keeping the boat moving and afloat are on the chopping block. After all, weight saved above the waterline can be reallocated as ballast, improving stability and permitting a design to carry more sail area. As a result, a racing yacht's freeboard tends to be as low as a rating rule and common sense will allow. In addition to saving weight in a portion of the hull deemed superfluous, reducing the freeboard also improves stability by lowering the position of the deck, all the hardware bolted to it, and the crew.

Transoms are raked forward for the same reason: to save weight. "Reverse" transoms cut away whatever aft deck isn't considered essential. The cockpit must be moved forward as a result, which is not a problem with a dedicated racer, as the crew's weight ideally should be more centrally located, and not

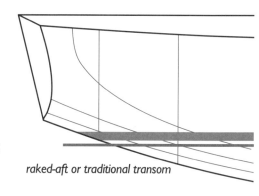

raked-aft or traditional transom

vertical transom

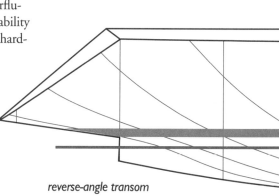

reverse-angle transom

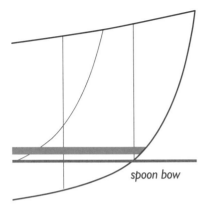

spoon bow

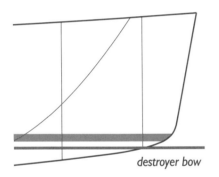

destroyer bow

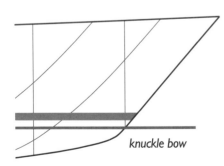

knuckle bow

bunched over the rudder, to reduce pitching. Moving the cockpit forward, of course, reduces the room available for the cabin and its trunk, but the priority for such amenities is minimal to nonexistent.

bow shapes: from·spoons to destroyers

Walk through any yacht club or marina and you will encounter any number of bow shapes—not unlike walking through a parking lot and studying the grilles of cars. As with cars, there is a definite aesthetic component to bows. A boat's bow profile conveys much about its character and purpose. By the same token, those profiles are steeped in design history and contradictions.

For many sailors, the elegant curve of the spoon bow harks back to "traditional" design values. But surprisingly, this bow form arose from rating rules that penalized waterline length; in response, waterlines were kept short and the hull length stretched above the waterline to produce more effective sailing length. Traditional Meter boats have this characteristic shape. The spoon bow carries an added benefit in a sea, in that pitching is reduced because of the huge reserve buoyancy sitting just above the waterline.

Many production racer-cruisers in the 1970s abandoned the classic spoon for a sharp knuckle. Again, a rating rule was behind the development. Under the IOR in the 1970s the forefoot (where the bottom of the bow stem meets the profile) tended to get deeper and sharper. This corner was below the waterline, which had the benefit of packing more volume and therefore sailing length into the boat without increasing the rating. The negative effect, however, was to make the boat difficult to steer in waves. The relatively sharp and deep entry would take control and cause the boat to round up into the wind. In the post-IOR era, the forward end of the forefoot moved up closer to the waterline, and sometimes above it, to improve steering characteristics. A knuckle above the waterline is not unlike a shortened Meter bow, providing some reserve buoyancy.

The near-vertical destroyer bow has been made popular by classes that measure overall length (like the MORC 30 and the Whitbread 60), but some other design types, like catamarans, have found their own reasons for vertical bows. Vertical bows are nothing new to yachting. Cutters and catboats already had "plumb" bows in the last century. British rating systems actually encouraged them, as the Thames Rule, used until 1878, measured rated length from bow stem to rudder post. The failure to distinguish overall length from waterline length, the true indicator of potential hull speed, encouraged shapes with no overhang forward (as any hull length above the waterline here would be measured as if it were waterline) and with extreme overhangs aft (as the yacht would pick up unmeasured waterline length as it heeled).

A vertical bow permits the maximum amount of waterline in a minimum overall length. Perhaps if the speed/dollars ratio is to be maximized, the vertical bow is the way to go. But with no overhang forward, the topsides near the bow are much more vertical than normal; reserve buoyancy (hull volume above the waterline) is lowered and with it resistance to pitching. This consequence contradicts one argument for eliminating bow overhang—the reduced weight is supposed to diminish pitching! Although traditional catamaran and trimaran hulls have quite spoon-shaped bows, many recent designs (perhaps inspired by weight-conscious racing multihulls) have gone to more vertical bows. Many designers have found that they then need to widen the deck substantially or add a flared chine near the bow to reduce the pitching tendency when the boat is hard pressed under sail or moving at speed through waves.

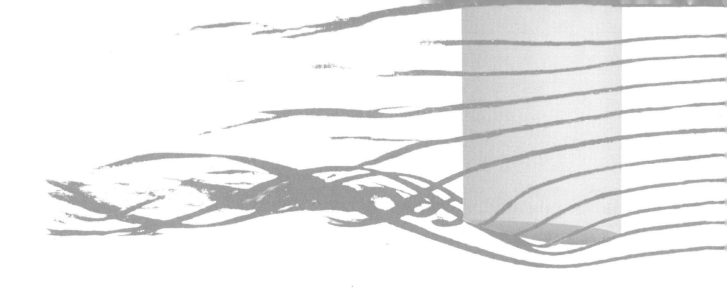

keels

The task of keeping a yacht moving to windward has fostered a long history of keel innovation. With progress in keel shapes have come fundamental changes in yachts in general.

giving a little leeway: the performance paradox

Keels are designed to resist leeway so that a yacht can sail efficiently against the wind, but without some leeway, a keel cannot function.

What is a keel supposed to do? When its role of housing ballast is left aside, the answer is deceptively simple. Like its unballasted cousins, the daggerboard and centerboard, it is there to stop the boat from going sideways. Thus a keel is said to improve performance by reducing the difference between the direction in which the boat is pointed and the direction in which it is actually going. This difference is called *leeway angle*.

Sailors detest excessive leeway. It forces them to take extra hitches to windward to get where they are going and threatens trouble on lee shores. The less leeway a keel permits, then, the happier the average sailor is. It follows that the happiest sailor would have a truly, perfectly efficient keel that permitted no leeway angle, no sideways motion at all. Course steered would be course achieved. But this dream, like ones that perpetually chase perpetual motion, is an impossible one. The paradox of keel performance is that for a keel to work—for it to prevent a boat from going sideways—the boat (at least as conventionally designed) must have some sideways motion. Leeway is what a keel is designed to reduce, but to reduce it, a keel requires leeway.

To resist sideways motion, a keel must generate lift, just the way the boat's sails do. Like a sail, a keel is a foil, and both operate according to the same scientific principle in their own viscous elements: the sail in air (where aerodynamics frame its performance), the keel in water (where hydrodynamics rule). Above or below the waterline, the foil obeys Bernoulli's principle, so named for its discoverer, the eighteenth-century Swiss scientist Daniel Bernoulli. Mr. Bernoulli made a name for himself by determining that the pressure of a fluid changes with velocity. The faster a fluid moves, the lower its pressure. It follows from Bernoulli's principle that a pressure difference can be created on an object if fluid flowing past it is moving faster on one side than on the other. (See Fig. 2.1.)

If you take, say, this book, with the spine pointing straight up, and hold it over the side of your boat while underway so that it is parallel to the flow of water, the water naturally flows along both sides with equal speed; there is no pressure difference between the two sides. If, however, you turn the book slightly, the water flowing around the downstream side must move faster than the water flowing past the upstream side, as it now must cover a greater distance in work-

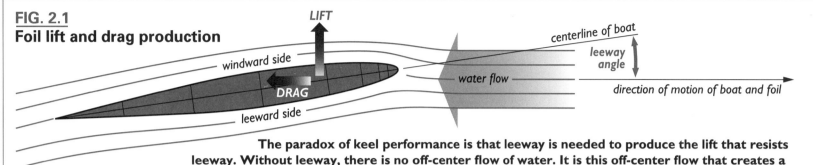

ing around the angled book. The downstream side experiences a drop in pressure relative to the upstream side. Lift has just been created—a greater pressure on the upstream side pressing the book in the direction of the downstream side. (Don't lose the book or you'll miss the next section.)

The angle to the flow of water you introduced in the book is known as the *angle of incidence* (sometimes called the *angle of attack*)—it is the off-centerline angle of flow a fluid requires to create a pressure difference, and thus lift, in an object. Note carefully that the object in our exercise wasn't the least bit aerodynamic (or hydrodynamic). No foil shape was required to conjure the effects of Bernoulli's principle. That is why many dinghies are able to use flat-as-pancake centerboards and daggerboards and still sail smartly to windward. But as we shall see, the foil's shape serves critical functions in making the keel perform as efficiently as possible.

In a conventional sailboat, angle of incidence and leeway angle are one and the same thing. The direction of the boat determines the direction of flow of the fluid; because the keel is fixed along the centerline, if the flow is not angled even a few degrees from the centerline no

lift can be generated. Thus the boat must slip sideways at least a small amount. It is leeway that creates the off-center direction of flow around the keel, for as the boat moves sideways ever so slightly, it makes the water flow approach the keel from the leeward side. This makes the leeward side of the keel the shorter route for the water flow and the windward side the longer route. The windward side experiences Mr. Bernoulli's pressure drop and lift is created, counteracting the lift force of the sails that is trying to push the boat sideways. Forward motion is created—with a little bit of necessary leeway thrown in.

Some of you no doubt are already getting bright ideas and thinking: Couldn't we get rid of leeway altogether if the keel wasn't fixed on the centerline, if the necessary angle of incidence was created by angling the keel itself? Well, yes, but there is some challenging engineering involved, some of it prohibitive, and we'll get to that later in this chapter.

Leeway is not constant. It changes according to the direction and speed of the boat. Fig. 2.2 shows a boat sailing three different courses: downwind, on a beam reach, and upwind. When it is sailing directly downwind, on the left of the illustration, the sail force

FIG. 2.2
Leeway angle and points of sail

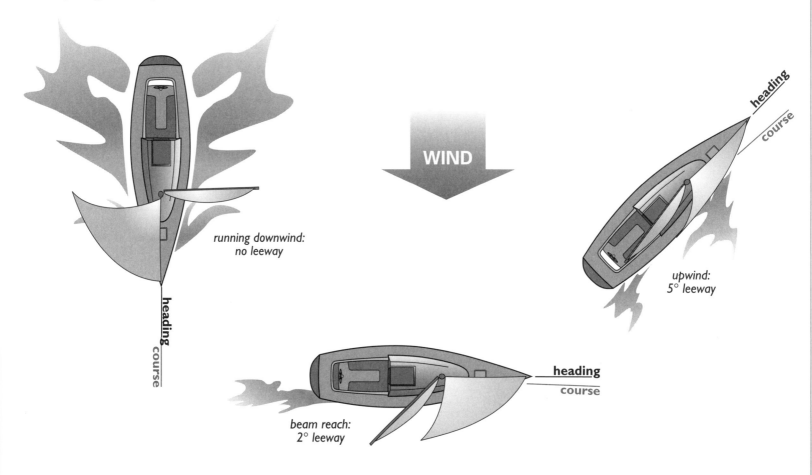

running downwind:
no leeway

WIND

heading
course

upwind:
5° leeway

heading
course

heading
course

beam reach:
2° leeway

Leeway varies according to the lift requirements of the keel. Running downwind, no lift is required (or desired), so leeway is nil. Reaching, 2 degrees of leeway may be needed to generate sufficient keel lift to offset the lift forces of the sails. Upwind, where lift forces on the sails greatly increase, 5 degrees of leeway typically is necessary to keep the boat tracking efficiently to windward.

pushes along the centerline of the boat; there is no tendency for the boat to turn, and consequently both the rudder and keel are producing no lift. The boat sails straight downwind, makes no leeway, and the wake is directly in line with the centerline of the boat.

In the middle, our boat is on a beam reach and the force on the sails no longer acts down the centerline of the boat. If the boat had no keel it would be pushed sideways until it reached a speed at which the resistance of the rapidly drifting boat equaled the side force of the sails. However, this boat does have a keel and consequently the keel generates the lift required to balance the sail forces. To generate the necessary amount of lift on a beam reach, the keel and hull must move through the water at a leeway angle typically of 2 degrees. This leeway angle will increase if the wind speed grows or the boat slows down. On the right, our boat has sails sheeted in hard and is going to windward, making a leeway angle of about 5 degrees. At this angle, the keel produces enough lift to match the greatly increased side force of the sails.

An efficient keel is one that produces the required lift at a very low leeway angle while creating minimum drag. The efficiency is controlled by the foil shape and finishing details like smoothness and fairness, but the most important factor is the aspect ratio (see below) of the keel itself. A keel with a deep, narrow profile, just like the high-efficiency wings on a glider, is the secret to superb upwind performance.

lift coefficient: why not just lift?

The relationship between the area of a keel, its speed, and the density of the fluid through which it is passing are all fundamental to keel design. Theoretical equations that address these relationships allow a designer to determine what size keel is appropriate for any boat.

Some of the relationships are intuitive, but others you might find surprising. Because water is denser than air, water logically produces far more force (800 times) on the same foil at the same angle. And if a keel's area is doubled, then the lift it produces is doubled—that seems intuitively acceptable. If, however, the speed of travel through the fluid is doubled, lift increases by a factor of four—the increase is proportional to the square of the velocity. Since speed is such a sensitive factor in the production of lift, a keel on an inherently faster hull does not need to be as large as one on a slower boat.

With the discovery of these relationships, a convenient way of presenting experimental lift and drag results was determined. The measured lift or drag is often divided by the fluid density, foil surface area, and speed squared, to remove the contribution to lift by those factors. The remaining value, called the *lift coefficient*, is an indicator of the efficiency of the foil. If lift were influenced only by these three factors, then the lift coefficient would be constant for all foils, keels, and sailing conditions. However, lift is further affected by the angle of incidence and by a list of less obvious factors, including aspect ratio, fairness, foil section type, and filleting details.

irresistible: drag and foil shape

Drag, the resistance to motion, is a critical concern when choosing the cross-sectional shape of a foil, commonly known as the *foil section*. Drag also demands attention when determining the area and aspect ratio of the keel, for they too affect the total drag.

With underwater appendages, the two compo-

Lift Coefficient

The lift coefficient is:

$$\frac{Lift}{0.5 \times rho \times Area \times Vel^2}$$

For imperial measure, the units of each term are:
Lift: pounds
rho (mass density of the liquid):
  for fresh water 1.94 slugs/ft³
  for salt water 1.99 slugs/ft³
  for air 0.00238 slugs/ft³
Area: square feet of keel area
Velocity: speed of motion in feet/second

For example, a 35-foot sloop traveling at 6.2 knots upwind in fresh water might have a lift coefficient as follows:

Lift: 1,020 lbs
rho: 1.94 slugs/ft³
Keel Area: 26 sq ft
Velocity: 6.2 × 1.688 = 10.47 ft/sec

Lift coefficient:
1,020/(0.5 × 1.94 × 26 × 10.47²)
= 0.369

FIG. 2.3
Keel drag types

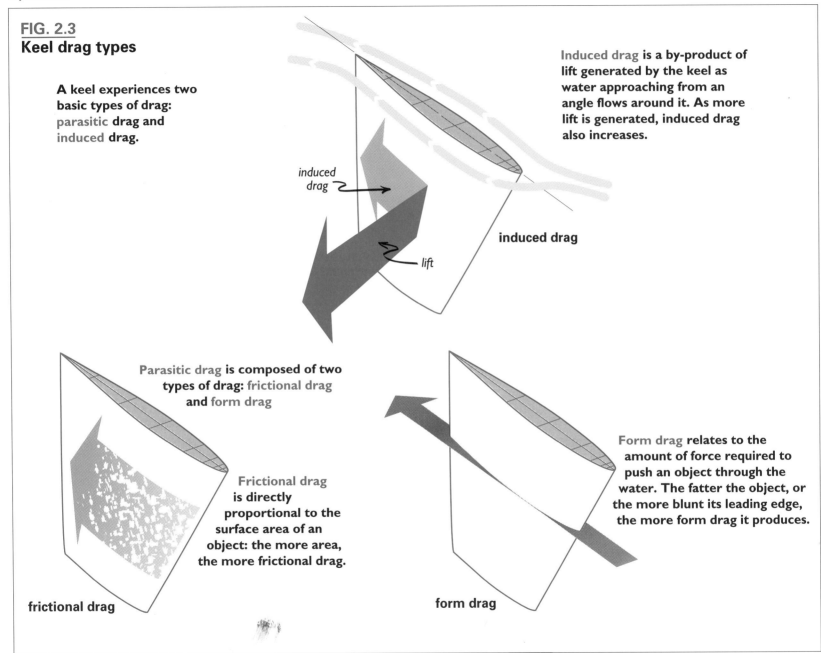

A keel experiences two basic types of drag: parasitic drag and induced drag.

Induced drag is a by-product of lift generated by the keel as water approaching from an angle flows around it. As more lift is generated, induced drag also increases.

induced drag

lift

induced drag

Parasitic drag is composed of two types of drag: frictional drag and form drag

Frictional drag is directly proportional to the surface area of an object: the more area, the more frictional drag.

Form drag relates to the amount of force required to push an object through the water. The fatter the object, or the more blunt its leading edge, the more form drag it produces.

frictional drag

form drag

nents of drag are *parasitic drag* and *induced drag.* (See Fig. 2.3.) Wavemaking drag, so important to minimize for hulls, is not a concern. Neither keels nor any other object totally immersed in a single fluid make waves.

Parasitic drag, so named because it is always present and always slows the object down, is composed of frictional drag and form drag. *Frictional drag,* the easiest of the drags to understand, is the resistance due to water (a viscous fluid) flowing past the surface of the object. The greater the surface area, the greater the frictional drag; other than making the object very small and very smooth there is not much that can be done to minimize frictional drag. Most designers will go to great lengths to reduce the wetted area of hull and keel to keep the frictional drag under control. If 1 square foot can be removed from the wetted area of a keel, then the benefit will be seen at all times—upwind, downwind, reaching, and even motoring. But caution flags should be set flying whenever the area of a keel is reduced for the purpose of lowering frictional drag. Those flags are a reminder that there are two other drag components, form drag and induced drag, which need to be observed at the same time.

Form drag is related to the thickness and, understandably, the form or shape of the object. Form drag is the reason it takes more force to push a fat foil than a thin foil through the water. Even if the foil type remains the same (an NACA 64A foil for example), the form drag will increase if the overall thickness is increased. Slightly more subtle than a thickness change, but nonetheless important, is the change in the foil section itself. Two keels that are of the same thickness may have quite different form drags because one used a 10-34 foil, which has a fine front end (low form drag), and the other a 64A foil with a much fuller forward end (higher form drag).

In discussing parasitic drag thus far, we have assumed that the foil is lined up directly with the water flow and no lift is being produced—the downwind scenario. If we were designing a keel to perform best in downwind conditions it would be squeezed down to a minimum area and would favor a foil with minimum form drag. However, since most sailboats need to move to windward at least some of the time, the final drag component, induced drag, must be added to the balancing act of keel design.

Induced drag is a by-product of the lift being produced by the foil. As a sailboat is turned up toward the wind, the angle of incidence of the keel increases and lift begins to grow—and so too does induced drag. Induced drag is influenced by the angle of incidence, the aspect ratio of the keel, and, like form drag, the foil section shape. The choice of a foil section thus is dictated by the lift and drag characteristics desired for the performance of a particular boat.

We will discuss properties of foil sections later in this chapter. For now, it is important to recognize that balancing parasitic (frictional and form) drag and induced drag is a significant part of the keel design process. As the area of a keel is increased, parasitic drag grows, because of added friction. But as the keel area becomes larger (and the lift it is required to produce remains the same), the lift coefficient drops and induced drag is lessened. So we have a growing parasitic drag and a decreasing induced drag—somewhere there will be an optimum-size keel that will produce a minimum drag overall.

tall tales: keel aspect ratio

Casually put, *aspect ratio* refers to how tall an object is compared to its width. But when airfoil data is being compared and keels optimized, it is important to have a consistent and precise definition. Unfortunately,

Viewed from below, this wind-tunnel foil vividly shows the tip vortices created as air "leaks" from the high-pressure (left) to the low-pressure (right) side of the foil by curling around the tip. Water behaves exactly the same way at the tip of a keel.

FIG. 2.4
Water flow in two and three dimensions

Two-dimensional flow:
Infinite aspect ratio

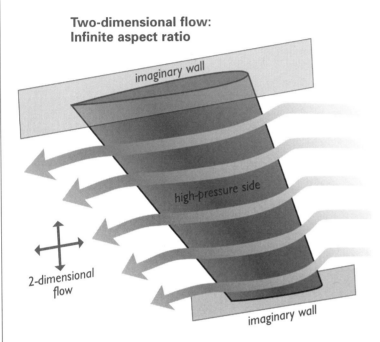

Bound by imaginary walls, this keel experiences flow in only two dimensions—no flow moves up or down the length of the keel. It is said to have infinite aspect ratio, with no losses at the root or tip.

Three-dimensional flow:
Significant tip vortex

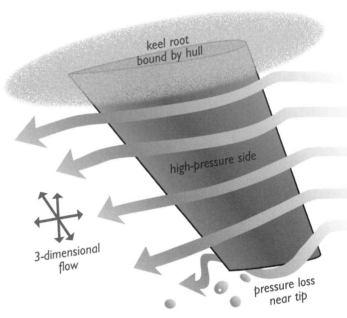

In real life, flow behaves in three dimensions. The hull surface at the keel root acts as an end plate to contain flow, but at the keel tip, flow migrates from the high-pressure to the low-pressure side, producing a significant tip vortex. The amount of tip loss depends on aspect ratio.

in the world of foils there are several different ways to define the aspect ratio, which can make for much confusion when yacht designers move between definitions without warning.

The ratio of the span of an object to its average chord length is called *geometric aspect ratio*. A measuring stick standing on end might have an aspect ratio of 12, while this book lying open on the table has an aspect ratio of 0.4. With a keel, the span is derived from its height, and the chord from its fore-and-aft width (for a straight tapering keel, this is the average of the chord at the hull and at the tip).

But for purposes of understanding keel performance, the geometric aspect ratio does not go far enough. Here is why. As Bernoulli revealed, a liquid flowing past a foil produces lift because it creates low-

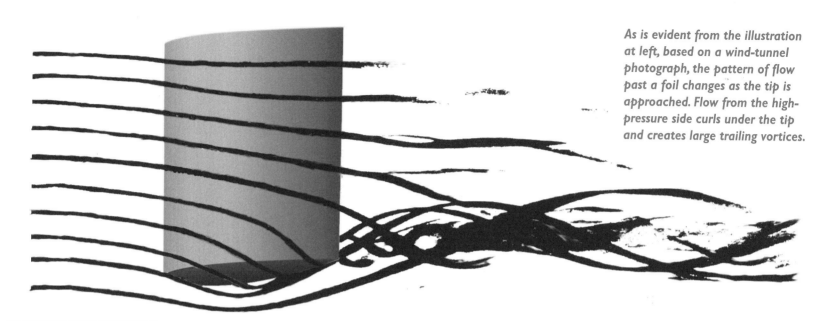

As is evident from the illustration at left, based on a wind-tunnel photograph, the pattern of flow past a foil changes as the tip is approached. Flow from the high-pressure side curls under the tip and creates large trailing vortices.

and high-pressure sides. The most efficient foil has either an extreme span (with a very high geometric aspect ratio) or has a "wall" or "fence" at each end to corral the flow. A perfectly fenced-in foil, which is a purely theoretical device, is said to have infinite aspect ratio. The drag of the fences is not included in an assessment of the performance of this perfect foil, as this is not a three-dimensional world. The liquid flowing over this ideal foil is two dimensional. It travels in the direction of motion (the first dimension) and is pushed out around the thickness of the foil (the second dimension), but does not have any motion along the length of the foil because of the end walls. (See Fig. 2.4.)

In the real world this situation seldom arises (although the addition of winglets and end plates to the bottom of keels is intended to get close to that ideal case, and aircraft wings often sprout winglets to minimize drag). When one wall is removed, as in the case of a conventional keel on a sailboat (which still has a wall

at the top of the keel, formed by the hull) the flow becomes three dimensional. Water near the tip of the keel no longer has anything preventing it from seeking the path of least resistance, around the bottom of the keel from the high- to the low-pressure side. Because of this leak in pressure the total force, and therefore the lift, is reduced.

These tip losses are indicated by the tip vortex, a turbulent flow that spirals its way around the bottom end of the keel. (See the illustration above and on on page 67.) The combination of the flow traveling from the high- to the low-pressure sides of the foil and the ambient flow past the keel produces the telltale oblique spiral. The greater this vortex is, the greater the loss in lift. Some of the largest vortices are produced by low aspect ratio keels with large chord lengths at the tip. The inverted 12-Meter keels made popular by *Australia II* are a good example. These low aspect

A winged keel created by Steve Killing for the 8-Meter Octavia, features high-aspect winglets designed to combat the enormous vortices the large keel tip otherwise would generate.

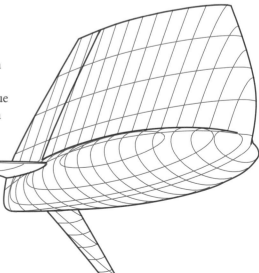

FIG. 2.5
The concept of an "effective keel"

The **aspect ratio** of a boat's true keel is calculated using a span measured from the tip of the keel to its base at the hull.

Research, however, has shown that the end-plate effect of the hull creates a larger **effective keel**, which has a span generally ranging from 85 to 99 percent of keel draft.

To gauge the efficiency of the keel and compare it to published wing data, the aspect ratio of the effective keel must be doubled, to arrive at the **aerodynamic aspect ratio**. Thus, the aspect ratio of the effective keel is more than double that of the true keel.

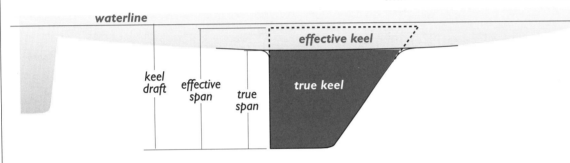

waterline

effective keel

keel draft

effective span

true span

true keel

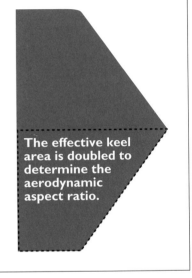

The effective keel area is doubled to determine the aerodynamic aspect ratio.

ratio keels (with a geometric aspect ratio of about 0.35) have very long bottom chords that, if left without wings or end plates, generate horrendous vortices. If the flow is contained, however, high degrees of lift can be produced. (The theory behind, and origin of, winged keels is discussed in Chapter 10.)

Most texts presenting experimental lift and drag data refer to aspect ratio as the span divided by the chord of a wing, with no hull, fuselage, or wall attached to the wing. In the analysis of sailboat keels or centerboards, though, it has been found that the "end plate effect" of the hull is very effective indeed and gives the keel the lift properties of an aspect ratio substantially higher than that calculated using the geometric aspect ratio. The drawings in Fig. 2.5 of a typical keel show the true keel and the effective keel profiles. The effec-

tive keel is taller than the actual keel because of the contribution of the hull to the performance of the keel. Effective keel depths usually vary from 85 to 99 percent of the keel draft, depending on the beam-to-draft ratio of the hull. This effective keel represents the area that is actually producing lift. To gauge the efficiency of the keel and compare it to published wing data, however, the aspect ratio of this effective keel must be doubled, to arrive at the *aerodynamic aspect ratio*.

The aspect ratio of a wing is technically defined as the span squared, divided by the area of its surface. The corollary for a boat's keel with straight edges is the span divided by the average chord length. Designers confuse the issue further by using the loose term "aspect ratio" to refer to either the geometric aspect ratio of the physical keel, the effective aspect ratio of the effective keel, or

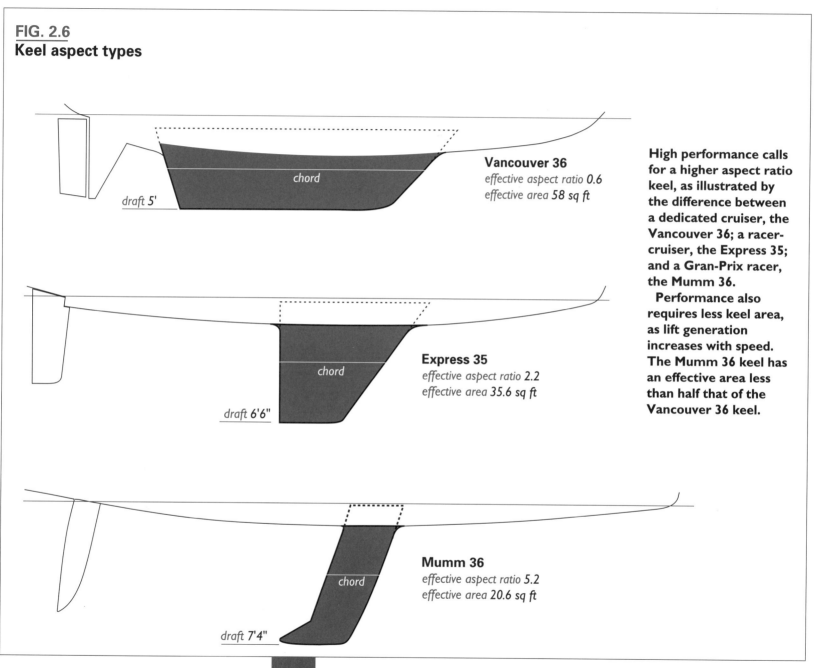

FIG. 2.6
Keel aspect types

Vancouver 36
effective aspect ratio 0.6
effective area 58 sq ft

chord

draft 5'

Express 35
effective aspect ratio 2.2
effective area 35.6 sq ft

chord

draft 6'6"

Mumm 36
effective aspect ratio 5.2
effective area 20.6 sq ft

chord

draft 7'4"

High performance calls for a higher aspect ratio keel, as illustrated by the difference between a dedicated cruiser, the Vancouver 36; a racer-cruiser, the Express 35; and a Gran-Prix racer, the Mumm 36.

Performance also requires less keel area, as lift generation increases with speed. The Mumm 36 keel has an effective area less than half that of the Vancouver 36 keel.

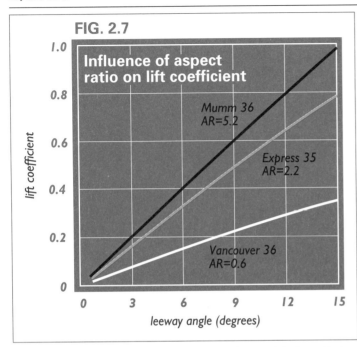

FIG. 2.7

Influence of aspect ratio on lift coefficient

Mumm 36
AR=5.2

Express 35
AR=2.2

Vancouver 36
AR=0.6

lift coefficient

leeway angle (degrees)

the aerodynamic aspect ratio (twice the effective aspect ratio). Any of these is useful in making comparisons with keels on other boats, but for analyzing lift and drag, the two important quantities are aerodynamic aspect ratio and the effective keel area.

Whether you refer to a keel's geometric or aerodynamic aspect ratio, the influence of the ratio on performance is still marked. Fig. 2.7, adapted from Abbott and Von Doenhoff's reference book *Theory of Wing Sections,* shows the strong influence of aspect ratio on lift coefficient, using examples of production keelboats with three distinct keel types: the Vancouver 36, a full-keel cruiser; Steve Killing's Express 35, a racer-cruiser; and the Mumm 36 racer. (See Fig. 2.6.) The higher the slope of that lift curve, the better. The angle of incidence, listed across the bottom of the plot, equates to a sailboat's leeway—the angle of the incoming flow to the keel. If the designer's goal is to produce the required lift (or *lift coefficient*) at the lowest angle of incidence (meaning with the least amount of leeway), then the highest aspect ratio keel looks desirable.

So why wouldn't every boat have a keel like the deep, narrow one of the Mumm 36?

There is a practical limit to the aspect ratio of a keel, that's why. To increase the aspect ratio while keeping the area of the keel constant, the keel span must increase. Racing boat designers know this, and a quick flip through sailing magazines will find 45-foot ocean racers with efficient keel drafts of more than 9 feet.

That depth of keel won't work for a lot of people. Every sailor has his or her own personal limit of depth. Docks, rocks, and favorite anchorages often won't permit anything that hangs more than 5 or 6 feet below the surface of the water. Marketing departments of production builders know that most boats with 9 feet of draft won't sell, so a designer has to make an intelligent trade-off between draft and aspect ratio.

The Mumm 36, designed by Bruce Farr, has a very high aspect ratio, deep-draft keel drawing 7.3 feet of water—prohibitive for many sailors, but it gives exceptional upwind performance appropriate to its role as a Gran-Prix racer. The Express 35 has a moderate aerodynamic aspect ratio of 2.2, as a compromise between performance and draft, which was limited by marketing concerns to 6.5 feet. The Vancouver 36, designed by Robert Harris with a draft of 5 feet, extends the cruising area even further, but pays a penalty in upwind performance. Neither solution is better than the other—each is suited to a specific type of sailing and works only within that genre. The Vancouver keel on the Mumm would be just as bad a pairing as the Mumm keel with the Vancouver

section solving: determining keel shape

Good experimental aerodynamic airfoil data is available and can be applied directly to yacht design. The great density difference between air and water alters the force that an airfoil produces but does not alter the lift coefficient characteristics. Many designers use the NACA foil section data compiled by Abbott and Von Doenhoff in *Theory of Wing Sections.* The text presents not only the lift and drag data for each foil section, but also the offsets to allow the foils themselves to be reproduced.

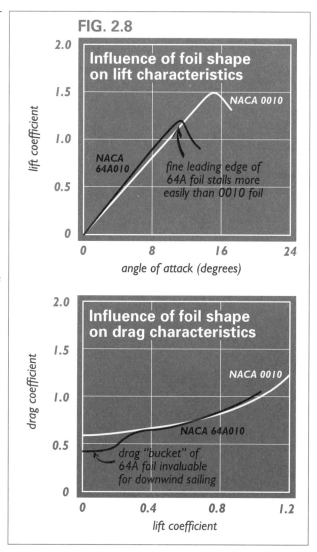

NACA 64A010
NACA 0010

The foils used for underwater appendages tend to be symmetrical: one side is the same as the other. With only a few special-purpose exceptions, boats must be able to operate equally well on port and starboard tack. (An exception is made with some high-performance multihulls that sport asymmetrical daggerboards. The boat needs only the leeward daggerboard in the water on any tack, so it can have a foil shape purpose built for maximum lift on that tack.) Although designers at times have been tempted by the enhanced performance of an asymmetrical foil, either the practical necessity of operating on both tacks or the complexity of changing the shape of a foil while underway eliminates it as a real performance solution.

The symmetrical foils for rudders, keels, and bulbs are slightly different shapes because of the different task each is expected to perform. (See Chapter 4 for a full discussion of rudders.) Rudders require large maximum lift coefficients, keels require low drag and high lift slopes, and bulbs require low drag and generally have no lift requirements.

Some typical keel foil sections include the 63A, 64A, 65A, and 10-34. The aerodynamic data for the 64A010 foil is presented in Fig. 2.8 and compared to the 0010 rudder foil. (See the sidebar on page 74 on foil label nomenclature.) Both sections have the same thickness, 10 percent of the chord length, but have quite different lift and drag characteristics.

The 64A010 foil section has a steeper lift slope than the 0010, which means that to produce the same amount of lift the foil would not need as great a leeway angle. The detriment to the lift curve of the "64A" foil is the lower stall point, which comes at a lift coefficient of 1.2 instead of 1.5 for the "00" foil. However, the keel will normally be operating down at a lift coefficient of less than 0.5, well away from the stall area. The only time a keel approaches stall is when it must produce a large side force at a low speed. That happens during a poorly executed tack—the boat has slowed considerably, the sails have been pulled in on the new tack, loading up the keel, and if the maximum lift coefficient of 1.2 is exceeded the keel will stall and the boat will slide sideways. A careful study of the two foil sections, 00 and 64A, will reveal that the front end of the 00 foil is thicker and the leading-edge radius is larger, both helping to prevent stalling.

It would be ideal to have a keel that when pointed downwind had no drag and produced no lift—perhaps a lifting daggerboard comes closest to this. But in a ballasted boat, weight is required for stability at all times, and lifting the keel is just not an option. In this case a foil section that can offer at least significantly reduced drag downwind is the one to choose. The 64A

FIG. 2.8

Influence of foil shape on lift characteristics

NACA 0010

NACA 64A010

fine leading edge of 64A foil stalls more easily than 0010 foil

angle of attack (degrees)

lift coefficient

Influence of foil shape on drag characteristics

NACA 0010

NACA 64A010

drag "bucket" of 64A foil invaluable for downwind sailing

drag coefficient

lift coefficient

Reading the foils

The U.S. NACA (National Advisory Committee for Aeronautics) conducted extensive research in the late 1940s into the properties of various airfoil shapes. In doing so they categorized the shapes by letters and numbers.

For example, the **0010** foil, reading left to right, indicates

0 – foil is symmetric

0 – location of asymmetry (still zero)

10 – thickness in percentage of chord

The **64A012** foil translates as

6 – series number

4 – location of minimum pressure aft of the leading edge (0.4)

A – indicates that from 80 percent aft the curve becomes a straight line

0 – indicates a symmetric foil

12 – thickness in percentage of chord (The maximum thickness of the 63, 64, and 65 foils is 35, 40, and 45 percent of chord respectively.)

foil demonstrates what is known as a "drag bucket" in the drag coefficient plot. At lift coefficients below 0.2 (which would be experienced downwind) there is a considerable drop in resistance, which results in an increase in boat speed. In a normal upwind sailing situation the lift coefficient would probably hover between 0.3 and 0.5, a range in which the 64A foil still has slightly less drag than the 0010 foil, making the 64A a better choice for both upwind and downwind work.

Choosing the appropriate thickness of the keel foil is a trade-off between the hydrodynamic requirements of lift and drag and the physical requirements of structure and ballasting. A keel whose chord thickness is around 10 to 12 percent of the chord length won't be far off the optimum, with 6 percent too thin and 18 percent too thick. As a keel gets thinner, the leading-edge radius tightens, promoting early stall—not good for tacking. As a keel gets thicker, the maximum lift coefficient before stall is increased but the form drag has grown, making the boat slow in all directions. Some designers have settled on 10 percent as a good trade-off, and maintain that percentage from top to bottom of the keel. Others feel that for several reasons the percentage thickness should increase near the bottom of the keel. There is an obvious ballasting benefit in increasing the thickness near the tip: more lead means more weight down low. A thicker tip (with a correspondingly larger leading-edge radius) also reduces the tip's stalling tendency.

Some classes of sailboats, for simplicity of construction or for historical reasons, use a flat metal plate for a centerboard. A flat-plate keel will still have an increasing lift coefficient with an increasing angle of attack up to about 8 degrees but is not an efficient producer of lift, and stalls at low angles of attack. To create a centerboard from a flat plate, the designer must keep the lift coefficient low, which means intentionally increasing the area of the board. In other

words, a keel or centerboard with no curve to its chord section must have more area than one with a proper foil shape. What is gained in simplicity of construction must be weighed against the increase in parasitic drag.

from scratch: a sample keel design

The output from the FastShip keel design program for a hypothetical 40-footer, as shown in the lower graph in Fig. 2.9, reveals the benefit of viewing the lift/drag trade-off when designing a keel. It is assumed for this exercise that the draft of the keel has been fixed at 6.88 feet. Thus, changes in aspect ratio also mean changes in area. A higher aspect ratio equates to a smaller area: because draft is constant, to increase the aspect ratio the chord must be reduced.

It can be seen that the parasitic drag for the low aspect ratio keel (AR=1.4) is about 40 pounds. As the aspect ratio is increased the parasitic drag drops, simply due to the reduced area and correspondingly reduced frictional drag. But in this design analysis the keel is required to hold a fixed amount of lead and therefore as the area gets smaller the thickness must increase. This increasing thickness jacks up the form drag, reflecting the difficulty of pushing a fat foil through the water. Once the aspect ratio exceeds 2.9 (for this particular keel) the form drag increase outweighs the frictional drag decrease, and the parasitic drag (the sum of the two) begins to rise.

The induced drag, which is the drag related to creating the 1,293 pounds of lift to oppose the sail forces, makes a predictable slow climb as the area decreases and the aspect ratio increases. The sum of the induced and parasitic drags—the total drag— shown by the solid white line, is the determining design factor. The minimum total drag (and it must be emphasized that this is true only for this keel draft and weight, on this boat) occurs at an aspect ratio of 2.7.

There is one other factor to consider before the final choice of keel aspect ratio is made. Although the total drag curve has a definite minimum, the penalty for straying from the absolute minimum is very small—an aspect ratio anywhere from 2.4 to 2.9 would give quite acceptable total drag figures. And there is a reason for choosing an aspect ratio slightly lower than that which produces the least drag. The leeway angle increases with the increase in aspect ratio, indicating that a small, high aspect ratio keel on this boat will produce more sideslipping. For a designer examining two keel options with the same drag—say, with aspect ratios of 2.3 and 3.0 and a drag of 80 pounds—the choice is clear. The lower aspect ratio has less leeway, with all other factors equal. A final aspect ratio around 2.4 would be a wise choice for this boat.

This is perhaps one of the most surprising things for sailors to grasp. A higher aspect ratio keel is not always the better performance choice, particularly when the amount of available draft is fixed.

torpedo running: bulb design

The simplest, and often the best, bulbs are torpedo shaped and slightly elliptical when viewed from the bow. These shapes are designed for minimum drag; although they probably provide some end-plate effect to reduce the tip vortex of the keel, they are primarily just a smooth housing for lead. Bulb shape varies with designer, rule, and fashion. Their foil shapes range from the large-volume NACA 10-34 to some of the laminar flow sections (see Fig. 2.10) with maximum thickness back as much as 55 percent of the chord.

Since these bulbs are just going along for the ride

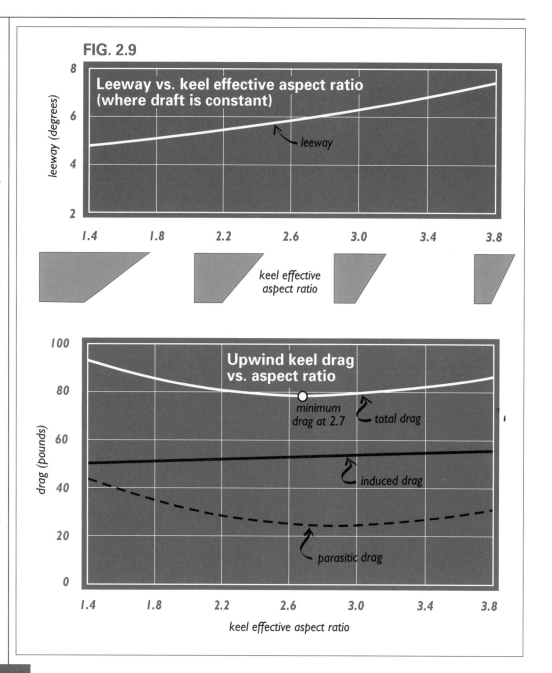

FIG. 2.9

Leeway vs. keel effective aspect ratio (where draft is constant)

leeway (degrees)

leeway

keel effective aspect ratio

Upwind keel drag vs. aspect ratio

drag (pounds)

minimum drag at 2.7

total drag

induced drag

parasitic drag

keel effective aspect ratio

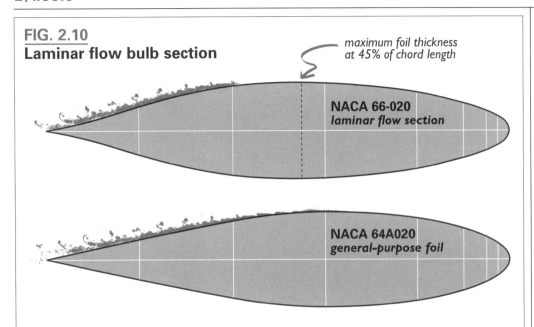

FIG. 2.10
Laminar flow bulb section

maximum foil thickness at 45% of chord length

NACA 66-020
laminar flow section

NACA 64A020
general-purpose foil

The foil section shape of a bulb has much different priorities than that of the keel to which it is attached. Generating lift is not important; minimizing drag is. A low-lift shape like NACA 66-020 delays the loss of laminar (nonturbulent) flow compared with a general-purpose shape like NACA 64A020.

FIG. 2.11
Round vs. elliptical bulbs

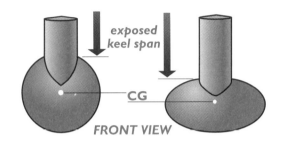

exposed keel span

CG

FRONT VIEW

Where the volume of lead to be contained in the bulb is constant, a circular bulb has a lower wetted surface than an elliptical bulb, producing less frictional drag. But the elliptical bulb on balance has greater performance advantages. Where keel draft is constant, it has a lower center of gravity (CG), improving stability. Its lower profile also exposes more keel span, which means more lift can be generated.

and cannot be efficient producers of lift, minimizing their drag is the design focus. Much like the optimal keel, the best bulb is a trade-off between chord length and thickness. Housing a particular weight of lead requires a given volume. That volume can be contained in a long bulb with a small diameter (large in wetted surface and frictional drag, but low in form drag) or in a short, fat bulb (low in wetted surface and frictional drag, but large in form drag). A plot of the thickness (as a percent of chord length) versus the total drag is the best way to visualize the trade-off. Shown in Fig. 2.12 is the frictional drag, the form drag, and the total drag, which is minimal at about 20 percent thickness.

When few other constraints are imposed, bulb

shapes on deep-draft keels tend to be flattened ellipses. From the simple calculations of surface area and volume it can be shown that a minimum surface area and therefore minimum frictional drag result if a bulb has a circular cross section—and some bulbs are designed that way. However, many designers have found it is a better trade-off to squash the bulb to an elliptical cross section, perhaps to a height only half of the bulb's width (Fig. 2.11). The resulting bulb, although it has a slightly larger wetted surface, has gained a lower center of gravity and has exposed more keel surface above the bulb that can be dedicated to producing lift.

Bulbs, just like hulls, masts, and interiors, are influenced by the rules governing the design of racing yachts, even when those yachts aren't necessarily raced at all. Once a design trend is set, even if it begins only because of the peculiarities of a handicapping rule, it often is followed by designers who have little knowledge of the reasoning behind the shapes they see. The IMS rating rule has had an influence on bulbs well beyond its own regime of racing. In particular, the IMS rule has inspired keel bulbs that are more triangular than elliptical in cross section. (See Fig. 2.13.) This is because the section of the handicapping rule governing bulbs was written to differentiate, in some concrete manner, the potential speed advantage of wings and extreme bulbs over normal keels. The rule as a result applies a penalty to the elliptical bulb and has led to the creation of many triangular bulbs on IMS boats. Having set the pace in the IMS system, however, these bulbs appear on boats that have nothing to do with the IMS—and, one suspects, with very little research to prove their continuing merit.

joint performances: fillets and dillets

Where a fixed keel meets the hull there is a confused flow. Because the flow is influenced by both surfaces, one of them perhaps producing lift, an additional drag (called *interference drag*) is present. Walk through a marina in the off-season and check out the various solutions to the problem. The fairing between the keel and hull varies from nothing to a quarter-round fillet as large as 10 percent of the chord length. To try to determine the best size of fillet to use on the keel/hull junction, undergraduate students at the University of Western Ontario conducted a wind-tunnel test. A 1:5 scale model of the underbody and keel of a 35-foot sloop was set in the tunnel and the forces measured at various angles of incidence,

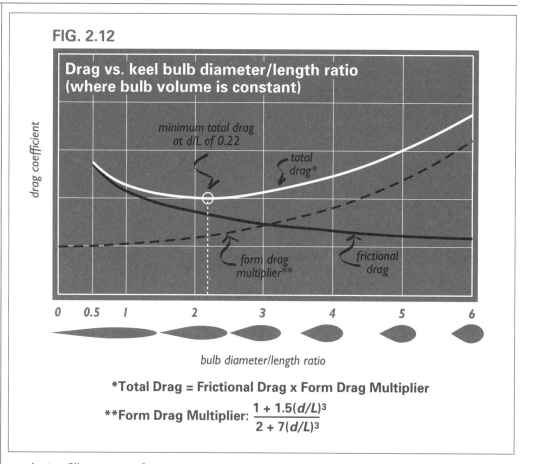

FIG. 2.12

Drag vs. keel bulb diameter/length ratio (where bulb volume is constant)

drag coefficient

minimum total drag at d/L of 0.22

total drag*

form drag multiplier**

frictional drag

0   0.5   1   2   3   4   5   6

bulb diameter/length ratio

*Total Drag = Frictional Drag x Form Drag Multiplier

**Form Drag Multiplier: $\dfrac{1 + 1.5(d/L)^3}{2 + 7(d/L)^3}$

employing fillets ranging from none to very large. The test was repeatable, but produced differences in lift and drag so small as to be inconclusive.

When scientific data doesn't provide the answers, the designer must dig into his bag of personal hunches. I tend to favor a moderate fillet in the junction to ease the transition in shape, but I haven't seen any conclusive data from any source to end the controversy.

While fillets enlarge the junction between two objects, dillets reduce the volume of the junction. Surprisingly, both attempt to do the same job—reduce

FIG. 2.13
Bulb types and the influence of racing rules

T-shaped keel with elliptical bulb

This example from an International America's Cup Class yacht shows the typical ellipse used when no bulb restrictions are imposed by a handicapping rule.

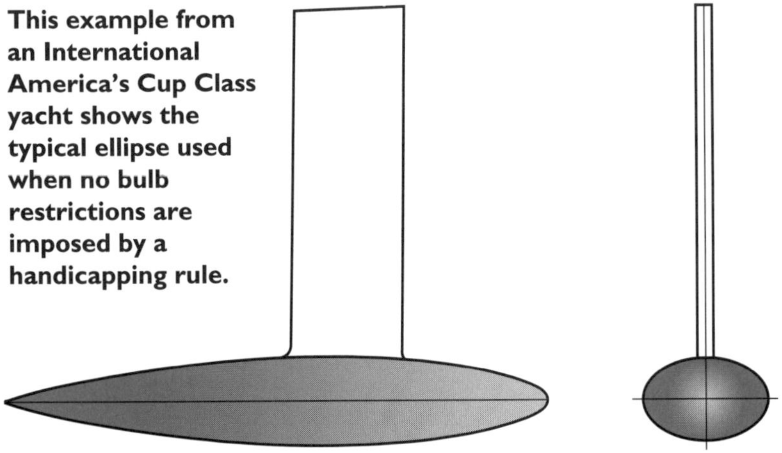

L-shaped keel with elliptical bulb (MORC)

The **MORC** rule for boats under 30 feet limits the height of the bulb to 50 percent of the width.

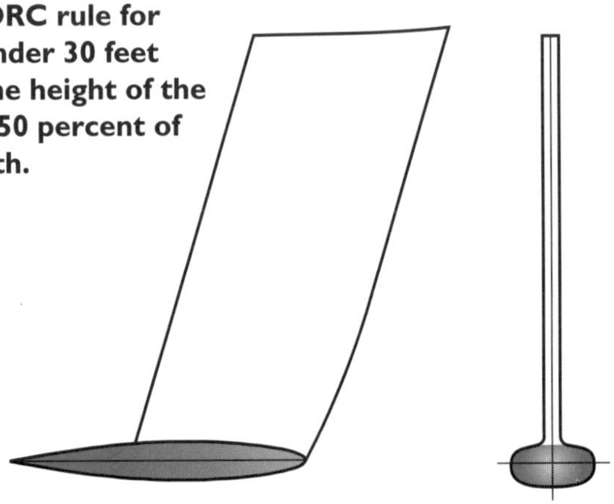

L-shaped keel with triangular bulb (IMS)

The International Measurement System (IMS) rule is written specifically to discourage keel wings, as well as bulbs that could deliver an end plate effect. To avoid having a bulb penalized, a designer must ensure that it can accommodate a triangle that fits entirely within the cross-sectional shape of the keel. The base of the triangle is set at the maximum width of the keel (within the bulb). The width of the bulb (dimension **A**) then determines the height of the triangle's apex, measured from the base of the keel.

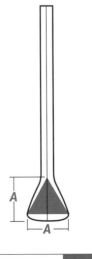

The keel bulb on the far right would draw a penalty under the IMS since its contours fall inside the controlling triangle.

Because the IMS is seen by some as a leading-edge racing design rule, the unusual triangular bulbs it stipulates are also seen as leading edge, even though there is no scientific basis for the IMS bulb configuration. The rule is meant to discourage bulb innovation, not to encourage it.

the interference drag. The most visible use of dillets is the keel/bulb intersection of some of the International America's Cup Class boats.

The theory of the *dillet* (a dimpled fillet) is to reduce the volume of one surface in the immediate area of the adjoining surface in order to alleviate any pressure buildup. If the geometry is arranged such that the recess on one surface is in perfect harmony with the adjacent volume of the other, then the pressure change, and therefore the interference drag, should be reduced. If the two surfaces are not in perfect concert, however, there will be a drag increase. The sensitivity required to get this match perfect is such that the technique is applicable only to the most sophisticated of racing-boat keels, and even then the variation in dillets and fillets from one designer to the next would indicate the problem is anything but resolved.

uplifting: the centerboard and daggerboard

The centerboard is an unballasted keel that can swing up into the boat to enhance the performance or simply reduce the draft. The daggerboard follows the same principle, except that it slides upward in its housing rather than pivoting.

In dinghies, a centerboard is a performance feature, permitting sailors to reduce wetted surface and frictional drag when sailing off the wind by raising some or most of it. In keelboats, though, their main purpose is to allow a boat to have a shallow-draft keel for cruising and a higher aspect ratio keel (by lowering the centerboard) for upwind work in deeper water. In smaller keelboats the centerboard, housed in a low aspect keel, is a design feature that allows trailering.

The centerboard also allows fine-tuning of balance and performance. When a centerboard is pivoted up

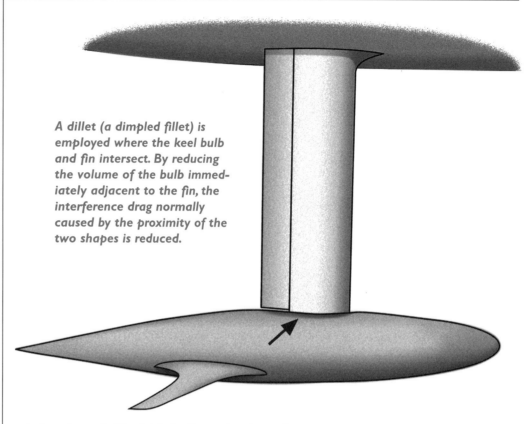

A dillet (a dimpled fillet) is employed where the keel bulb and fin intersect. By reducing the volume of the bulb immediately adjacent to the fin, the interference drag normally caused by the proximity of the two shapes is reduced.

and aft as shown in Fig. 2.14, the first major change is a movement aft of the center of lift. The result is a reduction in the weather helm—valuable for heavy-air reaches, but it is important to note that the area has been reduced very little. It is only when the board is pivoted aft at significant angles that there is a worthwhile reduction in area and frictional drag. On downwind legs, if control is not a problem, lifting the centerboard partway up will increase speed, but make sure it is raised 30 degrees or more to see some significant area reduction. In moderate wind conditions some of the board will need to be left exposed below the hull to act as a fulcrum, or pivot point, for the rudder. A

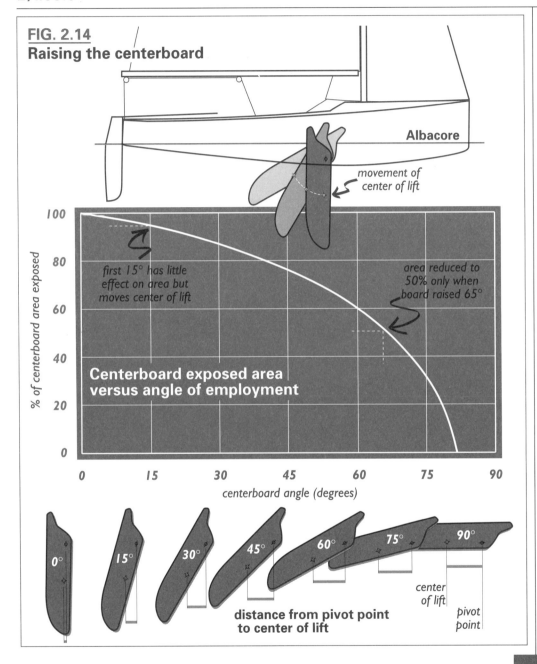

FIG. 2.14
Raising the centerboard

Albacore

*movement of
center of lift*

% of centerboard area exposed

*first 15° has little
effect on area but
moves center of lift*

*area reduced to
50% only when
board raised 65°*

**Centerboard exposed area
versus angle of employment**

100
80
60
40
20
0

0   15   30   45   60   75   90
centerboard angle (degrees)

0°   15°   30°   45°   60°   75°   90°

**distance from pivot point
to center of lift**

*center
of lift*

*pivot
point*

rudder tends to be very ineffective if it has no center-board around which to pivot. It's a bit like turning a car on a snowy road—the vehicle ends up pointed in the right general direction, but does a lot of undesirable sideslipping along the way.

Some centerboards can be pivoted, or canted, forward of vertical. This has two effects. First, the center of lift of the centerboard moves forward, thereby increasing weather helm. Some one-design classes that have been designed without enough weather helm can sail faster upwind when more weather helm is induced by the centerboard. The second effect is seen in medium air, when the board is under more pressure. Unlike keels, most boards have some measurable flexibility and when canted forward will twist to windward at the tip, reducing leeway. The twisting action is caused by the lift force acting well forward of the structural center up at the hull/board junction. The tip will see an increase in the angle of attack, but the root of the centerboard, next to the hull, will not. Care must be taken that the tip does not twist to such a high angle that it stalls, with an accompanying loss of lift.

draft proposal:
the keel-centerboard

When a keelboat's draft is limited and a full-depth keel is not a design option, a keel-centerboard can be used to gain some of the upwind performance exhibited by a deep keel. The shallow-draft fixed keel with a centerboard knifing from its lower edge can be more efficient than a shoal-draft keel or winged keel. It is important to note the caveat "can be more efficient," because the installation and details of the keel-centerboard are critical to its success.

When the centerboard is raised and hidden in its slot in the shallow-draft keel, performance is not usually the concern. With the centerboard retracted, the sailor will be heading to a dock or an anchorage, or perhaps sailing downwind. Keel depth is reduced with the centerboard neatly tucked away, but so is drag. For upwind sailing, the board is lowered by rotating it on a large-diameter pin in its upper forward edge. When the board is fully extended, the keel area is increased and the keel as a whole has a higher aspect ratio—a more efficient planform.

The hydrodynamics become rather complicated, however, when two foils, the centerboard and the keel, share the same water flow; both are producing lift but are considerably different in shape. The lift being produced by the bottom section of the keel is unlikely the same as the lift being produced by the neighboring top section of the centerboard. With varying pressure differences, unwanted flow makes its way from one foil to the other, reducing lift and increasing drag. Additional interference drag is precipitated at that same junction by differences in chord dimensions, with the thin centerboard right next to the thick keel.

Two keel-centerboard solutions to the shallow-draft problem are presented in Fig. 2.15. The first is a shallow-draft keel with a very high aspect ratio, deep-draft centerboard. This combination presents an efficient board working below a rather inefficient (as far as lift production is concerned), long, shallow-draft keel. The two foils have no choice but to operate at the same angle of attack to the water flow—they are after all connected to the same hull. However, the lift coefficient of the high aspect centerboard will be substantially higher, in this case perhaps six times greater, than that of the keel. With lift being the product of, among other things, the lift coefficient and foil area, the centerboard (at half the area but six times the lift coefficient) supplies more lift than the keel.

Hampering the efficiency of the underwater foils in this arrangement is the open slot left when the center-

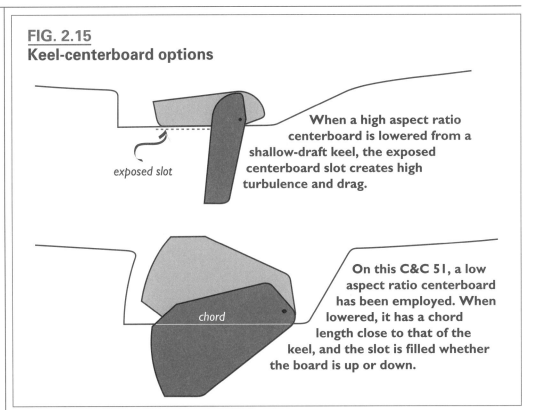

FIG. 2.15
Keel-centerboard options

exposed slot

When a high aspect ratio centerboard is lowered from a shallow-draft keel, the exposed centerboard slot creates high turbulence and drag.

chord

On this C&C 51, a low aspect ratio centerboard has been employed. When lowered, it has a chord length close to that of the keel, and the slot is filled whether the board is up or down.

board drops down. Unlike the centerboard slot in a dinghy, which can have a rubber or Mylar closing device to seal off the open case, sealing the slot in the keel's bottom is more problematic and ultimately impractical. There is seldom the opportunity to maintain a closing device on the bottom of the keel that can survive groundings against rocks and sand. Without a closing device, the open slot presents a large added area of turbulence and drag.

To address the added drag of the open centerboard slot, designer Rob Ball created the arrangement shown in Fig. 2.15 for the C&C 51, launched in Ontario, Canada, in 1993. The centerboard is noticeably less high aspect than the one just discussed. Rather than

FIG. 2.16
The gybing centerboard

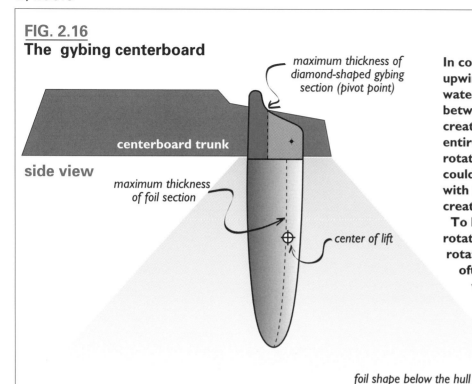

maximum thickness of diamond-shaped gybing section (pivot point)

centerboard trunk

side view

maximum thickness of foil section

center of lift

foil shape below the hull

centerboard angled 0°

top view

diamond shape inside centerboard trunk

pivot point

LIFT

centerboard angled 3°

In conventional sailboat design, leeway is a necessary part of upwind sailing. Without leeway and the associated angled water flow, no pressure difference would be observed between the two sides of the keel and no lift would be created. But instead of depending on the leeway of the entire boat to create the angled flow, if the keel alone were rotated, a better scenario could be developed. The hull could then travel through the water with no leeway (and with reduced drag) while the keel, cocked to one side, creates the lift.

To be of benefit on either tack, a keel would have to rotate to both port and starboard. The mechanics of rotating a heavy keel, not to mention the rules of racing, often prohibit these so-called gybing boards on larger vessels. In dinghy classes that permit them, there is often a restriction that the change in alignment happen without any mechanical persuasion. The ingenious solution was to create a centerboard with a diamond-shaped top portion featuring a pivot point aft of the board's center of lift.

As lift is generated by the centerboard, the forward part of the board tips to windward, swinging on the pivot point of the diamond-shaped top housed in the centerboard trunk. The lift forces keep the centerboard angled to windward 3 degrees, thereby allowing the boat to sail with 3 degrees less leeway than a conventional design. When the boat tacks, the lift force swings the centerboard into its new position.

Off the wind, where no lift is desired, the foil shape of the raised board, nestled firmly in the centerboard trunk, holds it in place along the centerline, preventing the board from gybing.

having a high-efficiency board produce the lion's share of the lift, this centerboard is essentially an extension of the keel itself. The difference in chord length at the junction of the two is much less dramatic, although for one to fit inside the other there still has to be a change in thickness. A significant benefit to this design is the slot, which remains mostly filled by the pie-shaped centerboard even when the board has been lowered. Less drag between the two lifting foils and from an open centerboard slot are the gains here.

No matter which centerboard style has been chosen, the mechanics of the hoisting and lowering remain the same: a wire connected to some point aft of the pivot leads to a winch or hydraulic ram to effect movement. Some of the simpler centerboard arrangements leave the wire hanging down in the water flow when the centerboard is lowered, a less than ideal arrangement. Others leave so little of the lowered board in the keel that the structure of the exposed centerboard is at risk.

A well-designed keel-centerboard is a viable option for good performance combined with shallow draft. Be aware, however, of the trade-offs—added drag from the open centerboard slot and the practical concern of maintaining the mechanical system.

losing leeway: the gybing board

Some design classes require that the centerboard fit tightly in the box, thereby limiting side-to-side movement. Other classes, like the International 14, permit gybing boards; consequently, sailors have spent many hours experimenting with the mechanics and the dynamics of centerboard movement.

If a board or keel is fixed to the hull, the leeway it experiences, say 5 degrees, is also experienced by 86 ▶

Keel-fairing basics

Fair but rough
The foil shape of this keel is fair, but the surface is rough. It needs to be sanded to reduce parasitic drag.

Smooth but not fair
This keel's surface is properly smoothed, but its foil shape is not fair. A wooden or plastic batten laid along its contours reveals hollows (exaggerated here) that will impede its performance.

Fair and smooth
This keel is properly prepared. Its foil shape is fair, and the surface is smooth.

If time and energy are limited, concentrate your fairing efforts on the forward one-third of the keel. This realizes the greatest performance gains for the amount of work, as it extends laminar flow and delays stall.

Keel myths and misunderstandings

catching stuff on the keel: the fears and realities

Almost without fail, when I am called upon to redesign a keel, the subject of running aground or catching weeds and lobster pots comes to the fore. Experienced boat owners with firsthand knowledge of hitting submerged objects and sailing through weeds tend to fear the unknown. If wings are added to my keel, will I find myself stuck on a sandbar until next spring's high tide? Will the new keel constantly be towing around miles of polypropylene rope?

Here are a few of my own experiences.

A keel with a leading-edge slope of 30 or more degrees to the vertical sheds weeds and other long stringy things. If your keel's leading edge is more vertical than this, then:

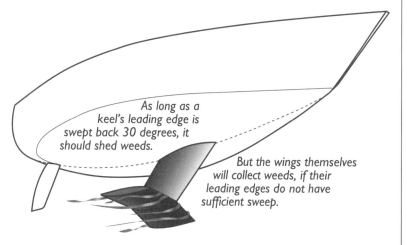

As long as a keel's leading edge is swept back 30 degrees, it should shed weeds.

But the wings themselves will collect weeds, if their leading edges do not have sufficient sweep.

a) if you are cruising, just live with it;

b) if you are racing, you will need either a kelp cutter or a flossing line.

Kelp cutters vary in design from a sliding knife set into the leading edge of the keel (an America's Cup trick) to a "rake"—a U-shaped bracket that wraps around the forward 3 inches of the leading edge of the keel and is connected to a push rod (see illustration on opposite page). The flossing line (named after the famous tooth-cleaning filament) is a long piece of rope, perhaps a jibsheet, looped over the bow when weeds are suspected. With the ends held by one crewmember on each side of the boat, the midsection of the line is allowed to drift back with the motion of the hull. Once it reaches the root of the keel it is sawed back and forth to loosen whatever might be caught and is finally retrieved by pulling it back on deck.

Performance advantages aside, many cruisers are afraid of winged keels. They dream at night about sandbars exactly 5 feet below the surface, waiting to put a bear hug on those wings, and about rock ledges narrowing on either side of the keel, wedging it in until the next Ice Age.

It could happen, but I have never heard of it. I have seen wings bent up at the tips from hitting rocks, but then I have seen a lot of standard keels bent sideways at the trailing edge. Don't bias your keel decision by its perceived sticking-to-the-bottom risk. This is not an issue.

feeding time: bulbs as weed-eaters

Bulbs are a great way to increase stability when no additional lift-producing keel area is required. They suffer, however, from some of the same perceived drawbacks as the winged keel, notably line catching and magnetism toward rocks. The only legitimate risk, though, is with the T-shaped keel, on which the nose of the bulb protrudes forward of the keel's main body. This arrangement is a great trap for weeds and lines and would be worth avoiding if my sailing grounds included perpetual weeds.

seakindly or lethargic: the full-keel debate

Full keels, those appendages that stretch from near the bow to the rudder, are the source of short debates. Short because sailors, although their opinions are strong, have little data to back up their arguments. The discussion usually revolves around directional stability: the argument for full keels is that the boat will almost sail itself—you never need to touch the wheel.

There is a marked difference in how a fin-keel and a full-keel boat feel, but it is a matter of preference, not a matter of seaworthiness or balance. I am sure you can accept the fact that a boat with a keel that reaches almost the full length of the hull will be harder to turn—it will tend to go in a straight line. This is definitely true, just as it is true that a short, deep keel will turn very readily. Agile turning ability is one of the reasons sailors enjoy the fin keel.

But when comparing the ability of various boats to sail for extended periods unattended, the difference is not that one style of keel permits better balancing—it is that the full keel dampens the movement; it slows the motion down. On well-designed boats, both styles of keel can be made to balance perfectly with the sails. And when the sails are unbalanced, say with some weather helm, both will turn into the wind. The full keel will take longer to turn to windward and longer to correct and bring back on course. Some sailors like that damped motion and some don't.

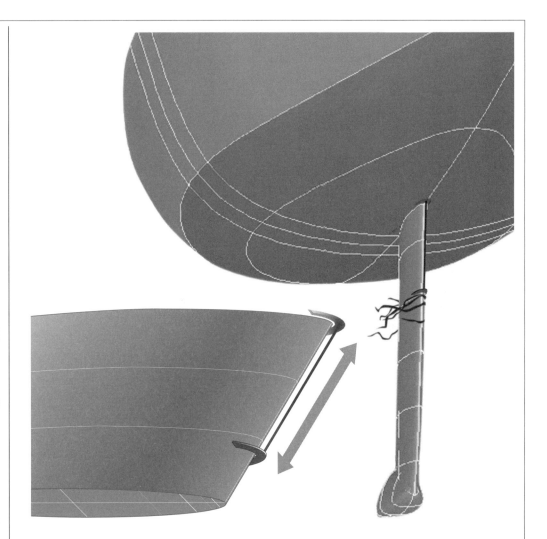

Cleanup detail: the weed rake

The keel on this IMS design is equipped with a "weed rake," which clears debris from the keel by pushing it down the leading edge. The rake is controlled manually from inside the boat, using a long rod. Pressure from the water flow keeps the rake sliding firmly along the leading edge. When not in use, it is pulled up into a hull recess so it doesn't create drag.

FIG. 2.17
Centerboard slot turbulence

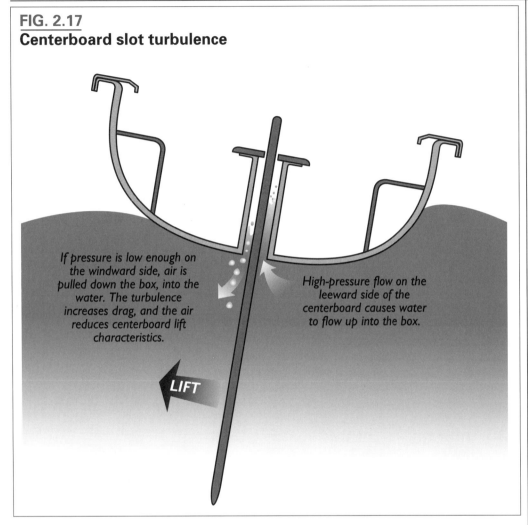

If pressure is low enough on the windward side, air is pulled down the box, into the water. The turbulence increases drag, and the air reduces centerboard lift characteristics.

High-pressure flow on the leeward side of the centerboard causes water to flow up into the box.

LIFT

Getting a gybing board to work consistently is a difficult job. If it occasionally gybes in the wrong direction, then it might as well not gybe at all. Classes that do permit a gybing board stipulate that it may not be forced mechanically to gybe—the movement must be a result of the natural action of the water on the board. To ensure this, the lift on the board must be forward of the point about which the board rotates in the vertical plane.

On centerboards this is usually achieved by making the board diamond shaped, as viewed from above, inside the centerboard case. (See Fig. 2.16.) The board can then flop back and forth with the leading edge always pointing to windward. But a gybing board downwind would be a great hindrance to performance—remember, because no lift is required, neither leeway nor gybing is desired. Gybing boards get around this by ceasing to gybe as they are retracted into the box. Once the board is pulled up partway, the foil shape, now inside the centerboard box, no longer allows the gybing movement.

The 41-foot *Evergreen,* designed under the International Offshore Rule (IOR) while Steve Killing was with the C&C design group in 1977 for the 1978 Canada's Cup match-racing event, had a rather ingenious gybing daggerboard. This particular design housed most of the ballast on the bottom of the hull, with the remaining 700 pounds bolted to the bottom of the daggerboard to (a) make the lightweight board drop when lowered and (b) provide a small amount of extra stability. It slid up and down on rollers that were set back about halfway along the foil. During upwind legs, the board would gybe to the windward side. In light breezes, when the forces were not large enough to make the board gybe, and for downwind sailing, a retainer bar could be pushed from inside the boat into a tapered slot at the leading edge. This would firmly lock the forward edge on centerline and stop it from

◄ **83**   the hull. But having the hull move through the water at a 5-degree angle produces extra drag and very little lift. If it were possible to angle the centerboard at 5 degrees to windward within the hull, then when the board took up its angle to the water, the hull would see an angle of incidence of nil. A board that can angle to windward on each tack is called a *gybing board.*

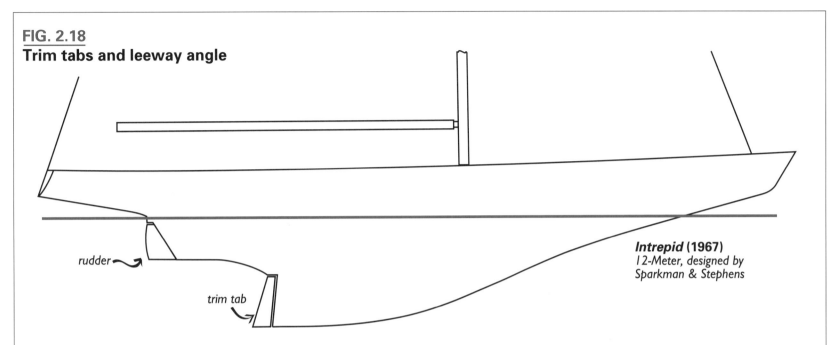

FIG. 2.18
Trim tabs and leeway angle

rudder

trim tab

Intrepid (1967)
*12-Meter, designed by
Sparkman & Stephens*

Introduced to yachting by the 1967 America's Cup defender *Intrepid,* the trim tab on the aft edge of a boat's keel acts just like the flap on an aircraft wing.

By setting the tab at an angle to the keel, an asymmetrical foil shape is introduced, improving lift characteristics. America's Cup match racers also learned to use the trim tab as a brake, setting it at high angles to slow the boat during starting maneuvers.

Published data on wing sections suggests that a trim tab occupying 20 percent of the keel's chord length, if set at a 4-degree angle, as shown below, will reduce leeway by half the tab setting. In this case, a leeway angle of 5 degrees has been reduced to 3 degrees. While a 2-degree improvement might seem small, it represents a 40 percent reduction in leeway, a considerable performance advantage for a racing yacht in an upwind duel or a cruiser attempting to avoid a lee shore. However, the trim tab's mechanical complexity, and restrictions in rating rules, have greatly limited their application.

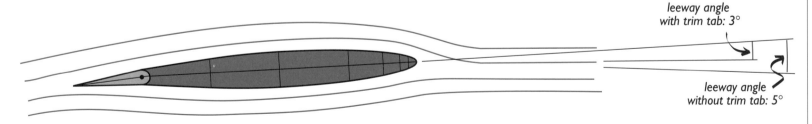

*leeway angle
with trim tab: 3°*

*leeway angle
without trim tab: 5°*

flopping back and forth. The daggerboard was very successful, but its superior performance depended on an effective seal where the board passed through the bottom of the hull.

Earlier in this chapter we noted that the presence of the hull greatly increases the effective aspect ratio of the keel. There is a risk with all centerboard and daggerboards, however, that the effectiveness of the foil will be reduced if careful attention is not paid to sealing the board slot.

When sailing upwind, the telltale sign that the board is not doing its job is the gurgling of water in the case. This indicates that the board is not well sealed at the hull junction and the pressures on the high and low sides cannot be maintained. If it were possible to see inside a poorly sealed centerboard case (with some classes, such as the Lightning, you can actually do this from the cockpit because the top of the case is open), you could see the water rising on the high-pressure (leeward) side and dropping, with perhaps an associated gurgling action, on the low-pressure side. Without a good seal, the lift produced by the top of the board will be greatly reduced.

When the complication of gybing a board is added to the already difficult job of sealing the slot, the task gets formidable. On *Evergreen,* the solution was thorough, but certainly not easy. Set into the bottom of the hull was a narrow channel that held horizontal pieces of Lexan on either side of the board. The edge of the Lexan next to the surface of the board was cut to match its contour, and a shock cord on the forward and aft ends ensured the Lexan was squeezed tight to the board. As the board gybed, the Lexan, still tight to the surface, would slide within the channel, keeping the joint sealed. The advantage of the daggerboard at that time under the IOR was large (a loophole permitted an extra 18 inches of draft through the use of a daggerboard) and was one of the contributing factors in *Evergreen*'s success in winning the Canada's Cup against the American defender *Agape,* which had a conventional keel. However, the loophole has now been closed and no new rules have opened any similar gaps. It is unlikely that many large racing boats with gybing daggerboards will be seen in the future.

loading up lift: the trim tab

A direct lift from the aircraft world, the trim tab on the aft edge of a sailboat's keel mimics the flaps on an airplane's wing. (See Fig. 2.18.) Typically, the aft 10 to 20 percent of the keel is hinged so that when sailing upwind the keel lift can be adjusted. By setting tab angles at 2 to 8 degrees, the windward performance of the keel can be altered and in extreme use a 20-degree tab angle can be employed to slow the boat quickly during match-racing maneuvers.

Lift increases and leeway decreases with increasing tab angle. There is an accompanying increase in drag with excessive tab angles, but by monitoring the performance carefully the best combination of trim tab, rudder, and sail trim can be reached. On 12-Meters, a tab setting of about 4 degrees was typical, but the optimum angle was influenced by changes in boat speed, wind velocity, and the keel configuration. Experimental data from *Theory of Wing Sections* shows that a flap of 20 percent of the chord length will reduce the angle of attack (leeway) by half the tab angle. Consequently, if the helmsman put on 4 degrees of tab, then the leeway would be reduce by 2 degrees—a significant change if total leeway is perhaps only 5 degrees. The complexity of the necessary shafting and waterproofing and in some cases the restrictions imposed by the racing rules, limit these extra rudders to the world of high-tech racing.

ballast

From human bodies to water tanks
to sacks of gravel to spent uranium:
a diversity of materials and
strategies has been enlisted in the
cause of keeping a yacht upright.

sinking in: the contradiction of weight and speed

The British yacht Winsome Gold executes a spectacular broach during the 1979 Admiral's Cup. As poor as Winsome Gold's prospects might appear, she recovered completely. Such a yacht must be heeled at least 20 degrees past horizontal to reach its limit of positive stability.

Any performance vehicle—racing car, space shuttle, aircraft, or bicycle—can be improved by making it lighter. Thus it seems contradictory to strap a chunk of lead to the bottom of a sailboat and claim this makes it faster. Yacht designers are well aware that lightness equals speed, even in marine vehicles, but just as removing the tires from a Formula 1 racing car will result in a lighter but ultimately slower machine, omitting the ballast from a 30-foot monohull sailboat will not make it go faster in any direction other than straight down.

The keel is essential to holding the boat upright, whether tied to the dock or sailing offshore in a 40-knot gale. Along with fulfilling the comforting role of maintaining the hull right-way up, the keel serves another, quite separate function: producing lift, or

resisting the side force of the sails. Without a winglike fin fixed beneath it, a sailboat working against the wind would simply blow sideways, regardless of the helmsman's intended direction. Enhancing performance, this second function of the keel, is quite a different issue from stability. Although the theory and practice of keel performance cannot be divorced entirely from ballasting when a designer creates a keel, these topics are dealt with separately in Chapter 2. As well, ballast is not the only significant factor in a boat's stability. Hull shape plays an extremely important role, and this is explored in Chapter 1. In this chapter, we will address the role ballast plays in stability and design.

Some of the basic relationships we now understand regarding length, beam, weight, and stability were foreign to early shipbuilders. As W. F. Stoot has written, "The application of science to naval architecture during the seventeenth century was almost non-existent…." And while tremendous interest in scientific ship design arose in the eighteenth century, rigorous (and lifesaving) application of this growing knowledge didn't come into widespread use in commercial shipping until the late nineteenth century.

The mathematical property of the *metacenter*—an imaginary point about which a vessel rotates, derived from the positions of the centers of buoyancy and gravity—was first explained by Frenchman Pierre Bouguer in his landmark *Traité du Navire* of 1746. In 1757, Daniel Bernoulli first addressed a vessel's transverse stability—how much effort is required to roll a ship to one side. The formula for calculating the righting moment, so vital to understanding the stability of a particular vessel, came in 1796.

In 1861, England's F. K. Barnes developed a geometric method of calculating stability; the simplified stability curves made possible by his work were first derived for designs of the British Admiralty in 1868, and were made compulsory for all Royal Navy designs after the loss in 1870 of HMS *Captain*. Launched in 1869, this sail-assisted battleship had a novel configuration—the hull had two gaping "windows" housing armored turrets, which created perilously low freeboard. In September 1870 she went down in a storm in the Bay of Biscay—473 men were lost, including her designer, Cowper Coles.

Although the science existed to create safer ships, commercial builders didn't necessarily pay any attention to it. From 1876 to 1892, 10,381 U.K. merchant ships were lost, along with 27,010 seamen and 3,543 passengers, according to the British Department of Transport's inquiry into the loss of the tall ship *Marques* in 1984. Many of these losses were probably due to poor stability. Shipbuilders who were ignorant (wilfully or otherwise) of the science of ship design continued to look at their last boat and make an educated guess as to the changes that would result in improved performance. (Intuition based on experience is still a vital component of the designer's tool kit, but now

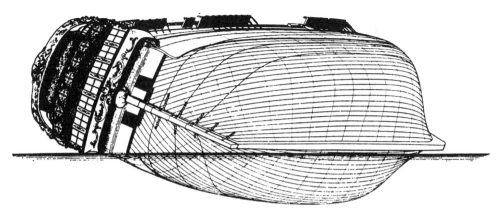

there is some math to keep the process on an even keel.) Early designers of pleasure craft were no less ignorant of scientific design principles.

The earliest innovators must have made the logical connection between lightness and speed, and perhaps noticed the parallel correlation between weight and stability. Stability can be confusing—a light ship is not always unstable and a heavy ship with adequate stability can be immensely unstable if laden high with stores and cannons. The fate of the warship *Vasa* illustrates the point. (See Fig. 3.1.) A new addition to the Swedish fleet, she set sail on her maiden promotional voyage in 1628 with dignitaries on board, but never left Stockholm Harbor. In an embarrassing and fatal demonstration of low stability, she capsized and sank in full view of thousands of spectators. Her stability was inadequate because of her high center of gravity, the result of some 64 guns strapped down to two gundecks. Her configuration was like that of a man trying to balance on stilts.

The *Vasa*'s fate was common to that of many early warships. Henry VIII's flagship *Mary Rose* toppled over in The Solent while setting forth to engage the French fleet in 1545. Originally a merchant ship, the *Mary Rose* was top-heavy with guns, which compromised her

Unlike the crew of **Winsome Gold**, *opposite, the sailors aboard this sailing ship could not be confident of their vessel righting itself. This drafting tour de force by Fredrik Chapman (see page 186), published in 1768, shows a ship heeled about 60 degrees, which was the limit of positive stability for traditional vessels. Their heavy rigs, deck-mounted cannons, and lack of an external ballasted keel sometimes spelled disaster even in seemingly innocuous conditions.*

FIG. 3.1
Vasa cross section

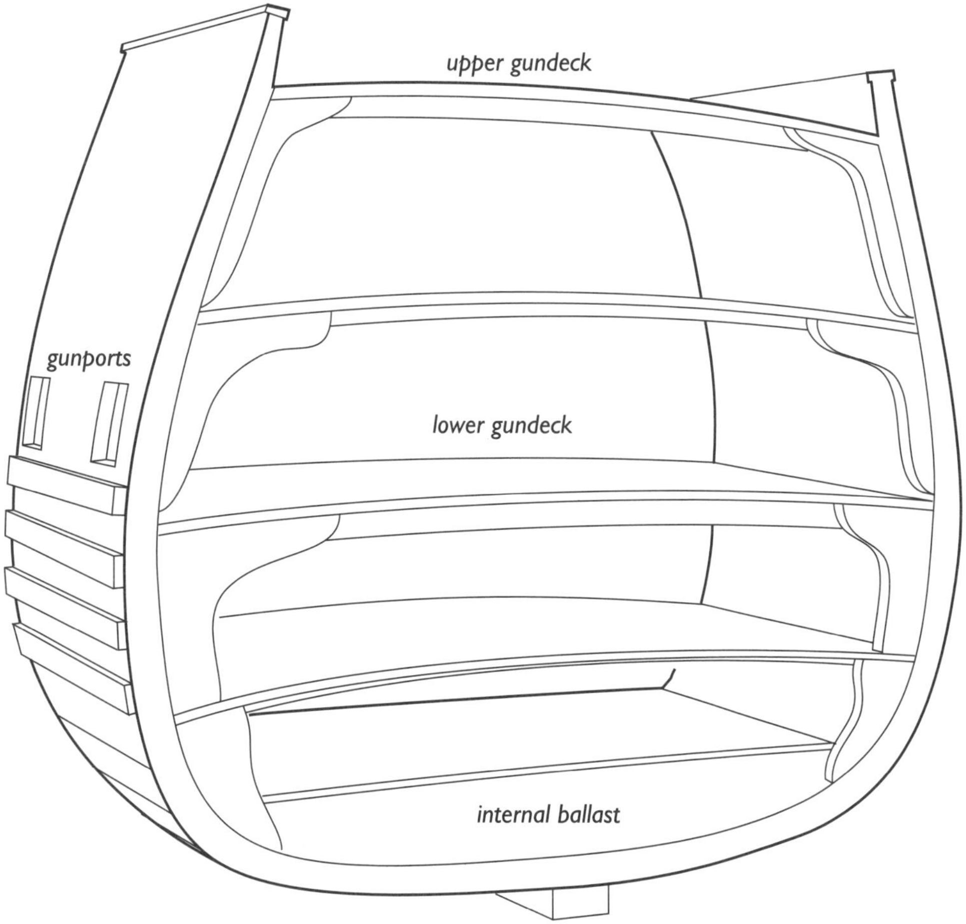

upper gundeck

gunports

lower gundeck

internal ballast

This sectional view of the Swedish warship *Vasa,* which sank on her maiden voyage in 1628, shows some of the features that made her vulnerable to capsizing. The use of internal ballast rather than an external keel was a stability shortcoming of traditional ship design. She was also made top-heavy with two gundecks, and gunports provided easy access for seawater when dangerously heeled. A heavy three-masted rig contributed further to her instability.

stability. Not all miscalculations of top-loading are consigned to distant ages, and we continue to risk allowing ponderous elegance to take precedence over seaworthiness. In 1984, the 117-foot sail-training barque *Marques* was lost in violent weather during a tall ships' race from Bermuda to Halifax, an accident that claimed 19 lives. A subsequent formal investigation by the British Department of Transport, which had allowed the vessel to sail without subjecting her to the normal procedure of formally determining her stability, revealed a twentieth-century twist on the fate of the *Mary Rose.* The *Marques* had been rerigged from her original two-masted schooner configuration to a taller, heavier barque rig, complete with a third mast (the mizzen) to make her more appealing for film work. As a result, the *Marques*'s vanishing angle of stability—the heel angle at which she was committed to capsizing—may have been as low as 57 degrees. (The investigation decided, however, that the weather was so violent that the ship's low stability made no difference to her fate.) The lesson of the *Marques* is that, while the science of sailing craft stability is well understood, that science must be applied rigorously to minimize the chances for disasters that best belong in centuries past.

During the design of the *Vasa* there was no way of knowing with absolute certainty if the boat would capsize. The *Vasa* being the first two-gundeck vessel the designer/builder had constructed, he had only his single gundeck creations for comparison. The task was not impossible, for subsequently ships were successfully built with even more gundecks, but at the time there was no easy way to calculate the required ballast and beam.

In some ways we have not left the age of the *Vasa* entirely behind, as the *Marques* sadly suggested. Even with the help of today's computer software and the knowledge gained by rubbing shoulders with the aerospace industry, the task of designing a wholesome sail-boat, though far more scientific, is not a simple one.

a moment's notice: the forces of stability

Imagine two children on a teeter-totter. One is heavier than the other, and finds that by moving closer to the pivot bar he can balance with his partner. The stabilizing effect of concentrating weight on the bottom of a boat is no more difficult to understand. The wind blows with a small force high above the water, while gravity tugs at the keel with a large force not far below the water. Designers take care that the ballast never loses the balancing contest, and the boat stays upright.

Just how that balancing act is conducted is revealed through the mathematical concept of a moment, which is a force times a distance. When a boat is under sail, two opposing moments are at work. The wind, pressing on the sails and trying to capsize the boat, creates the overturning moment, which is calculated by multiplying the sail force by the distance from the center of sail force to the center of keel lift. Meanwhile, the weight of the boat and keel, striving to return the boat to an upright position, creates the righting moment, which is calculated by multiplying the weight of the entire boat by the righting arm, the distance between the centers of gravity and buoyancy. (See Fig. 3.2; also 1.11.)

For the boat to be in equilibrium (i.e., to have stability), these two moments must be the same. Therefore, knowing the value of one, the designer automatically knows the value of the other. The easiest one to calculate from the drawing board or to measure when the boat is in the water is the righting moment, and thus it is used as the standard measure of stability.

Righting moment, however, is not static. Although the weight of a boat is constant, the righting arm

changes with the heel angle. This is because as a boat heels, the center of buoyancy shifts farther away from the center of gravity. The result is a longer righting arm, which increases the righting moment.

At large angles of heel, the righting arm no longer grows because the center of buoyancy moves no farther. Once the boat has rolled through 50 or 60 degrees, the deck edge is immersing and there is simply no boat left to provide buoyancy. Beyond this point, the righting moment decreases. The stability curve for a typical 35-foot sailboat (Fig. 3.3) shows the maximum righting moment value (for this boat) to be at 50 degrees heel.

Seldom will a boat perform at its best at heel angles of more than 30 degrees. The rare exception is a narrow

Dinghy sailors use their own weight to keep their craft upright and moving. The three-person crew of this Australian 18-Foot Skiff employs trapezes as well as hiking racks to create a tremendous lever arm. See Fig. 3.7 for the mechanics of dinghy stability.

FIG. 3.2
Stability and the righting arm

⊕ metacenter
● center of gravity
○ center of buoyancy

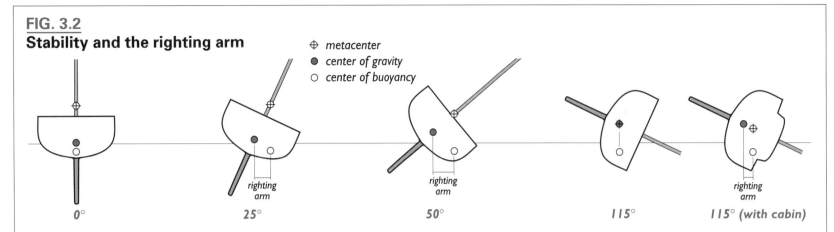

0°   25°   50°   115°   115° (with cabin)

righting arm (at 25°)   *righting arm* (at 50°)   *righting arm* (at 115° with cabin)

In this discussion of yacht stability, the center of gravity represents the yacht's weight, acting downward; the center of buoyancy represents the position of upward force; and the metacenter is the hull's current center of rotation, which is always directly above the center of buoyancy.

At 0 degrees heel, the centers of gravity and buoyancy are aligned, and the hull is stable. As heel increases, the center of buoyancy moves away from the center of gravity, creating a lever arm called the righting arm. This arm, multiplied by the yacht's weight, creates the righting moment, which counteracts the heeling moment imposed by the sails. (See Fig. 1.11.)

At 50 degrees heel, this yacht realizes its highest righting arm value. As the yacht heels farther, the righting arm steadily decreases until the centers of gravity and buoyancy are realigned, in this case at 115 degrees. The righting arm value is now zero and the positions of the center of gravity and metacenter are coincident. The yacht is "meta-stable": any small perturbation increasing or decreasing the heel angle will cause the yacht either to right itself or to flip upside down.

At this critical heel angle, the shape of the cabinhouse is a significant factor in ultimate stability. This flush-deck design receives no help from a cabintop, but some lifeboats and small oceangoing sailboats have intentionally oversized, rounded cabintops to provide additional buoyancy at high angles of heel. A sufficiently large cabinhouse can save a yacht from complete inversion. By adding a cabinhouse to our design (far right), a righting arm can still be produced at 115 degrees heel, extending the yacht's limit of positive stability.

racing boat like one of the Meter classes, but most cruisers will find comfort and speed by keeping the heel angle below 25 or 30 degrees. The portion of the stability curve for our 35-footer at heel angles below 30 degrees is relatively straight; this indicates that as the boat heels, stability increases in a predictable fashion. (The influence of hull form on stability is discussed in Chapter 1. For related stability curves, see Fig. 1.10.)

What happens when the wind increases, and with

it the overturning moment? Does the boat continue to heel until it is upside down?

There are extreme occasions when a boat will find itself upside down, but most sailors, thankfully, never experience such an event. The natural preference of humans for standing on a near-level platform is the first safety valve that prevents capsize—the sails usually get released by the alarmed crew. But a second, more scientific factor is involved. Looking at the sample stability curve in Fig. 3.3, we see that the significant features that relate to safety are the location of the peak of the curve (A), and the point at which the curve recrosses the zero righting moment line (B). The peak represents the greatest stability the boat can achieve. If the sail forces push it beyond this point, then something must change or the boat will continue to heel until the sails hit the water.

Fortunately, as the sails get closer to the water, the pressure of the wind diminishes for several reasons. The wind gradient phenomenon (see Fig. 6.3) causes the wind to blow less forcefully near the water, and because the rig is almost horizontal, less projected sail area is presented to the wind. The blanketing effect of the hull also reduces the amount of wind reaching the sail plan. The resulting reduction in load on the sails prevents most keelboat capsizes. But if the pressure cannot be released, or the momentum of the quickly heeling boat presses the sail and mast to the water, the yacht's stability still has one more card to play: the sails act like a huge sea anchor, stopping the capsizing motion. In the absence of any further forces, the boat will pop back up and carry on, provided the crew is still ready, willing, and able.

The angle at which the righting curve crosses the zero righting moment line is formally referred to as the "limit of positive stability," but a more evocative term is the "point of no return." It is important that this angle be as large as possible. Historic vessels with high topsides and little or no ballast had limits of positive stability as low as 60 degrees or less, which meant that once the heel angle exceeded 60 degrees, the boat would tip over and stay over (and, in their case, go down).

In today's sailboats, typical limits of positive stability are 110 degrees or greater. With values this high, the mast must be 20 degrees below horizontal for the boat to capsize. Although it seems impossible to achieve such a large heel angle, wave action in stormy

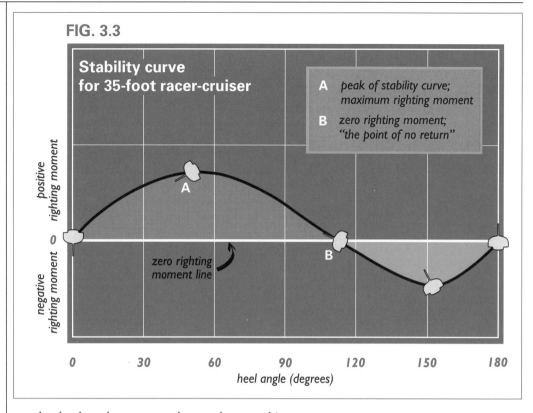

FIG. 3.3

Stability curve for 35-foot racer-cruiser

A peak of stability curve; maximum righting moment

B zero righting moment; "the point of no return"

positive righting moment

0

negative righting moment

zero righting moment line

heel angle (degrees)

0   30   60   90   120   150   180

weather has been known to push many boats to this point of no return. In the disastrous Fastnet Race off the coast of England in 1979 (which I sailed through in the 41-footer *Evergreen*), 15 lives were lost as modern racing yachts were overwhelmed by a storm in the Irish Sea. In response to the disaster, the Society of Naval Architects and Marine Engineers initiated an extensive study of capsizing in waves. The society's findings indicated that, although the wind (in that storm up to 70 knots) heeled the stricken boats, it was without doubt the short, steep, breaking waves—up to 30 feet high—that capsized them. Significant factors reducing the likelihood of this type of rollover capsize are initial stability (the more the better), the limit of

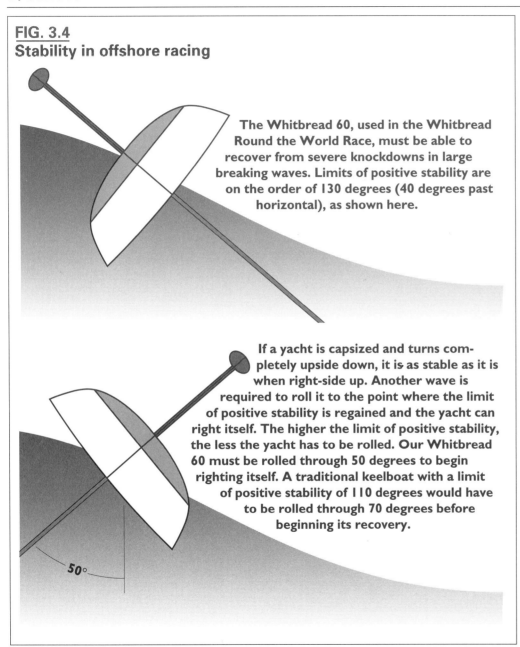

FIG. 3.4
Stability in offshore racing

The Whitbread 60, used in the Whitbread Round the World Race, must be able to recover from severe knockdowns in large breaking waves. Limits of positive stability are on the order of 130 degrees (40 degrees past horizontal), as shown here.

If a yacht is capsized and turns completely upside down, it is as stable as it is when right-side up. Another wave is required to roll it to the point where the limit of positive stability is regained and the yacht can right itself. The higher limit of positive stability, the less the yacht has to be rolled. Our Whitbread 60 must be rolled through 50 degrees to begin righting itself. A traditional keelboat with a limit of positive stability of 110 degrees would have to be rolled through 70 degrees before beginning its recovery.

50°

positive stability (the higher the angle the better), and mast integrity (if the mast is still standing, its inertia helps keep the boat upright).

Few sailors realize that sailboats, with only a few exceptions, are stable when upside down. If the boat manages to get completely inverted without significant flooding through deck hatches in the course of the capsize, it will remain afloat and inverted until some force flips it right-way up again. If there is enough power in a wave to roll a boat upside down, then the chances are great that in the same storm another wave will wrench the boat right-way up. The area under the top portion of the curve in Fig. 3.3 represents the energy required to capsize the boat. The area under the lower portion of the curve is directly related to the energy required to right the boat again. The ratio of the former to the latter is another important factor for a designer to consider, with capsizing energy to be held high and energy required to right the boat kept low.

The Whitbread 60 class designs used in the Whitbread Round the World Race are stable to an angle of about 115 to 130 degrees—that is, until the mast is pointing up to 40 degrees below horizontal. (See Fig. 3.4.) However, should the boat be rolled over by wind and waves, the large beam that provided such good stability when the boat was upright will produce an equally robust measure of stability when the boat is inverted. With boats that are very stable when upside down, provision must be made for an active system of ballast shifting to help right the boat, a sealed buoyant mast, or an effective escape hatch for the crew.

In sailing around the world, many adventurers report that their boats have been rolled over at some point during the trip. The 1996/97 edition of the Vendée Globe nonstop single-handed round-the-world race saw three of its 60-footers capsize and a fourth lost (along with its skipper) under unknown circumstances. The three capsized entries remained upside down with no thought of returning to upright. The skippers were rescued, but what does this indicate about the safety of these craft?

Because these beamy, flat-decked boats are very stable when upside down, they require another significant wave to roll them back up again. Their limit of positive stability has been the focus of much discussion, and it would help if the boats were all stable to 130 degrees—not because of an increase in the positive stability so much as a decrease in the inverted stability. If the boat is floating dead upside down, then a perturbation that rolls the boat through 50 degrees, to 130 degrees from upright, will be enough to allow the boat to right itself. A boat with a lower limit of positive stability would require perhaps a 70-degree twist to return to upright.

rocks to uranium: ballast materials

Most keels are cast from lead, a commonly available, dense metal. At 715 pounds per cubic foot, it can pack a lot of weight into a foil shape. But it's also soft. Because pure lead lacks the strength to resist the knocks and bumps of rocky bays, antimony or calcium is added to increase its strength. Occupying 2 percent of the casting, the additive brings the practical density down to about 700 pounds per cubic foot.

The quest for added performance can tempt designers from the logical path into a tangled thicket of bizarre thinking, and ballast is no exception. If heavy materials are good for sailboat keels, then heavier materials must be better, because they allow thinner, sleeker keels. (See Fig. 3.5 for a comparison of ballast material densities.) In 1972, portions of the keel of the Canada's Cup yacht *Mirage,* an IOR Two-Tonner designed and built by the Canadian company C&C Yachts, were cast

from spent uranium. (How do you get your lead-insulated hands on spent uranium? C&C Yachts was based in the province of Ontario, whose public electrical utility, Ontario Hydro, operates several nuclear power plants.) Only mildly radioactive (!) and with a density 70 percent greater than that of lead, the uranium did provide a slight performance edge when it was teamed with lead to produce a ballast package 15 percent more dense, but it came with higher costs and a risk to health and the environment. As it happened, the American yacht *Dynamite* won the match-racing event without triggering any Geiger counters. I was just beginning to work in the C&C design office when *Mirage* sailed against *Dynamite*. Shortly after that series, the use of spent uranium was, thankfully, disallowed, thereby removing radioactivity from my career path.

Back in the good old days of going down to the sea in ships, the average bilge carried as ballast the average heavy things of the day: rocks. Today, rocks can still be brought aboard as ballast in the form of concrete. While more practical and economical than uranium, its use is seldom recommended. Its cost is low, but so is its strength, not to mention its weight relative to lead—only 150 pounds per cubic foot. When a boat's performance is not critical, it fills the bilge quite well, but being low on strength it needs to be poured inside some other material; it's seen most often inside steel or wooden vessels.

A boat that has been partially filled with concrete allows no options for repair: the hull is inaccessible from the inside. Concrete ballast figured in the investigation of the *Marques's* sinking, as the impracticality of removing it discouraged a full load-line survey. And in the case of a wooden boat with concrete ballast, a portion of the hull is totally rigid, directly below a portion of the boat that (in the case of most wooden designs) is slightly flexible. The awkward interface between stiff and flexible is a potential source of structural failure.

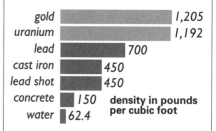

FIG. 3.5
Density of potential ballast materials

gold	1,205
uranium	1,192
lead	700
cast iron	450
lead shot	450
concrete	150
water	62.4

density in pounds per cubic foot

If density were the only criterion, then all keels would be cast from solid gold. But cost, strength, and regulations prevent the use of heavier-than-lead materials like gold and spent uranium. At the other end of the scale, water is free and readily available but rather inefficient as a ballasting material. Lead is the most dense material that is affordable for ballasting and the heaviest material that most rating rules permit. Cast iron is sometimes acceptable when keel volume is generous compared to the required ballast weight, but maintenance of cast-iron keels is troublesome. Lead shot in a polyester slurry and concrete are often used by do-it-yourselfers, but are inefficient users of space and invite maintenance problems.

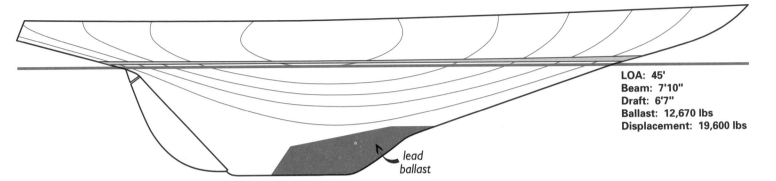

FIG. 3.6
Ballasting and full keels

LOA: 45'
Beam: 7'10"
Draft: 6'7"
Ballast: 12,670 lbs
Displacement: 19,600 lbs

lead ballast

Built in 1930 by Robert Jacob to a design by a young Olin Stephens, the 8-Meter *Conewago* was an unsuccessful contender in the Canada's Cup challenge trials held that year by the Rochester Yacht Club. She was, however, the RYC's successful defender of the trophy in 1932 and 1934 against challengers from the Royal Canadian Yacht Club of Toronto. She is shown here in her 1995 configuration while owned by Mr. James Flaherty of the RCYC.

Conewago exhibits the ballasting configuration typical of full-keeled designs, racer and cruiser alike. The keel has far more volume than is required to house ballast, and so only a portion of it is devoted to the task. The rest of the keel's volume consists of solid wood. Research subsequently revealed that these vintage designs had far more keel area than was necessary for generating lift. Modern 8-Meters as a result have much smaller keels (often winged keels) cast entirely from lead.

For an example of an 8-Meter winged keel, see page 69.

Compounding the problem in a wooden boat is the lack of ventilation under the concrete—the encasing wood will be constantly wet and susceptible to rot. One such victim is the famous Nova Scotia schooner *Bluenose II*. A replica of the great racing schooner of the 1920s, she was built in 1963 as a promotional vehicle by a brewery launching a new beer called "Schooner." Her construction followed traditional wood methods, but concrete ballast was used in select areas, and her keepers (she has belonged to the province of Nova Scotia since 1971) have tried with only moderate success to replace some rotted frames by removing planking and attacking the repair from the outside. *Bluenose II* will not be ballasted with con-

crete again, and others should learn from this lesson.

Sometimes (usually on smaller boats) a keel will be poured from cast iron. Cast iron can be cheaper than lead, but with a higher melting point, the molds into which iron is poured must be more complicated. Using cast iron would seem to make little sense. With a density of only 450 pounds per cubic foot, the cast-iron keel must be significantly larger or thicker than an equivalent lead keel to contain the same weight. There are, however, circumstances in which the use of cast iron is nonetheless appropriate.

Because of the two quite separate jobs that the keel has to perform, namely housing ballast and producing lift, usually one task will outrank the other.

The faster a boat moves, the less keel area it requires to generate lift (see Chapter 2), and this creates different ballasting considerations. The difference is exaggerated with a classic full-keeled cruising yacht, which has an incredibly large keel area—more than is really needed for lift generation. The keel in this circumstance needs only a fraction of its area for ballast, the rest being filled up with wood. (See Fig. 3.6.) Whenever the keel area provides more volume than is necessary for ballasting with lead, cast iron can be used to create some or all of the keel, saving money in the process.

Many midsize racer-cruisers face very different ballasting requirements. The keel area that a typical design requires for generating lift may not accommodate all the lead required for ballasting. The routine solution is to design a keel that is thicker than optimum lift performance would dictate, just to house the lead. In other words, a fatter keel in this circumstance is a better solution than a keel that is larger overall with still greater drag.

inside job: internal ballasting

Sometimes there just isn't enough keel volume to house all the ballast required, whether it is lead, cast iron, uranium, or kryptonite. This usually occurs when there is a significant limitation on draft, either because of a rating rule or cruising considerations. When ballast creeps into the bilge, the designer wants to keep it as central as possible, away from the ends, where the weight would contribute to pitching. Generally, ballasting within the hull to ensure stability is a last-resort or extreme-circumstances solution. The best place for ballast is always as far below the hull as possible. Because in-hull ballast reduces the righting arm by raising the center of gravity, more weight is needed in

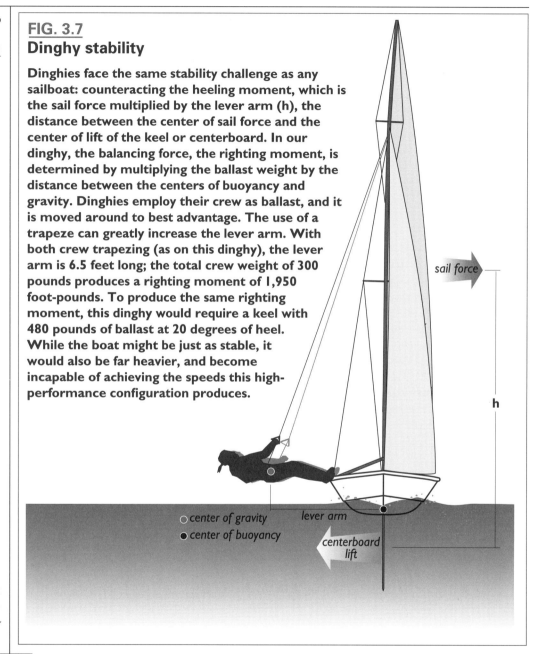

FIG. 3.7
Dinghy stability

Dinghies face the same stability challenge as any sailboat: counteracting the heeling moment, which is the sail force multiplied by the lever arm (h), the distance between the center of sail force and the center of lift of the keel or centerboard. In our dinghy, the balancing force, the righting moment, is determined by multiplying the ballast weight by the distance between the centers of buoyancy and gravity. Dinghies employ their crew as ballast, and it is moved around to best advantage. The use of a trapeze can greatly increase the lever arm. With both crew trapezing (as on this dinghy), the lever arm is 6.5 feet long; the total crew weight of 300 pounds produces a righting moment of 1,950 foot-pounds. To produce the same righting moment, this dinghy would require a keel with 480 pounds of ballast at 20 degrees of heel. While the boat might be just as stable, it would also be far heavier, and become incapable of achieving the speeds this high-performance configuration produces.

sail force

h

○ center of gravity
● center of buoyancy

lever arm

centerboard lift

FIG 3.8
Internal ballast

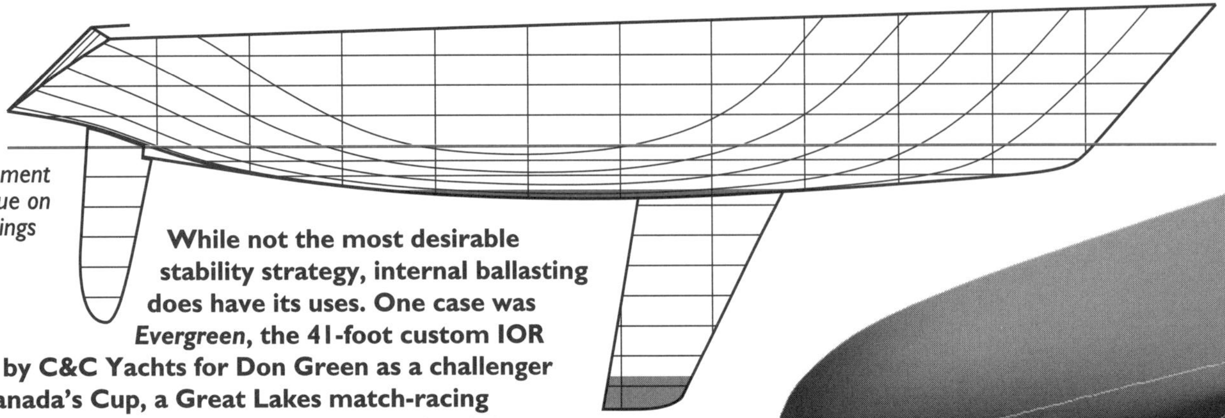

ballast placement shaded in blue on lines drawings

While not the most desirable stability strategy, internal ballasting does have its uses. One case was *Evergreen*, the 41-foot custom IOR design created by C&C Yachts for Don Green as a challenger for the 1978 Canada's Cup, a Great Lakes match-racing competition between Canadian and American yacht clubs. The use of a daggerboard limited traditional ballast placement to a 250-pound lead "shoe" at the daggerboard tip. The remaining 8,600 pounds of ballast was cast in a breastplate that was molded precisely to the contours of the hull bottom. With her flaring topsides, *Evergreen* also relied on crew weight for stability. *Evergreen* won the Canada's Cup for the Royal Hamilton Yacht Club; equipped with a "drop keel" (as daggerboards were subsequently heavily penalized under the IOR), she was sufficiently robust to survive the 1979 Fastnet Race.

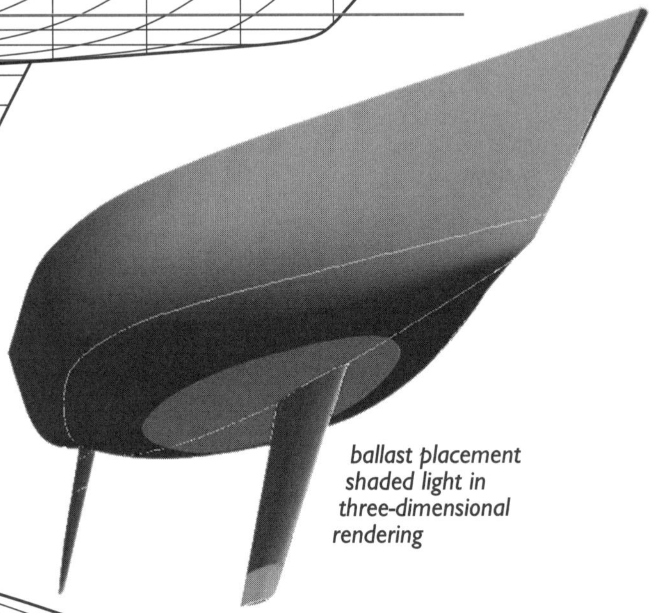

ballast placement shaded light in three-dimensional rendering

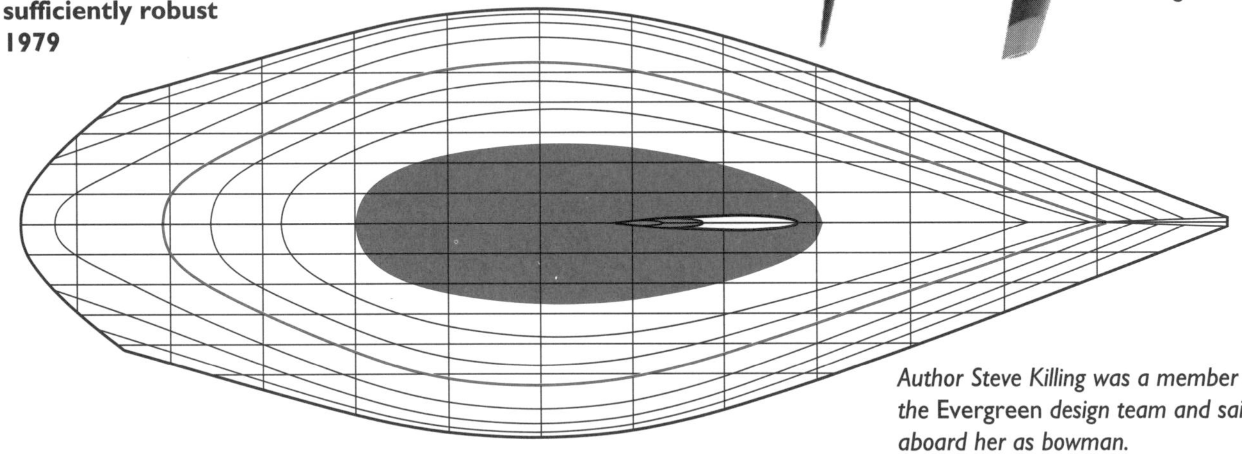

Author Steve Killing was a member of the Evergreen *design team and sailed aboard her as bowman.*

the hull than would be required in the keel to achieve the same stability.

But there are circumstances in which internal ballast is an acceptable, even desirable strategy. With the 1978 Canada's Cup winner *Evergreen*, a fairly radical 41-foot daggerboard design, displacement was kept low and much of her stability (she was purpose-built for match racing in light winds) derived from her flaring hull shape and the use of crew weight. She wore a breast plate of 8,600 pounds of "internal" lead on the lower surface of the hull, molded to exactly match the hull's contours. Another 250 pounds was fitted to the bottom of the daggerboard—this amount was limited by the lifting capacity of the manual hydraulics. (See Fig. 3.8.)

For this scheme to be successful, the remaining portion of the boat had to be built extremely light. The extensive use of Kevlar and honeycomb-core panels, as well as some carbon fiber, although more commonplace today, was revolutionary in 1978, and permitted a high ballast-displacement ratio (near 66 percent). With extensive "internal ballast," the boat had adequate, though not robust, stability, and the versatility of a daggerboard that could be lifted to reduce drag when sailing off the wind. This feature package gave *Evergreen* a significant performance edge over the competition.

weighty issues: ballasting and structure

Performance demands can increase to the point that structural requirements are the limiting factors in keel and ballast configuration. The now-famous *Australia II* winged keel, developed for the 12-Meter class in the 1983 America's Cup, was essentially an upside-down keel with winglets of solid lead. In the wake of the Australian innovation, designers of winged-keel 12-Meters like myself were forced to concern themselves as never before with structure. These inverted keels of up to 45,000 pounds were suspended from ever-shrinking attachment points on the hull—and the rest of the boat weighed only about 7,000 to 10,000 pounds. The tensile strength of the lead used to cast the keel was augmented with oversized stainless steel keel bolts and high calcium percentages. The trade-off, of course, was that as more foreign substances like calcium were added, the final product became less dense. (Winged-keel design is discussed on page 208.)

In high-tech racing boats, design ingenuity has

A radical match-racing design, the 41-foot daggerboarder Evergreen *achieved a 66 percent ballast-displacement ratio and adequate stability with mostly internal ballasting. (Author Steve Killing is standing on the windward rail.) See also Fig. 3.8 opposite.*

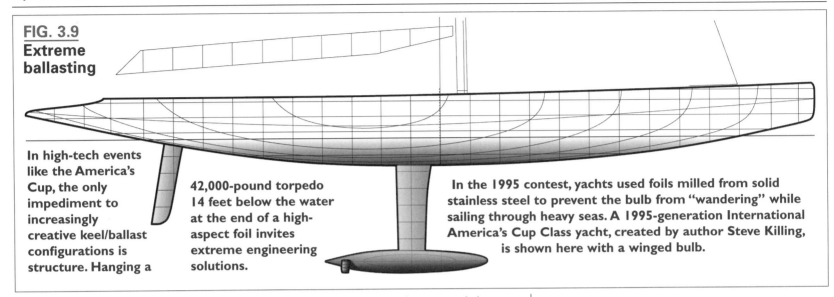

FIG. 3.9
Extreme ballasting

In high-tech events like the America's Cup, the only impediment to increasingly creative keel/ballast configurations is structure. Hanging a

42,000-pound torpedo 14 feet below the water at the end of a high-aspect foil invites extreme engineering solutions.

In the 1995 contest, yachts used foils milled from solid stainless steel to prevent the bulb from "wandering" while sailing through heavy seas. A 1995-generation International America's Cup Class yacht, created by author Steve Killing, is shown here with a winged bulb.

allowed the keel's lift function to be separated almost entirely from its normal role as a ballast container. The desire for high aspect, thin keels can get outrageous. The International America's Cup Class, developed in 1992, allows a depth of 14 feet for keels. Rather than sporting solid lead keels 14 feet deep, these yachts typically employ a deep, narrow fin with a heavy bulb on the bottom. (See Fig. 3.9.) The huge lever arm, combined with the desire for the lowest possible center of gravity, brought about the realization with early boats that lead was inappropriate for the fin. Molding the fin from carbon fiber over a wood or foam core did provide a stiffer member to support the lead torpedo. For the next contest in 1995, though, even more stiffness was desired, for it had been found that the bulbs (all 42,000 pounds of them) tended to wander around as boats sailed through heavy seas. The next generation of foils were milled from solid stainless steel—still with a lead bulb, which is regulated under the racing rules as the densest material permitted.

liquid assets: the water ballast innovation

To improve stability, the low-tech response is to increase ballast. This has unavoidable performance costs. While more ballast might improve upwind performance, the overall weight of the boat has increased, penalizing downwind performance. And a smaller boat that is meant to be trailerable is now harder to move around on shore.

It would be wonderful if you could maximize ballast deployment without increasing displacement. The answer, some flexibility in total ballast weight and distribution, is not impossible. The obvious choice in such flexible ballast is people. The crew is not only variable from day to day, but their position is changeable by the minute. If the breeze comes up, planting some stout bodies on the windward rail will flatten the boat a few degrees.

Ballast-displacement ratio: revealing or misleading?

Because a yacht's ballast-displacement ratio is simple to calculate—being nothing more than ballast divided by displacement—it is often cited in magazine boat reviews. Sailors have come to see this figure as the key measure of stability and often compare boats on paper with this figure as their sole indicator of sail-carrying ability.

But there is much to be considered besides this ratio when judging stability. Shown below is the same 39-foot hull with two different keel and ballasting considerations. The shallow-draft configuration has a ratio of 49 percent, while the deep-draft version has a ratio of 40 percent.

This is a substantial difference—but does that make the shallow-draft configuration more stable?

Not at all. As the calculations in the right side of the illustration show, at 20 degrees heel the two hulls have exactly the same righting moment. And from a performance standpoint, the deep-draft version is clearly superior. With its deeper bulb keel, it also enjoys a lower position for the center of gravity of its ballast. That means much less ballast is required to produce the same stability. A net reduction in displacement of 1,800 pounds delivers this configuration better all-round performance.

Of course, the shallow-draft version has its own performance advantages when seeking out anchorages. The deeper keel's lower center of lift also means a longer lever arm for the overturning moment, thereby increasing the heeling force it is designed to resist.

It is important to recognize that there are many factors affecting stability other than the ballast-displacement ratio. In addition to the depth of the ballast, the beam of the hull is vital in comparing different designs. Generally, boats sporting deep-draft keels with torpedo bulbs can get by with a low ratio, while classes like the 12-Meter boast 80 percent ratios, as they need to hold up a towering rig with keels of limited draft.

The moral here is never to compare published ballast-displacement ratios without a knowledge of hull beam and ballast center of gravity.

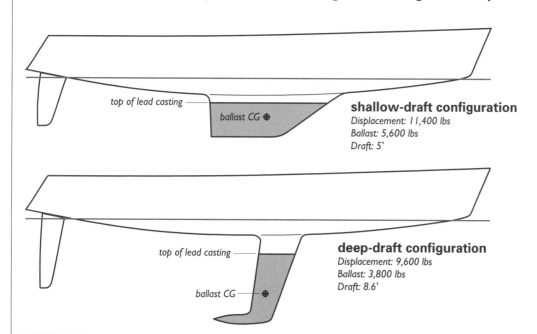

top of lead casting

ballast CG ⊕

shallow-draft configuration
Displacement: 11,400 lbs
Ballast: 5,600 lbs
Draft: 5'

top of lead casting

ballast CG ⊕

deep-draft configuration
Displacement: 9,600 lbs
Ballast: 3,800 lbs
Draft: 8.6'

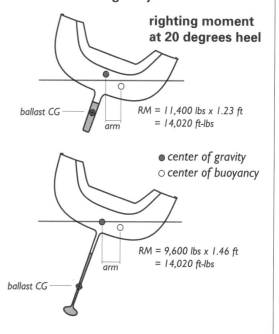

righting moment at 20 degrees heel

ballast CG

arm

RM = 11,400 lbs x 1.23 ft
= 14,020 ft-lbs

● *center of gravity*
○ *center of buoyancy*

arm

RM = 9,600 lbs x 1.46 ft
= 14,020 ft-lbs

ballast CG

Most racing boats from 10 to 60 feet still make use of crew weight in managing stability, but there are drawbacks. Some classes won't allow you to increase or decrease the number of crew according to the weather. And even when you can, the crew is often required for other jobs, just when you want them most on the rail. And unless you throw a few people overboard, it's impossible to reduce ballast while underway.

In the late nineteenth century, a peculiar high-performance centerboard design thrived called the *sand-bagger*. Generally between 20 and 30 feet overall and sporting enormous sail plans, these shallow-draft rockets augmented their lead and iron ballast (placed low in the bilge) with movable sacks of ballast. Contrary to the design type's nickname, the preferred ballast type was actually gravel, as unlike sand it tended not to rot the canvas bags in which it was stored. Upwind, the crew would pile sacks of gravel on the windward side. Tacking was not a spontaneous activity. As marine historian William P. Stephens noted, "A general rule was that all ballast must be brought home, but this was one cause of discussion in making a match, and in some cases it was permissible to dump ballast after turning the weather mark. Where this was not permitted it might happen that some bags slipped overboard, while a knife in a potato sack [filled with 100 pounds of gravel] served the same end."

Some owners today would not think twice about

In the late nineteenth century, an outrageous group of high-performance centerboarders flourished in the United States. Dubbed "sandbaggers," these overcanvassed, overcrewed racing craft used sacks of gravel as movable ballast, stacking them on the windward rail to remain upright.

chucking lead ingots overboard when moving downwind, were it not for the fact that racing rules forbid it. Similarly, competition regulations generally require you to finish the race with the same number of crew that you start with. And while sailors are free to shift gear around inside a boat for trim purposes while racing, rules tend to be quite strict about internal ballast being fixed in position.

The only movable ballast now seen in racing circles is water, and only in limited applications. Most competitive forums forbid it as an undesirable connivance, but it can be found in high-performance offshore events. (See Fig. 3.10.)

Water would not normally be a designer's first choice for ballast. Compared to the previously discussed materials, water isn't very heavy: salt water is 64 pounds per cubic foot, fresh water 62.4. But its weight is not inconsiderable. After all, human beings are almost entirely water and have proven their worth as movable ballast. And anyone who has hauled a bucket of water up into a boat knows that it packs some heft—a gallon of it weighs about 10 pounds.

The use of water ballast in round-the-world racing is the easiest to comprehend. Turning to water for ballast is understandable in this competitive forum. Long-distance singlehanders have no other options in movable ballast—their own weight is insignificant and they definitely cannot be spared from other jobs on the boat. With crewed boats, several months of rail-sitting in the extremes of snowstorms and searing sun has little appeal. The logical solution is to replace the weight of those bodies with water.

This movable ballast could be lead, concrete, rocks, or fish, but water has two inescapable advantages—it's abundant and easily moved. Tanks for the water are located where the deck meets the hull. Four tanks in total provide flexibility in positioning the virtual crew. When the boat is sailing upwind, the two

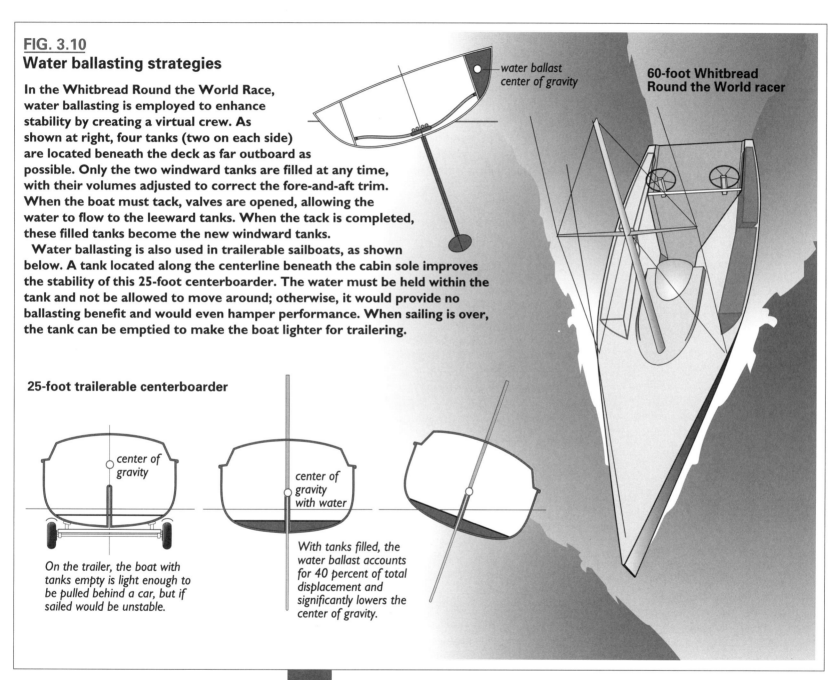

FIG. 3.10
Water ballasting strategies

In the Whitbread Round the World Race, water ballasting is employed to enhance stability by creating a virtual crew. As shown at right, four tanks (two on each side) are located beneath the deck as far outboard as possible. Only the two windward tanks are filled at any time, with their volumes adjusted to correct the fore-and-aft trim. When the boat must tack, valves are opened, allowing the water to flow to the leeward tanks. When the tack is completed, these filled tanks become the new windward tanks.

Water ballasting is also used in trailerable sailboats, as shown below. A tank located along the centerline beneath the cabin sole improves the stability of this 25-foot centerboarder. The water must be held within the tank and not be allowed to move around; otherwise, it would provide no ballasting benefit and would even hamper performance. When sailing is over, the tank can be emptied to make the boat lighter for trailering.

water ballast
center of gravity

**60-foot Whitbread
Round the World racer**

25-foot trailerable centerboarder

center of gravity

On the trailer, the boat with tanks empty is light enough to be pulled behind a car, but if sailed would be unstable.

center of gravity with water

With tanks filled, the water ballast accounts for 40 percent of total displacement and significantly lowers the center of gravity.

windward tanks are filled, their individual volumes adjusted to maintain proper fore-and-aft trim. Just before a tack, the valves connecting the windward and leeward tanks are opened, allowing the water to drain from one set to the other, momentarily increasing the heel angle. With the transfer of liquid complete, the valves are shut and the tack initiated. The new windward side now has full tanks to augment stability.

Carrying water ballast on one side of the boat at a time raises safety concerns. The weight that holds the boat flat on port tack will, if it is not transferred at the right time, increase the heel angle on starboard tack. In ideal conditions this is never an issue, but we all know that inadvertent tacks and gybes do happen—and often in the worst weather.

The regulations governing the design of round-the-world boats address this issue by limiting the heel angle induced by the water ballast to 10 degrees. It is tested by filling all the tanks on one side while the boat is at the dock and ensuring that the heel limit is not exceeded. Whether 10 degrees is an appropriate angle is a matter of ongoing discussion.

For water ballasting that is transferred from one side of the boat to the other to be a practical stability solution, the boat must sail on one tack for a long time. The mechanics of transferring ballast from one side to the other makes it poorly suited to sailing that involves a lot of tacking, such as cruising through islands, conventional course racing, and, especially, match racing. But water ballasting of a different sort is useful in small cruising boats.

Trailerable boats are a ballasting conundrum. They must be light for trailering, yet they need weight for stability. They need keel depth for upwind performance, yet no depth at all for the road. It is for trailerable boats that centerline water ballast makes the most sense.

A first glance at a sectional view of a trailerable, water-ballasted boat is a bit baffling. How can putting water in the bottom of a boat that is floating in water make any difference at all? The key to making centerline water ballast work is making sure it is enclosed. If the water is allowed to slosh around in the bilge, it adds nothing to stability. Even worse, its momentum can reduce stability as it rushes from one place to another. When the water is contained in a tank, however, it performs the same function as a casting of lead—although because of the density difference, you need 11 times the volume of water as lead to achieve the same ballast weight. As the boat heels, the center of buoyancy moves away from this fixed weight, and the righting moment is increased.

This ballasting system is also flexible. When winds are light, the water ballast can be left out entirely. If the wind does happen to come up, water can be taken on to improve stability by opening a plug in the hull and letting it fill the tank. After sailing with the water ballast on a breezy day, you can eliminate the weight by pulling the plug when the boat is on the trailer. And once on the trailer, the lighter boat is easier on the towing vehicle's gas mileage. The system, however, is passive—you can't actively pump water out of the tank while afloat, although there's no reason a boat couldn't be designed with this feature.

The other detriments to centerline water ballasting are the large volume of space taken up beneath the floorboards (which could otherwise be used for storage or interior space) and the rather inefficient location of the water, compared to lead in a keel below the hull. In pursuing a particular stability target, more weight is required when using ballast in the hull than would be needed if the weight were slung well below the hull. When you consider as well the volume difference between water and lead of the same weight, lead in a keel clearly is more efficient as ballast than water in a hull. But under the extenuating circumstances of trailer-sailing, water ballasting does have its place.

CHAPTER 4 rudders

Found alone or in pairs—or even at the bow—rudders are foils that generate lift to keep a yacht on course.

the rudderless myth: steering's true essentials

People use the word "rudderless" to describe someone or something without direction, be it physical, moral, or intellectual. The metaphor works because people assume any vessel without a rudder is out of control, in much the same way that someone who has lost their head cannot think properly. Rudders are indeed nice things to have, but to understand how they work you should first understand that you don't need a rudder to steer a boat. In the late nineteenth century the 20-foot St. Lawrence Skiff was a popular racing craft that sailed with no rudder at all. This slim (3.5-foot beam) canoelike hull had a single sail set well forward and a fan-shaped centerboard. John Gardner, in his book *Building Classic Small Craft,* quotes an August 1885 article from *The*

center of
sail force

lever arm

center of
lateral plane area

The 20-foot St. Lawrence Skiff of the late 1800s ably demonstrated that a rudder is not required to steer a sailboat. By moving his weight fore and aft, the sailor shifted the immersed hull's center of lateral plane area to effect course changes. Burying the stern (as shown here) moved the center of lateral plane area well aft of the center of sail force, creating lee helm and causing the boat to bear away.

Century Magazine that describes in some detail how to sail this skiff:

"The main peculiarity of the skiff under sail is that neither rudder nor oar nor paddle is needed to guide it. Some persons help themselves to come about on a fresh tack with the oars, but this is not at all necessary, and is held in great scorn by a good sailor. The latter walks unconcernedly up and down his boat, pays her off the wind, or brings her up close hauled as if by magic. The secret lies in distributing the weight of the sailor forward or backward. In order to bring the boat into the wind with the needed swiftness, he moves suddenly forward quite to the mast. This buries the bow of the boat, and the stern, shaped like the bow, rises up and is swung around by the wind. As soon as the sail shakes well in the wind, the skiff-man runs aft, thus raising the bow, which is helped about by the wind, and depressing at the same time the stern. All this without steering-oar or rudder, or the help of oars in the rowlocks."

How similar this description is to the technique of the modern sailboarder, who runs forward to step around the mast during a tack. Both rudderless craft depend on the mobility of the sailor to effect changes in direction. By shifting his weight forward, the skiff sailor moved with him the immersed hull's *center of lateral plane area,* causing the stern to swing away. The sailboarder does the same thing in tacking, but also uses another, more efficient strategy to manage the course of the craft. By standing in one position and slowly pivoting the sail plan forward or aft, he can move the center of effort of the sail relative to the daggerboard's center of lift. Moving the sail aft turns the bow into the wind; moving it forward causes the boat

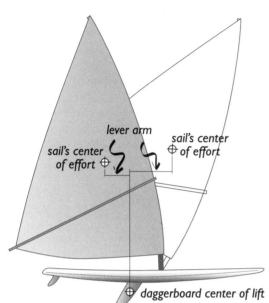

FIG. 4.1
The science of steering

Steering a sailboat is a matter of balancing the lift forces above and below the waterline. No rudder is actually required. Sailboards (left) are steered by moving the sail fore and aft. If the center of effort of the sail is moved aft of the daggerboard's center of lift, the lever arm (the distance between the two positions) causes the sailboard to turn into the wind. Moving the sail forward changes the lever arm so that the sailboard turns away from the wind.

sail's center of effort

lever arm

sail's center of effort

daggerboard center of lift

Large sailboats can also be steered with their sails, by changing sail trim so that their center of lift moves fore or aft of the keel's center of lateral resistance. Most boats have their sail plan's center of effort placed aft, giving them built-in weather helm: the boat naturally turns into the wind.

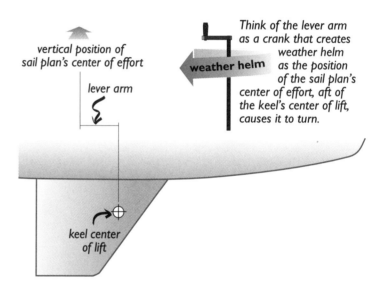

vertical position of sail plan's center of effort

lever arm

Think of the lever arm as a crank that creates weather helm as the position of the sail plan's center of effort, aft of the keel's center of lift, causes it to turn.

weather helm

keel center of lift

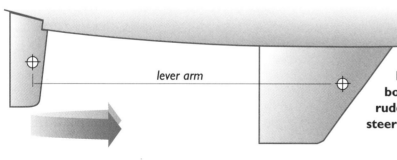

lever arm

A rudder is simply another lift-generating device below the waterline, and it creates another lever arm. This lever arm is determined by the centers of lift of the rudder and keel, and is powerful enough to pivot the stern, changing the boat's direction. (See also Fig. 4.2.) On a typical boat, the rudder is unquestionably a more effective (and far safer) way to steer than moving the sail plan's center of effort.

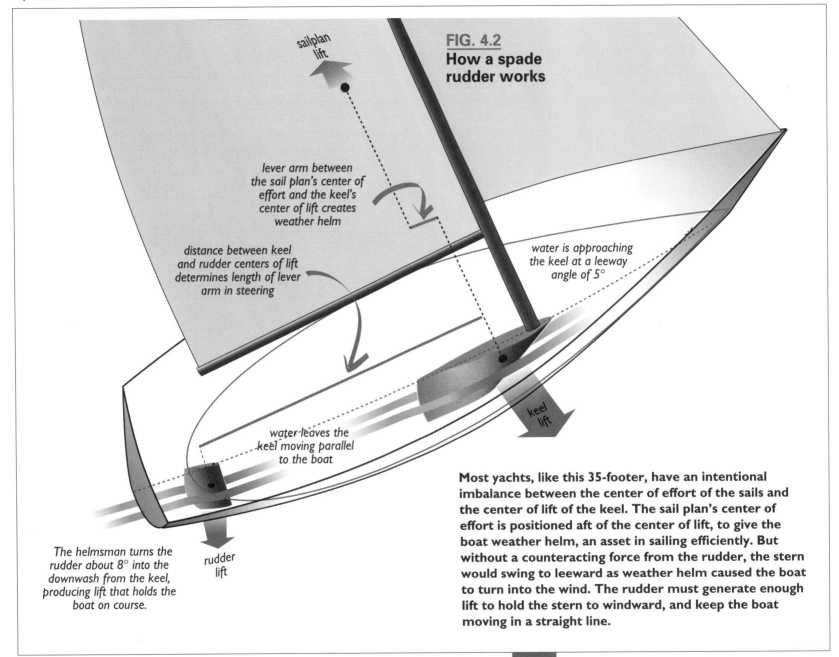

sailplan lift

FIG. 4.2
How a spade rudder works

lever arm between the sail plan's center of effort and the keel's center of lift creates weather helm

distance between keel and rudder centers of lift determines length of lever arm in steering

water is approaching the keel at a leeway angle of 5°

water leaves the keel moving parallel to the boat

keel lift

The helmsman turns the rudder about 8° into the downwash from the keel, producing lift that holds the boat on course.

rudder lift

Most yachts, like this 35-footer, have an intentional imbalance between the center of effort of the sails and the center of lift of the keel. The sail plan's center of effort is positioned aft of the center of lift, to give the boat weather helm, an asset in sailing efficiently. But without a counteracting force from the rudder, the stern would swing to leeward as weather helm caused the boat to turn into the wind. The rudder must generate enough lift to hold the stern to windward, and keep the boat moving in a straight line.

to bear off. Since a sailboard's rig can be tilted to port and starboard as well and fore and aft, the sailor has yet another, equally effective option for steering. Moving the sail to leeward pushes the center of effort out to the side, causing the board to turn. In strong breezes, when the force on the sail is great enough to support a good portion of the weight of the sailor, the sail plan can be pulled well to windward, above the sailor, in order to bear off.

The sailboard is excellent evidence that a sailing craft doesn't need a rudder to be steered with precision. In fact, many watercraft get along without one, canoes and rowboats foremost. Boats that use no rudder can travel through the water with a minimum of drag. Any sailboat with a rudder can be steered by adjusting sail trim, which moves the center of effort in the same way that a sailboarder does by tilting the entire rig. (See Fig. 4.1.)

Experience will tell you that, while it is theoretically possible to steer a 30-foot keelboat without a rudder, actually doing so is impractical and more than a little dangerous. Without a rudder to correct any misalignment of sail and keel forces, the boat, by definition, must be in perfect balance at all times (or it will turn). You would be forced to contrive a misalignment (most easily by fiddling with the sails) to effect a change in course, and then realign the sail and keel forces to return the boat's course to a straight line. Having a rudder to control the direction of the boat is a luxury that most of us have grown dependent upon. But whether the rudder is being used to steer an ideal course upwind or is hardly needed in light air off the wind, it is always adding extra resistance.

Steering a sailboat with a rudder, then, can be thought of as using an immersed mechanical device to introduce temporary misalignments in the lift forces at work above and below the waterline. The whole idea of steering is to get the craft to move its front end relative to its back end, or vice versa. There are just as many different "rudders" as there are different ways of getting these ends to move around.

Steering a canoe perhaps best illustrates the point that any moment (a force times a distance) will turn a boat. To turn a canoe to the right, the stern paddler can use his paddle to steer the aft end of the canoe to the left, thereby forcing the bow to the right, or the bow paddler can place his blade at an angle and draw the bow to the right. If speed is not an issue, the stern paddler can drag his blade on the starboard side, resulting in a slow right turn. The boat can also be turned without using paddles at all, by leaning the boat to port and making use of the asymmetrical heeled waterline to round the boat to starboard. Sailors can recognize these steering strategies in their own pastime: bow rudders, stern rudders, and twin rudders have all been used, and the turning ability of hull asymmetry when the boat is heeled is a tool dinghy sailors use in roll-tacking.

Whether using a paddle or a rudder, the essential force applied when steering is lift. The canoeist positions his blade at an angle to the passing water, creating high- and low-pressure sides. The resulting lift forces the blade in one direction, and takes one end of the boat with it as the paddler hangs on firmly. Only when the blade is set at a right angle to the flow is lift abandoned in favor of drag, slowing one side or one end of the boat and causing the craft to turn. Drag, however, is not an efficient tool for changing a vessel's course. The preferred tool of lift is the one all rudders employ. However, the location of the rudder—standing alone at the stern (or even at the bow) or attached to the trailing edge of the keel—dictates how those lift forces are used to make the boat turn.

While many ancient craft used steering oars at the transom to control their direction, the rudder on most recreational keelboats remained fixed to the trailing edge of the keel until after the Second World War. There seems to have been considerable confusion over how the rudder worked. In centerboard classes, the rudder was inevitably made a separate entity, but experimentation in keelboat design consistently frustrated attempts to separate the rudder from the keel, unless the keel was of such a shape that hanging a rudder from it was impractical. In other words, the standalone rudder was an alternative to the preferred practice of hanging one off the keel. It was left to advances in keel design, specifically the march toward high-aspect shapes over the last few decades, to promote the general use of a distinct rudder, located aft and independent of the keel.

A rudder that stands alone is very different from one that is attached to a keel. The leading edge of the freestanding (which we call a *spade*) rudder is fully exposed to the passing water (see Fig. 4.2), while the keel-mounted rudder has its leading edge tucked behind the trailing edge of the keel and experiences directly the high- and low-pressure water flow from the keel itself. (See Fig. 4.3.) When pondering how the traditional keel-mounted rudder operates, one can think of it in two ways: as a foil in its own right (even if it is board flat), and as a hinged extension of the keel, forming with it one large foil. The keel-mounted rudder survives in performance-oriented designs as the trim tab, and there may be some trim-tab qualities to how this rudder arrangement affects keel lift. But in all cases, we can explain the way the keel-mounted rudder works simply by describing it as a lift-producing foil in its own right, and leave its trim-tab qualities to secondary consideration.

As the boat sails along on starboard tack, the helmsman decides to bear off, or turn to the left. He turns the wheel or shifts the tiller so that the rudder is angled back to the left as well. The rudder produces lift toward the right, which spins the back end of the boat counterclockwise around the center of lift of the keel, located farther forward. Similarly, if the helmsman wants to turn to the right, the rudder is angled to the right far enough to create lift toward the left, spinning the back end of the boat clockwise.

When a boat is moving in a straight line, the sail plan's center of effort and the keel's center of lift are perfectly aligned. Most boats have some amount of *weather helm*—the center of effort of the sails is aft of the keel's center of lift, which makes the boat want to turn into the wind. The rudder counteracts this tendency by making its own lift contribution to that of the keel. The overall center of lift thus moves aft to align with the center of effort of the sails, and this allows the boat to sail in a straight line. (More on this below.)

In the middle of this century some of the finest design minds firmly believed that the best place for a racing boat's rudder was on the trailing edge of the keel. It may have been that boats with rudder-keel combinations were better than anything else designers had developed, but the science of rudder design still had a long way to go. It took until 1967 for the 12-Meter class to move away from the keel-rudder combination, when *Intrepid* revolutionized Meter-class design with a trim-tab-equipped keel and a separate rudder set on the end of a bustle.

What is most striking about old rudders, even those positioned on their own toward the stern, is how little they adhered to hydrodynamic concepts of efficient lifting foils—and in some cases how by modern standards they were actively inviting performance problems. It seems that designers were creating rudders with an entirely different mental picture of how they actually worked—perhaps by redirecting water flow, as on a powerboat or steamship, rather than by acting through lift forces.

Today, rudders and keels look very much of the same family, and in extreme cases, such as the 1992

FIG. 4.3
Full-keel and spade rudders

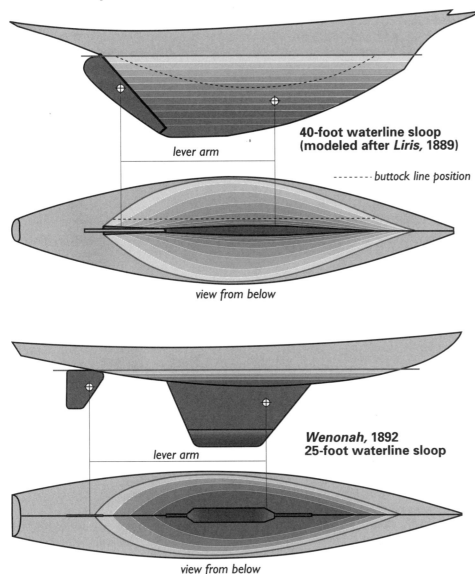

lever arm

**40-foot waterline sloop
(modeled after *Liris,* 1889)**

-------- *buttock line position*

view from below

**Wenonah, 1892
25-foot waterline sloop**

lever arm

view from below

Keel-mounted rudders operate in a very different environment than their spade counterparts. Traditional mountings feature tremendous aft rake in the rudder post, to accommodate tiller positioning in the cockpit. And a keel-mounted rudder's leading edge is not exposed to passing water flow, as is a spade rudder's; instead, it experiences the same flow as the keel to which it is attached. But the keel-mounted rudder still operates according to the same engineering principles as the spade: it creates a moment (a force times a distance) that causes the stern to swing.

As the drawing of the 40-foot waterline sloop at top shows, the lever arm (the distance component of the moment) can be quite long in a full-keel design. However, a spade rudder (as shown with the revolutionary *Wenonah* by N. G. Herreshoff) can produce an even greater lever arm, and the reduced area of the fin keel (in *Wenonah*'s case a plate with a bulb) means a smaller lateral plane underwater, and so more nimble steering.

Even so, fin keels with spade rudders were a long time finding broad acceptance. As late as the middle of this century, many designers and sailors felt the keel-hung rudder was the best performance configuration—possibly because of its trim-tab effect at low rudder angles.

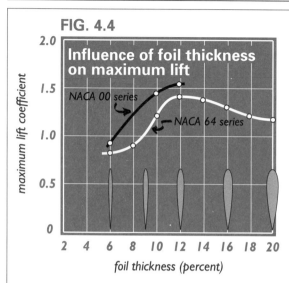

FIG. 4.4

Influence of foil thickness on maximum lift

maximum lift coefficient (vertical axis: 2.0, 1.5, 1.0, 0.5, 0)

NACA 00 series

NACA 64 series

foil thickness (percent) (horizontal axis: 2 4 6 8 10 12 14 16 18 20)

This graph shows why the NACA 00 series foil is used for rudders rather than the 64 series foil, generally used for keels. Although the data is limited (plotted here from data published in Abbott and Von Doenhoff's *Theory of Wing Sections*), the 00 series produces a higher lift coefficient when operating at typical speeds (Reynolds number 3 x 10⁶).

The graph also shows how foil thickness affects lift values. Data suggests a lift coefficient peak for the 00 series at a foil thickness of about 12 percent.

Rudders typically have foil thicknesses of 10 to 15 percent. The only reason for exceeding 12 percent is to accommodate the rudder shaft, and this is usually done only near the top of the rudder.

See also Fig. 2.8.

lift characteristics, foil thickness, and aspect ratio

The rudder experiences one of the most varied environments of all the parts of a boat. It sits in the outflow (technically called the *downwash*) of the keel, and is called upon to provide lift at very small angles of attack and yet not to stall when required to prevent a broach at high angles of attack. Sometimes the rudder is totally immersed in water, but when hard-pressed and heeled on a close reach it may have to keep the boat on course while its upper 20 percent is lifted clear of the water. Such a diverse series of criteria calls for some careful thinking in choosing both the foil section and planform shape.

The rudder's unique demands call for a foil section that produces a large lift force and yet can function at high rudder angles (angles of attack). The most common foil section for this use is the NACA 00 series, which differs greatly from the NACA 64 or 64A series often used for keel sections. (See page 74 for foil terminology.) A quick glance at a plot of the lift and drag of the two foil sections in Chapter 2 (Fig. 2.8) shows a marked difference both in the minimum drag at zero lift and the overall shape of the curve. The fine leading edge and forward section of the 64 foil contribute to the low drag at low lift—this drag "bucket" is very beneficial for a keel, which operates a good deal of the time at low leeway angles. However, when we examine the drag encountered outside this "bucket," the 00 rudder foil begins to shine. For a typical rudder angle of 8 degrees, the corresponding lift coefficient is 0.85 and creates a drag coefficient of 0.0075, while for the same lift coefficient, the keel foil would generate a drag coefficient of 0.0085—more than 10 percent higher. Not to be ignored is the physical shape of the

America's Cup challenger *New Zealand,* distinct roles for rudder and keel have been abandoned altogether in favor of steerable foils. (See page 125.)

Most sailors today prefer to have the rudder mounted well aft of the keel, either under the water or on the transom. The hydrodynamic behavior of a rudder traveling through the water is very similar to that of a keel or centerboard, with the added wrinkle that the angle of the rudder to the water can at times get rather large. In normal use, the rudder experiences an incoming flow of 3 to 10 degrees (compared with 2 to 8 degrees for the keel), but when hard-pressed it may be angled as much as 30 or 40 degrees, something a keel is never asked to do. These high angles change the parameters of design and influence the choice of foil section and aspect ratio.

two foil sections: the 00 foil is much thicker in the front and permits a 15 percent larger rudder shaft to fit within the foil.

The foil section, and more particularly the radius of the leading edge, affects how the rudder stalls and at what load. The 00 foil has a more gradual loss of lift at stall, a characteristic that most helmsmen appreciate. This predictable loss of lift can be felt through the tiller or wheel and serves as a warning that the rudder is about to stall, offering one more chance to ease off on the rudder, reattach the flow, and take another "bite" on the water. Although the choice of foil section can offer some advantages in the maximum lift and stall characteristics, these factors are even more influenced by aspect ratio and foil thickness.

One of the most critical decisions in designing a rudder is the foil thickness. If it is too thin, the foil will stall quickly under low load, and installation of the shaft is difficult; if it is too thick, drag will increase. The maximum lift coefficient, which is proportional to the maximum lift that the rudder generates, is shown in Fig. 4.4. The plot shows an almost linear relationship between thickness and maximum lift. With a 12 percent thick foil being able to produce 60 percent more lift than the 6 percent foil, it is very tempting to use a thick foil for a rudder. The penalty is an increase in drag, but it is not nearly as large as the increased benefit in lift. Rudder shapes on most boats will be found to range between 10 and 15 percent thickness.

As with keels, the aspect ratio of the rudder controls the overall efficiency of the blade. A higher aspect will produce the same lift with a lower angle of attack—not in itself a great benefit for a rudder, but the real advantage is in the drag reduction. The huge drag savings with increasing aspect ratio make the gains to be had in choosing the correct foil section look microscopic. Increasing a rudder's aspect ratio from two to four cuts drag in half.

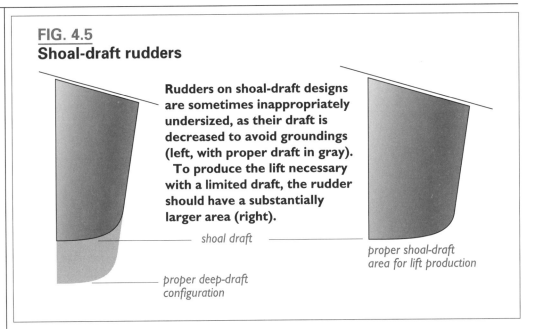

FIG. 4.5
Shoal-draft rudders

Rudders on shoal-draft designs are sometimes inappropriately undersized, as their draft is decreased to avoid groundings (left, with proper draft in gray).
To produce the lift necessary with a limited draft, the rudder should have a substantially larger area (right).

shoal draft

proper deep-draft configuration

proper shoal-draft area for lift production

It can be argued that such major changes in aspect ratio are seldom possible, but the real message is that any small aspect ratio improvement is worth striving for. Returns diminish as the aspect ratio is increased to very large values. Once the aspect ratio reaches five or six, there is little gain in pushing the tall-and-narrow philosophy any further, with its inherent problems of structure and loss of area.

better, not bigger: determining rudder area

In rudder design, a primary goal is to achieve the most lift for the least area, as rudder area translates directly into drag. The amount of lift required from a rudder to turn a particular boat is not absolute, as the rudder works through a moment, which is a force times a distance. (See Fig. 4.6.) The distance is the

FIG. 4.6
Rudder location and size

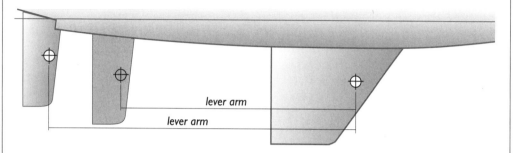

lever arm

lever arm

A rudder steers a boat by applying a moment—a force times a distance. It follows that as distance increases, the amount of force required to produce the same moment decreases. For a rudder, this means that the farther its center of lift is located from the keel's center of lift (measured as the lever arm), the less lift force it is required to generate—and thus the smaller the rudder can be made. Conversely, the closer the rudder is to the keel, the larger it must be made to achieve the same moment. In the above example, shortening the lever arm to 75 percent requires the rudder (in gray) to increase 33 percent in area. While the rudder's efficiency often improves as it moves forward and becomes more deeply immersed, its size increase creates more drag. Not surprisingly, spade rudders set at the very end of the waterline are the steering arrangement of choice in contemporary designs.

the brunt of the abuse from accidental groundings, the rudder is most often tucked up behind it and limited to 70 to 80 percent of the keel draft. In a boat that has a total draft of 6 feet, this would give the rudder a depth of about 4.5 feet. With the depth fixed, the area and the aspect ratio now go hand in hand. A large area can be achieved only by increasing the fore-and-aft dimension and therefore lowering the aspect ratio. (See Fig. 4.5.)

Here arises an interesting trade-off. For the same amount of drag, a higher aspect ratio rudder can produce more lift per unit area. However, when sailing a boat hard-pressed, it is the maximum lift that is critical, and that is little influenced by aspect ratio. Area, then, is still the fundamental design factor, no matter what the aspect ratio.

For this reason, methods of calculating required rudder area that ignore the foil section and aspect ratio are still very valid. Once the required area is calculated, the maximum lift production is also set for the rudder (assuming an average thickness), no matter what the foil section or aspect ratio. However, the aspect ratio is still critical for determining how much drag is produced along with that lift.

A simple relationship that I often use (and was used at the design office at C&C Yachts when I worked there in the 1970s) as a starting point for the rudder area calculation is:

$$\textbf{Rudder Area} \ = \ \frac{\textbf{C} \times \textbf{0.01} \times \textbf{SA} \times \textbf{BWL}}{\sqrt{\textbf{Lateral Plane Area}}}$$

Rudder Area is in square feet.
C is a coefficient—1.0 for absolute minimum area, 1.10 for better control. (In more recent years, as rudder areas have increased to become a larger part of the lifting surface, the coefficient **C** has increased from 1.0 to 1.10.)

lever arm that spans the centers of lift of the rudder and the keel. It follows that for a given moment, the amount of force required can be decreased if the lever arm is increased. Rudders consequently are usually placed at the aft end of the waterline (or beyond it, with transom-mounted rudders) to maximize the lever arm. The savings in rudder area are significant. A lever arm made 75 percent as long requires a rudder area 30 percent larger.

As with keels, rudders become more efficient as their aspect ratio increases and draft is usually the limiting design factor. In order to permit the keel to take

Sail Area (**SA**) is the 100 percent foretriangle plus mainsail sail area in square feet.

Beam Waterline (**BWL**) is in feet.

The **lateral plane area** is the profile (side view) area of the underwater portion of the keel and hull.

This formula recognizes that the rudder area is proportional to both the sail area being controlled and the beam of the boat (which increases the tendency of the boat to round up). Working to help the rudder (and therefore allowing the designer to decrease its size) is the lateral plane. While perhaps not technically correct, the keel and hull are lumped together as equal contributors to the longitudinal stability of the boat.

The required rudder area is also affected by its proximity to the water surface, as the loss in lift for transom-hung or surface-piercing rudders is significant. As shown in Fig. 4.7, significant lift is produced by the top of a rudder that is totally immersed in water. However, when the blade pierces the water surface, the lift must reduce to zero at the waterline and can build up to an appreciable level only some distance below the water. A transom-hung rudder is often increased in area by up to 20 percent to generate safely the same amount of lift as a totally immersed rudder.

As well as having less lift production, a transom-hung rudder is more susceptible to stall due to *ventilation*—the introduction of air onto the lifting surface of the rudder. This phenomenon, not to be confused with *cavitation* (a problem with propellers, when the pressure is lowered so much that the water on the low-pressure side of the blade vaporizes) can occur at high heel angles or when almost any rudder is brought close to the water surface. The effects of the pressure difference across the rudder blade become obvious to the naked eye. The high-pressure side will have a raised waterline and the low-pressure side will have a depressed waterline. If the low pressure is extreme enough, a small

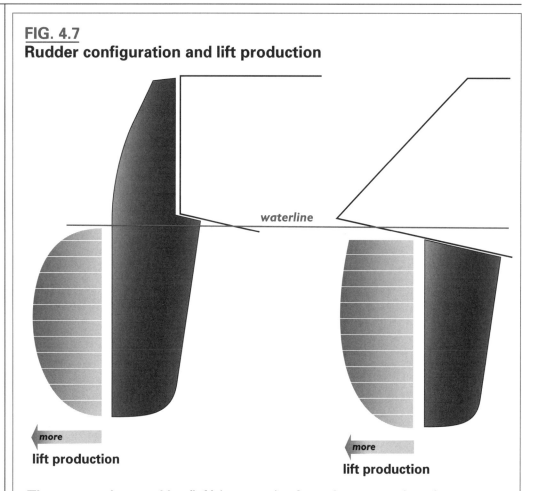

FIG. 4.7
Rudder configuration and lift production

waterline

more

lift production

more

lift production

The transom-hung rudder (left) is attractive from the perspective of construction and maintenance. There is no through-hull shaft, and the rudder can be easily removed while the boat is in the water. However, the fully immersed rudder (right) enjoys high lift values at its top due to the "end plate" effect of the hull. Because it breaks the surface, the transom-hung rudder generates far less lift in its upper immersed area. Thus, to generate the same amount of lift, the transom-hung rudder must have more area than a fully immersed one. As well, the transom-hung rudder is vulnerable to ventilation, as air migrates down the low-pressure side, reducing lift efficiency.

Placing the rudder at the very end of the waterline maximizes turning power while minimizing rudder area. But as the yacht heels or pitches in a sea, the upper part of the rudder can become exposed, reducing efficiency and even causing a loss of control. Here, an out-of-control spinnaker has helped expose the rudder blade.

amount of air can be pulled down next to the surface of the blade and begin to replace the water. A fully ventilated rudder has a column of air perhaps 10 inches fore and aft and the full depth of the rudder replacing what used to be the lift-generating section of water. Because this entire area is thus open to the atmosphere, it can no longer offer a significant low-pressure area and therefore most of the rudder's lift is lost. With the loss of lift goes the control the rudder holds over the boat.

This ventilation cannot occur if the rudder is fully embedded in the water, with the hull capping the rudder and nicely isolating it from the free surface. Ironically, it is when you need the rudder the most that it is most susceptible to ventilation. With increasing heel, the rudder, mounted on centerline, comes closer to the water surface. Compounding the problem is the tendency of boats to trim stern up as they heel because the aft end is wider than the bow; this brings the rudder farther out of the water. In this stressed condition, the boat develops the greatest amount of weather helm and needs the most control. If the rudder generates enough lift and the pressure drops low enough, ventilation will occur and the boat will round up into the wind.

To reduce the rudder's tendency to ventilate, it can be mounted more forward and lower down on the hull. This keeps the rudder farther from the free surface, but reduces the lever arm between the rudder and the keel, and the lever arm's size determines the boat's turning ability.

Another solution used to prevent ventilation on powerboat rudders, but seldom used on sailboats, is the *ventilation plate:* a horizontal fin projecting perhaps 2 inches from the rudder, a few inches below the water. This helps to separate the low-pressure area from the air above and makes it difficult for air to negotiate its way down around the ventilation plate to interfere with the lift production of the rudder.

a matter of balance: rudder shaft position

One of the most commonly misunderstood aspects of yacht design is rudder balance, yet the concept is simple and straightforward. The balance of the rudder has nothing to do with the balance of the boat. *Rudder balance* is the fraction of the rudder area ahead of the shaft line. (See Figs. 4.8, 4.9.) It affects the proportion of the rudder's load felt by the person holding the tiller or wheel.

The location of the shaft within the rudder is influenced greatly by boat size. In small dinghies, there can seldom be enough load on the tiller, and consequently the shaft line (represented by the pintles) is at, or forward of, the leading edge. (See Fig. 4.10.) Many older dinghy classes have swept-back rudders hinged on the transom, and the resulting moment created by the rudder's lifting force, set well aft of the pintles, requires a firm but comfortable hand on the tiller.

Although kick-up rudders are installed on many dinghy classes to permit launching in shallow water, they can also be used as a convenient demonstration of rudder balance. These hinged rudders have a set of cheeks, often metal, which incorporate the pintles, clamp the tiller, and house the blade. A pin connects the rudder blade to the cheeks and permits it to rotate when a retaining cord is released. The geometry of the rudder when the blade is down is significantly different than when raised. With the blade lowered, the rudder's balance is as designed, with the pintles just forward of the leading edge of the blade. The load on the tiller in this position will be moderate. If the blade is permitted to kick up while sailing (or in the excitement of launching has not yet been lowered) a noticeable increase in the load on the tiller can be felt, because the center of

FIG. 4.8
Rudder balance principle

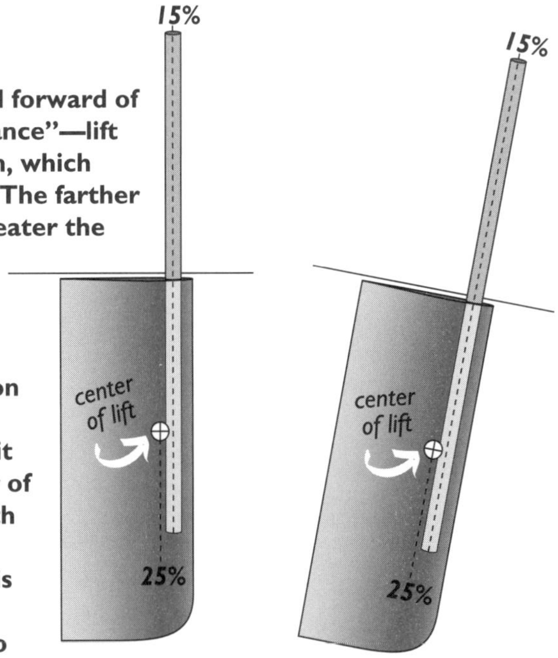

A rudder whose shaft is positioned forward of the center of lift has "positive balance"—lift pressure causes the rudder to turn, which gives the helm a beneficial "feel." The farther forward the shaft is placed, the greater the pressure. The shaft's position aft of the foil's leading edge is measured as a percentage of the chord length. A typical 30-foot keelboat rudder has a shaft position of about 15 percent. If the shaft is moved back to about 25 percent, it coincides with the rudder's center of lift. The helm is now balanced, with no sensation of lift pressure transferred to the helm. While this might seem to be desirable, it actually makes the boat difficult to handle. As seen at right, the angle of the shaft has no effect on the center of lift's position, provided the shaft and rudder centerlines are parallel.

effort of the blade is now well aft of the pintles. The rudder balance has just been increased.

If the rudder balance in a larger keelboat (like a 30-foot racer-cruiser) were left at 0 percent of the chord length, with the shaft line at the leading edge, the rudder load would be so large that it would be difficult for the helmsman to keep the boat on course. To reduce the load, the shaft within the blade is moved aft of the leading edge, typically to 15 percent of the chord length. Further movement of the shaft toward the trailing edge will continue to reduce the load until the 25 percent mark is reached. At this point, the shaft is positioned close to the center of hydrodynamic lift, and the load on the tiller or wheel becomes nil. This

FIG. 4.9
Behavior of a balanced rudder

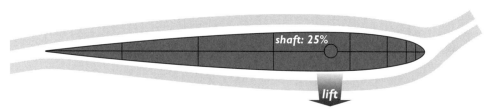

shaft: 25%

lift

This section through a balanced rudder shows the shaft positioned at 25 percent of chord length, aligned with the center of lift. None of the lift loads are transferred to the helm through the rudder post. This lack of feedback is disconcerting to most sailors.

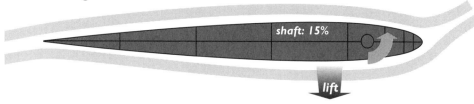

shaft: 15%

lift

The rudder above has positive balance; with the shaft at 15 percent of chord length, the center of lift is aft of the rudder shaft. Lift forces created when the rudder is angled to the incoming flow are transferred to the helm. Rudder balance, a measure of where the shaft lies within the blade, is often confused with weather helm, a term that refers to the rudder angle required to keep the boat on a straight course. Weather helm is determined by the position of the sail plan's center of effort, aft of the keel's center of lift.

best for the safety of the boat that the rudder follow the natural motion of the boat, just flagging along on the back end. I recall a capable amateur experimental builder assembling a replacement rudder for his boat. In a well-intentioned attempt to reduce the load on the tiller, he set the rudder shaft at the 25 percent chord line. This did indeed reduce the load, but it also gave the boat some new, rather unpleasant tendencies. Moving the tiller would start a turn as expected, but rather than producing some resistance to the movement, the rudder would push the helmsperson's hand, trying to turn the boat even more. The center of pressure of the rudder had moved forward of the shaft line, producing a negative load on the tiller. A third rudder, with the shaft about 15 percent back, solved the problem.

The condition most often confused with rudder balance is weather helm. Weather helm is not related to the load on the tiller so much as to the angle that the tiller must be turned in order to keep the boat on a straight course. One of the designer's fundamental tasks is to place the sail plan's center of lift aft of the keel and underbody's center of lateral resistance. The rudder produces lift in the direction of the wind to keep the boat on a straight course. This is achieved by pulling the tiller slightly to weather—hence the term *weather helm*. Optimum rudder angles upwind are usually in the range of 3 to 10 degrees of weather helm—less than that, the efficient rudder is not being used enough to minimize the drag of the keel/rudder combination; more than that, the rudder is too close to stall and paying too high a drag penalty. Although there is some correlation between tiller load (rudder balance) and the amount of weather helm (sailplan balance), the two can be confused. If the rudder angle is less than 10 degrees but the load is too large, then rudder balance is the culprit. If the rudder angle regularly exceeds 10 degrees, then weather-helm balance is the problem.

condition of no-load on the helm is disconcerting, as the person steering gets no feel for the true load on the rudder. Normally, if the rudder loads up, the mainsail needs to be eased or the boat must be allowed to point a little closer into the wind. With a perfectly balanced rudder, even a thousand pounds of lift will produce no telltale force in the helm.

Another detrimental effect of excessive balance in the rudder is the loss of the rudder's natural tendency to "weathervane." If the tiller or wheel is let go, it is

force and distance: tiller vs. wheel steering

According to some sailors, a tiller is the only acceptable way to steer. Every fluctuation of the blade, every increase in load, is felt through the finger-tips. For a small boat, I would agree. However, for sailing a larger boat, the inertia of a large rudder can slow the helmsman's reaction time and make steering a straight course difficult. I find it particularly difficult to steer 8-Meters with a tiller. These heavy, 40-plus-foot boats have good-size rudders, and many are still steered with a tiller. The combination of large loads on the rudder and the sluggish motion of a heavy boat makes steering and maneuvering difficult. The larger 12-Meter class designs are most often equipped with wheels, and while these boats are not thought of as sprightly in their motion, they are at least controllable with a wheel.

The mechanical advantage of a wheel is increased through the use of sprockets, a drive chain, and quadrants on the shaft. (See Fig. 4.11.) A typical 30-footer might have a 24-inch-diameter wheel and an 8-inch quadrant for a power ratio of 288 foot-pounds. To convert this power ratio to an equivalent tiller length, divide it by 40 pounds, the usual maximum comfortable load on a tiller. In this case, the equivalent tiller length is 7 feet. It would be unusual to be able to accommodate a 7-foot tiller on a 30-foot boat—another advantage of the wheel.

Since the mechanical advantage of a tiller is much less than that of most wheels, the balance of a rudder being used with a tiller must be greater than that for a wheel. The 15 percent used for a typical spade rudder with a wheel must be increased (the shaft moved aft in the blade) to about 18 percent for a tiller.

FIG. 4.10
Balance in transom-hung rudders

Seemingly small design changes can make big differences in rudder characteristics. The rudder at right has its pintles positioned a distance 15 percent of the chord length ahead of the leading edge. The resulting large distance between the rudder's center of lift and the pintles gives the rudder highly positive balance. By notching the rudder as shown at far right, the leading edge of the rudder lines up with the pintles, thus placing the pivot point at 0 percent of chord length. This rudder is still positively balanced (a desirable quality), but it requires less force on the tiller to steer.

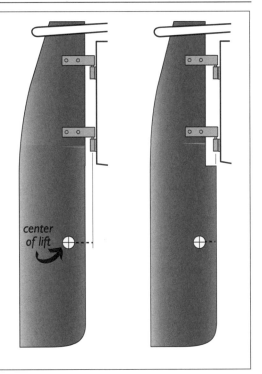

center of lift

spade vs. skeg: the performance debate

Name a position on a boat and there has probably been a rudder put there at some point—on the bow, amidships, on the trailing edge of the keel, at the aft end of the waterline, behind a skeg, on the transom, aft of the transom, or paired with another rudder off centerline. Some locations were a response to rating rules, others were aimed at controlling design considerations, and some were just experiments in being different.

The most common rudder position on a keelboat today is near the aft end of the waterline, either on its

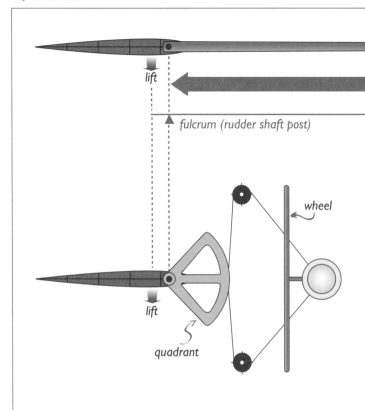

lift

lever arm: 7 ft

fulcrum (rudder shaft post)

wheel

lift

quadrant

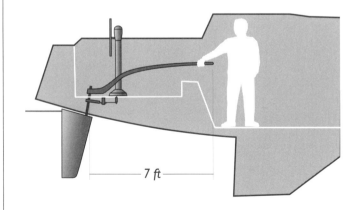

7 ft

FIG. 4.11
Tiller vs. wheel steering

Tillers and wheels are devices that provide the helmsman with the leverage necessary to manage the turning force placed on the rudder shaft by a rudder with positive balance. In this case, the shaft is at 15 percent of chord length.

The tiller (top) is a simple lever that transfers a moment (a force times a distance) to the rudder shaft to overcome the rudder's lift force. A lever maximizes distance to minimize force in producing the required moment.

Many sailors like the feel of the tiller, claiming it gives the best possible feedback of rudder loads and behavior. But as loads become larger, so must the tiller length, sometimes prohibitively so from the perspective of cockpit layout.

Wheel steering maximizes cockpit space by using two mechanical devices to manage loads. The first is a quadrant, a kind of minitiller set at the rudder shaft head. Cabling connects the quadrant with the wheel, which provides the second mechanical advantage. With an 8-inch quadrant and 24-inch wheel, our helmsman can deliver a moment of 288 foot-pounds.

To deliver the same power, the tiller (as shown at the top) would have to be 7 feet long. If mounted in the 30-footer at left, the helmsman would have to stand in the cabin to operate it. For practical tiller steering, the rudder shaft position must be moved back (right) so that there is less positive balance. This reduces the moment transferred to the shaft and permits a shorter tiller.

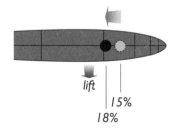

lift

15%

18%

own or hinged behind a skeg. This position has the convenience of being near the helmsman so that the tiller ends up in the cockpit and control lines for steering wheels are short. But primarily this location has become favored because the rudder's lifting surface is set well aft and control of the keel is excellent. The rudder force applies a moment, which turns the boat around the keel. If the rudder position is moved farther forward, the moment is reduced and the response to the rudder becomes more sluggish. If the rudder is slid farther aft, the chance of its lifting out of the water and losing its grip increases.

One of the remaining controversies is whether to locate the rudder behind a skeg or leave it on its own in the free-stream of the passing water. There is a perception that skeg-hung rudders are best for cruising boats, while spade rudders will perform better for the racer. (Designer L. Francis Herreshoff preferred transom-hung rudders for cruising, because they made repairs easy.) The skeg, which sits solidly in front of the rudder, performs two functions—the first hydrodynamic, the second structural. Because the skeg is mounted on centerline and is at a constant angle to the incoming flow, it never sees a very high angle of attack, and the likelihood of stalling is greatly reduced. When the rudder is turned, it forms with the skeg a shape approximating that of an efficient, cambered foil, which can produce high lift values. But the unfortunate reality is that during construction the joint between skeg and rudder is never perfect. In fact, it is usually so far from a smooth, well-sealed joint that when the rudder is highly loaded, stalling can be instigated by the discontinuity at the joint itself.

The real benefit of a skeg rudder is the increased tendency of the boat to travel in a straight line. Because the skeg is like a fixed rudder on centerline, it helps maintain a straight course in lumpy waves, with the rudder itself used only for course corrections. This benefit for some cruising sailors is the very argument that racers make against the skeg-hung rudder—it is much slower to react. Racers, or cruisers who like a more sprightly boat, want the boat to respond quickly to any movement of the wheel or tiller.

The heated "discussions" in the sailing club bar don't end when the conversation switches to the best structural arrangement for the rudder. A skeg assembly will usually house a third bearing in its lower end to support the rudder shaft at it lowest point. This permits the use of a smaller rudder shaft and also protects the lower end from damage. In the event of a hard grounding, the freely cantilevered spade rudder will most likely bend—I have heard of some that were bent a mere 1 or 2 degrees and others that canted off crazily at 30 degrees after hitting a shoal at 5 knots. The skeg proponents will say, "If you had a lower bearing mounted on a skeg, that wouldn't have happened." Just as fast, the spade rudder lovers will pull out a story about a friend who hit hard with a skeg rudder and knocked the lower bearing out of alignment so that the rudder couldn't be turned, making the boat inoperable.

twin rudders: a well-heeled solution

Twin rudders are typically installed on boats with very wide, flat hull sections near the transom. (See Fig. 4.12.) These boats, if fitted with a traditional rudder on centerline, will find the rudder lifting well out of the water as they heel. Because of the excessive beam aft, the boat's centerline, along with the attached rudder, will rise when the boat heels. To ensure control is maintained in this situation, the designer can move the rudder off centerline—perhaps one-quarter of the transom beam—so that it remains

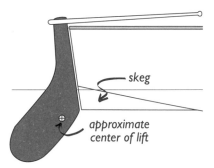

skeg

approximate center of lift

One-design classes will accept certain modifications over the years to keep pace with the times, but the class association for the 19-foot Lightning, a popular centerboarder designed by Olin Stephens in 1938, is particularly vigilant about not allowing modernization to make established boats obsolete.

In the 1980s, the class did consider updating its original rudder, which is mounted on the transom behind a skeg. Under high loads the blade is prone to ventilation, and blade breakage compelled the class association to investigate the possible use of a more modern blade shape. After testing prototypes, the class elected to stick with tradition.

FIG. 4.12
Twin rudders

A design with a wide, shallow hull form like the Open 60 class, used in singlehanded round-the-world racing, presents a special challenge in rudder configuration. At only 25 degrees of heel, a conventional rudder, mounted on the centerline, would encounter performance difficulties. The generous beam aft causes the stern to rise as the yacht heels, which would expose the top of the rudder blade (right), resulting in reduced control—or loss of it altogether.

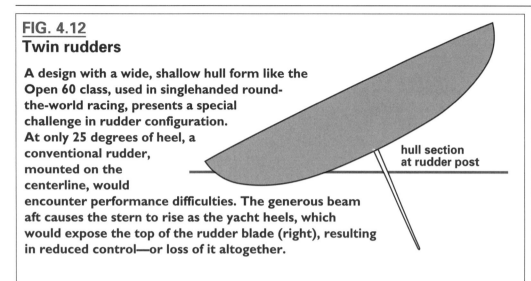

hull section
at rudder post

The design solution is to treat these craft like very large scows, which have similar hull forms and steering challenges. Moving the rudder off the centerline one-quarter of the transom beam and angling it about 20 degrees from the vertical ensures that when the yacht heels, the rudder is both fully immersed and near-vertical. Of course, a yacht must be able to operate on both tacks. Hence the use of twin rudders. The twin rudders have a shallower draft than a single centerline rudder, so that when the yacht heels, the windward rudder lifts clear of the water, reducing drag. Twin rudders also bring a beneficial redundancy factor to singlehanded ocean racing. Should one rudder fail, the sailor can maintain control with the surviving one.

hull section
at rudder posts

20°

in the water on the leeward side. Since it is specifically arranged to work efficiently on one tack, it can be installed at an angle to the vertical so that it remains close to perpendicular to the water when heeled. Twenty degrees is a common mounting angle.

A solitary off-center rudder is obviously of little use if one has any hopes of sailing on both tacks. So two rudders are installed symmetrically about the centerline. When heeled, the leeward one steers the boat and the windward comes clear of the water, to reduce the drag penalty of twin rudders. Downwind, both rudders are active.

There is a secondary safety benefit to twin rudders. Round-the-world racers, whose boats are often light and beamy aft, welcome the fact that some level of redundancy is added with twin rudders. If one rudder is damaged or lost, the other will sail the boat on one tack and reasonably well downwind while repairs are made. (Of course, having two rudders would suggest you have twice the odds of incurring rudder problems…)

closing the gap:
rudder shaft angles

With a rudder mounted beneath the hull, to maximize rudder lift, the designer strives to achieve a minimum space between the rudder top and the hull surface, a gap in the order of one-eighth to one-sixteenth of an inch. To accomplish this, the shaft must be perpendicular to the hull surface—otherwise the rudder top will bind against the hull when it is turned. For reasons I will explain, a perpendicular shaft alignment can seldom be attained, and a clearance of between half an inch and 1 inch must be left. This has the unwanted effect of permitting water to flow over the top of the rudder from the high-pressure

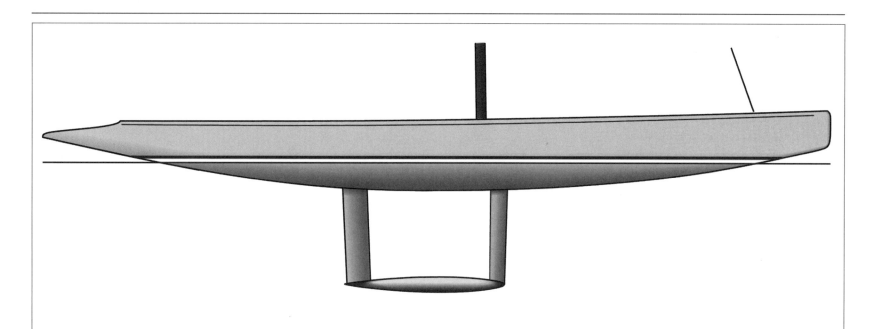

Because keels and rudders are both lift-generating foils, it is possible to merge their roles in a tandem keel-rudder. Two steerable foils support a lead torpedo bulb that contains all ballast. The forward foil can be locked into position with an angle of attack of about 4 degrees, reducing leeway, while the rear foil does the steering. Or both foils can be turned in unison about 8 degrees, allowing the boat to crab sideways to windward. This comes in handy in an upwind race, when the leeward yacht wants to move into a lee-bow position and feed its competitor disturbed air flow. A tandem keel arrangement similar to this was installed on the 1992 America's Cup contender *New Zealand*.

to the lower-pressure side, thereby reducing the lift produced by the top of the rudder.

The rudder shaft angle is usually dictated by factors other than hydrodynamic performance. If tiller steering is to be used, the top end of the rudder shaft must exit on deck in a convenient location, perhaps at the aft end of the cockpit or on the aft deck. If the rudder blade is located aft under the waterline, and that waterline ends somewhere under the cockpit, then the shaft must rake aft as it rises to meet the positional requirements of the rudder and tiller.

Traditional installations with the rudder mounted on the aft end of the keel had severely raked shafts.

For wheel steering, less restriction is put on the location of the top bearing of the rudder. Often mounted under the cockpit sole, the top of the rudder need not be located even remotely near the wheel pedestal. However, if the shaft is mounted perpendicular to the hull surface in this situation, it may incur too much sweep aft in the shaft. Many wheel-steering boats have their rudders swept slightly aft as a compromise between keeping the gap between the rudder and hull

FIG. 4.13
Rudder shaft angle

The "scimitar" rudder on this 41-footer built in the late 1960s shows the high shaft angle that can result when mounting a rudder shaft perpendicular to the hull surface. Rudders with such high shaft angles produce enough upward force when turned at angles of 20 degrees or more to raise the stern significant amounts, making the rudder more vulnerable to ventilation.

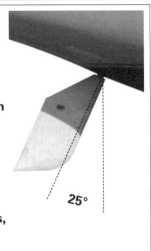

25°

sufficient and reducing the sweep to the shaft so that hydrodynamic performance does not suffer.

Why is shaft sweep a problem? Consider a not-uncommon shaft sweep angle of 20 degrees. In this condition, turning the rudder to large angles (20 degrees and beyond) will produce a significant upward force as well as a turning force. With a rudder that can produce a total force of 1,800 pounds in a 35-foot sailboat, the upward component of lift in a swept-back rudder can be equated to sitting a heavy crewmember on the bow. That is enough to raise the transom almost an inch and further expose the rudder in a position already vulnerable to ventilation. (See Fig. 4.13.) Reversing the sweep angle has the opposite effect—the rudder lift will tend to hold the aft end of the boat down. My own preference is to have the shaft angled at about 5 to 10 degrees from vertical, to concentrate all the rudder force into the turning motion and yet maintain enough sweep to keep the gap narrow between the hull and rudder.

leading the way: the bow rudder option

If a rudder works well 10 feet aft of the keel, why not 10 feet forward? The moment arm will be the same and all the hydrodynamics will function just as well.

There are some advantages to bow rudders—and some disadvantages. On the plus side, the rudder becomes more deeply immersed as the boat heels and the bow drops, which gives the rudder a solid bite on the water. However, since the yacht's center of pitching is aft of the center of the waterline, the bow experiences much more vertical motion than the stern, and much of the bow rudder ends up being pulled out of the water in rough conditions.

But there is also a primary difference in the behavior of a boat with a bow rudder. In order for the boat to progress at the best possible rate to windward, the lifting force on both the keel and the rudder should be in the same direction: to windward. With an aft rudder, this equates to having a boat with a nice bit of weather helm. If the sail plan and the keel are in the same position and the rudder is simply moved to the bow, the natural tendency of the bow to swing to windward would have to be resisted with a rudder force to leeward. This force, although it would keep the boat sailing in a straight line, would increase sideslip by adding an extra force to leeward, thereby negating the bow rudder as a sensible option. However, if the designed sail plan is located farther forward so that the natural tendency of the boat is to bear off, then the rudder can produce lift to windward once again and be of greater use.

One would then think that from a performance standard the situation is exactly the same as with the aft rudder, and it is—in flat water and steady-state sailing. But a bow rudder boat left to its own impulses will not round up to windward and stop—it will bear off, and the act of steering becomes active rather than passive. Any time the rudder comes partly out of the water in heavy air, the boat will head down, away from the waves, and lose some distance to weather. With an aft rudder, the boat will head up toward the wind. Over a long course, the two boats will separate as the aft-rudder yacht slowly makes more headway to weather.

CHAPTER 5 rigs

By providing a skeletal structure
to the sails, rigs transfer the
energy of the wind to the hull.
Designers must make sure that
what is up never comes down.

127

supporting role:
the rig as sailing's skeleton

It's the job of the rig to give the soft sails structure. It must be flexible enough to permit some shaping of the sails and yet rigid enough that the wind energy can be harnessed safely and efficiently into pushing the boat forward. The centerpiece of the rig is the mast. Whether it is supported with the help of a forestay, backstay, and side shrouds, or whether it stands on its own, held only at and below deck level, stiffness is paramount. For a given cross-sectional shape, the material of which the mast is constructed determines its stiffness. Carbon fiber, steel, aluminum, and wood have all been used with success to build masts but have significantly varied stiffnesses.

This International America's Cup Class yacht sports a five-spreader rig, one of the most complex in sailing. The comb of spreaders permits a small mast section diameter, which minimizes drag.

Technically, any boat can sail with an unstayed mast—that is, a mast without any supporting rigging. But with few exceptions, the mast would have to have cross-sectional dimensions and a wall thickness that invite more performance headaches than they solve. Just as building a radio transmission tower out of solid concrete is technically feasible, using metal and guy wires makes far more sense structurally. As it happens, it was Guglielmo Marconi's experimental radio towers that inspired the "Marconi" label for the sloop rigs, with their mass of rigging, pioneered at the turn of the century.

Generally, masts are designed with supportive rigging in mind, and the configurations of these elements are highly dependent on each other. While there are unstayed exceptions, most production sailboats have masts supported by rigging.

When rig designers consider potential failure, one of two things is susceptible: the supportive rigging, or the mast itself. If the rigging stays intact, mast failure is caused by buckling—the mast bends to one side between a set of spreaders and fails at the weakest point, often at a halyard exit, where a hole in the mast wall has created a vulnerable point. To avoid buckling, a mast can be made stiffer by either increasing the overall dimensions of the cross section (from an 8-inch by 5-inch mast to a 9 by 6, for example), or by shortening the panels, which are the lengths of mast between deck and spreaders, spreaders and spreaders, and spreaders and masthead.

Shortening the panels suggests that the designer is about to change the mast height in order to increase its strength, but if sailplan dimensions are fixed—a likely assumption—then changing the height of the mast is not an option. An exception is an especially large yacht for which it might make sense to divide the sailplan into a ketch rig, with two short masts, rather than try to support the towering rig a sloop configuration

FIG. 5.1
Essential rig elements

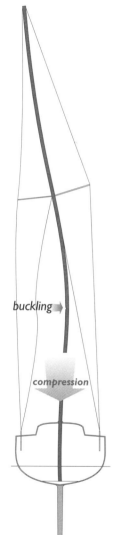

It is common to think that rigging is what holds up a stayed mast. Even though this is essentially true, as most masts would quickly go over the side without rigging, a stayed mast can (and usually does) fail by buckling, which can occur without any failure in the rigging. In fact, the rigging can be the source of failure.

Mast loads are produced by rigging tension. These loads are compressive, directed downward toward the mast step (left), and are an important factor in determining the likelihood of buckling.

Another important factor is panel length. Panels are the unsupported sections of mast (right), along which the mast section is free to deflect. The ability of the mast panels to withstand compression and not deflect (thus avoiding buckling) depends on the length of individual panels.

Introducing an additional set of spreaders and stays keeps the mast more securely in column and can allow the designer to reduce the mast section size, to the benefit of weight and windage. The staying base can also be reduced by moving the chainplates inboard to allow closer sheeting angles for the genoa.

buckling

compression

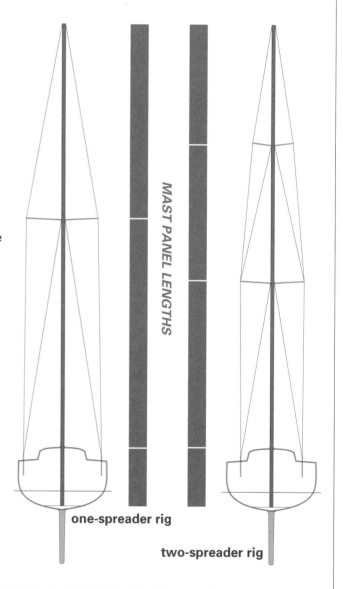

MAST PANEL LENGTHS

one-spreader rig

two-spreader rig

FIG. 5.2
Mast sections

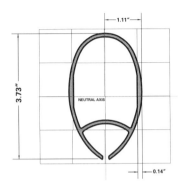

Super Shark 3822
Wall area: 1.10 sq in
Weight: 1.29 lbs/ft

Klacko 6243
Wall area: 2.74 sq in
Weight: 3.14 lbs/ft

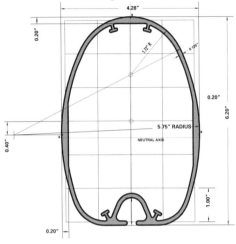

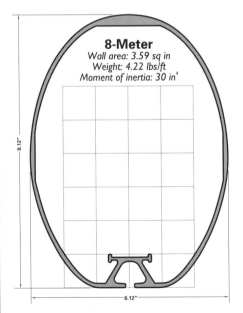

8-Meter
Wall area: 3.59 sq in
Weight: 4.22 lbs/ft
Moment of inertia: 30 in⁴

heavy-wall 3-spreader
Wall area: 5.18 sq in
Weight: 6.09 lbs/ft
Moment of inertia: 30 in⁴

Four mast sections, shown to the same scale (each square represents 1 inch), illustrate different approaches to section shape and wall thickness.

"Super Shark 3822" (top left) is a classic teardrop shape used by the one-design Shark class. "Klacko 6243" (top right, designed by author Steve Killing) follows the consensus on a sensible section shape: contoured forward and squared off aft, balancing low drag with desired stiffness.

"Heavy-wall 3-spreader" (bottom right) and "8-Meter" (bottom left, also designed by the author) display two distinct approaches to achieving the same performance goals. The heavy-wall section reduces area to minimize drag, but in doing so must increase wall thickness. The 8-Meter section uses a large section area to minimize wall thickness. The moment of inertia (a measure of the stiffness of the section) is the same for both sections. The heavy-wall section is 40 percent heavier but experiences less aerodynamic drag. Small and heavy sections were pioneered by American mast builder Tim Stearn in the 1970s.

requires. But if the sloop rig is to be maintained, the panel length can be changed only by moving the spreaders, or adding more of them. Fig. 5.1 shows a single-spreader and a two-spreader mast. Because additional stays and spreaders hold the mast more securely into column, the mast's load-carrying capacity increases. In a typical design problem, the goal is not to make the mast stronger, but to meet a target strength with the lightest or least expensive mast. In this case adding more spreaders permits the mast section itself to be reduced in size.

In a racing boat, the pressure is to reduce weight and windage aloft. Adding more spreaders permits the mast diameter to be reduced with each successive pair, and some racing boats have three-, four-, and even five-spreader rigs. One must do the arithmetic carefully, however, to ensure that gains are still being made with these extreme numbers of spreaders. When the extra weight and drag of the spreaders and additional shrouds and turnbuckles are taken into account, gains are reduced. In some cases, multiple spreaders cause more drag than a larger mast section with fewer spreaders. In an extreme situation, with a rail-skinny mast supported by a comb of spreaders, the design criterion becomes one of compression, not buckling. A mast so supported has no chance of buckling, and the pure compression in the mast caused by the forestay, backstay, and shroud loads will be the ultimate cause of failure.

steady states: section specifics

Wall thickness also controls the strength and stiffness of the spar. An aluminum spar with a constant outside dimension can be accompanied by a ⅛- or a ¼-inch wall thickness. There is a doubling of the

weight with the latter choice, and a corresponding increase in the stiffness. This has invited the intriguing trade-off in spar design, between a large, light section with a thin wall, and a small, heavy section with a thick wall.

In the 1970s, American Tim Stearn developed a number of mast innovations, among them the racing-boat section featuring a small outside dimension and thick-walled section. This approach accepted additional weight aloft to save windage over a larger, thinner-walled section. The 1978 Canada's Cup winner *Evergreen* (on which Stearn sailed) used such a section, with two sets of spreaders and substantial rigging to control

Most mast failures are due not to a break in the rigging, but rather to the compressive loads delivered to the mast by the rigging. The mast buckles at a vulnerable point, such as midway along a panel length, where it has the least support. Here, the crew of the Maxi Longobarda seeks shelter as the rig comes down.

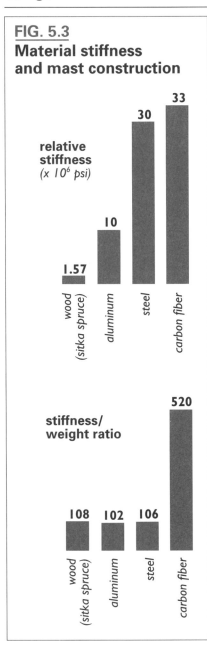

FIG. 5.3
Material stiffness and mast construction

relative
stiffness
(x 10⁶ psi)

33

30

10

1.57

wood
(sitka spruce)

aluminum

steel

carbon fiber

stiffness/
weight ratio

520

108 102 106

wood
(sitka spruce)

aluminum

steel

carbon fiber

its shape. Weight aloft obviously will reduce stability, but that can be accounted for in the initial design of a boat. The most detrimental effect, however, is felt when the boat is pitching through waves. Weight that is flailing around 50 feet above deck will increase the pitching of the boat and slow it down. But if the waves are small, the harm of the additional weight aloft is minimal, and the reduced windage of the smaller mast section, combined with the cleaner airflow on the mainsail, is advantageous. The 1978 Canada's Cup match was conducted on Lake St. Clair on the Great Lakes, where light winds predominate and the motion of the boat was expected to be relatively steady. As it turned out, *Evergreen* won that series on the strength of four course-race victories in the conditions for which her hull and rig were specifically designed.

Fig. 5.2 show a typical teardrop shape; a large, thin-wall section of an 8-Meter; a heavy, thick-wall section; and a more conservative compromise available in the 1990s. The 8-Meter section and the thick-wall section illustrate two different paths to the same destination: the *moment of inertia* (a measure of the stiffness of the section) is almost the same for both sections. The 8-Meter achieves its properties by having a large overall size, while the heavy-wall section uses a lot of material in a small package. The heavy-wall section is 40 percent heavier but experiences less aerodynamic drag.

Getting a consensus from designers on the best shape for a mast section is even less likely than getting them to agree on the optimum hull shape. The array of currently available sections tells the tale—they include the teardrop, circular, rounded rectangle, and D-section shapes. They have all been designed for the same purpose: as little disturbance of the mainsail airflow as possible while providing a maximum of stiffness and a minimum of weight and/or cost.

Some designers have argued that, no matter what you do, the mainsail will be disturbed on one side or

the other at some point of sail, so why not just make a rounded rectangle for an efficient structure? But others claim that a nicely contoured section shape is critical and find it is worth giving up some weight and structure to streamline the flow. Current wisdom favors a contoured section forward with a relatively flat back as a compromise between stiffness and windage.

The reason for such a variation in solutions to this one problem is that the analysis, like so many things on a yacht, is very complex. It is not simply a case of designing the section shape with the least amount of drag for a given stiffness, for the weight factor enters the picture. Once weight weighs in, the designer needs a way of assessing the trade-off between the detrimental effect of additional weight aloft and the bonus of reducing aerodynamic drag. And that is a difficult trade-off, one that depends on weather conditions. The fine differences between sections and the difficulty of making accurate assessments will continue to promote varied ideas in mast design.

giving good weight: section materials

Wood was the primary building material for masts right up until the 1960s, when mass production of sailboats in fiberglass was accompanied by cost-effective aluminum extrusions for masts and spars. Wood has some ideal characteristics: it is light, easily worked, and fairly stiff. I say "fairly" because if we stack it up against some alternatives, it doesn't fare so well. (See Fig. 5.3.)

The common measure of stiffness is the *modulus of elasticity*, quoted in pounds per square inch. Steel sits at 30 x 10⁶ psi and aluminum at 10 x 10⁶ psi, while wood has a lowly 1.57 x 10⁶ psi. Before we all start welding up steel replacements for our handsome varnished masts, let's realize that weight is the other critical factor. Steel has three times the stiffness of aluminum but also three times (3.03 to be exact) the weight. But even with additional weight considered, it would seem that steel is not so bad a choice.

For very large masts, steel has been used successfully. If the outside dimensions of a mast are kept constant, one could be designed from aluminum with perhaps a ⅜-inch wall thickness, or from steel with a ⅛-inch wall. The trade-off is plain; it is the product of material stiffness and a section shape that resists buckling. At one-third the thickness, the steel mast will weigh the same as the aluminum one and be of equal strength. However, for "small" craft (as naval architects define them) under 80 feet or so, the wall thickness for steel spars will become prohibitively thin if they are to remain light. The typical wall thickness on a 4-inch by 6-inch aluminum spar section is ⅛ inch; to remain competitive from a weight standpoint, a steel mast would have to knock that down by a factor of three to 0.04 inch. At this wall thickness, welding and attaching fittings become impractical, and so aluminum prevails in most pleasureboat applications.

With a stiffness to weight ratio only slightly less than that of aluminum, wood is now primarily used for spars on wooden boats, where the appeal of the material itself makes up for any small weight penalty. Well cared for, a wooden spar will last indefinitely. Most wooden spar designs take advantage of the versatility their material holds over aluminum. They can be shaped to match the required section shape for the entire length of the mast: smallest at the masthead, tapering gently to a maximum section somewhere above the gooseneck, then tapering down again to the foot of the spar. Aluminum and steel spars are generally tapered only at the masthead.

Carbon fiber is the one material that takes a huge leap ahead of the rest. Spun into shape and bonded with resin, this composite is ideal for many applications, boasting stiffness greater than that of steel and weight less than that of aluminum. Carbon fiber is available in many grades, each with its own stiffness and weight. A typical quality has an elastic modulus of 33×10^6 psi and a weight of 109 lbs/cu ft, for a stiffness to weight ratio five times better than that of aluminum. However, these composite spars took a long time to gain acceptance with sailors. The Freedom Yachts line of unstayed carbon fiber masts proved that the technology and reasoning is sound. The International America's Cup Class masts, stayed with a traditional shroud arrangement, are all carbon fiber laminates. A key issue that must be dealt with at the design stage is the transfer of high loads into the material's thin walls.

rig design priorities: the boat, not the sails

The two most significant factors influencing the loads imposed on a mast are the width between the chainplates and the boat's stability. The configuration of the sails is immaterial: if the boat has a lot of stability, the mast must be designed to be strong enough to heel the boat to its maximum righting moment, usually at about 45 degrees of heel.

Since the only items touching the deck that can impart that moment are the mast itself and the side shrouds, the distance between those two (the chainplate width, or *staying base,* divide by two) becomes critical. Dividing the maximum righting moment in foot-pounds by the half-chainplate width in feet gives the shroud load in pounds. A stiffer boat will have a potentially higher shroud load. Narrow chainplates, so desirable on a racing boat for close headsail sheeting angles, translate directly into higher shroud loads. (See Fig. 5.4.)

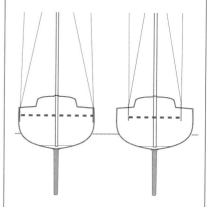

FIG. 5.4
Shroud loads and staying base width

Significant improvements in windward ability can be made by moving chainplates inboard (as shown at right) in order to permit narrower headsail sheeting angles. This smaller staying base (dashed line) carries with it greater shroud loads. A design's shroud loads are calculated by dividing its maximum righting moment (in foot-pounds) by half the staying base (in feet).

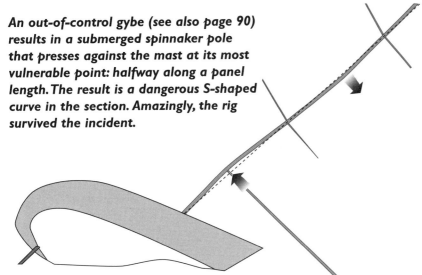

An out-of-control gybe (see also page 90) results in a submerged spinnaker pole that presses against the mast at its most vulnerable point: halfway along a panel length. The result is a dangerous S-shaped curve in the section. Amazingly, the rig survived the incident.

Adding spreaders was discussed earlier as a method to reduce the loads on a mast by permitting a lighter or smaller mast section. Additional spreaders can also be used to narrow the shroud base while keeping the mast section shape constant.

running backstays: help or hindrance?

There are infinite ways to support a mast: twin forestays, running backstays, multiple spreaders, stays to another mast, or no stays at all. In the 1970s Lars Bergstrom and Sven Ridder, two innovative sailor/engineers who developed the Windex that adorns almost every boat's masthead, created the B&R rig. Distinctive with its 30-degree swept-back spreaders, it permitted designers to eliminate the "baby stay," which pulled forward on the mast from about the height of the first spreader. Initially, the B&R rig was combined with a fixed backstay, but after some experimentation it was discovered that the rig could support the genoa and spinnaker without a backstay. Because they sweep back, the spreaders can exert fore-and-aft as well as side loads on the mast. An extra set of rigging wires extends from the outside end of the spreaders down to the mast at the next-lower spreader or the deck. These stiffen the mast and provide resistance to any tendency of the spar to "pump" aft in the middle. They also provide backup support. Should a windward shroud part, the leeward shroud will absorb some of the load.

Running backstays fall into the category of *running rigging*—that is, rigging that is adjustable rather than fixed, like shrouds. As shown in Fig. 5.5, a pair of running backstays are fixed at critical points on the mast and led back to the stern quarter on either side, their tension controlled by lines loaded on winches. They are used to keep small-section racing spars in column when working to windward, and only the windward one is cranked on at any one time. When tacking, the "old" windward one must be released and tension taken up on the "new" one.

Occasionally you will come across a production sailboat designed primarily for racing that sports running backstays, but generally they are found only in high-performance racing circles. For the average sailor, running backstays are a pain, one more task to attend to when tacking, a nuisance off the wind as they get in the way of the boom if they're not eased off properly. People also tend to fear the consequences of "not getting it right," that the mast will go over the side if they don't immediately set the running backstay to the proper tension when coming onto a new tack. So far, the boating industry has not convinced the typical keelboater that the headaches of dealing with running backstays are worth the payoff in a more sophisticated, better performing rig.

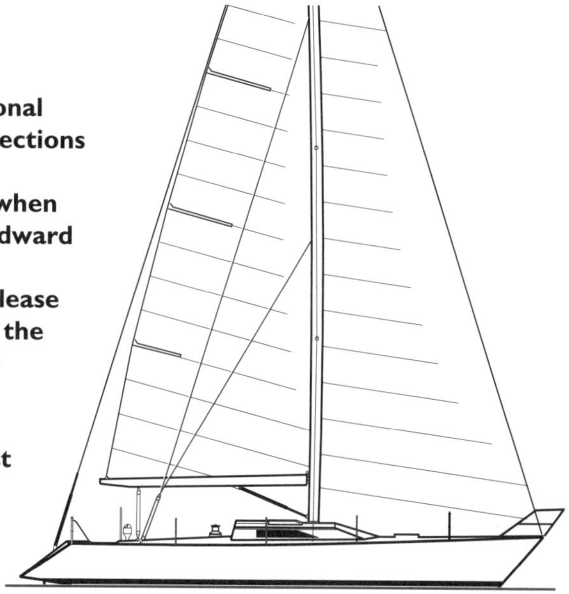

free to stand: unstayed rigs

Cat-rigged boats with freestanding masts provide a unique challenge to the designer. While a stayed mast fails by buckling, a freestanding mast fails by bending. The greatest load on a stayed mast is at its base, where the strength of the material (not its stiffness) and the size of the mast section determine the overall load resistance. Stiffness cannot be ignored, however, because the performance of the mast will not be adequate if the stiffness is insufficient.

With a stayed mast, the stretching characteristics of the rigging holding it up determine how far it deflects sideways under load. The unstayed mast's deflection is controlled by the stiffness of the material in the mast section. Unstayed masts have significant taper from top

FIG. 5.5
Running backstays

Running backstays provide additional support to small-diameter mast sections along their panel lengths, to help prevent the rig from "pumping" when sailing to windward. Only the windward set of running backstays is placed under tension, and the need to release and tighten the respective sets as the boat tacks is one reason why they are rarely seen outside racing circles. While their use would permit lighter mast sections, most cruisers and club racers prefer to live without their complexity.

to bottom, for the stiffness demands on the top are small and on the bottom huge. The loads imparted into the hull by the unstayed mast are significantly different than those sustained by typical chainplates of a stayed rig, for the unstayed load at the deck level and the mast step is horizontal rather than vertical. But the magnitude of the load is similar to that of a stayed rig because the distance between the chainplates of a stayed rig is about the same as the distance from deck to mast step in the unstayed rig; therefore, the moment arms are equivalent. (See Fig.5.7)

stress management: rig tuning techniques

Tuning a rig means adjusting the tension on the various shrouds and stays to reduce the deflection under load and keep the spar's overall shape smooth. **138 ▶**

FIG. 5.6
Mast bend and rig tuning

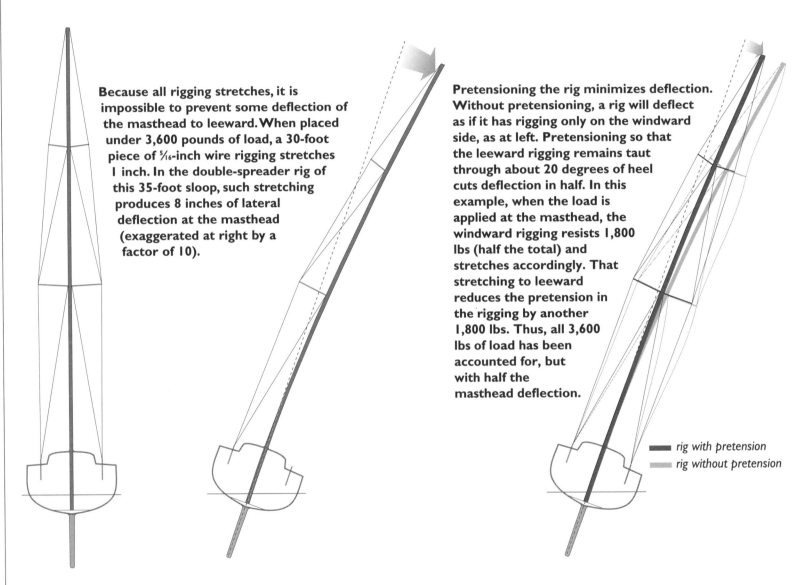

Because all rigging stretches, it is impossible to prevent some deflection of the masthead to leeward. When placed under 3,600 pounds of load, a 30-foot piece of ⁵⁄₁₆-inch wire rigging stretches 1 inch. In the double-spreader rig of this 35-foot sloop, such stretching produces 8 inches of lateral deflection at the masthead (exaggerated at right by a factor of 10).

Pretensioning the rig minimizes deflection. Without pretensioning, a rig will deflect as if it has rigging only on the windward side, as at left. Pretensioning so that the leeward rigging remains taut through about 20 degrees of heel cuts deflection in half. In this example, when the load is applied at the masthead, the windward rigging resists 1,800 lbs (half the total) and stretches accordingly. That stretching to leeward reduces the pretension in the rigging by another 1,800 lbs. Thus, all 3,600 lbs of load has been accounted for, but with half the masthead deflection.

rig with pretension
rig without pretension

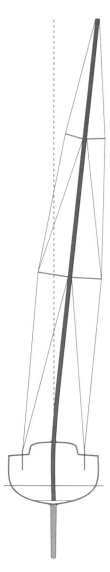

There are two theories on tuning the rig. The first holds that the deflected shape of the mast should be made as straight as possible (left). One must remember, however, that once under load the mast is not perpendicular to the deck. Most of the deflection is taking place around the deck level, placing disproportionate stress on the lower mast panels.

The second theory holds that to avoid this concentration of stress, pretensioning should evenly distribute deflection along the entire rig (right), so that no panel is more vulnerable than any another.

(Deflection in these examples is amplified tenfold for illustration purposes.)

In pretensioning the rig, care must be taken not to apply excessive tension. The upward pull on the chainplates, combined with the downward thrust of the mast, will cause the hull to distort (exaggerated at right, with original hull in blue). On most boats, the leeward rigging should begin to go slack at about 20 degrees of heel. If the leeward rigging never slackens, then there is too much tension.

FIG. 5.7
Stayed vs. unstayed rigs

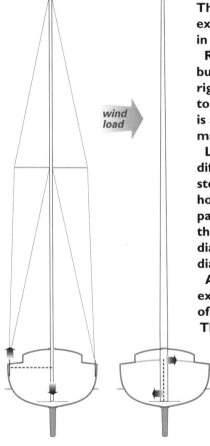

wind
load

The mast in an unstayed rig (right) experiences entirely different stresses than one in a stayed rig (left).

Rig failure in the stayed rig will result from buckling due to compression; in the unstayed rig, from bending by lateral forces. Resistance to overall sideways deflection in the stayed rig is a matter of rigging stretch; in the unstayed mast, bend is controlled by material stiffness.

Loads imparted to the hull are significantly different, being primarily vertical (at the mast step and chainplates) in the stayed rig and horizontal (at the mast step and deck partners) in the unstayed rig. To cope with these forces, an unstayed mast has a very small diameter aloft, tapering to an enormous diameter at deck level and belowdecks.

Although the stresses the two rig types experience are very different, the magnitude of the loads imparted to the hull are similar. This is because the distance (dashed blue line) between the chainplates and the mast in the stayed rig is comparable to the distance between the deck partners and the mast step in the unstayed rig.

◀ 135 An untuned mast may have an S shape when under load, or a tip that falls off excessively. Tuning is often a trial-and-error process of successive adjustments, yet the effects of changes are logical: simply tighten the shroud that is not giving the mast enough support.

The tuning factor that most readily eludes sailors is that the objective is not to prevent mast deflection; rather, it is to manage it. Deflection is impossible to eliminate, because all rigging stretches to some degree when under load.

In the good old days before wire or rod rigging, significant rig deflection was unavoidable, for even good rope stretches considerably compared with metal. A nylon anchor rode (in which stretching is desired, as it acts as a shock absorber) can stretch 10 feet for every 100 at 25 percent breaking strength. A nice 100-foot length, prestretched, 6-millimeter plaited halyard at the same breaking strength will grow 4 feet longer.

Wire is far less stretchy than rope, but it still stretches, in direct proportion to the load imposed on it. A piece of 5/16-inch wire 30 feet long will stretch 1 inch under a load of 3,500 pounds. That stretch translates into a sideways deflection at the masthead of approximately 8 inches on the 35-foot double-spreader sloop shown in Fig. 5.6.

The reality of stretching means that a well-tuned mast is not necessarily in a perfectly straight line. Once a sailor has a look at a sketch of a mast under load it is easy for him to see why. As the mast resists the side load of the sails, the rigging on the windward side of the boat must stretch. Knowing that at the base and deck level the mast is still on centerline, one must decide how best to allow the mast to reach the 8-inch deflected position at the masthead sustained with our 5/16-inch wire. Should the deflection all take place in the lowest panel and the rest of the mast be made straight? Should the deflection be all in the top panel? Or should it be evenly distributed?

There are two theories on the best solution. The majority of sailors will tune the spar so that it is straight, as determined by sighting up the mast from the gooseneck. The assumption made by most of them is that the entire mast is then straight, in column and strong. However, the reality is that most of the bend must be occurring in the lower panel, at the deck and below deck, because the mast or the hull must move to permit the deflection. Some argue (and I tend to agree) that the best deflected shape, which evenly distributes the deflection, has a very slight curve to leeward as one sights up the mast. Each panel then is only slightly out of column, and the resistance to buckling is maximized.

Once the mast has been tuned to a smooth, deflected shape, the decision must be made as to how much overall tension should be on the rig. The mast can be set up very loose or very tight, both with an acceptable curve when loaded. This pretensioning of the rig has a dramatic effect on the amount of deflection that occurs when the sails are set and the wind presses the boat over. On a lightly tensioned boat, by the time the heel angle has reached 15 degrees, the leeward rigging has gone slack due to the stretching of the windward rigging. This is a good indicator that the masthead really is moving to leeward. As more tension is put into the entire rigging, normally by tightening the main shroud at deck level, the rigging on the leeward side will become tighter.

It is easiest to tighten the loose rigging on the leeward side—then tack and tighten the new leeward rigging by the same amount. As this tightening occurs, more demands are being put on the hull. If continual tightening is not making any appreciable change in the tension of the leeward rigging, then tighten no further, as the hull is simply bending under the stress. But most boats will respond well, and the rigging can be tightened until it is just beginning to go slack, at about 20 degrees of heel.

Having a mast that stands up as straight as possible in the boat is important to windward performance. At the extreme, imagine a mast that simply gives up and lies almost horizontal in a 10-knot breeze. Any lift

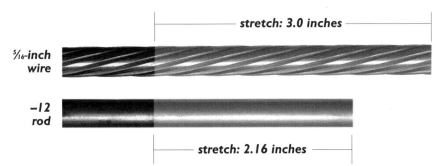

FIG. 5.8
Wire vs. rod rigging

⁵⁄₁₆-inch wire — stretch: 3.0 inches

−12 rod — stretch: 2.16 inches

Rod rigging offers a clear performance advantage over wire. With a diameter 10 percent smaller than ⁵⁄₁₆-inch wire, −12 stainless steel rod offers less windage and stretch. Manufacturer specifications indicate that, loaded to 25 percent of breaking strength, 100 feet of wire stretches 3 inches, while the same length of rod stretches 2.16 inches.

that is generated is well off to the side of the boat, increasing the weather helm. The overall wind speed that the sail encounters is reduced due to the wind gradient (see Fig. 6.3), and performance suffers.

To minimize mast deflection, both windward and leeward shrouds should be tight within the first 15 to 20 degrees of heel. While the leeward rigging is still tight, the mast is deflecting exactly one half the amount it would otherwise. The reason for this is fairly simple to understand. The case of a mast with loose leeward rigging is the same as a mast with rigging on only one side of the spar. As the wind and sails load up the rigging, it stretches until it can resist the applied loads. Let's say, as in the example quoted before, that a 3,500-pound load has caused a stretch of 1 inch. If we now examine a mast with rigging on both sides, with the leeward rigging still tight, this same 3,500-pound load will stretch the windward rigging ½ inch for 1,750 pounds, deflect the masthead, and unload the leeward rigging an equal ½ inch for another 1,750 pounds. With the help of the leeward rigging, which continues to relax as the windward rigging is tightened, the deflection of the entire rigging is cut in half.

Racers pay more attention than most sailors to pretensioning. Because their boats are built to be stiffer than cruisers, they will resist the high pretension loads and keep the leeward rigging tight longer and therefore reduce the deflection at the masthead.

If the leeward rigging never goes slack, there is too much pretension in the shrouds. The owner would do well to release some of the pretension and lower the load on the hull.

strength and stretch: rod size and materials

In calculating the rigging diameter required for a particular combination of mast and boat, the first order of business is strength requirement, not stretching. In my first 10 years of design practice, it was this strength requirement with an appropriate safety factor (1.5 to 3 times breaking point) that ultimately determined the shroud sizes. However, as it became more apparent that deflection of the rigging was a significant hindrance to boat speed, the shroud diameters in successive designs were increased to reduce stretch. In rod rigging a –10 rod would be increased to a –12, or in extreme cases to a –17. In particular the stretch of the lightly loaded D2 shroud (from the outboard end of the lower spreader to the base of the spreader above) often exhibited too much deflection.

Solid rod rigging is made of stainless steel or, for the Gran-Prix crowd, cobalt. Rod rigging's main benefit is the reduction of stretch compared to wire for the same strength—or, if stretch is your design criterion, a smaller diameter for the same stretch. Specific examples of rod manufactured by the firm Navtec illustrate the case. A 100-foot length of ⁵⁄₁₆-inch-diameter wire will stretch 3 inches when loaded to 25 percent of its breaking strength. A –12 rod with the same breaking strength (12,500 pounds) will stretch only 2.16 inches and is 10 percent smaller in diameter. (See Fig. 5.8.) The argument for smaller diameter rod with less stretch is hard to beat.

Cost used to be the big edge in favor of wire, but no longer, as rod is easily price competitive with wire. Cruisers will make one further argument: if they are sailing in some odd corner of the world and they have a problem with the rod rigging, they are not likely to be able to find someone to fix it. While wire is more readily available, sailors hooked on rod will counter with two arguments. In this ever-shrinking world, it is not that difficult to ship a shroud anywhere in the globe for a reasonable price. And whether it is rod or wire, some fittings will likely have to be shipped. If rod is for some reason difficult to find, a repair can still be made with wire because the fittings and pin sizes are the same.

Cobalt rod rigging was initially developed for the America's Cup racing yachts in the late 1970s. It has 18 percent less stretch than stainless steel rod, but a price that makes it suitable only for the most serious of racers.

Kevlar rod is manufactured with unidirectional strands of this high-tensile synthetic fiber (all running along the length of the rod), covered in a black plastic coating to protect them from the deteriorating effect of ultraviolet rays and abrasion. For the same stretch as a stainless rod, the Kevlar specifications indicate a diameter 50 percent larger, but a weight only 40 percent of the stainless steel. The breaking strength is also 20 percent higher. In an application where weight is critical, but windage is not, Kevlar rigging makes sense.

sails

In providing the yacht's horsepower, sails are a key design element in speed, safety, and practicality. There are almost as many ways to design the sail plan as there are to design the boat.

raiding to reaching: the sail plan's evolution

While yacht designers generally do not concern themselves with such sail design issues as chord shape and luff curve, the sail plan is a fundamental concern. How much horsepower is required, and how should it be distributed?

Sails are foils, just like keels or airplane wings, and they generate lift according to the same scientific principles. Sails, however, predate keels and aircraft wings, as well as human knowledge of what a foil even is or how one works. The first sails most certainly weren't foils at all—more along the lines of a square piece of goat skin that hurried a humble vessel along before the wind. Viking raiders and Phoenician traders, though many centuries apart, employed essentially the same square sail, and depended upon prevailing winds to press them forward and oars to make progress to windward. Chinese quadrilateral lug rigs

had windward capability, but Europeans did not make any significant gains to windward until they borrowed the triangular lateen configuration in the late fifteenth century from the Arab world, which had employed it since about A.D. 900. (This rig can still be found on recreational singlehanders like the Sunfish.)

The sloop's tall triangular sail plan is a relatively recent invention. The sloop itself is historically of somewhat flexible definition. (See Fig. 6.1.) Today we consider it a sailboat with a mainsail and one headsail, but traditionally refers to any yacht that has a single mast (to differentiate it from a schooner) and one or more headsails (to differentiate it from a cat or una-rig). What we call a *sloop rig,* with a single mainsail and headsail, was originally known as a *knockabout.* Technically, a *cutter rig* is a variation on the sloop, with a more elaborate arrangement of mainsail, topsail, and headsails (generally three), but in modern parlance any sloop with two headsails receives the "cutter" label. (See Figs. 6.1, 6.6.)

In the late nineteenth century, some racers got rid of the sloop's topsail to set large mainsails on a mast with a vertical gaff in a configuration known as a *gunter rig.* The single mainsail (called *leg o'mutton* in America) was a more efficient shape, and greater efficiency would result if the rig, too, could be reduced to a one-piece mast.

The late designer and marine historian William P. Stephens credited the first use in international competition of this rig, called a *Marconi* or *Bermuda/Bermudian,* to the Seawanhaka Cup defender *Ethelwynn,* a yacht whose hull he designed in 1895. Stephens would recall the criticism the novelty attracted from one correspondent in *The Rudder:* "I don't like *Ethelwynn*'s sail plan…. No form of sail will send a boat to windward like a gaff-sail, and any man who will take the trouble to closely watch a yacht with a well cut sail, when on the wind, will soon note the reason why."

FIG. 6.1
Evolution of the sloop

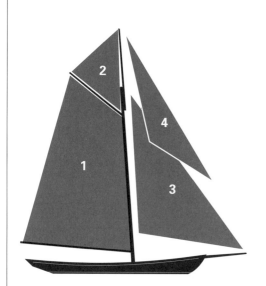

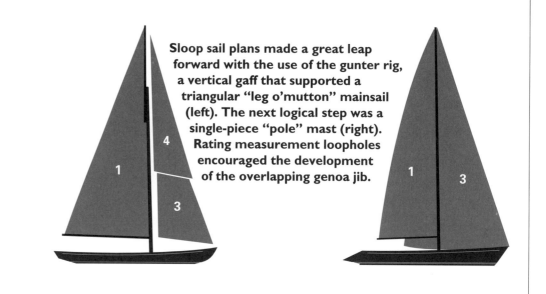

Sloop sail plans made a great leap forward with the use of the gunter rig, a vertical gaff that supported a triangular "leg o'mutton" mainsail (left). The next logical step was a single-piece "pole" mast (right). Rating measurement loopholes encouraged the development of the overlapping genoa jib.

Historically, a sloop is a single-masted rig (to distinguish it from a schooner) with one or more headsails (to distinguish it from a cat). Today, the term "sloop" is generally limited to single-masted craft with one mainsail and one headsail—a configuration once called a "knockabout."

1. Mainsail
2. Main topsail
3. Jib
4. Jib topsail
5. Staysail

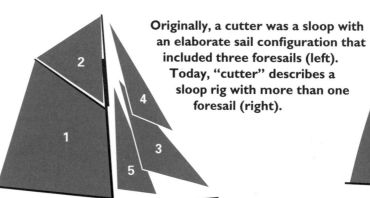

Originally, a cutter was a sloop with an elaborate sail configuration that included three foresails (left). Today, "cutter" describes a sloop rig with more than one foresail (right).

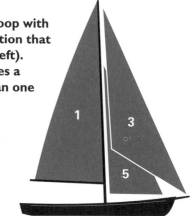

High-speed craft such as this DN-class iceboat generate so much apparent wind (the wind felt by an object in motion) that they are almost always sailing "upwind," regardless of the true wind's direction. Powerful mainsheet purchases and flat sails are required to keep drag low and speeds high.

But there was no reason why; the gaff-rigged sail was soon to be eclipsed. After the First World War, the Marconi rig's popularity began to spread. The rig's name was inspired by the radio transmission towers of contemporary innovator Guglielmo Marconi, who knew about as much about sailing as he did about black holes. Offended by the flippancy of the label, British yachtsmen turned to the term "Bermudian" or "Bermuda," co-opted from the traditional rig of the same name, which also had a single-piece mast but the boom extended ahead of the mast.

Stephens noted the influence of scientific advances spurred on by the new aircraft industry, which in turn had been spurred on by the First World War. A wind tunnel established at the Massachusetts Institute of Technology in 1914 was turned loose on sails in 1915,

and this initial work by Professor H. A. Everett was credited by Stephens with ushering in the modern era of scientific rig and sail design.

While sails are the engines that drive a yacht, they have also served as engines driving yacht design in general. Without advances in sail and rig design, advances in hull, and in particular keel, shapes and configurations would not have been possible, or possibly even contemplated. While yacht designers as a rule do not concern themselves with sail design issues such as chord shape and construction materials, the sail plan and the supporting rig still form a vital component of the yacht design process.

handling and horsepower: sail plan design issues

Sail plans are judged according to two basic characteristics: their efficiency in producing lift, and their ease of management.

The *unarig*—a single sail offering one leading edge—is simple, clean, and efficient. But two obstacles hurt its efficiency: the mast obstructing the clean flow into the leading edge, and the losses at both the top and bottom of the sail. Ideally one would want the lower edge of the sail glued to the deck, the upper edge somewhere up in the clouds, and a mast the size of the forestay to provide an efficient, high aspect ratio sail plan. Theoretical is one thing; practical is another. A sail plan cannot be called truly efficient if it is too fragile, too inconvenient, or too dangerous to be managed by the crew. Just as draft considerations and structural issues place practical limits on keel span, a host of real-world issues compels designers to come up with sail plans that are both efficient and practical.

While sails and keels generate lift according to the same basic scientific principles, they function in very different environments. The density of water flowing past the keel is essentially constant, as water cannot be compressed to any appreciable extent. Nor does the speed vary significantly from root to tip, as the water flow is determined by the speed of the boat. Sails, on the other hand, function in the quirky environment of wind, whose density can change with humidity and pressure, and whose speed differs significantly from deck level to masthead. Sails, unlike conventional keels, are designed to be *trimmed,* their angle of incidence adjusted to the breeze as the yacht's course changes. Trimming also adjusts in sometimes subtle but important ways a sail's aerodynamic shape, whereas a keel's sectional shape (leaving trim tabs aside) is fixed. Sail area must also be managed in many boats, through reefing or raising or lowering entire sails altogether, whereas keel area (unless a movable centerboard or daggerboard is involved) is unchanging. Finally, unlike a keel, a sail plan is not self-supporting. It requires a rig, composed of masts, spars, rigging, and sheets, to hold it up and control its shape. In summary, for most sailors the lift-generating foil below the water, the keel, requires little day-to-day consideration; while the lift-generating foil above the water, the sail plan, is a central focus of the art and science of sailing. When it comes to these complementary foils, not surprisingly sailors tend to have far more firsthand experience with and opinions about the latter.

For the designer, a sail plan begins with a simple requirement: to ensure enough area to generate the force necessary to move the boat. This area can differ significantly for a given hull if performance extremes are contemplated. A boat designed to excel in winds of 8 to 10 knots would be given far more sail area than the same boat tailored to 15- or 25-knot conditions. Most production-boat designs, however, are generalists, intended to perform well in midrange conditions, not plod in light winds, and not be overpowered in a stiff breeze.

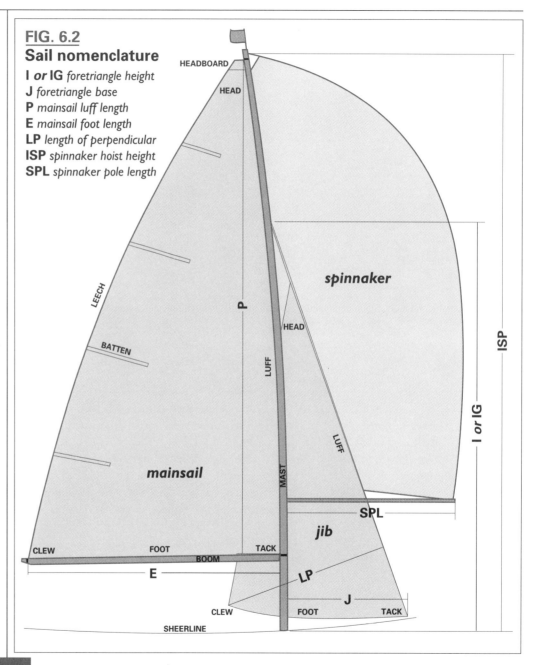

FIG. 6.2
Sail nomenclature
I *or* **IG** *foretriangle height*
J *foretriangle base*
P *mainsail luff length*
E *mainsail foot length*
LP *length of perpendicular*
ISP *spinnaker hoist height*
SPL *spinnaker pole length*

Sailors are always looking for extra downwind power. The "blooper," shown here being flown with the spinnaker, was technically a jib, because it was asymmetrical and had a narrow midgirth dimension. The IOR, though not enamored with it, permitted its use in the 1970s.

Modern sloop rigs follow the Marconi sail plan, which is a triangle divided into two main "white" sails: the mainsail and the jib. (Spinnakers and other downwind devices are considered separate from the upwind area.) A triangle of a given area can be shaped in many ways: long on the base and short in height, short on the base and tall in height, and with the lengths of the sides adjusted to distribute area to the left and right (or in a sailing scenario, fore and aft).

Changing the ratio of base to height, while maintaining a constant area, affects the sail plan's efficiency. For a given area a tall sail plan, with its high aspect ratio, is more aerodynamically efficient than a shorter one. A taller sail plan gets a double bang for the buck in lighter airs—not only is it more efficient because of

its shape, but its area is pushed up into a region of higher wind speeds. The *wind gradient,* which defines how wind strength increases with height above the water, is a more significant factor than many sailors realize. (See Fig. 6.3.) Immediately above the earth or water, the air, even on a windy day, is barely creeping along due to the friction with the surface. One foot above, the wind speed has increased significantly, but the intermolecular friction still keeps the speed well below the "free stream" velocity, often defined in nautical circles as the wind speed at a 10-meter height. The accompanying plot of the wind gradient for a typical day near Block Island shows that the wind speed on deck (5 feet above the water) reads 16 knots while the masthead (50 feet above the water) is in a stiff breeze of almost 21 knots. And because wind pressure varies with the wind speed squared, putting the sail area up high can lead to big gains, not only in raw velocity but in lift forces. The example cited above would produce over 70 percent more pressure at the masthead than at deck level. Get a lift in a bosun's chair while the boat is moored and you can feel the difference.

It is not uncommon for a production or semi-custom sailboat to be offered with different sail plans, recognizing that a customer sailing near Detroit on Lake St. Clair, where winds are routinely 10 knots or less, would need a different horsepower arrangement than one in San Francisco, where the wind chugs along at more than 20 knots. The heavy-air rig could afford to be smaller because sails follow the same basic lift principle of keels: the faster the flow past the foil surface, the greater the lift generated. Fast boats can get by with small keels; fast boats in heavy winds can get by with small sail plans.

Tall sail plans are not without complications, however. If they are employed in regions where the wind is stronger than what the boat's designer had considered to be "normal," an owner can spend an annoying amount of time shortening sail, or "powering down" the rig. It must be remembered that the term "tall rig," as used by a builder's marketing department for a particular model, usually means that the mainsail boom length and base dimension of the jib have remained the same, but the mast has been lengthened, resulting in a sail plan that is both taller and larger. Having more sail area, along with a higher center of effort, operating in the increased velocity of the wind gradient, all point to light-air benefits and heavy-air problems. A taller mast, unless engineered to maximize lightness and strength, is also heavier than a shorter one, and the all-up weight of rig and sails can further increase the heeling moment. Supporting a tall sail plan may require ingenuity in mast and rig construction—which, while feasible from an engineering standpoint, might prove too complex and too expensive from the perspective of the owner. (See the Rigs chapter for more.)

areas of concern: defining the triangle

While we refer in simplistic terms to the components of a sloop-rig sail plan as triangular, a glance at most yachts with this configuration reveals that this provides at best a rough estimate. And yet it is good enough to be the standard by which designers size the sail plan. What is referred to as the "100 percent" sail area figure is calculated by adding the area of a triangular mainsail to the area bounded by the forestay, the mast, and the deck, known as the *foretriangle*. (See Figs. 6.2, 6.4.) Missing from this area is any overlap of the headsail with the mast and any curvature to the edges of the sails.

The curve of the mainsail leech, called the *roach*, which depending on the design can be fairly subtle or quite pronounced, can increase total sail area by up to

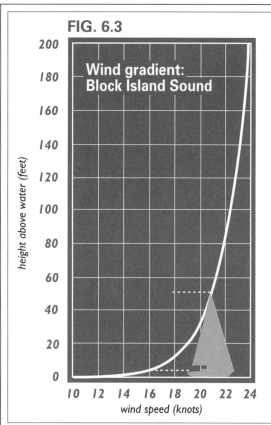

FIG. 6.3

Wind gradient: Block Island Sound

height above water (feet): 0, 20, 40, 60, 80, 100, 120, 140, 160, 180, 200

wind speed (knots): 10 12 14 16 18 20 22 24

Due to the phenomenon of wind sheer, a 32-foot sailboat on Block Island Sound encounters dramatically different wind speeds at the deck and at the masthead. The deck, 5 feet above the water, is experiencing a breeze of about 16 knots, while at the masthead, 50 feet above the water, the wind is blowing at about 21 knots—almost one-third faster. Because wind pressure varies with the wind speed squared, the pressure is 72 percent higher at the masthead than at the deck. Sail plans with higher aspect ratios take advantage of this additional wind pressure without increasing area. However, higher aspect ratios also mean a higher center of sail force and a longer heeling arm, reducing the yacht's stability.

40 percent. But the most noticeable discrepancy in this simple triangular assessment is found in the jib. Most sloop-rigged keelboats carry an overlapping jib known as a *genoa*. Practically speaking, then, the sail plan is not one large triangle subdivided into two triangles, but rather is composed of two overlapping triangles. A genoa might overlap the mainsail 150 percent or more—that is, the length of the perpendicular (LP) from the clew to the forestay of the genoa is 150 percent the length of the foretriangle base, the distance along the deck from the forestay terminus to the mast (commonly referred to as the "J" measurement). (See Fig. 6.2.)

FIG. 6.4
Determining sail area and the center of sail force

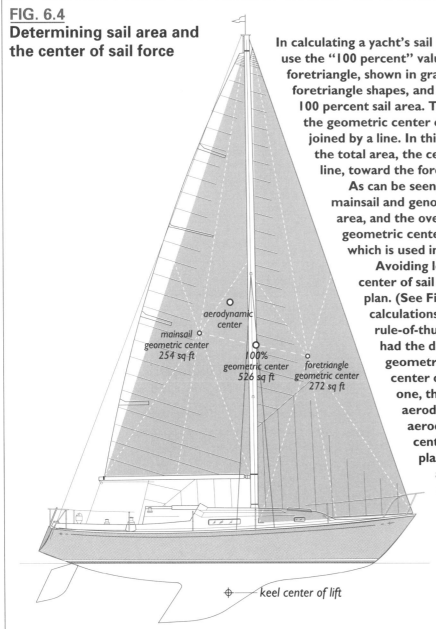

aerodynamic center

mainsail geometric center 254 sq ft

100% geometric center 526 sq ft

foretriangle geometric center 272 sq ft

keel center of lift

In calculating a yacht's sail area to determine raw horsepower, designers traditionally use the "100 percent" value, the sum of the geometric areas of the mainsail and foretriangle, shown in gray. Simple triangles are drawn for the mainsail and foretriangle shapes, and their areas are calculated. The sum of these areas gives the 100 percent sail area. To locate the geometric center of the 100 percent sail area, the geometric center of each triangle is first plotted. These centers are then joined by a line. In this case, because the foretriangle accounts for 52 percent of the total area, the center of sail area is located 52 percent along the connecting line, toward the foretriangle center.

As can be seen, the geometric method does not reflect the true area of the mainsail and genoa. The mainsail roach contains significant unmeasured sail area, and the overlapping portion of the genoa is ignored. Nor does the geometric center represent (as some people think) the center of sail force, which is used in determining heeling moment and helm balance.

Avoiding lee helm is an important reason for accurately locating the center of sail force, represented by the aerodynamic center of the sail plan. (See Figs. 4.1, 4.2.) Before computer programs could make precise calculations to assist in locating the aerodynamic center, designers used rule-of-thumb procedures with the geometric center to ensure a yacht had the desired helm balance. One method was to place the geometric center 15 percent of the waterline length forward of the center of lateral plane. Invariably, in a masthead rig sloop like this one, the geometric center is farther forward and lower than the aerodynamic center. This method (hopefully) ensured that the aerodynamic center was aligned with, or just astern of, the keel center of lift. As it happens, the geometric center of the sail plan on this C&C 35, designed in 1969, was well placed. The aerodynamic center is perfectly aligned with the keel center of lift. A small amount of mast rake would introduce the desired weather helm.

Computer programs can now help accurately locate the centers of sail force and keel lift, making guesswork employing the geometric center of the sail plan unnecessary. In present-day designs, locating the aerodynamic center 2 to 4 percent of the waterline length aft of the keel center of lift ensures a desirable amount of weather helm.

That said, depending on the purpose for which sail area is being calculated, varying amounts of the true sail area will be included. As discussed above, the designer may simply use the 100 percent sail area, but many rating rules restrict measurement to basic dimensions that do not incorporate mainsail roach, genoa overlap, or even the basic 100 percent area.

The purpose of calculating any sail area is to use it as a guide to the power available to drive the boat. Designers need to know this in order to ensure the boat meets certain performance parameters; rating rules need to know this in order to assess the design's potential speed. Designers have their own charts to help them size the sails, based on the 100 percent sail area and personal experience. Some early rating rules used proportions of the sailplan dimensions to estimate their effectiveness. The Universal Rule, popular in the 1920s and 1930s, used the triangular area of the mainsail, but only 85 percent of the area of the foretriangle. It was felt that the percentage fairly represented the actual size of a typical jib. Designers, however, saw the opportunity for unrated sail area, and overlapping jibs were born. By the time the IOR became the handicapping tool of choice in the 1970s, the true mainsail and genoa areas were being analyzed for their speed potential, although the relative effectiveness of the two sails was still not well understood. An error in the weighting of the genoa and mainsail performance abilities led to a trend of smaller and smaller mainsails, as designers exploited the fact that genoas were much more powerful than the rule considered them to be.

The interaction between mainsail and genoa is a continuing subject of debate, its focal point the phenomenon called "slot effect," which holds that the slot between the mainsail and genoa creates its own airflow that improves overall lift. (See below for more.) At the very least, there is known to be a decreasing benefit as genoa overlap becomes increasingly large. While a genoa with an LP of 130 percent will see a proportionate increase in speed over a nonoverlapping jib, extending that overlap to 170 percent will produce little additional gain.

As yacht design evolves, it has become more common to measure actual sail area during the design process to determine raw horsepower. This is because of innovations in sail plan shapes—nonoverlapping jibs in keelboats are increasingly common—and because performance prediction programs incorporate more sophisticated aerodynamics and therefore can make use of the actual areas and overlaps of the individual sails.

parceling power: mainsail vs. jib

In a sloop rig, the proportion of sail area assigned to the mainsail and genoa is not just a matter of performance. The ease of sailing the boat is important, whether racing or cruising. The crew on a racing boat with an easy-to-sail rig may be able to keep the boat at 95 percent of its performance potential, while a theoretically more efficient design may go slower because the crew can seldom tweak it to anywhere close to its optimum.

Fig. 6.5 shows a 40-foot sloop with two different sailplan approaches to the same total sail area. Changing the ratio of mainsail to jib area carries with it important handling considerations, as the sail types are trimmed very differently. The modern jib, loose-footed and fixed along the luff to the forestay, is controlled from a single point, the clew, where the foot and leech meet. While the sheet's trim angle can be adjusted fore and aft, and inboard and outboard, the jib's range of controls is generally limited to creating the most efficient foil shape for the wind and sea conditions.

As demonstrated by the 80-foot Matador *during the 1990* Miami Maxi Regatta, *mainsail and genoa work together in a phenomenon known as the "slot effect" to create more power than they would individually produce. The effect's name derives from the slot between the sails through which air flows to leeward of the mainsail.*

The mainsail is far more dynamic in its controls. Constrained by the boom along its foot, the trim of the sail can be greatly adjusted by tension on the sheet and the vang, which controls how high the boom can rise. In most yachts, the sheeting point position can be adjusted from one side of the boat to the other with the traveler. This control comes into play significantly when managing sail power. If a keelboat becomes overpowered, the immediate reaction is to ease the mainsheet and/or traveler, as these are the simplest sail controls on board to adjust. The genoa too can be released, but because the sheet controls both the depth of the sail and the angle of the sail, an unfortunate increase in power results as the depth increases, before a reduction in power can be realized as the sail begins to luff. Bringing the genoa back in after the puff takes far longer than with the mainsail because of the increased loads on the genoa sheet.

If a high proportion of the functioning sail area is tied up in the genoa, cracking off the mainsail—the desired technique for power reduction—may have little effect on a boat's manageability. Worse, once the mainsail's drive is lost, the center of sail force moves forward into the genoa, creating lee helm and hampering the helmsman's efforts to "pinch" the boat into the wind and lessen the pressure on the sails. Dinghy sailors know that if the mainsail is released in a heavy gust and the jib is left driving, it can capsize the boat on its own by generating excessive lee helm that prevents the helmsman from rounding the boat into the wind.

The more sail area that is in the mainsail, the more efficiently total sail power can be managed in oscillating wind conditions. The traveler can be eased down, the sheet released, and adjustments made in the rig that flatten the mainsail and reduce total power without one's having to resort to reefing. This is a great advantage in any design with particularly sensitive trim characteristics.

There are, however, limits to the proportion of sail area one desires in the mainsail. A reduced jib size can affect acceleration in light winds, and the jib continues to be an important companion to the mainsail in developing lift. Because of the slot effect phenomenon, a combination of a main and jib is more effective than either sail on its own; if the jib is reduced to a pocket handkerchief, the effect is lost. In my own wind-tunnel studies on a $\frac{1}{6}$ scale model of an Albacore dinghy, the main and jib working together produced 20 percent more driving force than the two individual sails. This effect was most pronounced at an apparent wind angle of 90 degrees, but I would expect it to be valid whenever there is attached flow on the sails. Downwind, there is little beneficial interaction between the sails.

balancing act: the center of sail force

The fore-and-aft positioning of the sail plan plays a crucial role in a sailboat's handling characteristics. If the rig is too far forward, the sail plan's center of sail force is positioned ahead of the keel's balancing center of lift. This creates the undesirable, even dangerous, condition known as lee helm. If the skipper releases the helm of such a boat, it will naturally want to bear away from the wind. This can be a significant problem in a breeze, as the helmsman must fight the boat's tendency to bear off. As the boat turns itself to leeward, the sails become oversheeted and heeling moment increases—a disconcerting feeling.

If the two centers are perfectly aligned, the boat is considered balanced and the boat tracks in a straight line. An excellent exercise in appreciating your boat's characteristics is to exploit the influence of the sail plan's center of force by steering the boat with the sails alone. If you ease off the jib and trim in the main, the center of sail force moves aft and the boat turns into the wind; conversely, sheeting in the jib and easing the main will cause the boat to bear off. If you get the sails' trim balanced properly (on a close reach for best results), the boat will steer itself in a straight line. You may not want to sail a Wednesday evening race or negotiate a rip tide without a rudder, but this exercise will make you appreciate how good—and bad—sail trim affects the way your boat behaves. The powerful control that sail trim has on handling varies from design to design. In 12-Meters, for example, which have a large portion of the sail area in the mainsail, the trimmer's job is an especially important one. Simply by oversheeting the main in a strong breeze, he can force the boat to tack.

Most sailors and designers prefer a boat's helm to have some amount of "feel" and deliberately introduce weather helm by adjusting the rig's fore-and-aft position so that the center of sail force moves aft of the keel's center of lift. This can be accomplished by changing the position of the mast step or by raking the mast aft.

There is more than just "good feel" to be gained from sailing with weather helm. Placing the center of sail force aft of the keel's center of lift requires the helmsman to turn the leading edge of the rudder to weather in order to keep the boat traveling in a straight line. The rudder is now producing lift in the same direction (to windward) as the keel and therefore reduces the amount of lift the keel is required to develop. (This is what is known as *unloading the keel,* or *loading up the rudder*). The optimum proportion of lift to have the rudder contribute is the subject of continuing research, but most designers feel from 10 to 30 percent of the total lift of the boat is appropriate. The range just quoted is large, but so is the variation in rudder sizes from designers. The IMS boats designed in the 1990s carry large, high aspect rudders that are more efficient than the keels they steer. Loading up these rudders can have obvious benefits. But low aspect rudders with uninspired hydrodynamic characteristics would do well to give most of the lift production to the keel.

There will be those who argue about the optimum size of the rudder loads, but none will argue that having *lee helm* (a negative lift) is good. Lee helm increases the load on the keel and consequently the leeway. Placing the center of sail force in the correct location to ensure weather helm is a fundamental requirement of the designer.

Two methods are in common use by designers to locate the center of sail force, and both have seen success. One is traditional and uses the geometric center of the sail area, while the other uses an estimate of the true aerodynamic center of the sails and takes into account the interaction of the sails.

To calculate the geometric center, a line is drawn from the midpoint of the sides of each triangular sail to its opposite corner, which is called the *vertex.* These three lines cross in the geometric center of the triangle. To find the center of the combined areas, draw a line between the two centers and measure its length.

Competitors round the leeward mark at the 1995 470 Women's World Championships. Like most sloop-rigged dinghies, the Olympic 470 features a fractional rig. Most of the "white" sail area is in the mainsail, which can be fine-tuned easily in this performance-sensitive class.

Rather than attempt a description of the computer calculations, let's look at the difference between the geometric and aerodynamic centers, shown in Fig. 6.4. As with this C&C 35, the geometric center is almost always lower and farther forward than the true aerodynamic center. Designers know that the geometric center does not reflect the true center of sail force (any more than the geometric center of the keel reflects its center of lift), but it can still be of use in locating the sail plan fore and aft on the hull.

From experience, designers have found that if the geometric center of the sail plan is placed about 15 percent of the waterline length ahead of the center of lateral plane, then the weather helm should be comfortable. Intuitively, this technique is wrong, for the real center of sail force must be aft, not forward, of the center of keel lift in order for the boat to have weather helm. The technique is appropriate, however, if you remember that the aerodynamic center of the sail plan is not represented by its geometric center. That said, knowing the actual location of the aerodynamic center of sail force is much more confidence inspiring. The designer can see it on the sail plan and know its physical relationship to the keel center of lift.

Locating a sail plan so that the center of sail force is 2 to 4 percent of the waterline length aft of the keel's center of lift of the keel is a standard that many designers now use. The C&C 35 shown in Fig. 6.4 (designed in 1969) has the two centers almost directly aligned vertically, indicating very light helm in light to medium air. It should be noted that controlling the weather helm in heavy air is not a function of the fore-and-aft location of the sail plan as much as the heel angle and immersed hull shape. In a heeled condition, the sail plan, with its sail force now well out to the side of the hull, has a large moment arm and will tend to push the bow of the boat into the wind.

The center of sail force is also important for

Divide the line in two portions, using the ratio of the areas of the sails, with the shorter section closer to the larger sail (See Fig. 6.4.) The point so determined is the geometric center of the combined sails.

Determining the aerodynamic center is a more complicated procedure. Jerry Milgram was instrumental in assessing the lift, drag, and centers of effort for a variety of sailplan combinations. His paper, presented to the Society of Naval Architects and Marine Engineers in 1971, was entitled "Sail Force Coefficients for Systematic Rig Variations," and calculated the lift and drag of mainsails and jibs of varying aspect ratios and combinations. It was a theoretical, rather than a physical analysis, but the results have been proven to be a useful tool for designers.

determining the design's true heeling moment. The geometric center in our example produces a heeling arm noticeably shorter than the one indicated by the aerodynamic center. As a result, the yacht would appear to be much stiffer than it actually is.

Getting the sail plan's location right is important, because the helm cannot be balanced otherwise. That comfortable feel on a wheel or tiller, although it can be adjusted by sail cut and trim, is determined more by the boat's designer than anyone else.

settling for less: the fractional rig

Sail plans in which the jib hoist does not reach the full height of the mast are known as *fractional rigs*. In this arrangement the mainsail occupies an even greater proportion of the overall sail plan, and the headsail is often (but not always) limited to a "blade" that fills only the foretriangle area. Fractional rigs are categorized, for example ¾ or ⅞, to reflect the proportion of the mast height the forestay reaches.

Fractional rigs, most common in dinghy designs, place the bulk of the sail area where it is most easily trimmed and adjusted, in the mainsail. And because the forestay does not reach all the way to the masthead, the upper section of the mast can be quite bendy, allowing for considerable control over mainsail shape. The upper section can be bent to flatten the upper sail area, reducing power in a breeze and with it heeling moment.

Fractional rigs are not limited to dinghies. America's Cup 12-Meters employed a ¾ fractional rig, which was imposed by the design rule. This created an enormous, low aspect overlapping genoa that at times seemed to make the mainsail superfluous. In one breezy race during the 1983 America's Cup challengers'

trials, *Canada 1* suffered damage to the mainsail halyard that reduced the rig to a solitary genoa while the crew attempted in-race repairs. They thought the boat actually sailed better without the mainsail.

The reduced jib hoist height can be a drawback in light winds, as the yacht is denied the long leading edge of a masthead rig's genoa, an important source of horsepower coming out of a tack. And because the jib hoist height is lower, so by extension is the spinnaker hoist height. Combined with the reduced spinnaker girth that comes with the shorter "J" measurement of a fractional rig, the configuration means the spinnaker overall is much smaller than would be possible in a masthead configuration. However, current rating rules that govern so much of a yacht's development have relaxed the restrictions on spinnaker hoist height and more fairly rate the resulting sail plan. Although it has not yet become commonplace, many fractionally rigged boats now fly their spinnaker from the masthead.

two for one: the modern cutter rig

In the march toward the modern two-sail Marconi sloop rig, the overall sail plan we know today was often broken up into smaller components for the sake of management. The upper mainsail area was dedicated to a separate topsail (as was the case in the great J-class yachts of the 1930s), and the foretriangle was occupied by more than one headsail. Although the main topsail has essentially vanished, the parceling approach survives today in a sail plan recreational boaters know as the cutter rig. (See Fig. 6.6.) The modern cutter borrows its name from a complex sail plan sported by plumb-bow British racing yachts of the nineteenth century, which used three headsails. The only similarities between the historic cutter and the

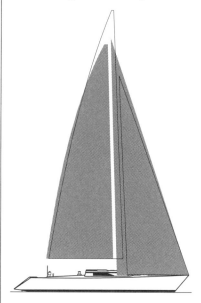

FIG. 6.5
Parceling the sail plan

Once a designer has determined the sail area a yacht requires, it can be apportioned a variety of ways. This 40-footer employs the same sail area (represented by the mainsail and foretriangle area) in two configurations: a masthead rig (solid blue), and a fractional rig (black outline). Note the fractional rig's larger mainsail, shorter "J" measurement, and taller rig.

FIG. 6.6
The modern cutter

The traditional cutter boasted three foresails and a topsail above the gaff-rigged main. Today, most recreational yachts are sloop-rigged with a single large genoa, and "cutter" generally refers to any yacht with more than one headsail— an arrangement that technically still qualifies as a sloop.

The twin headsails shown on this 41-footer give passage-makers more reefing options, and the double slot effect can be beneficial when reaching. However, when sailing to windward, the headsails interfere with each other, and are less efficient than a single large headsail.

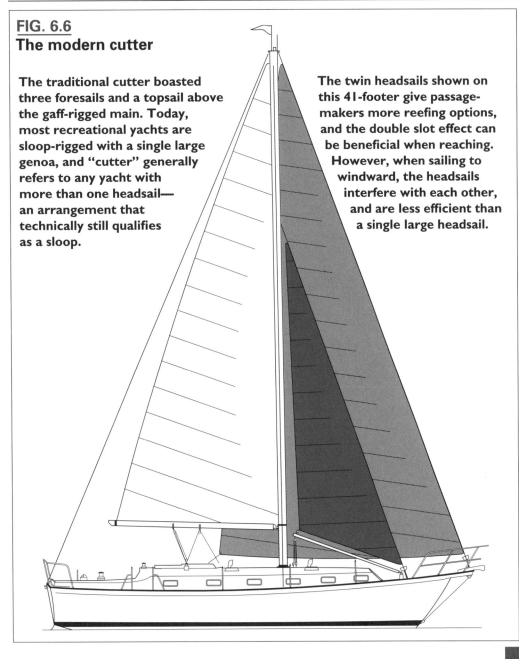

modern configuration is the presence of more than one headsail and the occasional use of a bowsprit or bow platform, which increases the foretriangle area by extending it ahead of the actual bow.

Cruisers like the cutter configuration for the way it parcels sail area into smaller, more manageable pieces. What might have been a daunting genoa for a cruising couple or singlehander has been divided into two sails that are much easier physically to trim—easier still if the staysail is rigged (sometimes club-footed) to be self-tacking. Because there is no overlap with the mast, the staysail can be sheeted to a block and cleat on a deck track that allows the sail to tack itself from one side of the boat to the other. (This arrangement can be used with any blade-type jib where the deck will accommodate a track.) When it comes to reefing down, the crew can do away with the main headsail and carry on with the smaller staysail.

The cutter rig has its critics, though. Some don't like the fuss of having to trim two headsails instead of one. Although a self-tacking staysail minimizes this problem, the arrangement is not always possible on smaller cruisers whose cabin trunks extend well forward. Fundamentally, the cutter rig gains most of its detractors when it is applied to yachts under 35 feet. Part of the rig's appeal tends to be nostalgic rather than practical, and in smaller craft the fuss involved with trimming and managing two headsails instead of one can make for more bother than they are worth. Because a second stay is required to be set inside the foretriangle for the staysail, the main headsail must squeeze through the space between the forestay and staysail when tacking. This can be cumbersome and even somewhat hazardous in a smaller boat, as a crew must go forward to help the headsail through the gap if it becomes snagged. This problem will not arise if the main headsail is cut with minimal overlap with the staysail, but in a smaller boat this can mean that the individual sails are approaching hankie size. At this point, one can argue serious performance criteria are being sacrificed for purely aesthetic reasons.

The performance gain for the cutter rig is on a reach, when both sails can be set efficiently and present more area than a single genoa can. The performance loss is one that some cutter-rig owners cannot accept—sailing hard on the wind with two headsails set is just not efficient. Rather than having one sail help the other, as with a genoa adding lift to the mainsail, the two sails create significant interference. The forward jib backwinds the staysail, or requires it to be sheeted so tightly that it backwinds the mainsail.

doubling up: ketches and yawls

Just like the cutter rig that divides the sail area into smaller, more manageable packages, the ketch or yawl rig keeps more sails comfortably attached to masts. The resulting sails are lower and smaller than in a sloop rig of the same area.

As with a cutter, I find that some sailors' attachment to a schooner, yawl, or ketch rig is nostalgic rather than scientific, but I must remember that much of the rationale behind owning a boat is not scientific. We own boats because we like the way they look, feel, and sail.

It might come as a surprise to sailors who are attracted to the "traditional" look of ketches and yawls that their popularity, which began late in the nineteenth century, was due partly to an oversight in rating rules. Over the years, rating rules minimized their horsepower assessments of aft rigs, tempting designers to pick up unrated sail area by installing them. Once such loopholes closed up, this sail plan all but disappeared in smaller racers, although its continued use in large offshore racing designs reinforces its practical aspects.

The line between ketch and yawl, with the latter having the mast aft of the rudder post, is a fine one. The yawl made its way into recreational sailing in England in the nineteenth century, having been borrowed from fishing craft. By setting just the mizzen sail aft of the rudder, the vessel could hove-to with sufficient steadiness to tend to nets.

In yachting applications, when all sail is set nothing magical happens if the mizzenmast is located aft rather than forward of the rudder, other than a little more weather helm being generated when the sail is sheeted in. The discussion of ketches and yawls then becomes a single one. When the mizzen sail is very small, its effectiveness in generating lift is limited. Some racing ketches have been built with the ketch rig almost the same height as the mainmast in an effort to divide the sail area while keeping both pieces as effective as possible. This has meant both rigs flying their own spinnakers and other downwind sails.

single-minded: the unarig option

Initially, recreational craft devoted little or no sailplan area to headsails. When they were used, they tended to be small, or at least secondary to the mainsail. After the Second World War, with advances in construction materials and the influence of rating rules that measured only foretriangle area, headsails increased tremendously in area, reaching the point under the IOR in the 1970s that the mainsail seemed almost an afterthought to the powerful overlapping genoas.

Big genoas present engineering challenges, as they are set on a piece of rigging, not a solid mast. The power of these sails places considerable loads on rigs,

The modern cruising ketch owes its existence to racing designers who once exploited the arrangement to take advantage of the unmeasured sail area of the second rig. With this Dickerson 37, designed by George Hazen, the rig offers the practical benefit of parceling the sail plan into smaller, more manageable pieces, but creates one more sail to trim.

as efficient headsail performance can demand considerable tension along the sail's luff. They can also be a challenge to trim, as the large overlapping sail must be ground into position by winch power after every tack. It's entirely possible that the bother of dealing with great genoas on even modest-size racer-cruisers whose designs were inspired by the IOR drove more than a few cruising couples out of sailboats altogether.

Sailors don't have to put up with hulking genoas. The cutter rig, as we have seen above, is one long-standing, if imperfect, alternative. In recent years, yacht designers and production-boat manufacturers have provided large mainsail/blade jib configurations that make the sail plan far more manageable. But for some sailors, the sail plan is considered manageable only when the headsail is eliminated altogether. For ease of handling, there isn't much that beats a unarig. One mast, one sail, one halyard, and one sheet. A small singlehander like the Laser doesn't even bother with a halyard—the sail just slides over the unstayed mast with a sleeve.

The unarig has been around recreational boating for more than a century. Many people know it as the *cat rig*, so called because of its use in *catboats,* those handsome plumb-bowed craft made popular in New England.

In the 1970s, cat rigs found a new following when two North American production yacht designers brought them to the mass market. Gary Hoyt and Freedom Yachts began producing single- and two-masted (cat ketch) models that employed fully battened sails, an unstayed carbon fiber mast, and a wishbone boom. Then Mark Ellis created a custom 30-foot cat with an unstayed aluminum mast and a wishbone boom called *Nonsuch*, which blossomed into a full production line from 22 to 36 feet under the Nonsuch name; about 1,000 would be turned out by the builder, Hinterhoeller Yachts.

winging it: the hard-sail innovation

For those striving for the last ounce of power, there are more exotic developments than the "soft" sail held up by a solid mast. Catamarans that operate in a higher speed regime made it apparent that the drag of a conventional mast excessively inhibit performance. Their masts became longer fore and aft, eventually occupying as much as 20 percent of the chord of the sail. Wing masts have an efficient foil shape that feeds the air onto a fully battened, nicely cambered fabric sail. These sails are often so tightly sprung by the battens that they have to be popped into shape on each tack.

The Little America's Cup, an international match-racing challenge series sailed in C-class catamarans, has inspired much of the exotic sail plan development. Recent events in both the Little and "Big" America's Cup have led to the next level of sail efficiency: the hard sail.

Impractical by its very nature, the *hard sail* is a rigid wing mounted vertically on the deck, usually on a multihull. Its efficiency stems from its versatile set of controls, which can vary the twist, the camber, and the angle of attack, permitting high lift coefficients for downwind sailing and low drag for upwind sailing.

For recreational sailors, hard sails are not the answer to improved performance. While efficient during a race, their efficiency unfortunately continues when they are tied to the dock. They cannot be reefed, hoisted, or doused, as they remain erect and anxious to power the boat. During competitions, these rigs must be removed at night. In the case of *Stars & Stripes*, the 60-foot America's Cup catamaran, the entire boat was strapped to a hydraulic platform, which tipped it onto its side for a well-deserved rest after each race.

design types

Sailing craft designed for distinct
purposes naturally show distinct
characteristics. The five design
types presented here run the
gamut from cottage dinghy to
round-the-world record setter.

Albacore: cruising/racing dinghy

There are many boats struggling for a market share in the cruising/racing dinghy class, but I have chosen the now well-aged Albacore for its stamina. A design by the late and legendary Uffa Fox, the Albacore has remained strictly one-design over the years, shunning innovations like trapezes and spinnakers that could make it faster, in order to keep the boat simple and affordable.

The philosophy of a one-design class is distinctly different from that of a measurement or restricted class rule. As the name implies, the one-design class requires that all hulls, centerboards, and sail areas be of the same design. Most classes require that fiberglass hulls be built in an approved mold, and the tolerances on hull dimensions are quite tight. Some one-design classes, like the singlehanded Laser, require the sails to be cut to approved templates and therefore have identical depth as well as area, although the Albacore requires only the outside dimensions of the sails to conform to the rules. With a one-design class the emphasis is on close, evenly matched racing in which the difference in performance is all due to the sailors.

This boat is forgiving—it has enough stability provided by the hull shape that an error in judgment or a slow transition of the crew from port to starboard during a tack won't result in a capsize. This is a sharp contrast to the International 14 (see page 160), which has a narrow waterline and little hull form stability. The Albacore is normally raced with two, but is just as happy with one or six on board. It has enough sail area powering its 250-pound hull to get up on a plane, but be warned—the rounded hull shape provides a wet ride. Albacore fanatics (and I was one) will exclaim that the flying spray is all part of the thrill of the boat.

When the Albacore or any boat with rounded bilges starts to plane, its bow is lifted up and the initial contact point with the water moves back to about 3 feet aft of the bow. The water that is being pushed aside hugs the surface of the hull, travels up around the turn of the bilge, and finally, when it can hold on no longer, breaks off as spray. Depending on the speed of travel, that spray lands in the lower torso or

Albacores drive off the starting line at a Canadian championships in the 1980s.

face of the aggressively hiking crew. The water adhering to the boat increases hull drag, and the spray on the crew slows the boat as well. Modern dinghies, which spend more of their time planing than does an Albacore, have incorporated a hard chine in the middle and aft sections of the boat to shed the spray cleanly from the bottom.

The class continues to have an active racing fleet and, without a spinnaker to enhance off-the-wind performance, emphasis is placed on finesse and delicate movements. In light to medium downwind sailing, the reduction of the speed-robbing wetted surface is the principal factor in getting to the leeward mark first. Moving crew weight forward in any dinghy will lift the transom and the aft portion of the bottom of the boat out of the water. With the loss of contact with the water, so goes the frictional resistance. In low-speed sailing, the waterline length, which is being reduced with this technique, is not an issue. The relationship between waterline length and speed is a wavemaking consideration—when a nonplaning hull is traveling fast, the effective waterline length is one of the primary speed limiting factors. In light air, however, wetted surface is the culprit, and the water-line length is insignificant. The sailor who manages to reduce the wetted surface to a minimum will be the winner downwind in light breezes every time. The limiting factors in raising the transom will be loss of control as the rudder leaves the water, and excess wave drag as the bow begins to bury—as with many sailing optimizations, time on the water is the best way to determine the fastest trade-off.

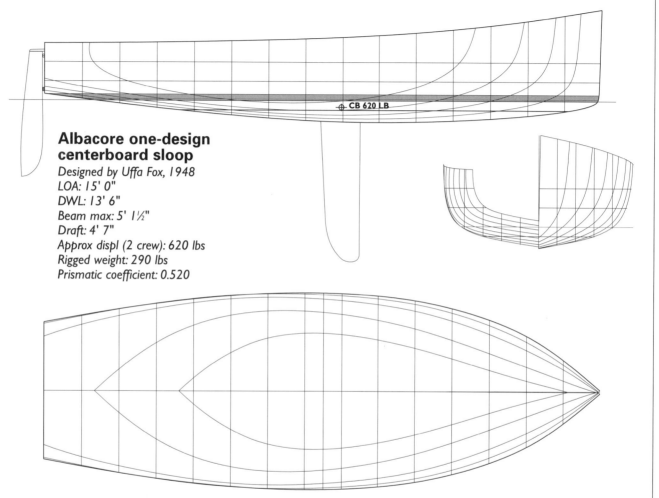

Albacore one-design centerboard sloop

Designed by Uffa Fox, 1948
LOA: 15' 0"
DWL: 13' 6"
Beam max: 5' 1½"
Draft: 4' 7"
Approx displ (2 crew): 620 lbs
Rigged weight: 290 lbs
Prismatic coefficient: 0.520

CB 620 LB

International 14: decades in development

With ink that seldom has a chance to dry, the International 14 rule has endured since 1929 in a continuously evolving format. This is a restricted-rule class, which is distinct from a one-design rule. A restricted rule permits some variation in a boat's design as part of the contest, whereas under a one-design rule (see the Albacore on the preceding spread), minimal construction tolerances are employed so that all boats are essentially identical. A restricted-rule boat must fit within an imaginary box in order to be legal, and the designer's job is to create the fastest shape within those limitations. To be more precise, the International 14 rule should be termed both a development (it changes over time) and a restricted (the boats must fit within certain dimensions) rule. Sailors of this dynamic 14-foot class, never a group to sit on the fence, have always set their sights on owning the fastest boat in its size category, and consequently even the rules themselves are continually in a state of flux.

Dinghy-racing at the 14-foot level had been occurring around the world since the late nineteenth century when Britain's Yacht Racing Association secured International status from the International Yacht Racing Union (IYRU) for its version of the 14-Foot class in 1928. In 1933, the Seawanhaka Corinthian Yacht Club of Oyster Bay, New York, arranged to have sailors from the Royal Norfolk and Suffolk Yacht Club participate in a racing series in which the British 14s could be compared with existing North American dinghy types. Sailors from Rochester Yacht Club in Upstate New York and the Royal Canadian Yacht Club (RCYC) in Toronto were invited to join in as well. The Canadians won the racing, and were sufficiently intrigued by the International 14 to invite the British sailors to the RCYC for more comparisons the following summer. In 1934 Canadian and American sailors formally joined the International class association, and the RCYC launched its first home-built 14s the following year. It would take the Canadians until 1959 to produce boats that met all the parameters of the British-based class rules.

Britain's innovative Uffa Fox set the 14 standard in the 1930s with a series of designs incorporating a trademark V-shaped hull. His veed bows, quite different from today's well-rounded forward sections, gave the early 14s a good bite on the water for upwind work, while the huge overlapping jibs performed well

A double-trapezing International 14 competes at the Open 14 World Championships in San Francisco in 1989.

in light air but were more of a hindrance in anything one might call a breeze. With its amazing ability to recognize limitations in its own rules, the class consequently permitted higher forestay positions on the mast to redistribute the sail area and reduce overlap.

This philosophy of continually looking around the world for new speed-producing elements, and adopting them if they promise good racing, keeps the 14 at the fore of the high-speed dinghy. Although to some outside the class this tends to categorize the current 14 sailors as followers rather than innovators, their attitude is still to be commended.

One can imagine that designing and sailing to a rule that is continually changing leads to tensions within the class. If the rules change, owners of existing boats must spend more money to update their craft or watch them become obsolete. Over the years, the 14 has steered through the gray area between a restricted rule's fundamental disinterest in obsolescence and a class association's concern that changes not be so frequent or so radical that enthusiasts can ill afford to keep up with them, thereby killing the class and disbanding the fraternity. Added to the mix with the 14 have been old-guard/young hotshots dissensions and geocentric perspectives on the design's proper evolution. British, American, and Canadian 14ers battled with and lobbied each other either to accept rule proposals or defeat ones that were deemed suicidal for the fraternity.

The class's modern reputation as a high-tech innovator was anything but deserved for several decades. In hindsight, the class's darkest hour came when it refused to embrace the trapeze, invented by one of its own, Britain's Peter Scott, in 1938. While trapezes did come into use in North American 14s, it wasn't until 1969 that the International class rules finally allowed them. In the meantime, the door had been left open for the postwar development of a host of exciting new one-design trapezing classes such as the Fireball, 505, and Flying Dutchman, which was used in the Olympics from 1960 to 1992. In the great dinghy-sailing boom of the 1950s and 1960s, the 14 was far from cutting edge.

Things began to look up again in the 1970s, after the formation of a class World Council in 1968, the trapeze approval of 1969, and a complete overhaul of the class rules, which were finally approved (amid controversy) in 1975.

When the trapeze was accepted in 1969, the effect of having a crewmember suspended on a wire with feet braced on the outside of the gunwale was significant. The 1970s and 1980s saw feverish activity from designers, primarily in England and Canada, to produce boats optimized to the changing rules. Bruce Kirby, Jay Cross, and Rob Mazza from Canada and Ian Howlett, Phil Morrison, and Chris Benedict in the UK all had their moments of fame. Many of the advancements in centerboard sailing classes, like the planing hull form, the tiller extension, and the trapeze, had their beginnings in the 14 class.

The performance boost provided by the single trapeze of 1969 proved to be only a hint of what the design would become capable of 15 years later, when both crewmembers took to the air. The increase in stability afforded by having two stout bodies hanging 7 feet off centerline permitted designers to change the way they shaped their hulls. Less beam was required at the waterline since the stability was now supplied by the crew, not the hull, and flatter bottoms proved advantageous now that planing was a more frequent activity.

It can be safely said that in the 1980s and 1990s the main impetus for change in the class has come from outside its ranks. The Australian 14, a close cousin with slightly more liberal rules and faster speeds, eclipsed the International version of the boat

The British International 14 Canute *participates in a competitive demonstration at the Royal Canadian Yacht Club in 1934, in this photo that survives in the club's* **Annals.** *That year, Canadian and American sailors joined the class association as the "14" phenomenon crossed the Atlantic. It would take another 62 years to bring Australian and New Zealand 14 enthusiasts into the International family.*

Mazza III
International 14

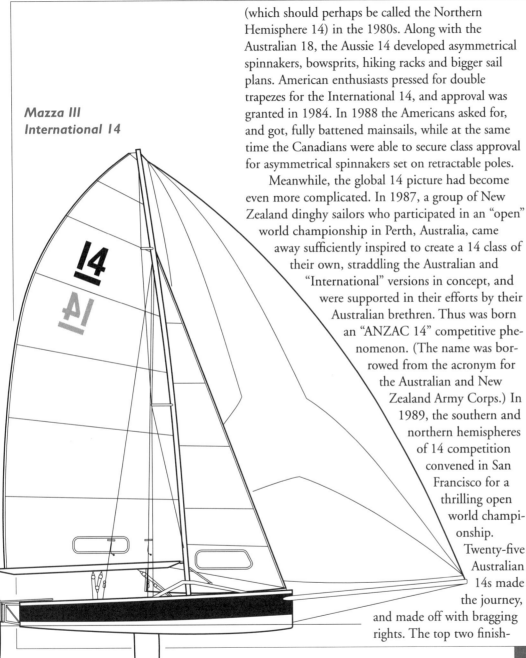

(which should perhaps be called the Northern Hemisphere 14) in the 1980s. Along with the Australian 18, the Aussie 14 developed asymmetrical spinnakers, bowsprits, hiking racks and bigger sail plans. American enthusiasts pressed for double trapezes for the International 14, and approval was granted in 1984. In 1988 the Americans asked for, and got, fully battened mainsails, while at the same time the Canadians were able to secure class approval for asymmetrical spinnakers set on retractable poles.

Meanwhile, the global 14 picture had become even more complicated. In 1987, a group of New Zealand dinghy sailors who participated in an "open" world championship in Perth, Australia, came away sufficiently inspired to create a 14 class of their own, straddling the Australian and "International" versions in concept, and were supported in their efforts by their Australian brethren. Thus was born an "ANZAC 14" competitive phenomenon. (The name was borrowed from the acronym for the Australian and New Zealand Army Corps.) In 1989, the southern and northern hemispheres of 14 competition convened in San Francisco for a thrilling open world championship. Twenty-five Australian 14s made the journey, and made off with bragging rights. The top two finish-ers—in all, five of the top eight—were from the Australian contingent in the 113-boat fleet. The design momentum was unequivocally Down Under.

More pressure arrived from the IYRU (which renamed itself the International Sailing Federation, or ISAF). The sport's world governing body was calling for a new high-performance class for the 2000 Olympics in Sydney. The International 14 rules were further liberalized in 1995, to prevent the class from being overrun by the new designs springing up to vie for Olympic selection, and to move the "world" 14 closer to the "ANZAC" boats. While selection as the new Olympic design eluded the International 14, an important breakthrough was made in 1996 when the Down Under enthusiasts agreed to join the International class and begin harmonizing the rules governing 14s the world over.

The class rules for the International 14 as they stood in 1996 permitted a length of 14 feet, an enlarged beam of 6 feet, and a slimmed hull shape at the midstation that rises no more than 8 inches over a width of 44 inches. There was also a limit on sail area of 200 square feet, a mast height of 25 feet, and a hull weight minimum of 164 pounds. Freedom still afforded to the designer included the hull shape (within the maximum beam and midsection shape restrictions), sail area aspect ratio, and centerboard shape, with no limitations on width or draft.

In January 1997 a revised set of rules was issued, to make possible a harmonized world fleet, with a phase-in period running until 1999.

The greatest weakness of the class has also proved to be its greatest strength. As rules have evolved to keep up with the latest speed-enhancing developments, a dynamic class with a small but incredibly enthusiastic following has evolved with them. Thanks to the 1997 initiative, the International 14 following truly can be called "international."

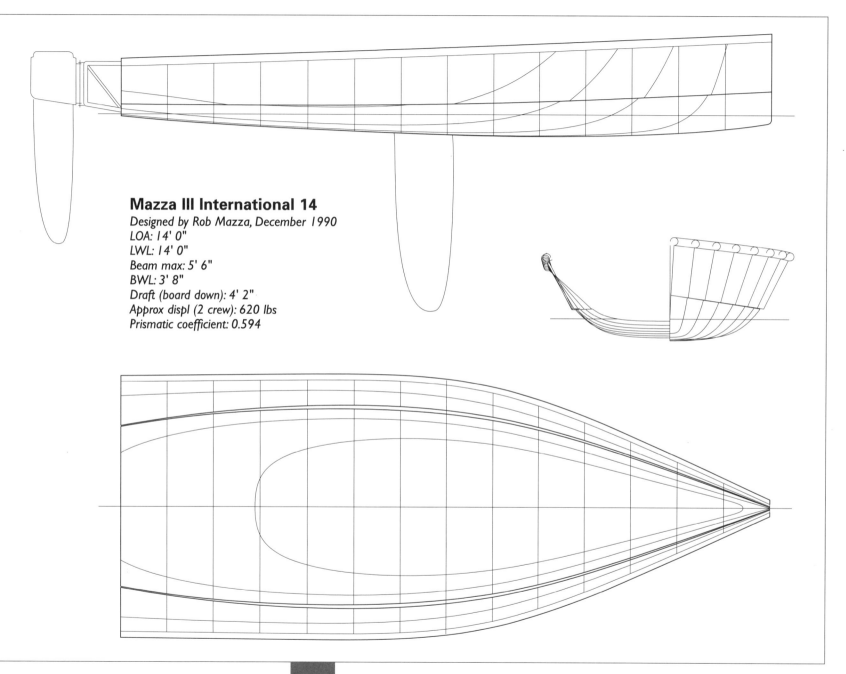

Mazza III International 14

Designed by Rob Mazza, December 1990
LOA: 14' 0"
LWL: 14' 0"
Beam max: 5' 6"
BWL: 3' 8"
Draft (board down): 4' 2"
Approx displ (2 crew): 620 lbs
Prismatic coefficient: 0.594

C&C 35 Mark I & II:
a classic racer-cruiser

The C&C 35 that once rolled off the assembly line of the C&C Yachts production plant in Ontario, Canada, has survived successive waves of yachting trends. The boat is no longer the fastest on the lake, nor the most striking, but it has a whole-

A 1972 C&C Yachts brochure asserted the C&C 35 was "designed to come first with the family—and first at the finish line."

someness that reminds one of how every detail was designed for a reason and therefore is still acceptable and useful several decades later. Indeed, for many boaters, the styling and practicality of the C&C 35 continues to make this design, approaching its thirtieth anniversary, more attractive to them than anything built since.

The boat was the brainchild of the Canadian design team of George Cuthbertson and George Cassian and first built in 1969 as the Redwing 35 by Hinterhoeller Ltd. of St. Catharines, Ontario. Before the year was out, the Cuthbertson and Cassian team joined forces with Hinterhoeller and two other Canadian builders who were producing their designs to form the company C&C Yachts. The Redwing 35 was duly renamed the C&C 35. Most of C&C's production was exported to the United States, and the C&C 35 became known as one of the classic North American club racer-cruisers of the 1970s. In all, 351 were built (including 15 in England) in Mark I and II versions before production ceased in 1975.

Although it was created when Cuthbertson and Cassian were heralded as purveyors of world-class racing designs, the C&C 35 harbors none of the distortions associated with a "rule" boat. The CCA (Cruising Club of America) rule, which promoted wide transoms, and the ensuing IOR (International Offshore Rule), which permitted boats to gain an advantage by locally "bumping" measurement points on the hull, were given only token attention during the design phase. The boat above all still had to be a yacht—good looking, solid, and stable.

Designers of the time were learning how best to use the new fiberglass technology. The material permitted cabins to be contoured in every direction, unlimited by the practicality of wood joinerwork. Some designers and builders leapt at the chance to round everything in sight, regardless of the aesthetic

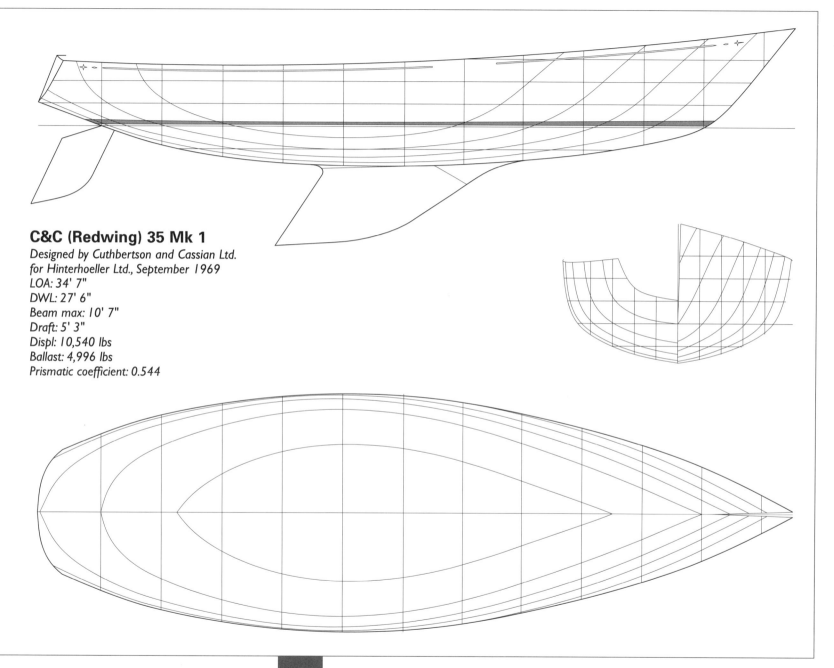

C&C (Redwing) 35 Mk 1

Designed by Cuthbertson and Cassian Ltd.
for Hinterhoeller Ltd., September 1969
LOA: 34' 7"
DWL: 27' 6"
Beam max: 10' 7"
Draft: 5' 3"
Displ: 10,540 lbs
Ballast: 4,996 lbs
Prismatic coefficient: 0.544

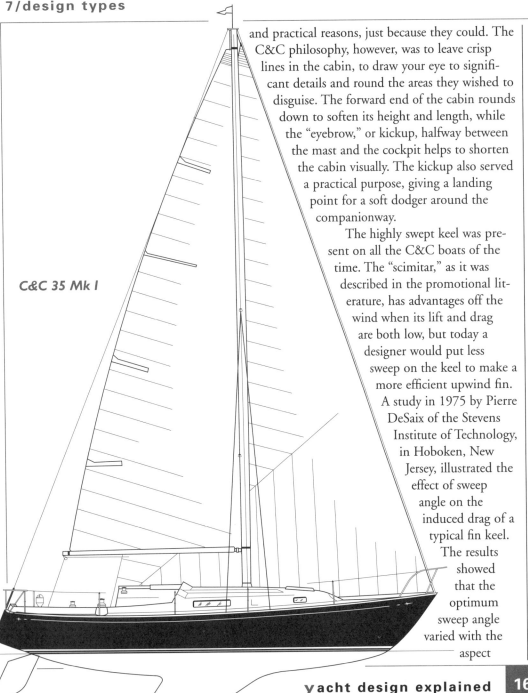

C&C 35 Mk I

and practical reasons, just because they could. The C&C philosophy, however, was to leave crisp lines in the cabin, to draw your eye to significant details and round the areas they wished to disguise. The forward end of the cabin rounds down to soften its height and length, while the "eyebrow," or kickup, halfway between the mast and the cockpit helps to shorten the cabin visually. The kickup also served a practical purpose, giving a landing point for a soft dodger around the companionway.

The highly swept keel was present on all the C&C boats of the time. The "scimitar," as it was described in the promotional literature, has advantages off the wind when its lift and drag are both low, but today a designer would put less sweep on the keel to make a more efficient upwind fin. A study in 1975 by Pierre DeSaix of the Stevens Institute of Technology, in Hoboken, New Jersey, illustrated the effect of sweep angle on the induced drag of a typical fin keel. The results showed that the optimum sweep angle varied with the aspect ratio. It would suggest for the C&C 35 a sweep angle of 35 degrees rather than the 50 degrees shown here.

The rudder shown is the original Mark I rudder, which has a small area near the waterline, concentrating the bulk of the area farther below. This rudder probably loses a little performance because of its low aspect ratio and lack of end plate effect at the hull. A rudder that was larger at the top but was located farther forward and sat completely under the hull would provide more lift for the same rudder angle. In the Mark II version, which began production in 1973, the C&C 35 was equipped with a rudder with a more vertical post, set closer to the keel. (Sail area was also shaved 54 square feet as the rig was shortened about 2 feet, and displacement was reduced slightly.)

George Cuthbertson, the man behind the hull and overall concept of this boat, had very strong and well-founded convictions about the shape a boat should have. Paramount to the visual success of a boat was its sheerline. This design's sheerline has significant curvature, with its lowest point well aft, at about 75 percent of the waterline length. A highly curved sheer will give a boat a classic, somewhat jaunty look and is most likely to produce a line that is pleasant when viewed from any angle. The most difficult sheerlines for which to guarantee beauty are not the straight-line racing sheers, but the slightly curved ones of the "modern" racer-cruiser, which if not sculpted properly can take on an unpleasant S-shape when viewed from beside the bow. This boat looks happy from any angle.

Though it ceased production in 1975, the C&C 35 is a widely praised hallmark design that continues to be popular in the used marine market. Many cared-for or refurbished hulls are still strong and well-behaved vessels.

high-speed cruising: the PDQ 36 catamaran

PDQ Yachts has found a successful niche in the cruising multihull industry with boats that provide significant interior amenities without pushing displacement into the sluggish category. Founded in 1987, the Canadian company sells its product to an international clientele, most of them in the United States.

Light weight equates to speed more directly in a catamaran than in any monohull. The racing-cat sailor knows this well, but cruising-cat aficionados often leave this knowledge somewhere astern in their quest for more interior or an extra refrigerator. PDQ has managed to maintain a light displacement with its PDQ 36 through the sensible use of vacuum bagging, Kevlar, and carbon fiber where necessary. I say "sensible use," because they are quite cost conscious and use more exotic (and more expensive) materials only if they help to keep weight down, not just because they sound good in the brochure.

Alan Slater designed the boat with symmetrical hulls and shallow keels to aid windward performance. Since these boats travel faster than an equivalent-size monohull, the area of the fins can be significantly reduced and still provide the required lift. Rudder area can be also be reduced because heel angle, which redirects and reduces the effect of the rudder lift force, is not the factor it can be on a monohull routinely laying over 20 degrees or more. The rudder force in a cat pushes horizontally—the way you want it to.

Cruising multihulls pose one of the biggest visual challenges of all boats. They must provide usable space between the hulls, and yet the cabin sole level is some 18 inches above the water. Compare this to a monohull, or even the hulls on the very same multihull that offer a sole level perhaps 12 inches below the waterline. The multi then by definition is either a tall boat or one that lacks headroom between the hulls—the norm is a compromise between the two. But the reason to put up with the height of the boat is the floor space that it offers. The PDQ 36 is a good example, and a comparison with the C&C 35 illustrates that these are quite different boats. The multihull has a beam of more than 18 feet and a weight of 8,000 pounds, while the C&C has a beam of less than 11 feet and a weight of 10,500 pounds. The catamaran's huge increase in square footage is devoted to a large lounging and dining area between the hulls that short people will be able to stand up in, and a large double cabin forward in each hull. The catamaran, don't forget, derives its stability from its beam, not ballast. Therefore, its weight can be reduced significantly or put into more furnishings.

The other deception when viewing a catamaran sail plan is the rather tall-looking cabin, which is actually sitting on a very wide hull. In reality, the beam helps to lower the aspect ratio of the deckhouse and

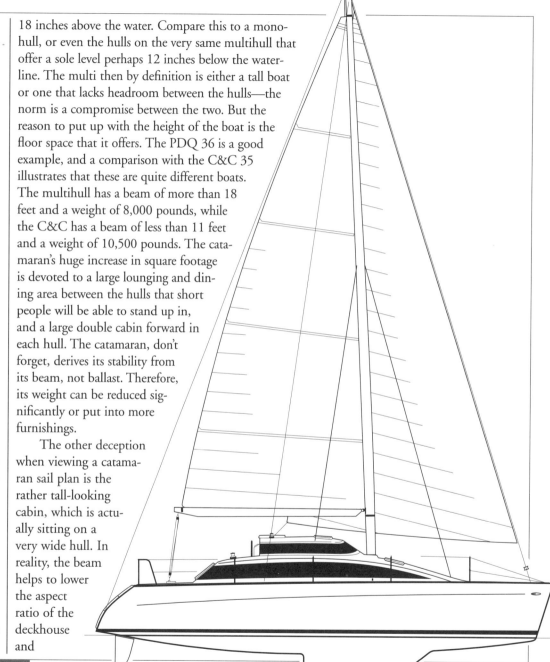

improves the appearance considerably. Monohull sailors will have some trouble appreciating the grace of this boat from the sail plan, but hold your judgment until you see the boat on the water.

The remarkable difference in state of mind when sailing a cat is due to its stability. A cruising cat because of its weight and moderate sail area seldom has a significant heel. In most cases 10 degrees is an absolute maximum—the windward hull never comes free of the water. So when a puff comes along the boat speeds up, but little else changes—the response required by those on board is minimal. A monohull, however, will heel significantly, and easing of the sails may be necessary to keep life comfortable.

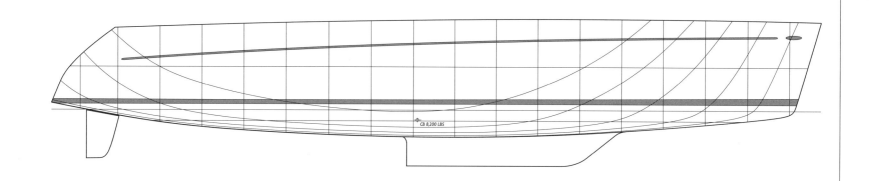

PDQ 36

Designed by Alan Slater
for PDQ Yachts, April 1989
LOA: 36' 5"
DWL: 34' 4"
Beam overall max: 18' 3"
Hull beam max: 5' 1"
Draft: 2' 10"
Displ: 8,200 lbs
Prismatic coefficient: 0.580

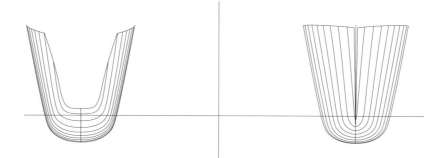

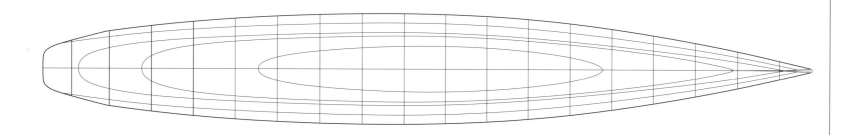

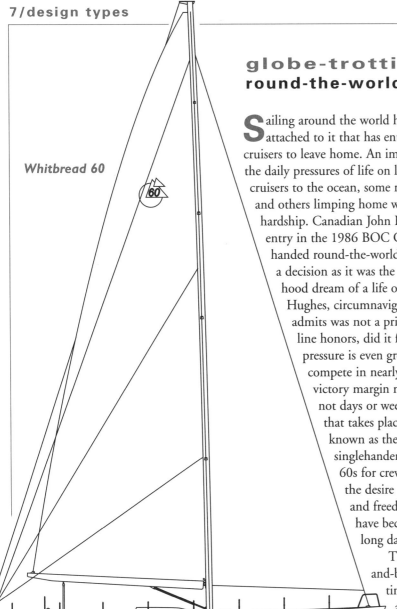

Whitbread 60

globe-trotting: round-the-world racers

Sailing around the world has a romance firmly attached to it that has enticed both racers and cruisers to leave home. An imagined freedom from the daily pressures of life on land has pulled many cruisers to the ocean, some reveling in life at sea and others limping home with tales of unending hardship. Canadian John Hughes describes his entry in the 1986 BOC Challenge, a single-handed round-the-world race, as "not so much a decision as it was the culmination of a boyhood dream of a life of adventure at sea." Hughes, circumnavigating in a boat that he admits was not a prime candidate for finish-line honors, did it for the adventure. The pressure is even greater for those who now compete in nearly-identical boats for a victory margin measured in seconds, not days or weeks. Certainly the racing that takes place in what are today known as the Open 60 class for singlehanders and the Whitbread 60s for crewed boats has surpassed the desire for peace, tranquillity, and freedom at sea. The events have become intense, months-long day races.

The purpose-designed-and-built boats have a distinctive wide, low, and aggressive look and incorporate many features not found on other boats. It is not the fact that these boats have to endure extreme conditions that forces them to be different; rather, they are a response to an opportunity unveiled by the length of time that they spend on one tack. The skipper of an inland racing yacht on a triangular course thinks nothing of changing direction every five minutes on the windward leg, but a round-the-world-racer will easily spend five hours and could spend five days on one tack. A crew has the time, and even welcomes the opportunity, to delve rather deeply into optimizing for a particular tack, wind speed, and wind angle. Designers therefore, in looking for those hundredths of a knot that will add up to hours ahead at the finish, provide water ballast, movable keels, and twin rudders and daggerboards, which can be used to great advantage.

The particular event dictates which gadgets are permitted, but for most contests water ballast is a minimum requirement. Since the efficiency of the sail plan and keel are both degraded with increasing heel angle, if water can be pumped up to the windward side of the boat to do the hiking task of 20 or 30 invisible sailors on the rail, then speed will jump. And so tanks, hoses, and valves placed well outboard in these wide, dinghy-shaped hulls are put to good use pumping water to the most advantageous spots. (See Fig. 3.10.)

Unique to the singlehanded boats is a hull shape that is as clever as it is odd. The triangular deck gives the impression that the back half of the boat is missing—the maximum beam is virtually at the transom. According to conventional yacht design wisdom, this sounds like an invitation to bad performance. The flat sections aft will add immense wetted surface, but the worst effect of this radical hull shape is the response to heeling. At 20 degrees of heel the centerline of the transom is well above the water, and a rudder in the normal centerline location will be useless.

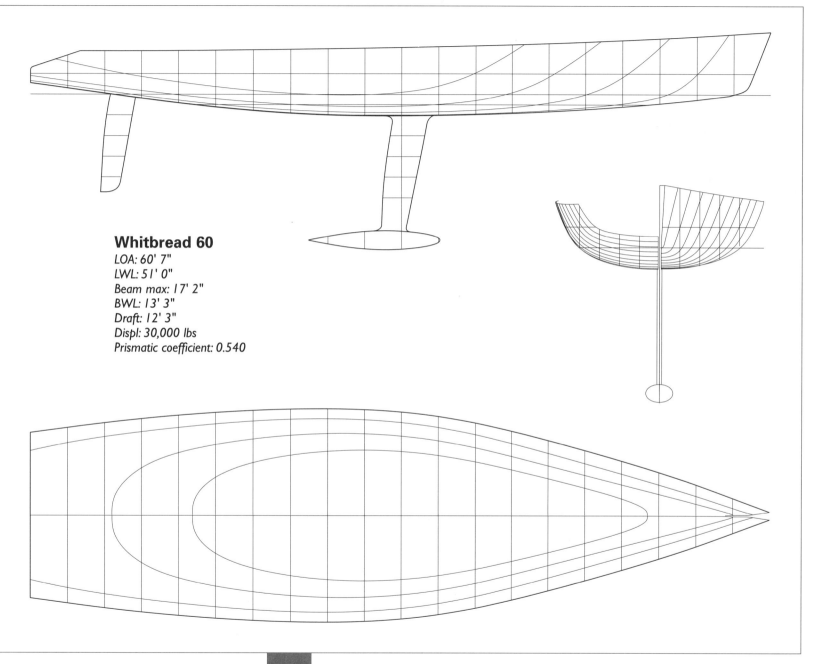

Whitbread 60
LOA: 60' 7"
LWL: 51' 0"
Beam max: 17' 2"
BWL: 13' 3"
Draft: 12' 3"
Displ: 30,000 lbs
Prismatic coefficient: 0.540

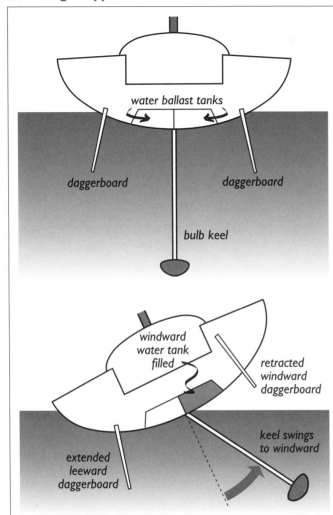

water ballast tanks

daggerboard   daggerboard

bulb keel

windward
water tank
filled

retracted
windward
daggerboard

keel swings
to windward

extended
leeward
daggerboard

The Open 60 Team Group 4, designed by Groupe Finot, relies on twin daggerboards for lift. A bulb keel can be swung to windward to increase righting moment. Stability is augmented by water ballast.

Now the clever part. The heeled waterline shape of this boat is narrow, its centerline angled at several degrees to windward, and is as different from the upright shape as one can imagine. Resistance will be low, but the real innovation is the placement of twin rudders and daggerboards off-center and canted outward. When heeled, the windward rudder is lifted well clear of the water, while the leeward rudder is deeply immersed, vertical, and in control. The versatility of this system is quickly evident. With the ballasting function left to a central keel and water ballast, the lift generation can be made efficient and variable. By raising the daggerboard progressively, one can optimize the balance of the boat for upwind, reaching, or downwind sailing.

The Open 60 *Team Group 4* shown here has included one additional performance—and, as it turns out, safety—feature. The keel swings on a longitudinal shaft at the bottom of the hull, permitting it to pivot up to 45 degrees to either side. Unlike the daggerboard, which is arranged to be vertical when the boat is heeled, with the swing keel the ballast is pushed even farther to windward when the boat heels. Divorcing the functions of leeway prevention (now handled by daggerboards) and ballasting (taken care of by the pivoting keel and some

internal water ballast) permits this extreme motion of the bulb. The fin above the bulb no longer is used to resist the side force of the sails. With added stability, the sail plan can be supported in heavier winds, and the speed increased.

One detriment to the wide hull shapes that have now become the norm in round-the-world racers is their inherent stability when inverted. The wide hull gives so much form stability to the boat that once flipped by wind and waves, it will remain resolutely upside down. Once again, the pivoting keel comes to the rescue—by forcing it off to one side, it can unbalance the boat enough to cause it to right itself.

Round-the-world racers are no longer isolated individuals testing their own personal strengths. As the speeds of these boats, whether solo or fully crewed, reach upward to a common plateau, they will spend more time racing within sight of each other, and that will cause them to push the boats even harder and inevitably take larger risks. When Joshua Slocum made the first solo passage around the world in 1895, there was neither competition nor regulations. It was common sense and the learned thought that "one should go understandingly about his work and be prepared for every emergency" that kept him safe. Now that we have rules that govern the shapes of these round-the-world boats, designers and sailors tend to lean on them and often push them to the limit, assuming if they follow the regulations for design and construction, the boats will be safe.

But rules are written only to make the competition fair and sometimes to prevent designers from moving into the ridiculous zone. They guarantee neither safety nor structural strength. It still remains the duty of the designer to engineer the boat's shape and materials for the safety of the crew; once you are on the ocean, the rules don't matter.

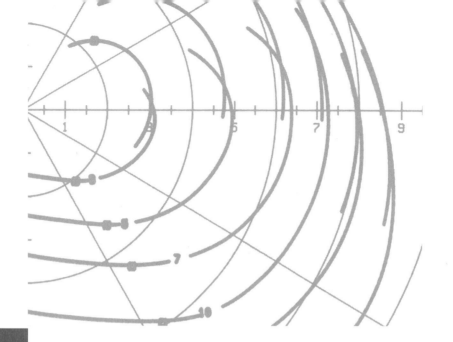

performance prediction

**Computer modeling can provide valuable
answers to questions about a design's
sailing characteristics, and give boat
owners an edge on the racecourse.**

finding out fast: predicting performance

Designers are constantly fielding performance questions from boat owners. What if I add 6 inches to the bottom of my keel—how much faster will the boat be? What if I increase both the sail area and the stability of my boat—will it make up for the increase in my racing handicap?

If the proposed change is large enough, the experienced designer can make an educated judgment as to whether the boat will be slower or faster, but predicting the amount of change is a risky business without further analysis. And for small changes in several

Computer performance prediction gives a designer a reliable assessment of a new yacht's potential, and a boat owner a precise understanding of how his boat should be sailed.

parameters, even predicting whether they are good or bad for boat speed is a risky business.

Several analytical techniques are available to help the designer estimate performance: computer performance prediction, tank testing, and full-scale boat testing. Such tools are valuable to varying degrees in beginning a design from scratch, modifying an existing design, and understanding the performance parameters of a boat so that it can be sailed as efficiently as possible.

Computer performance prediction stems from an ambitious research project at the Massachusetts Institute of Technology (MIT) in the 1970s. This research combined the theoretical work of a systematic series of tank tests with full-scale speed measurements from a yacht called *BayBea*. I am slightly oversimplifying the process in saying that this project used tank-testing analysis to predict the resistance of *BayBea*'s hull, keel, and rudder, while the full-size measurements indicated how fast the boat sailed in the real world. The only missing ingredient was the power supplied by the sails. However, with the first two ingredients in hand, the sail force coefficients (lift and drag) for various wind speeds and angles could be calculated.

In reality, determining sail force coefficients from full-size testing data is a tedious and difficult job. Recording such data while sailing is fraught with challenges—some expected, some totally unexpected. Since sailboats have a large inertia, even when precise data points are collected they may not reflect real steady-state conditions. It is easy for an unfeeling instrument to take measurements that are meaningless. Most helmspersons know that pointing the bow closer to the wind for 5 to 10 seconds while sailing upwind can give an exaggerated impression of performance. During that time the boat speed will change very little, but the velocity made good (VMG) in the direction of the wind—the vital measurement of

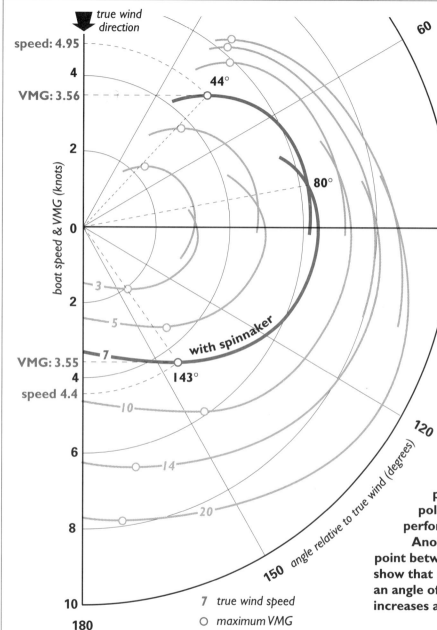

speed: 4.95

VMG: 3.56

44°

80°

true wind direction

boat speed & VMG (knots)

with spinnaker

VMG: 3.55

143°

speed 4.4

3

5

7

10

14

20

60

90

120

150

180

angle relative to true wind (degrees)

7   true wind speed

○   maximum VMG

FIG. 8.1

VPP and polar plots

One of the most eloquent uses of velocity performance prediction data is the polar plot, which presents VPP results in a graphic format. The plot at left is for author Steve Killing's Reliance 12M one design and was generated using FastYacht VPP software. Boat speed for each selected wind strength is plotted as a curve through a full range of compass bearings; off the wind, the speed curve reflects the use of a spinnaker.

By focusing on the information for performance in 7 knots true wind, we can examine the practical information a polar plot delivers to not only a designer, but a boat owner as well. The plot reveals that when sailing to windward, a maximum velocity made good (VMG) of 3.56 knots is achieved when steering a course 44 degrees to the true wind, with the boat moving through the water at 4.95 knots. (For more on windward performance and polar plots, see Fig. 8.4.) Off the wind, VMG reaches its peak of 3.55 knots when steering a course of 143 degrees, with the boat moving at 4.4 knots.

Note how the increase in wind from 10 to 14 knots produces a large change in the angle steered for maximizing downwind VMG. For racing sailors, knowing precise steering angles on the run is crucial to success, and a polar plot for their boat can deliver large gains in downwind performance. (See Fig. 8.2.)

Another useful item the polar plot provides is the transition point between genoa and spinnaker performance. Our 7-knot curves show that using a spinnaker instead of a genoa is more effective up to an angle of 80 degrees; this angle grows significantly when the wind increases above 10 knots.

FIG 8.2
Polar plots and downwind tactics

A polar plot produced by a velocity prediction program (VPP) makes it simple to visualize the relationship between raw boat speed and actual progress.

As the blue line on the polar plot indicates, in 20 knots of true wind this particular yacht will reach its highest speed, 9.5 knots, when sailing at 120 degrees to the true wind. However, our yacht is racing in the fleet at right, on a downwind run with a rhumb line of 180 degrees to the true wind, and her crew needs to know the course that will get them to the leeward mark the quickest. They look for the point on the blue curve that is farthest down the polar plot, which represents maximum velocity made good (VMG) to leeward, and determine the

bearing with which this point corresponds. In this case, the fastest bearing is 171 degrees, traveling at 7.8 knots. This dictates a gybing angle of 18 degrees—the angle through which the yacht can gybe back and forth while maintaining maximum VMG. The plot also shows that for this yacht in these conditions, there is little difference in VMG to leeward if the tacking angle is from 165 to 175 degrees. This means their gybing angle can be made as wide as 30 degrees if tactics or navigation call for it. Other yachts might have a polar plot that reveals a much different gybing angle range if VMG is to be maximized. Generally, as the wind lightens, gybing angles must increase to maintain high VMG values to leeward.

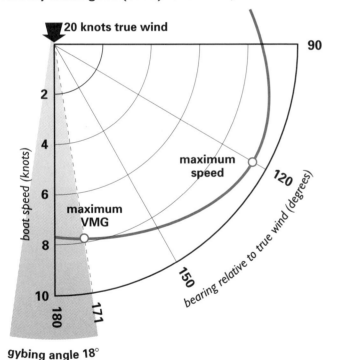

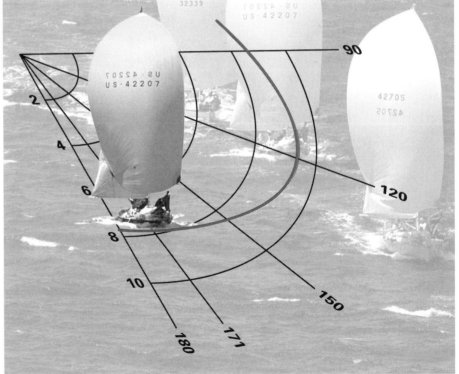

windward performance—will soar. When the boat resumes its more normal upwind course, the VMG will drop well below the steady-state level and then will slowly build again. When full-scale measurements are collected, there is no way to tell whether the boat is in a steady-state or an instantaneously better-than-real condition. The technician sifting the data is compelled to use some fairing technique to put a line through the mass of dots on the page. In my own experience, it is much better to collect less data, but only in conditions that the sailors know are close to steady state, to simplify and give credence to the validity of the numbers.

Once the data collection for *BayBea* was complete, sail force coefficients were developed that could be applied to other sail plans. Hull resistance data from a series of tank tests that varied beam, length, and hull shape were massaged into mathematical formulae that could, with good creditability, model any hull form. These two tools formed the basis of a software called the Velocity Prediction Program (VPP). This program takes the known characteristics of a boat—the hull, sails, and keel—and combines them numerically to predict how it will sail.

Two challenges must be resolved in a program like this. The first is determining the individual formulae that govern hull drag, keel lift, the side force of the sails, the righting moment of the hull and keel, the overturning moment of the sails, and more. With these settled, the second challenge is to find combinations of those values that maintain equilibrium in the boat—that is, conditions that relate to a real boat, for many conditions can be analyzed that are not "real." For example, speed could be predicted for a sail overturning moment that is much greater than the hull righting moment, but this condition cannot exist in nature, because a real boat will increase its heel angle until the two moments do agree. This second chal-

lenge, of ensuring that all forces are in equilibrium, is one of mathematics rather than design, but is paramount to the successful use of VPP software.

Early solution techniques were developed at MIT by then graduate student George Hazen, who, along with professors J. E. Kerwin and J. N. Newman, laid the groundwork during the North American Yacht Racing Union/MIT Ocean Race Handicapping Project. This project, and the solution techniques it developed, evolved into the Measurement Handicapping System (MHS) and later the International Measurement System (IMS) with only minor modification.

To make the program for predicting sailboat performance useful, the procedure for bringing the boat into equilibrium must be efficient, as it is directly related to the speed required to run the program. Although this is an internal operation of the software that the yacht designer cares little about, it is fundamental to the successful use of the program. The factors involved in bringing a boat into equilibrium are interrelated. For a given wind speed, the boat speed is a function of the drag of the hull, but the drag of the hull is a complex function affected by the heel, the sail forces, and, yes, the boat speed. So the solution to the problem is by necessity an iterative one—in other words, keep repeating the calculation until neither the heel angle nor the boat speed changes. Then the boat is in equilibrium and the next condition can be analyzed.

As computers continue to increase in speed, and solution techniques become more refined, the time required to "sail" a boat through a performance prediction drops. The first prediction run on a desktop machine in the early 1980s would take about 20 minutes to calculate boat speeds for 6 wind speeds with 10 wind angles for each. Recent developments have dropped that time to a matter of seconds. In fact, the FastShip VPP refined by Peter Schwenn runs in "real time" as a boat's hull shape is altered on the screen.

FIG. 8.3
Windward performance plot

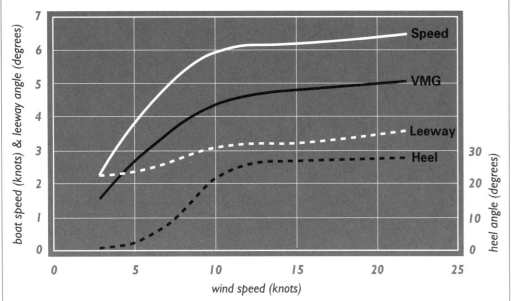

Not all VPP data can be presented satisfactorily in a polar plot. Traditional graphs can show revealing trends in individual performance characteristics. Here, data relative to a yacht's upwind performance in varying wind speeds is grouped.

The VPP, originally developed as a method of fairly handicapping boats of varying designs, has become a key analytical tool for the designer. Although it took some time (as happens with many innovations) for designers to gain faith in its predictions, the VPP is now an indispensable part of the designer's office. Whether the goal is to optimize a new boat for its intended use or to modify an existing one, the procedure is exactly the same. The current hull or base boat is run through the performance prediction program as it stands, the modifications are made, and the new boat is analyzed and compared with the original. The com-

parison can be made in terms of elapsed time around a racecourse, around the world, or in degrees of heel in a given wind condition.

shaping a prediction: design analysis

The designer's analysis of a hull begins with a hull shape drawn either by hand or with the aid of a computer. Discrete sections of the hull, usually 20 or more, are used to define with some accuracy how the shape changes along the length of the hull. The design program will use this numerical definition of the hull to calculate displacements with various amounts of gear on board, effective sailing length, and stability at various heel angles. Freeboard measurements are used to predict the hull's windage. The keel shape is defined as a separate entity by its planform (the side view), thickness, and distance below the waterline. The keel's lift characteristics are based on standard wing theory, and its efficiency is moderated by the presence of the hull above it—a flatter, shallower hull will make the keel more efficient than will a deep round one. The rudder is defined in much the same way as the keel, but most VPPs simply use the rudder volume to determine the correct flotation of the hull, and do not evaluate it as a lifting surface.

Sail specifications include the basic dimensions of the mainsail and foresail and, if they exist, the spinnaker, gennaker, and mizzen sails. The original sail algorithm was applicable only to sloops with similar proportions to *BayBea*, the yacht from which they were derived. In 1980 Hazen devised a model that would work for diverse rig types, including downwind sails and ketches and yawls. The spar dimensions are input, including the length and size of the taper at the top, to more accurately model the mast drag. The propeller, shaft and strut dimensions permit the calculation of prop drag. Included are models of the resistance of solid, folding, and feathering propellers.

The final block of information required by the VPP is flotation specifications. One of the most difficult of these to provide is the vertical location of the center of gravity—either an estimate or the end result of a long document totaling up its location in each part of the boat. With the center of gravity modeled, the program can calculate the hull's righting moment. The weight of the crew and extra equipment are added to the basic weight of the boat to find the *sailing flotation*—the position of the waterline when the boat is rigged and ready to sail. During the iterations to predict the sailing speeds, the software will move the crew weight outboard on deck to the rail to help reduce the heel angle in stronger winds.

showing results: output presentation

The VPP produces tables of data that describe a hull's sailing behavior. While all relevant information is present in these tables, many performance characteristics are not obvious until plotted in another format.

The polar plot, for example, shows how the yacht's speed varies with the true wind angle and velocity. As shown in Fig. 8.1, the polar plot is drawn as if the true wind were blowing in from the top of the page. Since boats cannot sail directly into the true wind, there are no points on the plot in that direction. The horizontal line across the page is the 90-degree reach line, while the vertical downward position represents 180 degrees (dead downwind).

Valuable performance indicators can be determined from this plot. The most obvious indicator is that as the wind speed increases, so does boat speed.

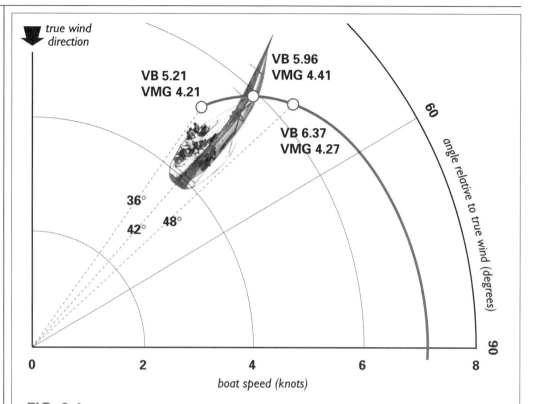

FIG. 8.4
VMG to windward and polar plots

A polar plot is useful in determining a bearing that strikes the perfect compromise between heading and raw boat speed (VB) in maximizing velocity made good (VMG) to windward. Sailors are often left guessing as to whether they should "foot" or pinch" when sailing upwind. The polar plot, based on VPP data, can tell them precisely what course to steer relative to the true wind angle. And the plot allows them to visualize the effect of bearing on performance the way a column of numbers never would.

For this yacht, a speed curve in 10 knots true wind shows, as expected, how boat speed decreases along with the steering angle relative to the wind. Of course, as this angle decreases, the yacht makes more progress to windward, as expressed by the VMG. This plot reveals an ideal heading of 42 degrees, at which VMG reaches a maximum value of 4.41 knots.

FIG. 8.5
Downwind performance plots

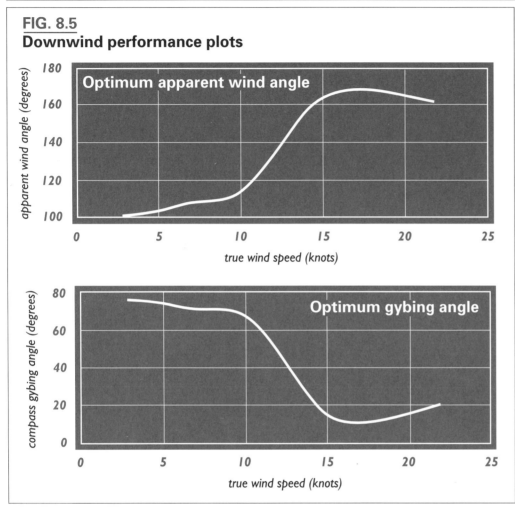

velocity made good (VMG). If you simply wanted your boat to go fast under main and jib to impress your friends, you would probably sail downwind at about 135 degrees to the true wind in a 28-knot breeze—but that will not get the boat to windward very fast. A polar plot makes clear how to maximize VMG in different wind speeds, as the vector drawn directly up the page is greatest at the crest of the polar curve by the white circles. In 10 knots of true wind, the yacht in Fig. 8.4 should be sailed at a true wind angle of 42 degrees for maximum VMG.

Polar plots can also reveal design shortcomings. Boats lacking stability will have this weakness show up on a polar plot by successive upwind "polars" nesting close together, or even overlapping, as the true wind speed increases. Normally, you would expect the polars to expand outward with increasing wind. If the upwind VMG at 28 knots of wind is the same as for 20 knots, then low stability is the limiting factor.

I find polar prediction plots very helpful in sailing a boat off the wind. In a racing situation, the fastest possible route to the leeward mark is not always obvious. Just like upwind, there is an optimum VMG downwind that occurs at a specific wind angle. (See Fig. 8.2.) Only in exceptional cases does a boat reach the leeward mark quickest by sailing directly for it, and determining proper downwind gybing angles is one of the most critical tasks overlooked by racing sailors. Gybing accurately through some angle, dependent on wind speed, can bring substantial gains. The optimum gybing angle decreases as the wind speed increases, indicating that in heavier winds one can sail more directly toward the mark. But the surprising thing to most sailors is how large the gybing angles are when the wind is below 10 knots. As seen in Fig. 8.1, a bearing of 143 degrees from the true wind angle in 7 knots of wind, representing a gybing angle of 74 degrees, is not unusual. Using the predicted values from a polar

The plot's mapping of upwind performance illustrates precisely the trade-off between *pinching* (sailing closer to the true wind direction than is optimum) and *footing* (sailing lower). (See Fig. 8.4.) The goal for any sailboat going to windward is to travel not necessarily fast through the water, but to make the most efficient progress in the direction from which the wind is blowing. This vector directly into the true wind is called plot is a good way to learn quickly how to sail a new boat, or to optimize the performance of the one you already have.

Other information valuable when sailing downwind, such as the relationship between true wind speed and apparent wind angle, and true wind speed and gybing angle, can also be summarized in graphic form, as shown in Fig. 8.5.

The upwind plot in Fig. 8.3 is a handy summary of information, and can be augmented by a plot of compass tacking angles. Leeway and compass tacking angles, which depend greatly on keel efficiency, are often used by navigators to estimate the course required to a landfall. Since the compass reading on board represents the direction the boat is pointing, not the direction it is actual going, the leeway (the difference between the compass course and actual course) is vital. With upwind leeway angles varying from 4 degrees in a racing boat to 12 degrees in a shallow-draft cruiser, the effect of the actual course sailed on navigating is important. With the information provided by a VPP, the navigator can adjust the desired course by the leeway angle to give the helmsman a target course to steer. In similar fashion, the compass tacking angle is the total angle through which the boat will tack when heading onto a new upwind course, and will usually decrease as the wind increases. Knowing these values can save considerable embarrassment when tacking to make a headland or channel marker.

strength in numbers: how much to believe

While the computer VPP is an incredible tool, it should be relied upon only when the parameters it is assessing are within the range of a "normal" boat. Within that recommended window of design types,

predictions are very accurate—often more accurate than the instruments on board the boats. Sailors regularly criticize the predictions as being "way off," only to find after the designer assured them of his confidence in the predictions that the yacht's instruments required calibration. I have great faith in the predictions of a well-executed VPP. I emphasize the qualifier "well-executed," for much care is needed in preparing data for a VPP. If inexact information is presented for analysis, then only inexact results can be expected. As the old computer software saying goes: garbage in, garbage out.

There are also some limitations to the VPP itself that, if not understood, can lead to unexpected results. The basis of the VPP is a systematic series of tank tests that were performed on a series of models with incremental changes in beam, displacement, length, and (more recently) cross-section shape. In analyzing the data, complex relationships were recognized. These were approximated by equations to allow the computer to predict the performance of future hull shapes. Problems will arise in a prediction if there were weaknesses in the original tank data, or if the hull shape being analyzed is well beyond the original test series.

I have seen examples of both problems. One weakness of tank testing is in the data produced by very full aft-end configurations. Transoms that extend below the waterline and hulls with very large bustles just forward of the rudder are not interpreted correctly in the tank, and consequently will not be analyzed properly in the VPP. It is possible to design additional volume into the aft end of a boat and watch the performance improve according to the test tank and the VPP, when in reality the full-size boat would see a speed loss. (See Chapter 9 on tank testing for more on this.)

Other sirens leading designers onto rocky shores are boats that are well outside the matrix of yachts tested, or are beyond the limits of good sense. Yachts with very low prismatic coefficients, which typically means they have large midsections and fine ends, will give inaccurate results. (They would be predicted faster than they really are.) The severe shape change in the boat's middle will not be assessed fairly because the current VPP cannot determine when flow separation will occur. Keeping prismatic coefficients in the range historically called "normal" will ensure good results.

The VPP does not perform a microscopic scan of the hull surface, nor does it check to see if the hull is fair. It records the distribution of volume, but if you were to glue half a football on the bottom of the hull, it would analyze the shape as if that bump were distributed around the entire middle of the boat. The lesson is not to stick objects on the bottom of your boat. At a more microscopic level, the surface finish of the hull is modeled on some VPPs, and either a smooth bottom or a fouled bottom equivalent to heavy barnacles on an old ship can be selected.

As the shapes of hulls evolve—and they will continue to do so as long as there are designers, cruisers, and racing rules—the VPPs will be updated to follow and more accurately predict those shapes. Each year that an America's Cup is held, VPPs make another leap forward, although usually only in the direction of shapes emerging in the International America's Cup Class yachts. But some features found on those boats are common to other sailboats, and a spin-off benefit is found. In particular, as bulbs and wings are found on more boats, so the analysis of those appendages will become more exact. In the first VPPs that blossomed in the 1980s, the only type of keel truly addressed was a straight-sided, tapered foil. Keels outside this realm had to be approximated, and if there was extra drag or lift to be accounted for, that was added by a rather cumbersome process. Elliptical, bulb, and wing keels are just beginning to be added as standard items, thanks to the America's Cup, and these features have already begun to show up in the racer-cruisers of local yacht clubs. Soon other developments will be required to cover the entire realm of possible shapes. Maybe even footballs glued to the hull.

a surer thing: improving VPP accuracy

When more analytical accuracy is called for, and the research budget is on hand, the VPP can be combined directly with tank testing. The first section of the VPP, often termed the *LPP* (for lines processing program), digests the hull surface and appendage definition file and reduces it to a bank of numbers representing the equivalent lengths and the righting moments for each heel angle. Normally, these are then used to predict the lift and drag of the boat as various sailing conditions are analyzed. But if towing tank results of the specific hull are available, their lift and drag data can be substituted for the mathematical model. The VPP then throws out the mathematical model of the hull, keel, and rudder, and substitutes the presumably more accurate data from the tank. The software then continues with its analysis of the design's performance.

Any or all of the discrete sections of the software can be replaced by hard data obtained from the tank, the wind tunnel, or the real world. Sail force coefficients can be measured in a wind tunnel and used in place of the computer model. In every case the VPP operator determines the most reliable source for his data. Typically the substitution of tank data for math models only occurs for very large cruising boats or specialized racing boats (America's Cup, round-the-world racers) and miscellaneous big-budget campaigns. For most fin keel sailboats, the VPP will give exceptionally good results without having to resort to the additional expense of tank testing.

tank testing

An analytical tool with centuries
of development, the test tank
continues to be refined in an
elusive search for perfect data.

modeling performance: the test tank challenge

Without the benefit of analytical tools, predicting how a particular design will perform once built and launched is a largely intuitive process. Unfortunately, understanding the resistance of a hull, heeled and yawed while traveling through water, is anything but intuitive.

Designers are often caught by surprise when their latest racing hull lumbers near the back of the fleet. While a designer can make intuitive changes to a

A design by C&C Yachts negotiates the Davidson Labs test tank in New Jersey in the early 1970s.

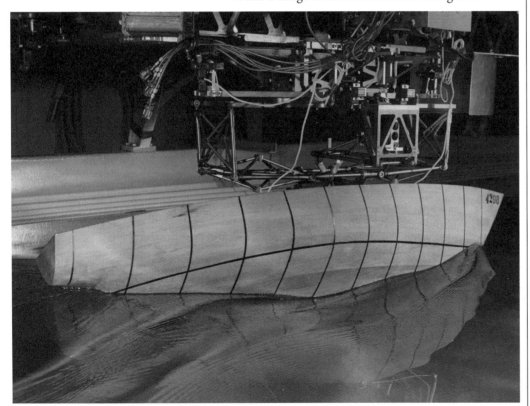

design based on watching a hull in motion, it is almost impossible to assess the effect of those changes—not only their magnitude, but even whether they will improve or hamper performance. Knowing that yacht A is 5 percent faster that yacht B, and knowing that yacht B produces a confused waveform, is the closest a designer can get to cause and effect without analytical help. Smoothing the buttock lines just forward of the transom may help the water flow more cleanly in that area, but knowing whether this will make the boat go faster or slower is mere guesswork. The reduction in turbulence aft might result in a drag reduction, but at the same time the shape change might shorten the effective sailing length, increasing drag overall.

Such conundrums require an authoritative bridge between the design as a collection of lines on paper and the design as a finished yacht. A design's performance can certainly be measured by studying the finished boat, but this is a case of closing the barn door after the horse has escaped. Before computer performance prediction techniques (see Chapter 8) could give credible answers, tank testing was the only way to assess numerical analysis and realistic waveforms of a new design prior to construction. Even now, with computers able to assess the potential of most hulls and rigs, the tank still has a role to play.

The premise of tank testing is simple: tow a scale-model hull down a tank of water in a controlled environment and measure all the forces and moments acting on the boat. Enlarging these values to full size can produce a prediction of the design's speed. Compared to full-size testing—sailing a completed boat out on the ocean—the procedure is much simpler. The tank requires no helmsman or crew, nor does it have to endure the accompanying variables of human fatigue and inconsistent action in steering and sail trim. The tank eliminates the varying wind conditions (there is no wind at all) and provides a solid platform from which to reference directions, speeds and forces.

Tank testing has a long history in design science. It was only logical that models, which had been used for some time to determine the shape of a ship, would be used to predict their speed. By the time Swedish shipbuilder and designer Fredrik Chapman died in 1808, he had significantly enlarged the envelope of scientific knowledge related to ships. His theories of buoyancy, stability, and performance, rounded out by practical ship designing, were far beyond those of his peers. In his efforts to better understand the flow of water around hulls and the resulting drag forces, he built one of the first testing tanks (actually a towing apparatus in a pond) to help prove his theories. This initial Chapman device handled geometric models about 28 inches long. (See Fig. 9.1.) His second facility, a wooden tank about 68 feet long, could test 8-foot models to refine the shapes of ships.

In Chapman's first test facility, lines connected to the bow and stern of a model led to pulleys at opposite ends of the towing area. From there the lines turned upward to another pulley at the top of supporting towers and finally were attached to weights that were free to fall under the force of gravity. (This method of model propulsion had been around since at least the previous century.) For a model weight of 27 pounds, a typical Chapman test run would involve a forward weight of 20 pounds and a restraining weight of 13 pounds for a net forward force of 7 pounds. By recording the time required for the model to traverse a 74-foot span, a measure of its resistance could be made. His models varied the center of maximum beam and the curvature in the ends of the boat—some parabolic and some conic.

In the test tank, physical results are correct, no matter what knowledge exists of why resistance is low or high (although, as experience would prove, those results are absolutely correct only for the model, not

necessarily for the full-scale design). And so Chapman could extract practical knowledge without fully understanding (a quest we are still pursuing) all the physics behind the results. Because his results are of interest even today, the data from one test are presented in Fig. 9.1, adapted from the original table of values.

While the mechanics and instrumentation are greatly refined, modern towing tanks follow the basic mechanical principle used by Chapman and his eighteenth century contemporaries: haul a model in a straight line through the water and make sense of the data. Two other tank configurations, however, are worth noting. One is the water tunnel, in which the model is held stationary and the water flows by, just like a model is held stationary before a breeze in a wind tunnel. (A test facility using a stationary object and moving water is known to have existed in the mideighteenth century.) This tunnel, completely filled with water, is used primarily for testing propellers and other submerged objects, which do not produce waves. Its advantage is that a test can be run continuously for data logging or viewing, with no waiting time while the model is reset to its starting position. But it is not applicable to boat hulls, which must sit on the free surface.

Some simple tests can also be done in circular tanks, in which the floating model is towed from the end of a rotating arm. Interfering wave patterns build up, which will most likely influence results, but for large variations in hull configurations some meaningful data may be acquired.

Full-size tests on canoe hulls have been successfully made by towing them behind a powerboat. Two hulls that are to be compared are attached to either end of a pivoting bar. The bar's geometry determines the percentage change in drag required to pivot the bar 1 degree. Although absolute results are not obtained in this fashion, quite accurate comparative values can be documented.

FIG. 9.1
Mr. Chapman's investigations

While Swedish shipbuilder and designer Fredrik H. Chapman (1721–1808) was not the first person to conduct tank-testing experiments, he is acknowledged to be the first to apply rigorous methodology and glean practical knowledge from his experiments.

Sir Isaac Newton's *Principia* of 1687 introduced the concept of a "solid of least resistance," a mathematical shape that could produce an ideal ship form. This concept inspired the first test-tank experimenters pursuing Newton's mathematical grail to focus on shapes that were geometric, rather than attempt to assess scale versions of actual vessels. Chapman was one of them.

Chapman was drawn to tank testing to seek physical proof for a geometrical method he had developed for determining a ship's resistance. His first towing tank (shown below) was not a tank at all, but rather a pond, in which he erected towers 100 feet apart that supported a pulley and weight system, the standard model-propulsion strategy of the day. The larger "moving" weight would pull on the line at the object's "bow," towing it down the tank, while a smaller "retarding" weight steadied its course. Chapman timed the transit by starting a stop watch when a cloth marker on the towing line passed the pointer at the "towing" end of the tank, and stopping it when another marker 74 feet back passed by. In this way, Chapman applied a simple but consistent method of measuring relative drag. Objects with low drag values would transit the tank the quickest, and objects with high drag values the slowest.

"moving" weight

"retarding" weight

flag marker

flag marker

timing pointer

Chapman's investigation of three-dimensional shapes used careful scientific parameters. He tested three categories of shapes: nonstreamlined (in blue), sharp-bowed streamlined (in dark gray), and blunt-bowed streamlined (in light gray). A double-ended model (shown dark gray, fourth from top) straddled both groups, as the blunt-bowed models were the sharp-bowed models towed in reverse. Each model category used a progression of fore-and-aft positions for maximum beam, a focal point of his investigation into drag. The models were 28 inches long, with a circular cross section, and were ballasted to float with their upper surface just emerging from the water.

In his investigation, Chapman varied the towing speeds by using different weight combinations. Because the models did not all weigh the same, he selected towing weights according to their fraction of the individual model's weight. In the results plotted here, Chapman used moving weights three-quarters the model weight and retarding weights one-half the model weight. For each model and weight combination, six test runs were made to ensure consistent results.

While Chapman's work, the results of which he published in 1775, might seem crude by today's standards, it is nonetheless impressive for eliciting reasonable data through uncomplicated yet rigorous means. Most insightful was his conclusion that the optimum shape varied with the towing velocity. Chapman concluded that sharp-bowed objects were faster at low towing speeds (as illustrated here with his slowest towing results), moderate speeds favored no particular shape, and high speeds favored a blunt bow.

Chapman's experiment was admittedly flawed in that he was towing almost entirely submerged objects to determine the best underwater shape of a hull form. Chapman was working at the dawn of realization of the different drag components affecting a ship, and wavemaking drag was particularly unappreciated. To his credit, Chapman observed the waveforms his models produced and attempted to explain them mathematically.

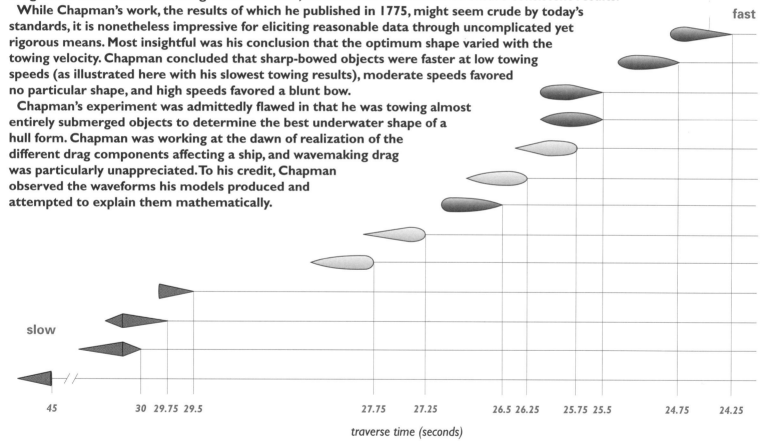

fast

slow

| 45 | | 30 | 29.75 | 29.5 | | 27.75 | 27.25 | | 26.5 | 26.25 | | 25.75 | 25.5 | | 24.75 | | 24.25 |

traverse time (seconds)

FIG. 9.2
"Captive" towing apparatus

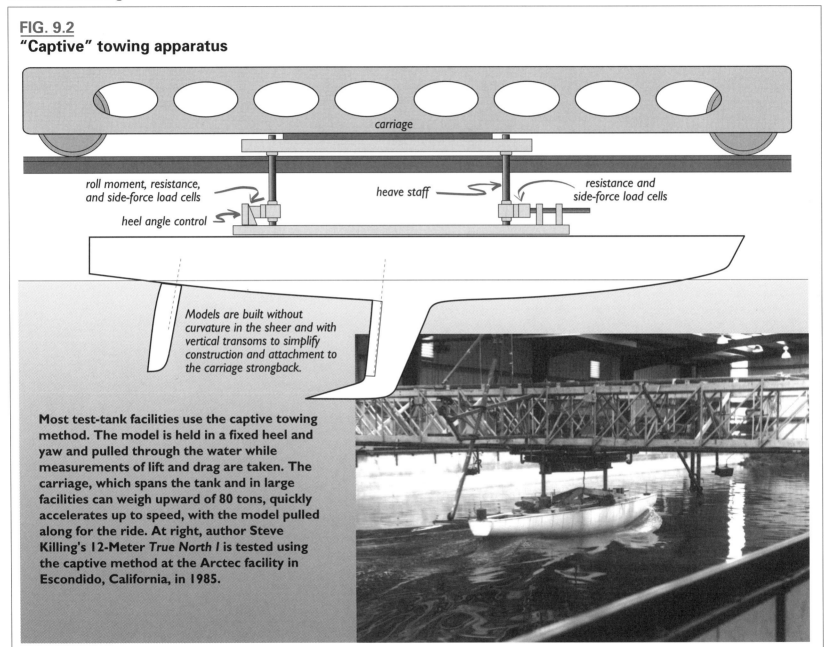

carriage

roll moment, resistance, and side-force load cells

heave staff

resistance and side-force load cells

heel angle control

Models are built without curvature in the sheer and with vertical transoms to simplify construction and attachment to the carriage strongback.

Most test-tank facilities use the captive towing method. The model is held in a fixed heel and yaw and pulled through the water while measurements of lift and drag are taken. The carriage, which spans the tank and in large facilities can weigh upward of 80 tons, quickly accelerates up to speed, with the model pulled along for the ride. At right, author Steve Killing's 12-Meter *True North I* is tested using the captive method at the Arctec facility in Escondido, California, in 1985.

captive and free: tank towing methods

In North America, much of the development and refinement of test-tank techniques came at Davidson Labs, part of the Stevens Institute of Technology in New Jersey. In the Davidson configuration, a towing carriage runs above a tank of water and holds a model captive in heel and yaw, but allows it to pitch and heave. (See Fig. 9.2.) By running at a combination of different heel, yaw, and boat speeds, the entire range of possible sailing conditions is covered.

Yacht towing tank facilities around the world operate in one of two modes—captive, as described above, or free-sailing. (See Fig. 9.3.) When I was working in the design office of C&C Yachts, I spent the 1975 calendar year at the National Research Council (NRC) towing tank in Ottawa developing an apparatus for free-sail testing of yacht hulls. (This tank has since been replaced by a new NRC facility in St. John's, Newfoundland, with a tank 650 feet long, 40 feet wide, and 23 feet deep. I have used both tanks, among others, in testing America's Cup designs.)

Whether free-sailing or captive, the tank and main carriage remain the same. The free-sailing technique developed in Ottawa required a hull model about 10 feet on the waterline (three times the size of models C&C had used at Davidson Labs), correctly ballasted and fitted with a mast. The mast was placed not where the full-size mast would be, but at the center of effort of the sails. To propel a free-sailing model down the tank, a string is led from the mast at the height of the center of effort to a force-measuring block on the carriage. Encoders (angle measuring devices) on the mast and force block record towing and leeway angles. Before each run, the rudder angle is set to a predeter-

mined value. The carriage is run up to speed and the model "sails" down the tank. Because the stability is modeled correctly, the combination of lift, drag, heel, and yaw is automatically obtained. Even with a firm knowledge of the theory of the forces at work in sailing, it is still rather amazing to watch a scale-model yacht heeled over and traveling straight down the tank, pulled by a single string well off to one side.

The benefit of the free-sailing technique is that it minimizes the amount of tank time for each run, as it is a realistic sailing condition. However, its benefit is also its weakness—it gives little general information. It is difficult to separate the effect of various parameters—for example the increase of lift with yaw or the increase of drag with heel—which individually are so valuable for later use in a velocity prediction program (VPP). If the model's performance with a different sail plan or stability is required, the boat must be re-run down the tank. You also discover when running the tests that there are some conditions in which the boat will sail itself (nicely balanced upwind), and others in which the boat is "meta-stable"—any perturbation will push it off course, and it will continue to veer off course. This wandering results in a bad run: the boat will not balance as it travels down the tank.

For the above reasons, most tanks use the captive method, in which the boat is held in a fixed heel and yaw and pulled through the water while measurements of lift and drag are taken. The carriage, which spans the tank and in large facilities can weigh upward of 80 tons, quickly accelerates up to speed with the model pulled along for the ride. During the "constant velocity" portion of the tank run, measurements are taken and averaged before the carriage must decelerate at the end of the tank. It then reverses, slowly runs back to the start, and waits for the water to settle before starting the next run. Typical data sampling times are 30 seconds for a low-speed run down to perhaps 5 seconds for a high-speed test. Once the entire matrix of sailing conditions (some real, some not) is covered, the data is exported to a software program to find, with a given sail plan, which conditions represent a balanced sailboat. Those values of lift and drag are then used to predict the full-size performance.

The author tested several C&C designs at Davidson Labs in the 1970s to confirm their behavior before construction. As noted, the use of small 3-foot models then was quite common. Occasionally the resulting data did not reliably predict the performance we saw in full-size hulls. In particular, these tests encouraged shallow-draft keels. When the depth of a keel was reduced, the lift and drag characteristics would change—as expected, lift for the worse, drag for the better. But the drag improvements were grossly overpredicted by the tank. Having a disproportionately large drag component assigned to the keel meant that reducing the area of the keel would appear to be very beneficial, as some loss of lift could pay off in significant improvements in drag. Unfortunately, when these shallow keels were applied to the real boat, they would not exhibit such optimistic results. General wisdom even then said that keel draft is paramount to good performance, but we believed the tank and followed its advice.

number crunched: the rise of tank data error

We weren't the only designers heeding the tank's pied-piper call. For the 1970 America's Cup, tank testing encouraged a potentially fatal trend in the designs of all American defense candidates—the new *Valiant* by Sparkman & Stephens and *Heritage* by Charles Morgan, and the modified 1967 defender *Intrepid,* reshaped by Britton Chance. Results from Davidson Labs on the small models (about 4.5 feet) encouraged fuller aft sections, which resulted in large bustles and heavier designs. *Valiant* was also equipped with a tiny rudder, a result of the tank's exaggerated assessment of drag savings with small appendages. Once launched, *Valiant* was unmanageable and had to be equipped with a larger rudder. *Intrepid* won the defense trials and in the finals defeated through superior sailing the Australian challenger *Gretel II,* designed by Alan Payne, which was generally accepted to be a lighter—and faster—yacht.

The warning signs were gathering around the potential for serious miscalculation in the test tank. Both Olin Stephens and Charles Morgan said they felt their designs *Valiant* and *Heritage* hadn't performed the way the test tank had promised. But Chance remained confident of its results, and his decision to follow the assurances of the Davidson Labs data led him to create the radical shape of *Mariner* for the 1974 defense.

Just as the tank had encouraged Morgan, Stephens, and Chance to equip their 1970 contenders with full aft ends, the tank now encouraged Chance to equip *Mariner* with a bizarre "fast back" underwater bustle. (See Fig. 9.4.) Intuitively, the shape was entirely wrong, promising horrendous turbulence. But the tank promised a design breakthrough, and Chance chanced it. Once built, *Mariner* produced the speed-sapping turbulence the test tank entirely overlooked.

Halfway through the defense trials, Britton Chance and Pierre DeSaix, head of the Davidson Labs tank, conceded defeat and bewilderment. According to Roger Vaughan's book *The Grand Gesture,* when DeSaix arrived at the Derecktor boatyard to announce the plan to give *Mariner* a conventional transom, the tank expert confessed, "We've found out we can't predict the performance of the stern in the tank, and we don't know why."

FIG. 9.3
"Free-sailing" towing method

Rather than simply pull a model down the tank, the free-sailing method reproduces the actual sail forces experienced by the yacht. A mast positioned at the sail plan's center of effort allows the model to be "sailed" down the tank, with the keel providing the necessary opposing lift to heel the model and with the rudder set to the angle required to counteract weather helm.

While the free-sailing method impressively reproduces the actual forces a yacht experiences under sail, it also invites problems in assessing hull performance. The models can wander, making it difficult to collect reliable data. While efficient in testing a specific hull and ballast configuration, the free-sailing method fails to give the breadth of data available from a captive test. For this reason, the free-sailing procedure is not the preferred towing strategy.

At right: Steve Killing (kneeling on platform) oversees the testing of the 12-Meter design Canada 1 *in 1982 at the National Research Council tank in Ottawa, using the free-sailing method.*

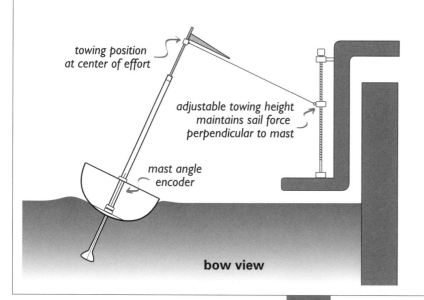

towing position at center of effort

adjustable towing height maintains sail force perpendicular to mast

mast angle encoder

bow view

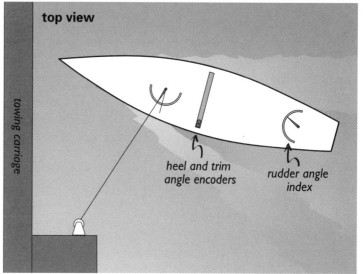

top view

towing carriage

heel and trim angle encoders

rudder angle index

A 4-foot model awaits the next data-collecting run at the Stevens Institute tank in the early 1970s. The scale distortion inherent in such small-scale tests was revealed through painstaking analysis in 1974.

Froude number

$$Fn = \frac{V}{\sqrt{(gL)}}$$

V is the speed in ft/sec

g is a constant (32.2 ft/sec/sec, acceleration due to gravity)

L is the length of the model in feet

That fall, the reasons for the *Mariner* mishap, and other design foibles experienced by people like me, were made clear in a paper delivered by Karl Kirkman and David Pedrick at the annual meeting of the Society of Naval Architects and Marine Engineers (SNAME) in New York. Kirkman, then a researcher at Hydronautics Inc., a tank-testing facility in Maryland, and Pedrick, then of the Sparkman & Stephens design office, had been studying the scale effects present in testing techniques. In an interview published in *Yachting* shortly before *Mariner*'s launch, Britton Chance had said, "Do boats perform as predicted in the tank? I think the answer is 'yes.'" But by midsummer 1974, Chance had a much different answer to his own question, and by that fall Kirkman and Pedrick could say why. They had suspected for some time—and had put together the data to prove it—that there was more going on under the water in towing tanks than designers were led to believe.

big and little: scaling error exposed

The culprit lay in a profound scaling problem. Every detail of a test-tank model is a miniature version of the real hull, except for one vital part—the water molecules used to float the model. (See Fig. 9.6.) While the model of a 12-Meter would be about one-thirteenth actual size, the water molecules were still life-size. These "oversized" molecules also have a density and viscosity that is out of proportion to the model. But because no fluid exists with the correct scale characteristics, tanks are stuck with standard tap water to float the models. Unless something is changed in the way models are towed or built, a tank will give results that bear little relation to the real world. *Mariner* would have been fine if the water molecules in Rhode Island Sound were

scaled-up versions of those used in the tank.

Recognizing this scale problem was only the beginning of more test headaches. Of course, if all tests are done on full-scale models, there can be no scaling problems—you simply have to tow the boat down the tank at various heel angles and yaws. The resistance figures will relate directly to the resistance the boat will experience when sailing. However, for most projects, testing a full-size model is not practical. To test a scale model, some thought must be given to relating the speed and forces in the tank to those of the real world.

To compensate for the irresolvable water scaling problem, you can change the towing speed of the model to correctly scale the drag produced by either wave formations or friction—but not by both simultaneously. That is because scaling the towing speed for these distinct types of drag requires adjustments in opposite directions.

The fact that speed must be scaled along with hull sizes to produce accurate drag values was far from unacknowledged in the early 1970s. William Froude, a brilliant English scientist with a keen interest in boats and drag, correctly proposed in the late nineteenth century the division of the drag into the two components of wavemaking and frictional drag. (Froude's pioneering work in frictional drag compelled an enthusiastic overreaction by George Lenox Watson in his design of the 1887 America's Cup challenger *Thistle*. In 1901 he conceded to marine historian William P. Stephens that in an effort to reduce drag he "had cut the wetted surface to a point where he sacrificed both lateral plane and stability.") Froude observed that if a scale model is run at "corresponding speeds" to the full-size design, the wave patterns along the sides of both boats are identical. That corresponding speed is determined by what is now known as the *Froude number* (see margin).

FIG. 9.4
The *Mariner* miscue

Sometimes intuition is safer than science. For the 1974 America's Cup defense, Britton Chance designed the contender *Mariner* with a radical "fastback" bustle that ended abruptly just behind the rudder, as shown in this rendering based on photographs interpreted by Steve Killing. At far right is a conventional 12-Meter hull. Anything as square as *Mariner* below the waterline would seem to invite horrendous turbulence—and it did. *Mariner* was painfully slow, but she was only the latest (albeit the most spectacular) example of design miscalculations that arose from tank testing in the early 1970s. Chance had been misled by tank-testing data from a 4.5-foot model that could not accurately reflect water flow in the radical after third of the hull.

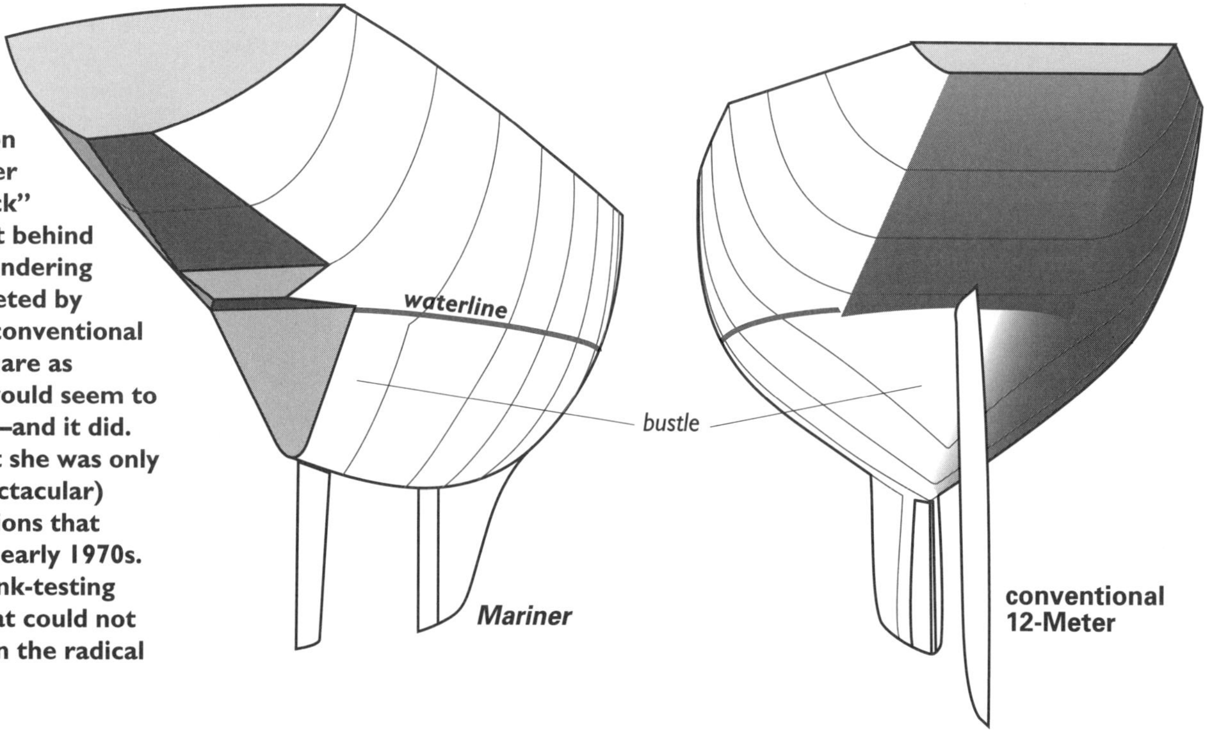

waterline

bustle

Mariner

conventional 12-Meter

If the Froude numbers of the model and full-scale boat are matched, the waveforms will be matched. That means the speeds of the two hulls should be proportional to the square root of the length factors. For example, if the full-size boat is 16 times the length of the model, then the scale speed should be multiplied by 4 (the square root of 16) to represent the boat at sea. In the case of a 12-Meter (actually about 60 feet long) tested with a 1:13.3-scale 4.5-foot model, it would have to be towed down the tank at 2.2 knots to replicate the waveforms present when the actual boat was sailing at 8 knots.

But in order to scale correctly the second drag component, frictional drag, the speed should be the inverse of the same length scale. The guiding formula is called the *Reynolds number,* named in honor of Osborne Reynolds, who devised the calculation in 1883. It is the product of the length and the velocity of an object divided by the viscosity of the surrounding fluid. This relationship needs to be maintained from model to ship in order to scale the frictional drag, and in particular the critical transition point on the hull from laminar to turbulent flow.

A model must be towed more quickly than the full-size boat to reflect true frictional drag values, and the smaller the scale of the model, the greater the

Steve Killing uses a 1:2.5 model of the 5.5-Meter Antiope *to calibrate the National Research Council test tank in Ottawa in 1974.* Antiope *served as a benchmark design in the investigation of scaling error in tanks around the world.*

speed. To scale the Reynolds number experienced by the full-size boat when sailing at 8 knots, a 1:13.3 model would have to be rocketed down the tank at 106 knots. This speed would have both the model and the full-scale boat experiencing the same proportion of laminar and turbulent flow, but with such a high speed, the frictional drag would be dwarfed by the unrealistically high wave drag. At these speeds, the boat would be planing, or digging an immense hole in the water; either behavior is unacceptable.

There is no way to reconcile the scaling problems of drag in model testing. A hypothetical solution would be to somehow create a liquid with the proper values of molecule dimension, density, and viscosity for the given model size. But while this liquid (cur-

rently beyond our technological grasp) might provide the proper results in terms of frictional drag, it's questionable if it would behave properly in terms of wave drag. Since the opportunity to model both the components of drag accurately at the same time does not (and probably never will) exist, tank technicians choose to model the one they understand the least and correct for the one they understand the most. Wave drag, still on the fringes of our comprehension, is the one chosen to be modeled correctly by running the test model at a scale-corresponding speed. Frictional drag—the resistance due to the surface area of the boat rubbing shoulders with the surrounding water—is the component that gets corrected. This is also the most reasonable solution because the speeds required from a model for accurate frictional drag results would mechanically challenge a test-tank apparatus.

To correct for the error in the frictional drag present in test results of total observed model drag, the frictional and wavemaking drags must be separated before expanding them to full size. The frictional drag (the one technicians are comfortable predicting) is calculated for the model, with its value then subtracted from the total observed model drag to get the model wave drag. To project the drag value to its full-size equivalent, the wave drag is scaled by the length factor cubed, and the frictional drag is scaled by a correction that accounts for varying drags with Reynolds numbers.

The Davidson Labs technicians were fully aware of the scale issues and faithfully applied the Froude and Reynolds calculations in the tests of *Mariner*. Without question, the Davidson Labs were employing the most advanced tank-testing knowledge of the day. The errors that manifested themselves so spectacularly with *Mariner* lay in the murky realm of water flow in scale testing. And the clue to the problem came in Kirkman and Pedrick's analysis of frictional drag results in scale testing. 198 ▶

FIG. 9.5
Testing the tank

Research into problems in scale-model tank testing in 1974 led to the *Antiope* Project, in which different-length models of a 5.5-Meter design by A. E. Luders were tested to determine how model size affected results. At 31.6 feet overall, the actual *Antiope* was small enough to be tank-tested at full scale, to provide a benchmark for results from the scale models. Those results gave textbook consistency in testing error.

The most significant information in the data collected by Karl Kirkman and David Pedrick, plotted at right, is on the left-hand side of the graph. Here, the lower Froude number range would coincide with hull speeds in light to medium winds. As model size decreases, it can be seen that the tank results steadily overstate frictional drag, as represented by the resistance coefficient. Small-scale models do not consistently overstate resistance, however; with a different design they can just as easily understate it.

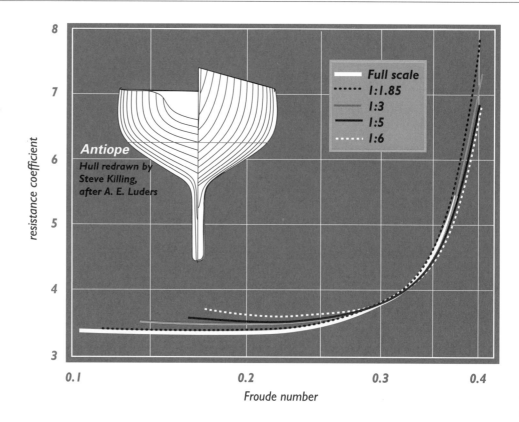

Antiope
Hull redrawn by
Steve Killing,
after A. E. Luders

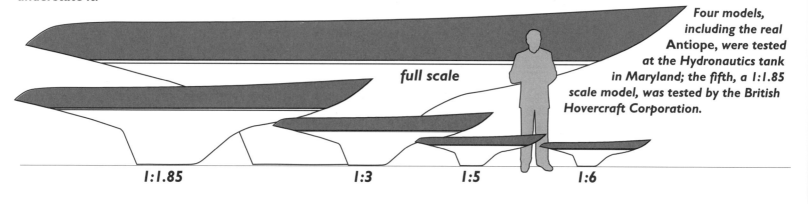

full scale

*Four models,
including the real
Antiope, were tested
at the Hydronautics tank
in Maryland; the fifth, a 1:1.85
scale model, was tested by the British
Hovercraft Corporation.*

1:1.85   1:3   1:5   1:6

FIG. 9.6
Coping with water scaling problems in tank testing

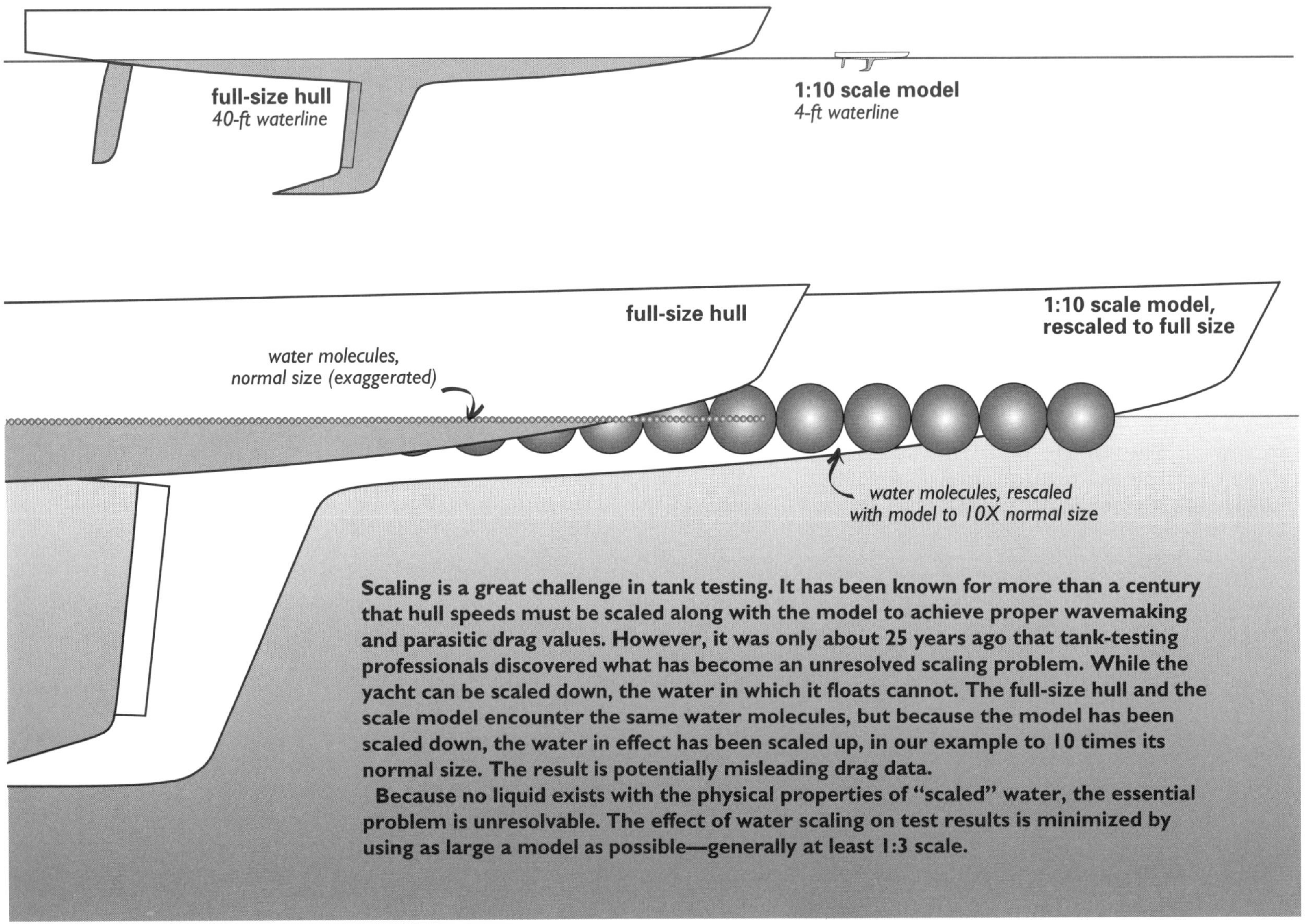

full-size hull
40-ft waterline

1:10 scale model
4-ft waterline

full-size hull

**1:10 scale model,
rescaled to full size**

*water molecules,
normal size (exaggerated)*

*water molecules, rescaled
with model to 10X normal size*

Scaling is a great challenge in tank testing. It has been known for more than a century that hull speeds must be scaled along with the model to achieve proper wavemaking and parasitic drag values. However, it was only about 25 years ago that tank-testing professionals discovered what has become an unresolved scaling problem. While the yacht can be scaled down, the water in which it floats cannot. The full-size hull and the scale model encounter the same water molecules, but because the model has been scaled down, the water in effect has been scaled up, in our example to 10 times its normal size. The result is potentially misleading drag data.

Because no liquid exists with the physical properties of "scaled" water, the essential problem is unresolvable. The effect of water scaling on test results is minimized by using as large a model as possible—generally at least 1:3 scale.

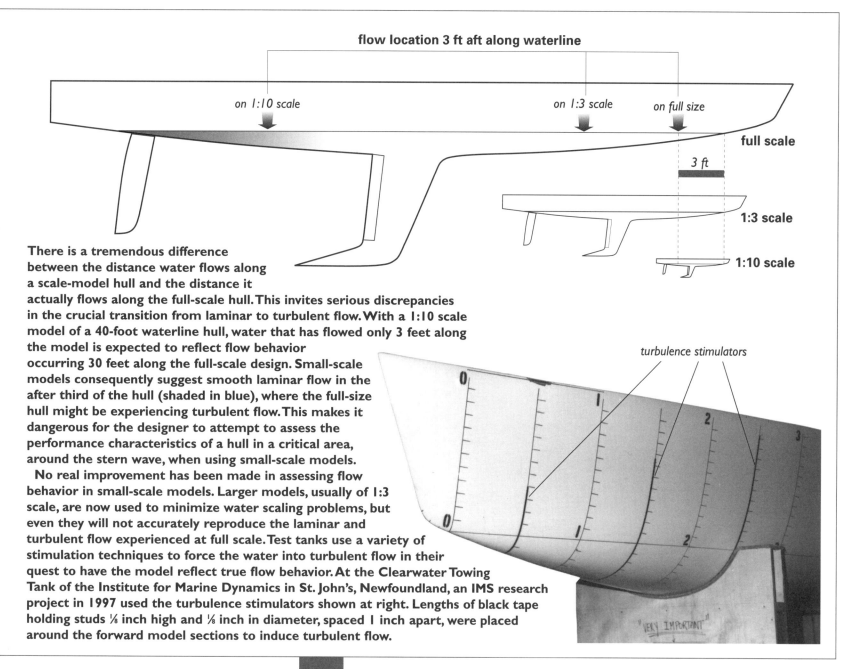

flow location 3 ft aft along waterline

on 1:10 scale   *on 1:3 scale*   *on full size*

full scale

3 ft

1:3 scale

1:10 scale

turbulence stimulators

There is a tremendous difference between the distance water flows along a scale-model hull and the distance it actually flows along the full-scale hull. This invites serious discrepancies in the crucial transition from laminar to turbulent flow. With a 1:10 scale model of a 40-foot waterline hull, water that has flowed only 3 feet along the model is expected to reflect flow behavior occurring 30 feet along the full-scale design. Small-scale models consequently suggest smooth laminar flow in the after third of the hull (shaded in blue), where the full-size hull might be experiencing turbulent flow. This makes it dangerous for the designer to attempt to assess the performance characteristics of a hull in a critical area, around the stern wave, when using small-scale models.

   No real improvement has been made in assessing flow behavior in small-scale models. Larger models, usually of 1:3 scale, are now used to minimize water scaling problems, but even they will not accurately reproduce the laminar and turbulent flow experienced at full scale. Test tanks use a variety of stimulation techniques to force the water into turbulent flow in their quest to have the model reflect true flow behavior. At the Clearwater Towing Tank of the Institute for Marine Dynamics in St. John's, Newfoundland, an IMS research project in 1997 used the turbulence stimulators shown at right. Lengths of black tape holding studs ⅛ inch high and ⅛ inch in diameter, spaced 1 inch apart, were placed around the forward model sections to induce turbulent flow.

FIG. 9.7
Scale error in model testing

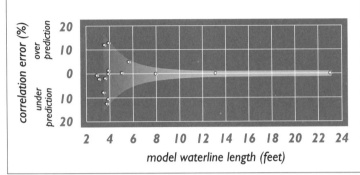

The landmark study by Karl Kirkman and David Pedrick established an irrefutable link between model size and test-tank error. Their results, published in the fall of 1974, revealed how tank testing had been fooling designers of America's Cup yachts as well as production racer-cruisers.

Results from testing upright drag with existing scale models of a variety of designs (replotted here) revealed that with increasingly smaller test models came increasing margins of error between the performances of the test model and the actual yacht. Yacht designs were routinely tested with models of 3 to 4.5 feet, a range in which the study showed correlation errors of greater than 10 percent. Kirkman and Pedrick recommended that models be made at least 10 feet long to avoid this problem—advice that was promptly heeded.

◄ 194 By comparing tank-test results of different-size models of the same hull design, trends were observed, which indicated that model size influenced results beyond the corrective framework of Froude and Reynolds numbers. The small models that were standard at the time gave results that were sometimes low in frictional drag for one design, sometimes high for another, but certainly had more variation than the larger models. The reason the discrepancy was able to snakebite designers like Britton Chance was that the results on a particular small model, although in error, met a fundamental requirement of experimental science: they were totally repeatable.

There was no fault to be found with the integrity of the towing tank—the *Mariner* data appeared wholesome and confidence inspiring. If the model were taken to another tank, that facility would also deliver, within experimental accuracy, the same answers. What makes the detective work difficult in trying to discover the causes of erroneous data, is the variation from one hull design to the next. The results from *Mariner's* tests were too optimistic, while, for example, the predictions for *Antiope,* a benchmark 5.5-Meter design, were too pessimistic. Unless you know the real answer before you start, there is no way to know whether the tank will under- or overpredict the drag of a particular small-scale model.

Part of the investigative work by Kirkman, Pedrick, and the Hydronautics tank involved testing, in concert with others around the world, a "geosim" (geometrically similar) series of hulls. *Antiope,* an A. E. Luders design, was chosen as the standard and was tested at scales varying from full size down to 1:6 (a 4-foot waterline). The trend of these results, as shown in Fig. 9.5, was unmistakable. The drag at low speed, which one would hope would remain independent of scale, marched steadily upward as model size diminished.

The *Antiope* data is so steady and seemingly well behaved that one is tempted to say that surely some sort of correction could be made to bring all the results into line. Indeed, an empirical adjustment could be made to improve the correlation, but unfortunately it would be valid only for *Antiope,* for the model of another design could easily predict trends in the opposite direction. The other obvious conclusion to reach from this plot is that the larger the model, the closer the results relate to the full-size boat. The results from the 1:3 model (8-foot waterline) are encouraging, and those of the 1:1.85 model (13-foot waterline) are truly confidence inspiring.

Some blame in the errors of small-scale testing, it could be argued, lay with the limits of the instrumentation—a small model in which the actual forces measured are on the order of 5 pounds requires more precision than the 200-pound loads on a larger model. But the real culprit was the modeling of frictional drag.

Part of the problem was the separation of flow at the aft end of a hull. (See Fig. 9.6.) The initial flow of water over an object is laminar: smooth streamlines of water begin to pass along the hull. But as the water moves aft, the layer next to the hull is slowed and disturbed by the hull's presence, and this so-called "boundary layer" grows thicker, until the flow detaches or separates.

Our ability to predict separation, a somewhat random phenomenon, from a scale model is far from perfect. Separation of flow from a three-dimensional object like a hull is dependent on many factors, including the shape of the model (presumably the same as the full-scale boat) and the fluid in which the boat is floating (which unfortunately cannot be scaled).

Critical is the actual distance of the separation point from the forward end of the boat—significantly different on the boat and the model. The thickness and turbulence level within the boundary layer depend on (among other things) the distance from the leading edge of the submerged object. If you look at the thickness of the boundary layer 3 feet back from the forward edge of the waterline on a full-size hull, you will find it is the same thickness as the boundary layer 3 feet back on a scale-model version's waterline. It is important to realize that this is not a scaled distance on the model—it is a real 3 feet. Too much of the model is covered with laminar flow. In the case of a 12-Meter tested with a 4.5-foot model, this 3-foot example point with its thin boundary layer would rep-

resent a point 40 feet back on the actual hull, where the boundary layer should be much thicker—in the range of the bustle. It is not a coincidence that this is the area where misleading flow characteristics led to the unusually full shapes of the 1970 defense contenders and the extreme shape of *Mariner* in 1974.

Kirkman and Pedrick's research recommended that the minimum size of models be enlarged to 10 feet to increase the confidence level in results, advice that was duly heeded. The accompanying plot based on their work (Fig. 9.7) shows the rapid deterioration of results with decreased model size. It has now become standard on high-level projects (America's Cup contenders and large cruising yachts) for large models to be used. The upscale tank testing comes with upscale budgets. In 1997, model costs run in the order of $12,000 with testing charges of $3,000 per day. But

The 12-Meter True North I is prepared for testing. Large models have minimized historic problems with misleading tank data, but test tanks must use data-gathering methods with extremely low error margins to achieve reliable results.

a large, more costly model is always better when accuracy is the goal.

Their research raised several other issues that are still being addressed. The first is that frictional drag does not have a simple, direct relationship with Reynolds numbers; rather, there is a certain 3-D component to drag. While the Froude equation treats friction experienced by a surface without regard to its shape, there is significant evidence that a flat plate and a football of the same surface area experience different degrees of frictional drag. As well, conventional wisdom holds that once the Froude number is scaled correctly, wave drag will be modeled correctly. But it appears that wave drag may depend on factors other than the Froude number. Lastly, there is growing concern that laminar and turbulent flow over a hull are not well modeled.

It is a testament to the difficulties of small-scale model testing that we really don't understand their laminar flow problems today much better than we did a quarter-century ago, when *Mariner* refused to sail as her test-tank model predicted. We have not solved the problem of small-scale testing so much as put it behind us simply by using larger models. But even larger models must contend with the unavoidable scaling problem of water behavior, and the solutions are far from definitive.

To attempt a better representation of flow over the hull and the buildup of the boundary layer, turbulence stimulation is often added to the forward edge of the hull and keel with today's models. (See Fig. 9.6.) Each tank has its favorite technique. They vary from sand strips (a 0.5-inch-wide strip of "sandpaper" glued on the forward edge of the hull and keel) to trip wires (approximately 0.05-inch-diameter wires attached for the same purpose) and studs (0.12-inch-diameter by 0.1-inch-long cylinders spaced along the leading edges).

These turbulence stimulation techniques strike the uninitiated as crude. A finely finished model, shaped with milled accuracy, is slathered with glue and sprinkled with sand in order to model the turbulence correctly. Indeed, without care the turbulence generated could just as easily be too great as too little. Judging how much sand, how long a wire, or how many studs should be added to a model is a matter of experience and judgment—an unfortunate situation in a scientific test. Assuming that the turbulence stimulation has been appropriately executed, there is still another hurdle to be jumped. The stimulation technique adds its own extra unwanted drag, which must be corrected for. Various techniques are used to subtract out this drag, but suffice to say here that getting reliable answers from the tank is no simple matter.

As the mathematical model in computer performance prediction software improves each year, the accuracy of predictions that can be made of a yacht's performance follows along in harmony. More diverse yacht types can now be predicted with amazing accuracy, without ever venturing into the tank.

The future of the towing tank, however, is still secure. The mathematical models used in performance prediction software have been built using tank testing, and will not give good predictions unless the boat being analyzed falls within the range of knowledge used to create the software. Predictions for a four-hulled boat with twin keels will not be reliable if the data used to create the program included no such hull form. An unwise designer expects the software to correctly predict the speed of a hull that is radical in nature. The performance of most general-purpose designs can be reliably predicted with software, but the leading edge of the sport has always been, and will continue to be, a prime area for new development. New keel appendages, subtle changes in hull shape, and radical combinations all require the physical modeling that the test tank affords.

CHAPTER 10

America's Cup

Since 1851, yacht racing's
grandest prize has been an
unparalleled focal point of design
innovation—and controversy.

the auld mug: born in controversy

The America's Cup competition began with controversy in 1851 and has deviated little since then, sailing through patches of ill-will and subterfuge. In that hotly contested loop around the Isle of Wight, the schooner *America* raced alone against 14 English rivals—poor odds in anyone's books. With good fortune and excellent speed she won the event. The fairness of the race was never contested, but adjusting the odds of success has turned out to be a commonplace occurrence in the race for the Cup.

Trying to gain the upper hand before the race begins is routine—witness the aggressive jockeying for position at the starting line. But at other times the maneuvering has begun long before any start sequence, back on dry land, as contenders strive to bend the rules of the contest in their favor. High stress levels and big egos ensure that all contestants will explore every avenue, legal and quasi-legal, to win the ornate Auld Mug. For designers, though, the focus is on design. While there have been stories of desperate syndicates diving into competitors' garbage bins to discover their research secrets, the security employed at towing test tanks, computer centers, and design offices ensures that secrets are not shared before the boats hit the water. Those who want to win without getting involved in the politics and bickering of the America's Cup concentrate on producing a better design. Although it is not a guarantee of victory (*Gretel*, a decidedly faster boat, lost to *Weatherly* in 1962 due to superior sailing, as did *Gretel II* to *Intrepid* in 1970), it is the one solid advantage that no one can take away.

Making advances in yacht design invariably occurs within some framework. If a designer is requested to create a faster boat, his immediate reply is, "Faster than what? And with what restrictions?" If there are no restrictions, the boat will simply grow longer, with more draft and more sail area, than what has gone before. In the America's Cup contest, as for most yacht racing events, a measurement rule is used to control the size of the boats. They don't have to be exactly the same, but they must fit within dimensional limits, and relationships between various parameters must be maintained.

After the original contest, the America's Cup organizing committee of the New York Yacht Club, under whose burgee *America* sailed, introduced a measurement rule to attempt to ensure a fairer competition in 1870, but with every passing year limitations in the rule were discovered and a new "perfect" rule was instituted. The rulemakers, who have a task as difficult as that of the designers, have always tried to assess the

The schooner America *triumphs in an 1851 race around the Isle of Wight. A grand sporting tradition, and more than a century of design controversy, is thereby launched.*

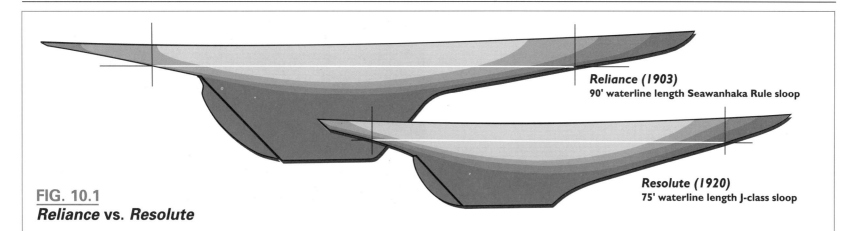

FIG. 10.1
Reliance vs. *Resolute*

FIG. 10.1
Reliance vs. *Resolute*

Reliance (1903)
90' waterline length Seawanhaka Rule sloop

Resolute (1920)
75' waterline length J-class sloop

N. G. Herreshoff's 1903 defender *Reliance* took long overhangs to the extreme to give the yacht an effective waterline when heeled that was far greater than her measured waterline. With an LOA of 144 feet and a LWL of 90 feet, her forward and aft overhangs accounted for more than 50 feet of her overall length.

Herreshoff was instrumental in creating the Universal Rule, the design rule that essentially outlawed the excesses of *Reliance*. His 1920 defender *Resolute,* designed to the "J" category of the new rule, showed much more conservative overhangs and a deeper midsection than *Reliance*. She was also much smaller, measuring 75 feet LWL and 106 feet LOA.

qualities that produce speed in a sailboat. After several modifications the prime factors surfaced—length was introduced into the governing design rule in 1876, sail area was added in 1885, and displacement finally weighed in during the early 1900s. Those three factors have remained in succeeding design rules in varying ratios, but always with the same implications: sail area supplies the power, length permits the speed, and displacement is simply a drag.

the early challenges: the defense never rests

Inequities in the early challenges can be attributed to handicap rules that just weren't up to the job, and to defense organizing committees that wanted to bend if not warp the rules to serve their own best interest of retaining the Cup. The 1871 challenge, for example, saw the British yacht *Livonia* pitted against no less than four American schooners. Each day the Americans would select their best boat, based on the wind and wave conditions, to sail against the lone challenger. If the breezes were gentle they would pick *Columbia,* but for stronger winds the heavier *Sappho* was a better choice. The last two, *Dauntless* and *Palmer,* were held in reserve, but their services were never required—*Columbia* and *Sappho* brushed off the challenger in five races. Also open to constant criticism was the rule requiring the challenger to submit the dimensions of his boat to the defender 10 months before the event, permitting the defending designers to create a boat specifically targeted to trounce the challenger.

The rulemakers struggled to keep pace with the

Measure for measure:
the Universal and International Rules

J-Class
(Universal Rule)

$$\frac{0.18 \times L \times \sqrt{SA}}{\sqrt[3]{DISP}} = 78 \text{ ft}$$

12-Meter Class
(International Rule)

$$\frac{L + \sqrt{SA} + 2d - F}{2.37} = 12 \text{ m}$$

The J-boats, used in four America's Cup matches between 1920 and 1937, were designed to the Universal Rule, an American rating system, while the 12-Meters that competed from 1958 to 1987 were designed to the International Rule, a Euro-pean creation. Despite the great separation between the Cup years of the Js and the Twelves, both eras used design rules that were contempo-raneous when created before the First World War—the Universal Rule in 1903, the International Rule in 1906.

Both rules asked designers to trade off the main ingredients of performance: displacement, sail area, and waterline length.

The Universal Rule took an important step forward for design rules in making displacement part of the rating calculation. While the International Rule's creators did not insert displacement right into their formula, it was nonetheless represented by setting minimum displace-ment levels for waterline lengths in a calculation "outside" the formula.

Both rules also placed length and sail area, the governing determinants of raw power, in the numerator, the top part of the equation, requiring designers to trade one off against the other. The International Rule employed a

Above: 12-Meter Stars & Stripes, 1987 America's Cup winner. Left: restored J-class yacht Shamrock V, 1930 America's Cup challenger. Though separated by more than a half-century, these yachts were designed to similar rules that were created before the First World War.

more complex formula, however. It injected two factors not found in the Universal Rule: girth differ-ence *(d),* which controlled the cross-sectional shape of the hull at its midsection, forcing designs to be deep-bodied and heavy, and freeboard *(F),* which discouraged designers from letting decks get too close to the water—which would beneficially lower the yacht's center of gravity while compromising seaworthiness.

designers. They would watch each successive America's Cup race (and other events that used the same handicap rules) and assess what trends were developing. The Seawanhaka Rule, used from 1885 to 1903, measured only sail area and waterline length and was easy to exploit. Factoring in waterline length was meant to assess the speed potential of the boat, since length has such an influence on the maximum attainable speed. However, waterline length alone is not a good performance indicator. As Nathanael Herreshoff and other designers of the time knew, keeping the waterline length short but extending the ends of the boat in long, low overhangs produces a boat that is faster than the waterline length would indicate. His boats, of which the mammoth 144-foot *Reliance* is a prime example, had huge unmeasured overhangs that would immerse as the boat heeled under a press of canvas. (See Fig. 10.1.) When more hull was immersed, more waterline was naturally created. A rule that measured a single dimension, like waterline length, when the boat was sitting level in the water had no chance of assessing the effective waterline length when it heeled over. This wasn't cheating so much as the designer applying common sense to take advantage of the simplicity of the rule. Success for the designer lay in minimizing the measured waterline, indicating to the rule the boat was slower than it actually was, while maximizing the "real" waterline, which made the boat as fast as possible. This practice, of making boats longer/faster/more powerful than the rules would otherwise perceive, has been at the heart of decades of revisions in design rules.

Reliance's outrageous length illustrated that things were getting out of hand, and not just in terms of design issues. The boats were becoming too big and too expensive. Consequently, the next series in 1920 was contested in what were to become J-class sloops, boats built to the Universal Rule, an American-based measurement rule that exercised much more control over

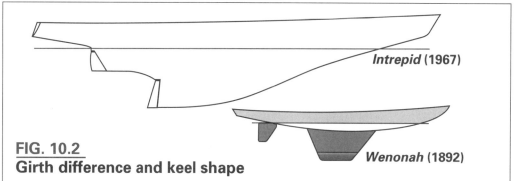

Intrepid (1967)

Wenonah (1892)

FIG. 10.2
Girth difference and keel shape

It's a myth that the International Rule governing 12-Meter design harks back to an era when designers were ignorant of the benefits of a sleeker hull form. The 37.5-foot *Wenonah,* designed by N. G. Herreshoff in 1892, 14 years before the International Rule was written, displayed an elegant, shallow-draft hull with the keel starkly separated from the hull, and a bulb carrying much of the ballast. *Wenonah* belonged to the era of the Seawanhaka Rule, when only waterline length and sail area were measured. The International Rule was written deliberately to encourage hull forms with deep midsections and a minimal separation between hull and keel. The controlling mechanism was the **Girth Difference** penalty. A designer who attempted to tuck up the hull to create greater separation from the keel paid dearly. More keel span meant having to give up sail area or waterline length under the 12-Meter formula. Consequently, the typical Girth Difference settled upon by designers of prewinged keel Twelves, such as *Intrepid,* was minimal, generally around 40 millimeters. Even though she was only about half their size, *Wenonah* had as much or more keel span than the 12-Meters, whose cross-sectional shapes were so restricted by the Girth Difference penalty.

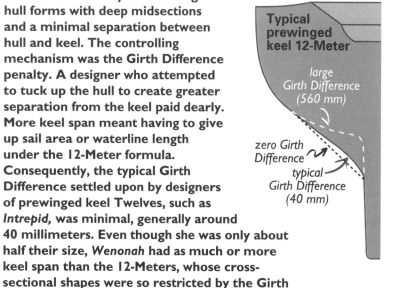

Typical prewinged keel 12-Meter

large Girth Difference (560 mm)

zero Girth Difference

typical Girth Difference (40 mm)

Wenonah

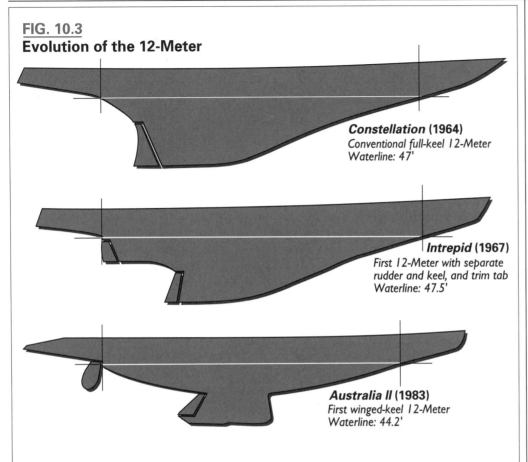

FIG. 10.3
Evolution of the 12-Meter

Constellation (1964)
Conventional full-keel 12-Meter
Waterline: 47'

Intrepid (1967)
*First 12-Meter with separate
rudder and keel, and trim tab
Waterline: 47.5'*

Australia II (1983)
*First winged-keel 12-Meter
Waterline: 44.2'*

Design rules used in high-profile competition typically begin by encouraging "ideal" designs. As the rule comes under more creative pressure, yachts begin to evolve in extreme directions. The evolution of 12-Meter design during the America's Cup is a textbook example. Created in 1906, the International Rule governing 12-Meter design was first used by the America's Cup in 1958. *Constellation* was an "Ideal" Twelve, while *Intrepid* sent the class in a new direction with a separate rudder and keel, employment of a trim tab, and a bustle for better distribution of hull volume. With *Australia II*, Ben Lexcen realized an elusive design dream of producing a small, light Twelve by equipping her with a revolutionary winged keel.

hull shape and brought displacement into the formula. Herreshoff himself helped author the new rule, knowing best what limits designers needed to keep them producing (as the rules committee of New York yacht owners stated) "a wholesome type of yacht." The long overhanging ends seen on *Reliance* would no longer pay off, for example, because the Universal Rule made a more complex calculation of length. Waterline length was now averaged with deck length, and both were measured one-quarter of the beam off centerline to prevent designers from distorting the overhangs.

moderation, please: the Twelves arrive

After the Second World War there was another call for moderation in the design rule governing the America's Cup. The J-class boats were still too expensive to build and maintain and required more than 20 crew. The International Rule, developed in Europe in 1906, was of the same era as the Universal Rule. It had been used with favor in other contests and was promoting good racing in different rated length categories from the 5.5-Meter right up to the 12-Meter. With girth measurements (measured around the hull from one sheerline to the other) controlling the shape of the ends and a minimum displacement calculated for a given waterline length, the measurement committee felt the resulting yachts would be a "healthy" breed.

The 12-Meter, with an overall length of about 70 feet, was chosen for the first America's Cup to be held since 1938, in 1958. With the new class came a new, more exciting style of competition: level racing. Prior to the 1958 match the boats, even though they were designed to a handicap rule, were only required to be within a certain rated size range. Consequently the rating of each boat was not the same, and the elapsed time of each yacht was adjusted after the race in proportion to its rating. If the rating difference was great, the adjustment would be great. This system of time handicapping tended to be confusing for spectators and frustrating for the competitors because stopwatches and mathematics determined how much one competitor was ahead of the other. It could mean that one competitor was actually losing when it looked, boat-for-boat, like it was winning. To eliminate this problem, the new 12-Meter class would provide racing without handicap. Each yacht would have to rate 12.00 meters or less under the International Rule, and the boat that crossed the finish line first would be declared the winner.

To the dismay and confusion of casual observers, the designation of this elite racing class as the "12-Meter" has nothing to do with its overall length, or the length of anything, for that matter—the boom, the waterline, the amount of line on board, or the depth of the competing syndicate's overdraft statement. The limit of 12 meters is governed by a simple formula (see "Measure for measure," page 204) that calls upon the designer to trade off those principal speed-producing factors: length, sail area, and displacement. Because the length and the sail area are in the same part (the numerator) of the equation, if one is increased the other must be correspondingly decreased to maintain a result of 12 meters. The displacement, although not explicitly mentioned in the formula, is controlled by imposing a direct link between length and displacement. For a given waterline length the volume displaced by the hull when floating at the dock (without crew) must be more than

(0.2 x *LWL* + 0.15)³ cubic meters

This means a typical 12-Meter with a waterline of 45 feet would be required to weigh at least 54,736 pounds (displacing 24.2 cubic meters of salt water).

The Girth Difference, which is weighted by a factor of two in the 12-Meter formula, applies to the shape of the midsection. (See Fig. 10.2.) During the measurement process a wire is stretched from a point on the sheer just aft of the middle of the hull, down to another point 1.5 meters below the waterline (usually this point is at the top of the keel). The difference between the length of this wire and the length of a tape measure that travels along the surface of the hull between the same two points is recorded on each side of the yacht. The sum of the two differences is termed the Girth Difference. A hull that has no hollow between the sheer and the bottom of the Girth Difference measurement will have a Girth Difference of zero. But once hollows are introduced into the hull shape, the wire will begin to bridge the gap and the Girth Difference will begin to grow. And as it grows bigger, something else, something beneficial, has to grow smaller.

Because the Girth Difference factor has such a great influence on the rating, it essentially forces the hull to be very deep in the midsection, severely penalizing hulls that are less than 1.5 meters deep. I recall in 1983, as an enthusiastic neophyte in the 12-Meter game, attacking the rule with a childlike

¼" plating

6" radius

2" diameter lightening holes on 5" centers

³/₁₆" plating

24" radius

¼" plating

Designers who dreamed of reducing an aluminum 12-Meter's displacement, or at least of moving some of that displacement out of the hull structure and into the keel, were handcuffed by strict construction standards set down by Lloyd's Register of Shipping. Here is a construction detail for web frame 31 from the author's 12-Meter True North I, showing Lloyd's' exacting specifications for details such as corner radii, the size and spacing of lightening holes, and minimum permissible hull plate thicknesses.

The winged keel was introduced to yachting by the 1983 America's Cup winner **Australia II** *(top). Winged keels became must-have components of all subsequent 12-Meters, including Steve Killing's* **True North 1** *(bottom).*

glee. Viewing the deep, heavy shapes of *Intrepid* and *Courageous,* the Cup winners from 1967 to 1977, it seemed obvious that the way to jump ahead of the competition was elementary: build a boat that has a dinghy-like hull, less volume overall, and a much flatter midsection. The resistance would be reduced, and in particular the wavemaking drag caused by the deep center section and the heavy weight could be greatly improved. But the reality of the rule takes a grip even before the pencil draws its first curve on the Mylar. The Girth Difference holds the midsection deep, while the displacement rule weighs down the boat. Boats drawn to the International 12-Meter Rule cannot stray far from the mold set by the rulemakers back in 1906. With less glee, but the same enthusiasm, I went back looking for smaller gains.

revolution below: the winged keel

From 1958 to 1964, the 12-Meter rule served the America's Cup class well. Over the course of three matches, the successful defenders—*Columbia,* designed by Olin Stephens, *Weatherly,* designed by Phil Rhodes, and *Constellation,* designed by Stephens—were progressively but conservatively improved to become what the designers of the rule had hoped. The boats were getting marginally faster each year but still had deep hulls and full keels with rudders attached to their trailing edge. Then, for the 1967 match, Olin Stephens and his supporting cast of designers at Sparkman & Stephens launched their latest Twelve, *Intrepid,* causing fellow designers to take note. (See Fig. 10.3.)

Stephens had pulled the rule farther than it had ever been stretched before. In truth, 12-Meter design was striving to catch up with advancements in the rest of the yacht design world. Developments in other keel-

boat classes, like a rudder distinctly separated from the keel and a trim tab on the trailing edge of the keel, led Stephens to experiment with the same configurations on a Twelve. With confidence built by scale-model tank testing, he convinced the *Intrepid* syndicate to build the first Twelve to have a separate rudder and a more distinct keel. *Intrepid* also sported a "bustle"—an enlarged skeg between the rudder and keel. The bustle was Stephens' solution to the International Rule's insatiable demand for hull volume, given how much boats designed to the rule were required to displace. Designers toiling under the International Rule were always looking for convenient places to tuck that extra displacement. If volume could be taken out of the hull proper and placed in this new bustle, then the hull could be slimmed and the drag reduced a corresponding amount. *Intrepid,* with her innovative hull shape, won the America's Cup easily in 1967 and again, after modifications by Britton Chance, in 1970.

This was the beginning of a new phase for the 12-Meter rule. With most every design rule, the first few contests employing it see designers creating conventional boats that conform well to each clause of the regulations. But successive generations of boats push the speed and the rule a little further. America's Cup designers wished in vain that they could design exactly what the rule was written to prevent: lighter boats. The only avenues left open to designers were the ones on which the rule's creators, working before the First World War, had not thought to set up roadblocks. The move was on to exploit the design areas the rule did not control. Keels became still more distinct from the hull, with razor-sharp lines at the 1.5-meter measurement depth designed to minimize the Girth Difference factor. Bustles absorbed even more hull volume; graceful bow and stern overhangs were chopped short to minimize weight in the ends. Very soon designers found they were producing boats that were faster by the yardstick of this particular rule, but they were not necessarily more efficient boats.

The America's Cup had become a strange enclave of the yacht design world. While the America's Cup continued to boast of being the ultimate sailing event, the rest of the yachting world was marching steadily into the lead. Although fiberglass had revolutionized the boatbuilding industry in the 1960s in custom and mass-production applications, and had become commonplace by the 1970s, the International 12-Meter Rule still required the boats to be made from wood. In 1974 aluminum was cautiously permitted as a building material. Designers immediately saw the advantages in stiffness, durability, ease of modification, and, to a lesser extent, in weight. The problem wasn't that using aluminum couldn't make Twelves a lot lighter than an equivalent wooden vessel. The problem was that the society governing the construction regulations, Lloyd's Register of Shipping in Southampton, England, wouldn't permit it. They were concerned that the existing boats built in wood retain their competitive status (and value) and therefore set the aluminum weights higher than engineering would seem to call for. In retrospect however, viewing the 12-Meters that sailed in the extreme conditions in Australia in 1987, the aluminum scantlings were not excessive. Many boats exhibited stressed hull plating in the chainplate area after sailing in heavy seas. As aluminum plating flexes over the 16 inches between ribs, the yacht takes on the "hungry dog" look—every rib can be seen. Even *Liberty,* the first American yacht to lose the Cup in 1983, looked strikingly battered while sailing in the comparatively benign conditions off Newport, Rhode Island. But excessive or not, the scantlings were all encompassing, permitting designers freedom to innovate.

Under Lloyd's' "Requirements for 12-Meter International Rating Class Yachts Constructed Of

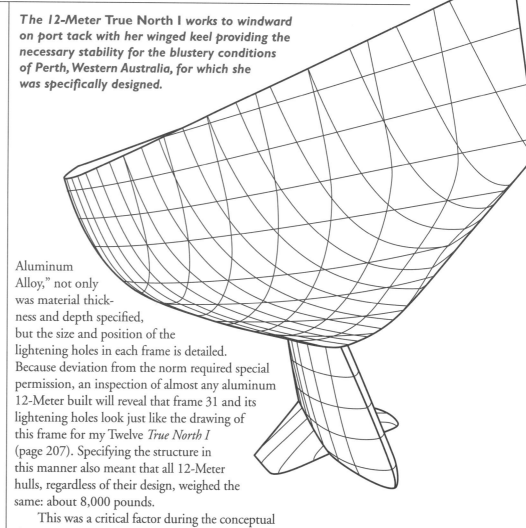

The 12-Meter True North I works to windward on port tack with her winged keel providing the necessary stability for the blustery conditions of Perth, Western Australia, for which she was specifically designed.

Aluminum Alloy," not only was material thickness and depth specified, but the size and position of the lightening holes in each frame is detailed. Because deviation from the norm required special permission, an inspection of almost any aluminum 12-Meter built will reveal that frame 31 and its lightening holes look just like the drawing of this frame for my Twelve *True North I* (page 207). Specifying the structure in this manner also meant that all 12-Meter hulls, regardless of their design, weighed the same: about 8,000 pounds.

This was a critical factor during the conceptual design phase of a 12-Meter. When a designer is dealing with the displacement of a boat, he knows that it is not simply some number in a rating rule. It will ultimately take physical form. The boat will weigh something, and its weight will be the sum of its parts. The 12-Meter rule already told him he couldn't have less weight within a given waterline. His instinct then was to take the

FIG. 10.4
12-Meter keel center of gravity

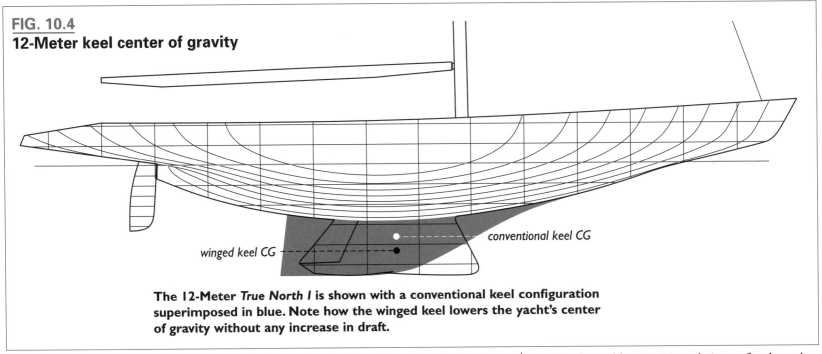

winged keel CG

conventional keel CG

The 12-Meter *True North I* is shown with a conventional keel configuration superimposed in blue. Note how the winged keel lowers the yacht's center of gravity without any increase in draft.

weight he was forced to live with and put it where it would do the most good. Fundamentally, he wanted that weight as low in the boat as possible, so that it was contributing to the stability and hence the power of the boat. He wanted it out of the ends, where it contributed to pitching motion; this is why Twelves started losing their graceful bows and sterns. He wanted it as low as possible overall, which meant hulls started getting lower to the water as freeboard was reduced—a strategy that also lowered the position of the crew's weight. He could take volume (hence displacement) out of the drag-inducing beam of the boat and stuff it down in the bustle, where it caused less trouble. And if he could, he would take as much of the boat's displacement out of the structure of the hull, cast it in lead, and put it deep down in the keel, where it would actually do some good by helping keep the boat upright.

But the problem 12-Meter designers faced wasn't just that the rule tied a given displacement to a given waterline. Lloyd's' scantlings wouldn't let them take weight out of the structure of the hull and put it in the keel. The only unblocked avenue the designers had left to explore in the battle with displacement was the keel itself. By changing the very nature of the keel, perhaps the designer could find a way to put more of the boat's weight where it would do the most good.

The Americans had staged yet another successful defense in 1980 with the Sparkman & Stephens design *Freedom,* although for a moment it had looked like there would be a true design breakthrough. *Australia,* modified from her 1977 challenge, sprung on the American defenders a radical bendy-rig sail plan copied from the British contender. A flexible fiberglass top section on the mast allowed her to carry a huge amount of unmeasured mainsail area. It allowed her to win one light-air race and give the Americans a scare. But when the series was over the guardians of the 12-Meter rule promptly outlawed the device. And while innovative, it had no substantial effect on the basic hull shape of the competing yachts. In 1983 rumor had it that the America's Cup 12-Meters, as magnificent as they were to look at, had pegged the speedometer and there was no room left for improvement.

Designers were busy sanding and polishing an old concept that really needed some major rework with a chainsaw. Chop off the hull to a shallower depth. Deepen the keel. Widen the hull. In effect, replace the 12-Meter rule with something altogether more modern. But the conservative sailing establishment wasn't ready to abandon the class, and while the Twelve was still active, the Australians wanted another chance to squeeze some more speed from the rule. Guided by syndicate leader Alan Bond and designer Ben Lexcen (who had tried the bendy-rig caper together in 1980), they launched a well-shrouded secret called *Australia II*.

When Ben Lexcen tackled the 12-Meter rule yet again (*Southern Cross* in 1974 and *Australia* in 1977 and 1980 were his first efforts), he was still stifled by the limitations on hull depth and weight but decided to make a direct attack on the shallow keel draft. The rule limited the maximum depth of the keel below the waterline to 16 percent of the waterline length plus 500 millimeters. A 45-foot waterline boat would thus have a draft limit of 8.8 feet. To imagine what would have happened if the draft limit were deeper, just consider the America's Cup class yachts of 1995. Even with a generous draft limit of 4.0 meters (13.1 feet), every boat designed to this rule had a keel that stretched down to within millimeters of the limit. Designers know that the span of the keel is directly linked with upwind performance. The extra efficiency (meaning low leeway and low induced drag) of the high aspect

ratio keel allows its area to be reduced compared to a medium or low aspect ratio keel on the same hull, which in turn lowers the parasitic (skin friction) drag. Unless some other restriction prevails, like structural strength, then keels under any design rule will always be stretched to the maximum permitted draft.

If Lexcen had the luxury of making the keel deeper he would have taken it, but he didn't, since the design rule forbade him. Instead he set about to improve a keel that is limited in draft. He needed some way to overcome both ballasting and performance weaknesses of a shallow-draft keel.

In 12-Meters there is a special impetus for designers to improve stability. The stability is not measured, and so it is not a factor in calculating the rating. The more stable the boat is, the faster it will be in heavy air upwind, because the designer does not have to pay a rating penalty for the improvement in performance.

With a shallow keel, the center of gravity of the lead ballast is closer to the hull than desired. By increasing the length of the bottom of the keel and reducing that of the top, the center of gravity drops. Simply by reshaping the available ballast, the designer can increase stability to a value equivalent to that of a much deeper keel, but a new problem now arises: hydrodynamic efficiency. The water flow around this "upside-down" keel is not clean and tidy; in particular, the lower section produces little lift due to a large quantity of water that flows around the bottom of the keel from the high- to the low-pressure side, which is why keels aren't upside down in the first place. The drag of this new configuration negates any benefit from the increased stability. Without further work the inverted keel profile would not be a winner.

As it happened, syndicate head Alan Bond insisted that for the 1983 Cup summer Lexcen design a second, more conservative Twelve, eventually campaigned by the Royal Yacht Club of Victoria. *Challenge 12*

One of New Zealand's fiberglass Twelves leads the fleet into the leeward mark at the 1986 12-Meter Worlds off Fremantle, Australia. The New Zealand challenge built a pair of identical sisterships from this material, the first—and last—of their kind.

flow slipping around its bottom, but a careful analysis had to be made of their appropriate size and angle. If the wings were too big, the additional wetted surface drag would slow the boat. If they were angled down too much at the forward edge, the induced drag (drag due to lift) would hurt the downwind performance. By adjusting the angle of the wings to approximately 3 degrees bow-down, they would align with the direction of local water flow passing under the hull so that they produced no lift when sailing downwind. As long as the wings gave some positive lift when the boat was heeled, an overall benefit could be realized. A secondary but nonetheless significant advantage to the wings was their weight. Casting them in lead moved another 4,000 pounds to the bottom of the keel, increasing the stability another notch. The final keel, small in area with a low center of gravity and only slightly larger wetted surface area than usual (due to the wings), when mounted on an appropriate hull could significantly enhance performance.

In continued tank testing during the *Australia II* design phase, this keel began to show promise, but it would not excel on just any hull. For the light airs off Newport, Rhode Island, it had to be matched up with a small hull and a large sail plan. Reducing the length of a 12-Meter would normally have significant stability implications. In the same year, Johan Valentijn produced a boat for the American Freedom syndicate called *Magic,* perhaps the smallest and lightest Twelve ever built. Light 12-Meters can get that way only by reducing their ballast weight and in turn their stability. With rigging and mast weights regulated and structure not open for interpretation, the only heavy object left to lighten was the keel. *Magic*'s performance in a breeze was so disappointing, presumably because her stability was so low, that shortly after she was launched, the boat was offered for sale to help pay for a replacement.

But in the case of *Australia II,* another small, light

addressed the stability issue by sporting a "fat keel," a fairly conventional keel that had a much thicker chord measurement to pack as much displacement as low in the boat as possible. What the keel gave up in hydrodynamic performance it was expected to surpass in overall performance through increased stability. *Challenge 12* proved to be a good Twelve, and her ultimate shortfall in the challenge selection trials that summer owed more to her syndicate's financial straits than any performance problems. But she was not the breakthrough Lexcen was looking for. At the same time he was designing *Challenge 12,* Lexcen was pursuing a radical improvement for Alan Bond's effort by figuring out how to make an upside-down keel work.

For Lexcen, the solution to the hydrodynamic efficiency problem lay in wings. Mounted to the keel's lower end, they could be used to reduce the amount of

Twelve, stability was more than adequate because of the low center of gravity of the winged keel. *Australia II* weighed in at around 52,000 pounds, compared to 55,000 pounds for a typical 12-Meter. Without each of the parts fitting the philosophy as it did—the inverted keel, the wings, the light weight, and the short hull—the boat could not have been a success. And a success she certainly was, becoming the first non-American yacht ever to win the America's Cup. The upside-down keel capsized a 132-year winning streak, and sent the Cup Down Under for 1987.

plastic fantastic: the fiberglass Twelves

In 1984 Lloyd's Register of Shipping received several requests for fiberglass (also known as glass-reinforced polyester, or GRP) scantlings for 12-Meters. The recreational sailing yacht market had boomed in the 1970s with fiberglass being the material of choice, and now the world was full of these long-lasting easy-to-form sailboats. But the America's Cup wasn't quite sure yet. During the startup phase for the *True North* Challenge in 1984 I sent a request for what I assumed would be a standard copy of Lloyd's' fiberglass scantlings and received a telex from Lloyd's Register of Shipping that included the following:

> "...The society has not contemplated writing rules for G.R.P. construction as it is considered that no material advantage could be gained by designing in G.R.P. without using high strength reinforcements (.i.e. Kevlar, Carbon fibre etc.) the use of which were not considered acceptable to the I.Y.R.U. Keel Boat committee in 1981.
>
> "...if we received a submission in G.R.P.

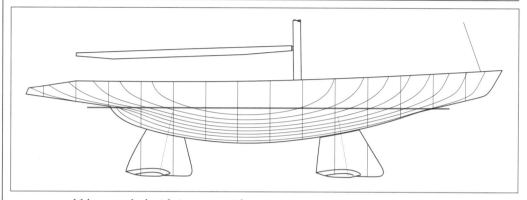

we would have to deal with it as a special case, equating it weight-wise and strength-wise to aluminum...."

Although fiberglass was to be regulated to equate to aluminum in strength and weight, the advantage Lloyd's failed to recognize was the local panel stiffness of fiberglass. Because the boat could have a thicker cored hull (perhaps 1-inch thick compared to the $\frac{3}{16}$-inch aluminum), the deflection between frames would be greatly reduced. The only fiberglass 12-Meters ever built were launched for the 1987 series by the New Zealand challenge, which had essentially written its own scantlings and had Lloyd's approve them. This began the often vocal conflict between the New Zealanders and Dennis Conner, who was in Australia to win back the trophy he had lost in 1983.

The New Zealand team felt they had built a superior boat with the "new" material while Conner, echoing Lloyd's' claim that advantages due to a better material are not permitted, blurted out at a press conference "...why would you build a boat out of fiberglass... unless you wanted to cheat?" That comment, although not atypical for the event, didn't win Conner any friends, especially after the New Zealand boat was remeasured and declared perfectly legal.

The rest of the world never got a chance to find out

Wild and crazy is the order of the day when brainstorming breakthroughs as an America's Cup designer. Steve Killing investigated the possibility of twin "steerable" winged keels for his 12-Meter True North I, and went as far as producing an engineering study. But performance evaluation concluded the concept would produce too much drag with the extra wetted surface, and the concept was scrapped at the drawingboard.

The 1983 America's Cup winner Australia II (KA 6) paces with True North I in windy Western Australia during the last-ever 12-Meter Worlds in 1986.

After the America's Cup was shipped back to the San Diego Yacht Club by Dennis Conner, the New Zealand team, whom he had so annoyed with his "cheaters" press conference—and whom he had defeated in the 1987 challengers' finals—put a magnifying glass to the original deed of gift of the trophy and responded with its unorthodox "Big Boat" challenge. The 110-foot New Zealand monohull, which fit none of the existing design rules, was slapped in the face by the American multihull *Stars & Stripes*.

That 1988 skirmish, which spent more time in courtrooms than on racecourses, would prompt the sailors and organizers of the Cup to tighten the rules and provided the impetus to create a new rule: the International America's Cup Class.

front-row seat: designing for the Cup

For the 1987 Canadian *True North* America's Cup Challenge, I was the leader of a small design team that included Bill Goman concentrating on construction details and John Hemingway researching keels and wings. We had technical backup from DeHavilland Aircraft and the Ontario Research Foundation (now Ortec), and computer support from Hewlett Packard and Control Data.

At the outset of a design project as huge as the America's Cup, most designers would admit there is never a shortage of ideas to investigate—the problem is finding some way of weeding out the bad ones, of finding that rose amongst the other prickly bushes. The bundle of ideas are pulled from the "investigate this someday" file that builds up over years of designing, from unsolicited mail that just floats in, and from conversations that get out of hand during late-night research. I could categorize the bulk of the mail that

if fiberglass 12-Meters made any sense. After Conner, sailing the aluminum *Stars & Stripes,* won the America's Cup that year, 12-Meters were never again used for Cup competition. Once out of the Cup limelight, the class's entire raison d'être since 1958, all design and construction activity ceased in these elegant high-tech anachronisms. I have no doubt, however, if the 12-Meter class had continued as the vessel of choice for the America's Cup, that Canada for one would have chosen dependable fiberglass as its building material, if for no other reason than the pool of skilled fiberglass boatbuilders dwarfs the aluminum labor force.

gets sent to an America's Cup designer as "well beyond left field"—my collection includes keels that move fore and aft to balance the boat, keels that remain vertical while the boat heels, masts that remain vertical while the boat heels, inflatable keel foils that can form efficient asymmetric foils, surface coatings that reduce drag, hull shapes that resemble whales ("nature must be right"), and lightweight carbon fiber masts. Some ideas, like carbon fiber masts, canting keels, and surface coatings you might recognize as innovations that did find acceptance, but not in the 12-Meter class, where they were specifically prohibited.

Since the depth of America's Cup experience in Canada was limited (the only challenge in recent history before the *True North* Challenge was *Canada 1* in 1983, in which I worked on the design with Bruce Kirby), we decided to approach the event with a two-boat campaign. We simply did not have the budget of a Dennis Conner–style five-boat research institution. One conservative boat and one more radical development to push the envelope would be the limit of our resources.

In 1983 *Australia II* had just wrestled the Cup away from the United States in a tense 4-3 battle. Technology, tank testing, and a winged keel had won the event for Australia, and the United States, proud of its high-tech industries, was ashamed of the loss. The rest of the world, however, was encouraged to see a boat win the event without the familiar stars and stripes ensign flying from the transom—if Australia could win the Cup, then so could we.

The conservative *True North I* was my version of what *Australia II* needed to be to excel in the windy waters off Fremantle, Australia. Applying the winged keel philosophy to a longer waterline hull, I arrived at a heavier boat with less sail area.

While our evolutionary process of design continued in the *True North* Challenge, we investigated one

"revolutionary" detail with help from the Ontario Research Foundation—a surface coating that passively, not actively, released drag-reducing chemicals into the boundary layer of the hull. The goal was to reduce the skin-friction drag of the water passing over the hull surface, and long-chain polymers have been proven to be able to do that. However, the only successful applications of these slippery liquids have involved actively dripping them into the water just forward of the bow or letting them ooze from perforations in the boat. That practice had been outlawed for all sailboat races. However, we hoped to develop a coating that could be painted onto the hull the night before the race (the boats are lifted out of water each night) that contained the polymer held in a carrier, much like a soft paint. On the way to the race course the carrier would slowly dissolve and start to release the polymer, which could then do its job of reducing drag during the race. In drag tests in the laboratory, the coatings did reduce the drag for a time, but once the polymer had been released, the remaining surface resembled sandpaper,

To establish ideal waterline lengths for his 1986 12-Meters **True North I** *and* **II,** *the author "sailed" the designs around a computerized virtual racecourse using meteorological data from the actual race site off Fremantle, Australia. In typical conditions there was little to choose between designs with waterlines of between 44 and 46 feet—all completed the course within seconds of an elapsed time of 3:42:00. With a wind speed increase of 40 percent, however, the longer waterline designs gained an increasing performance advantage. The lesson: a "big" Twelve, around 46 feet LWL, would suffer no performance penalty in typical conditions, and offer up a huge advantage when the wind really blew. The author set the waterline of* **True North I** *at 44.75 feet, of* **True North II** *at 46 feet.*

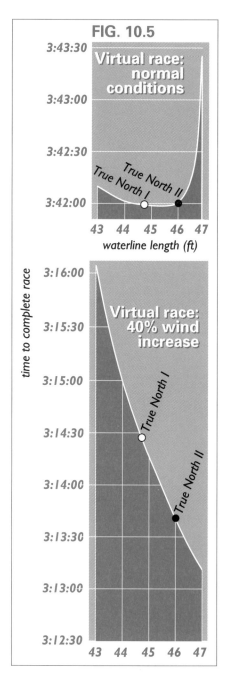

FIG. 10.5

Virtual race: normal conditions

waterline length (ft)

time to complete race

Virtual race: 40% wind increase

with small pockets where the grains of polymer, now washed away, had been held. That remaining rough surface had significantly more drag than a conventionally prepared smooth hull. The chance of getting the benefit of the reduced drag during the time period of the race and avoiding the added drag of the depleted carrier was slim—the timing was too critical. We did not apply the coating to any of our hulls.

Now, 10 years later, and away from the America's Cup hype, the idea looks rather unethical. We were circumventing a rule in both detail and intent and had we succeeded I am sure the following year a rewording of the rule would have been brought into place to prevent even the "passive" use of friction-reducing coatings. But in the America's Cup arena such radical schemes were, and still are, all part of the game.

Coincidentally, we were not the only team thinking of reducing the skin friction. Just before the finals of the 1987 series in Australia, Dennis Conner's program applied a 3M self-adhesive product called riblets to the outside hull surface of *Stars & Stripes* to reduce drag. The grooves on these sheets are reminiscent of the surface of a vinyl phonograph record, except that they run fore and aft, not in a circular pattern. When lined up with the direction of flow they alter the boundary layer and reportedly reduce the parasitic drag by up to 10 percent. Their application had been so successful in rowing shells, where the direction of flow is well defined, that they had been banned, but the sailing world had yet to experience them.

If any sailing conditions were not meant for riblets, it was the rough rail-down waters off Fremantle. With hulls pitching and slamming through waves, it is unlikely that the grooves were even close to the required alignment with the water flow of 30 degrees or less—with streamlines misaligned, research showed the riblets would cause more drag, not less. No one really knows if the high-tech covering helped Conner

win the event in 1987 (my suspicion is that at best it was an even trade-off), but one outcome was predictable. Riblets were later banned.

The International Yacht Racing Rules were modified in 1989 to read:

63 Skin Friction
A yacht:
(a) shall not eject or release from a container any substance (such as polymer); or
(b) unless otherwise prescribed by her class rules, shall not have specially textured hull or appendage surfaces; the purpose of which is, or could be, to reduce the frictional resistance of her surface by altering the character of the flow of water inside the boundary layer.

I suspect that our *True North* design process paralleled many other syndicates in our quest for speed. It is quite common to find most design groups working with the same tools—most have access to the same historical data and software since the market is now international. For example, it is probably safe to say that the Velocity Prediction Programs (VPP) used by every syndicate stemmed from the MIT Pratt Project, a series of systematic tank tests conducted to determine hull parameters that influence lift and drag, and most of the computer code for theoretical analysis began with a program called VSAero.

The Velocity Prediction Program (see Chapter 8) is the real workhorse of any yacht development program. In an America's Cup program it would be used to assemble performance data of various parts of the boat into a "sailing" model. For example, if tank testing (see Chapter 9) were used to predict the lift and drag characteristics of the hull, and a wind-tunnel study was completed to predict the sail forces, the VPP would combine those values to determine how fast the boat would sail in any wind speed and direction.

In the early stages of a project, and *True North* was no exception, neither tank nor wind-tunnel testing has been performed and consequently internal computer models must be used—equations that relate hull, keel, and sail shape to lift and drag. The accuracy of these math models is critical to the success of investigations, and proprietary changes are made by each designer or VPP specialist to fine-tune their program to better analyze a specific style of boat. Improved versions of the VPP are both coveted and marketable.

The VPP internal math model can usually be used with confidence to investigate major size variations. A systematic series of length changes was made to my base 12-Meter hull shape to vary the waterline from 43 to 47 feet, which was beyond the then-popular range of lengths. At this stage of the analysis it was important to ensure that each candidate boat was designed to rate as a legal 12-Meter yacht so that when the length was altered, the beam, depth, and sail area had to be massaged to keep the rating at a steady 12.00 meters. Each hull was matched with three different keels and sailed with three stabilities to attempt to find an optimum from the entire matrix.

The output from the VPP can be viewed in many ways, but one of the most useful is by postprocessing the performance data through a race analysis program in which you virtually "race" the boat around a particular course. For the 1987 Fremantle event, the program would "race" the boats (one at a time with no interboat tactics) around the America's Cup course starting at 1:00 P.M. in a building wind (from the his-

Top to bottom: **True North 1, Courageous,** *and* **Victory 83** *compete at the 1986 12-Meter Worlds off Fremantle, Australia. The World Championships, held exactly one year before the America's Cup, were used by designers as a testing ground.*

torical Australian weather data) and predictions made of elapsed time.

The wind speeds expected on the racecourse have a profound effect on the parameters of the boat to be designed. The influence of wind speed can be seen in the preliminary analysis to determine the waterline length of *True North I* and *II.* (See Fig. 10.5.) The time required to sail an 8-leg, 24.3-nautical-mile America's Cup course was predicted for each length of boat. This analysis used the average daily wind speed for each hour of the day with a race start of 1:00 P.M. and indicated that the difference between a 44-foot waterline and a 46-foot waterline was slight, but the penalty for a 47-foot waterline could not be ignored. However, if the same analysis was performed with a higher wind strength (40 percent higher taken as an example), the analysis showed that the larger boat was heavily favored.

The sizes of the two *True North* challengers were selected based on a wind spectrum similar to the lower one shown in Fig. 10.5. The first boat, typified by me as a conservative improvement of *Australia II,* was built with a waterline length of 44 feet, 9 inches—longer than I believed the original *Australia II* to have been, with the intent that the resulting boat would be a heavy air version of the successful winged keel 12-Meter. At the World Championships in Australia the year before the America's Cup, this prediction turned out to be true. We handily beat *Australia II,* but ran in the middle of the rest of the fleet.

The choice of a 46-foot waterline length for *True North II* was, at the time, a bold move. This was I believe the longest 12-Meter designed since *Intrepid* in 1967, a wise choice I thought for what was predicted to be the windiest America's Cup ever held. Since the second *True North* never got to see the waters of Australia (lack of funds halted the project in the spring of 1986) the design loop, comparing the actual to the predicted performance, could not be closed. If I were

to rationalize I would note that the reported waterline length of *Stars & Stripes,* another large 12-Meter and the eventual winner that year, was within 4 inches of *True North II*'s. Perhaps significant, perhaps not.

Many people have commented to me that launch day must be a great relief for the designer: his work is now done and he can relax a bit while the crew learns how to get the most out of the boat. Unfortunately, here the most difficult part of a designer's job begins.

The designer must piece together the performance puzzle to determine in what conditions the boat is not reaching its potential and, more important, why not. Pride and egos must be left aside (a difficult task for some people) for the good of the project. If the hull is bad, then change it; if the keel needs longer wings, then bolt them on; if the sails are too deep aft, then re-cut them; if the crew doesn't have the necessary skill, then train them.

At the end of the 1986 12-Meter World Championships, we all agreed that *True North I* could perform better—on the "to change" list were the keel (by a casting error it was made too thick), the wings (too large in area and too short), and the mast (which flexed too much while sailing in heavy seas). I was also convinced that the longer waterline length of *True North II,* scheduled for launch about four weeks later, would be an asset.

None of the hopes for improvement ever came to fruition. Upon our return to Canada, the funding for *True North* stopped, and despite an attempted merger with the other Canadian syndicate, *Canada II, True North* never went as fast again. Four months later *True North I* and a still unfinished *True North II* sat lonely and forgotten in a trucker's yard.

Happily, today *True North I* and *II* are sailing in St. Maarten with *Canada II* and *Stars & Stripes* at the 12-Meter Challenge, where anyone can join in for a modest fee and sail in a 12-Meter match race.

agreeing to disagree: the 1988 mismatch

In the 1987 America's Cup, New Zealand was the new kid on the block, for although the country had long excelled in international sailing events it had never before entered the best-known of yachting competitions. Michael Fay, the merchant banker who launched the country's first Cup challenge, had a spirit that suited the competition well: quietly but fiercely competitive. He entered Cup competition in what turned out to be the last year of the 12-Meter era—an ending that was facilitated by Fay himself.

New Zealand made a seemingly invincible Cup debut with its two fiberglass "plastic fantastic" Twelves and was the odds-on favorite to become the challenger, but was beaten in the trials finals by Dennis Conner in *Stars & Stripes*. The harsh words exchanged between Conner and the New Zealand camp over the course of the challengers' elimination series set the stage for a rivalry that would last for at least the next 10 years.

Having come so close to winning in 1987—for if the New Zealanders had gotten past Conner they would almost certainly have defeated the Australian defenders—Fay didn't want to wait the usual four years until the next scheduled Cup event. Instead, he and his lawyers had a close look at the 1887 Deed of Gift. (The original invitation for challengers was issued in 1857; the Deed was amended in 1956 and 1985). The document lays out in somewhat casual fashion the rules governing the challenges for the America's Cup. Fay's camp discovered that the document makes no mention of four-year intervals, 12-Meter yachts, or multiple challengers sailing off to see who will win the privilege of racing against the defender. Most important, the language of the deed suggested that the

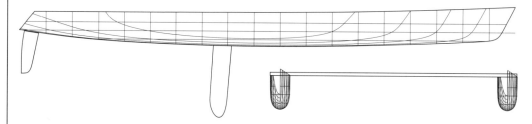

Author Steve Killing practiced "forensic yacht design" for the 1988 New Zealand challenge, analyzing photographs of the catamaran Stars & Stripes. Mylar overlays were drawn (as shown in this composite image) to estimate her shape so that her performance could be predicted. From this analysis, tactical options for the New Zealand "Big Boat" could be derived.

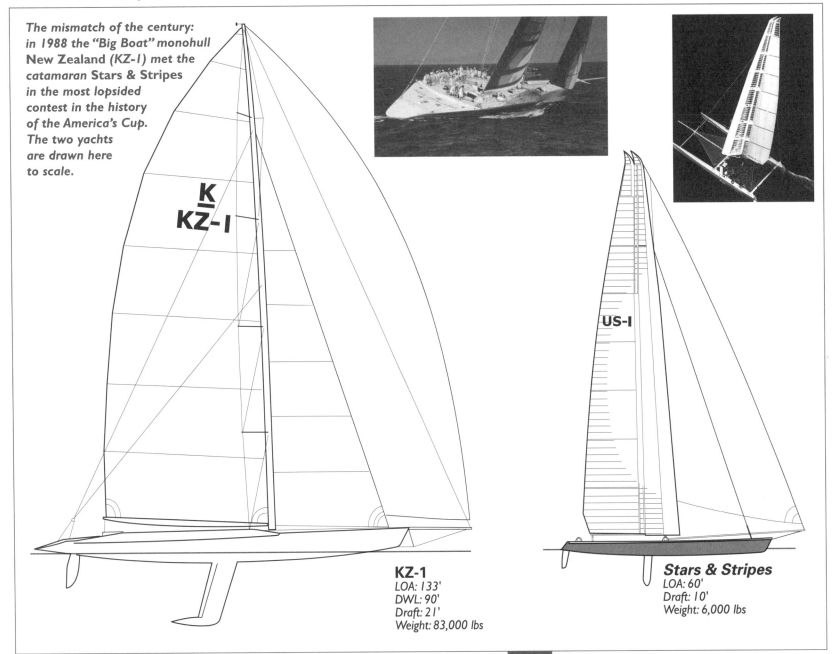

The mismatch of the century: in 1988 the "Big Boat" monohull New Zealand (KZ-1) met the catamaran Stars & Stripes in the most lopsided contest in the history of the America's Cup. The two yachts are drawn here to scale.

K̲
KZ-1

US-1

KZ-1
LOA: 133'
DWL: 90'
Draft: 21'
Weight: 83,000 lbs

Stars & Stripes
LOA: 60'
Draft: 10'
Weight: 6,000 lbs

America's Cup was supposed to be a challenger-driven, and not a defender-driven, contest. As a challenger, Fay was not interested in taking directions from a back-seat driver—the new defender of record, the San Diego Yacht Club.

The eligible boats and the challenging procedure are described simply in these excerpts from the 1887 Deed of Gift:

"This Cup is donated upon the conditions that it shall be preserved as a perpetual Challenge Cup for friendly competition between foreign countries. [This is a clause all competing nations should reread once in a while.]

"The competing yachts or vessels, if of one mast, shall be not less than forty-four feet nor more than ninety feet on the load waterline; if of more than one mast they shall not be less than eighty feet nor more than one hundred and fifteen feet on the load waterline.

"The Challenging Club shall give ten months' notice, in writing, naming the days for the proposed races; but no race shall be sailed in the days intervening between November 1st and May 1st if the races are to be concluded in the Northern Hemisphere; and no race shall be sailed in the days intervening between May 1 and November 1 if the races are to be concluded in the southern hemisphere. Accompanying the ten months' notice of challenge there must be sent the name of the owner and certificate of the name, rig, and following dimensions of the challenging vessel, namely, length on load water-line; beam at load water-line and extreme beam; and draught of water; which

dimensions shall not be exceeded; and a custom-house registry of the vessel must also be sent as soon as possible. Center-board or sliding keel vessels shall always be allowed to compete in any race for this Cup..."

With this seemingly straightforward document at hand, the New Zealand challenge prepared their attack. Designer Bruce Farr was commissioned to create a boat optimized to the light winds off San Diego that would satisfy the Deed of Gift's length restrictions. Farr's resulting boat was long for maximum ultimate speed, narrow on the waterline to reduce both the skin friction and wavemaking resistance, wide on deck for maximum use of the crew's weight while hiking, and deep in the water to permit an efficient keel. The official challenge from New Zealand included the following information:

Waterline length: 90 feet
Beam waterline: 14 feet
Beam max: 26 feet
Draft: 21 feet

As required by the Deed, 10 months' advance warning was given by the challenger and a three-race match was suggested: two windward-leeward races and one triangle race.

It took the San Diego Yacht Club some time to respond to New Zealand's request for a race in 1988—they were busy organizing what they thought was to be the next America's Cup race for 1990 or 1991 in 12-Meters. Conventional challenges had begun to flow in from countries around the world, and the Fay gauntlet was thought to be a bit of a joke. But Fay was not laughing, and with the help of the courts forced the San Diego Yacht Club to listen. The New Zealand challenge was legitimate and all other countries, annoyed and

In the 1988 series, the small American catamaran had a speed potential almost twice that of the New Zealand super-monohull. To avoid further such nonevents, all interested parties agreed on a new design rule and terms of competition for 1992.

stunned, were forced to sit on the sidelines.

San Diego's battle plan, once it was forced to accept the Fay challenge, was to accommodate the rogue New Zealand challenge with a minimum of fuss and risk of losing, and get on with holding a "real" America's Cup in 12-Meters. Later Fay and San Diego tried to ease the pain by offering challengers' slots to other nations, but neither could agree on what dimensions these boats must have. (A U.K. syndicate, in a move not unlike that of Fay, decided simply to build a boat, called *Blue Arrow,* that in their mind was appropriate for the event. The radical machine, with a single hull stabilized by twin outriggers and hydrofoils, was as distasteful and unacceptable to Fay as the catamaran San Diego came up with.)

Meanwhile, the designers and builders were under way. In New Zealand the challenger was nearing com-

pletion. The daring "big boat" intrigued sailors as the first construction photos made their way into the press. A rather open attitude at the launch revealed even more. Farr had picked a weight of about 83,000 pounds for his 90-foot waterline racer, which gave a displacement-to-length ratio of 50.8—radically light for a monohull yacht. A light boat would mean good acceleration and surfing potential, but not necessarily good stability. The stability requirement was tempered by the expected low winds in San Diego of 10 knots or less, and Farr had two other ways to hold the boat up straight. The wings that flared out on each side of the boat had room for 30 crewmembers to put their cumulative 5,200 pounds to good use as movable ballast. The permanent ballast was set at 21 feet below the waterline and was estimated to have been 57,000 pounds. Farr knew it was important for safety considerations that all the stability not be supplied by the crew. If an unexpected wind shift caught the crew hiking on the wrong side of the boat, a capsize would be inevitable. To avoid this, Farr limited the contribution of the crew's stability to 15 percent of the total when the boat is heeled 20 degrees. Another risk he took, banking on light winds, was installing the permanent deck wings, as they limited the heel angle to about 25 degrees. Any greater heel and they would be immersed in the water, severely slowing the boat.

The hull construction of *New Zealand,* designated KZ-1 as the first of a new K-class yacht, was carbon fiber and Kevlar, using epoxy resins baked at elevated temperatures—55°C for the first 24 hours and then 60°C for another day (according to *Seahorse,* May 1988). The mast was also carbon fiber to provide light weight where it is so vital: well above the deck. A light mast contributes significantly to stability—or, perhaps better stated, a heavy mast can severely reduce stability. To shave more weight from the mast, the spar's cross section was reduced in size by altering the staying arrangement. The side shrouds, the lower diagonal, and first vertical stay were pinned to chainplates buried into the forward outer corner of the deck wings. This spread of almost 25 feet between the supporting stays meant the compression loads on the mast were lower than on a boat with a narrower chainplate base. The headsail, often at odds with a wide shroud base, didn't project aft past the mast, and consequently there was no interference.

Once the San Diego Yacht Club realized, with help from the courts, that New Zealand was serious about their 90-foot waterline challenge, the Americans started designing in earnest. With New Zealand's four principle measurements in hand (and assuming the boat was going to be a monohull) they began optimizing a boat to fit that specific envelope. As John Letcher pointed out in his paper "Monitoring Performance of the Sloop *New Zealand*" (1990 New England Sailing Yacht Symposium), the American team did not need to re-create the New Zealand boat, but simply optimize the design of a boat to fit the New Zealand dimensions. This would represent the fastest boat that New Zealand could assemble. However, once this fictional boat was designed (by Letcher), information on the real KZ-1 began to filter in. Combining published photos of the boat under construction and ready for launch with a few reference dimensions led to better estimates of what New Zealand had produced.

The Americans had two options: design a boat to match their estimate of KZ-1 and do their best to make it a fraction of a percent faster, or pursue their unorthodox idea and build a catamaran with almost twice the speed. The choice was made even more obvious after realizing they didn't have the 12 months it would take to design and build a 90-foot waterline monohull. And so a smaller, lighter multihull was the answer. The only question remaining was a common one being considered that summer—was it legal?

Back in 1857, the New York Yacht Club's original invitation for challenges had promised "the strictest fair play." That promise no longer appeared to apply. The Americans felt they had been blindsided by a literal reading of an arcane document, a reading that ignored the consensus of modern participating nations that the America's Cup was, until everyone agreed otherwise, a 12-Meter event. If Michael Fay was going to be line-by-line literal, then so were the Americans. There was nothing in the original deed that said you couldn't use a catamaran. With their own lawyers telling them it was worth the risk, the Americans began the design process.

Catamarans and monohulls often excel in opposite conditions, making competition between them essentially meaningless. (And multihulls, for that matter, already enjoyed their own international match-racing contest, called the Little America's Cup.) A catamaran does not perform well in light airs, with the excessive wetted surface of both its hulls gluing it to the water. Once the wind is strong enough to lift the windward hull, though, the wetted area drops and the speed rises dramatically. A single-hulled ballasted sailboat might be a full knot faster than a similarly sized multihull in light wind, but 5 to 10 knots slower in strong breezes. Such varied performance characteristics make a mono-multi contest so weather dependent and so skill independent that a match with two such boats is simply inappropriate. But "inappropriate" is exactly what the Americans wanted, and if they could eliminate the light-air weakness of the catamaran, then they could almost be assured of victory.

The *Stars & Stripes* design team homed in on a 60-foot catamaran, weighing one-tenth of the New Zealand challenger, with a high-tech carbon fiber articulating wing mast. The wing was mounted vertically with eight independently controlled sections, one above the other. Each level could be made to camber

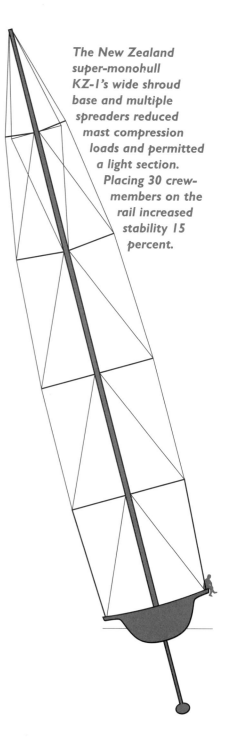

The New Zealand super-monohull KZ-1's wide shroud base and multiple spreaders reduced mast compression loads and permitted a light section. Placing 30 crewmembers on the rail increased stability 15 percent.

and twist to provide an appropriate shape for each wind speed. Observed top speeds hovered around the 30-knot range—limited mainly by the spunk of the crew.

In the 1988 America's Cup I was employed by the New Zealand challenge to reconstruct the drawings and analyze the performance of the catamaran *Stars & Stripes.* It was a unique opportunity to observe the design development of a high-speed multihull built for one purpose: to beat the New Zealand big boat. Once that analysis was complete, the speed prediction would let the sailors know their chances on the racecourse and therefore what their strategy should be on any particular race day.

The New Zealand management wanted to leave no stone unturned in their quest for knowledge. I used a combination of their own photographs, press clippings, and hearsay to begin the drawing re-creation process. Once a few reference dimensions in a photograph are known, the perspective of the photo can be determined and other dimensions previously unknown can be measured. For example, an overhead shot combined with the knowledge that the length is 60 feet and the beam 30 feet, permits one to pick out the mast location, sail foot length, hull beam, hull sheer in planview, and daggerboard chord length. Slowly, as more pictures are gathered, the confidence level builds. Drawings produced were replotted by the computer in true perspective to match the original photograph, laid on top, and compared (see page 219).

Just as in creating an original America's Cup design, the performance analysis of the completed redesign took place in two stages, the first by numerical analysis in the computer and the second by tank testing. In 1988 the performance analysis software for catamarans was not yet perfected and predictions were at best a good estimate. Looking for better estimates, we built two models: one of the re-created *Stars & Stripes,* for which we wanted a speed reading, and the

other of a D-class catamaran that the New Zealand team owned and was using as a reference. We knew how fast the D-class cat could sail, and therefore its predicted performance served as a confidence test— if we got the correct answer, then the *Stars & Stripes* values were most likely good as well.

Additional confirmation was required to indicate how accurate the tank-testing process was. Towing tank facilities are always struggling to improve the accuracy of the resistance predicted by scale models, and we needed a way to check that the analysis of these pencil-slim catamaran hulls was still good. Since the D-class cat was only 35 feet long, a typical length for ship models, it could be tested full size and the results compared with the predictions from the one-third scale model of the same hull. The *Stars & Stripes* hull could then be tested at one-third scale and expanded to full size with some confidence. With the plan in place, the models were built and tested at Arctec, a tank test facility then located in Escondido, California.

Unfortunately, the correlation between the full size and one-third scale model of the D-class catamaran was disappointing. Even when all the corrections for scale and turbulence stimulation were applied to the model, the hull was predicted to be 5 percent faster than it actually was. These errors are beyond what one would expect for a model of that size, and in spite of our best efforts this issue was never resolved. Fortunately, the margin of performance difference between the catamaran and the Kiwi monohull was expected to be much greater than 5 percent and therefore comparisons could still be made with some confidence.

During the summer of 1988 (both sides had finally agreed to a match in September) the *Stars & Stripes* team realized they might have trouble beating the challenger in light winds and so increased the height of their wing mast by 18 feet. With the extra sail area they could now lift the windward hull out of the water ("fly a hull") in as little as 5 knots of wind, thereby eliminating their vulnerability in light airs. In winds of less than 5 knots, races would most likely not be completed within the time limit, so performance in that region was not an issue. My analysis of performance curves reflects this rig change, with the speed of *Stars & Stripes* improving in all wind conditions. The only performance loss relative to the shorter rig was in heavy air upwind—not a concern, since *Stars & Stripes* could throw away several knots of upwind boat speed and still stay well ahead of *New Zealand.*

Because of the extensive research done by the New Zealand team, they knew the probable outcome of the race well before the starting gun fired. The theory said there were no conditions under which the big boat could beat the nimble little cat. The racecourse proved the theory. Both boats sailed the necessary two races in the saddest series I have ever seen—the cat going at half speed, just keeping safely ahead of the magnificent but significantly slower *New Zealand.* Multihull enthusiasts were outraged by this "sandbagging" by Conner. It was as if he had designed a Formula 1 car and was cruising it around in second gear against a bicycle. For these aficionados, *Stars & Stripes* was a mockery of cutting-edge multihull technology, not a celebration of it.

The competing yachts were two examples of superb engineering and design. If either one had been matched with a similar vessel, the event would have been dynamic. On September 7, 1988, the catamaran won the first race by 2½ miles—18 minutes, 15 seconds—and could easily have doubled that margin of victory. Race two was even more lopsided as *Stars & Stripes* successfully defended the America's Cup for the San Diego Yacht Club.

The trophy was briefly awarded to New Zealand after Michael Fay cried "foul" to the courts, claiming the catamaran design was illegal. That decision was overturned for good by the State of New York Court

of Appeals on April 26, 1990, in 51 pages of legal opinion. The appeals court decided that Fay's complaints that the match was unfair were unfounded. Nowhere did the Deed of Gift say that the defender must respond with a like-minded craft, nor did the wording preclude a catamaran, provided it stayed within the overall dimension limitations.

Sailors, designers, and managers were happy to end the chapter of the 1988 Cup races. Victory remained with Dennis Conner and the San Diego Yacht Club, but all parties had a major task before them in getting the America's Cup back under control. The procedure for challenging needed clarifying, and a new class of yacht was required to bring the majesty

*The second-generation IACC design **OneAustralia** drives for the windward mark during the 1994 class World Championships in San Diego, California. Longer and narrower than the 1992 designs, the contenders built for the 1995 event excelled in rough conditions like these.*

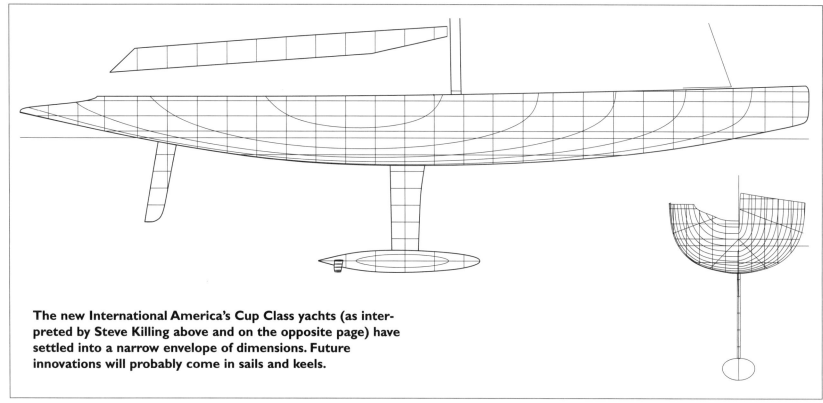

The new International America's Cup Class yachts (as interpreted by Steve Killing above and on the opposite page) have settled into a narrow envelope of dimensions. Future innovations will probably come in sails and keels.

back to the event. If there was good to be found in the "Big Boat" rebel challenge, it was that some fresh thinking began in the minds of those that race for the Cup, and their primary thoughts revolved around the boats. Despite the farcical nature of the 1988 match, the sheer bravura of design technology meant that the 12-Meter class, heavy and outdated, could not resurface. The managers of America's Cup efforts who had been scratching their heads over the modern relevance of the Deed of Gift had gained some taste of what their designers were enduring in creating contemporary racing machines out of the 12 Meter's 80-odd-year-old International Rule. The next America's Cup, in 1992, would see some revolutionary changes.

starting over: the IACC Rule

The 1988 America's Cup event between the New Zealand "Big Boat" and the American catamaran *Stars & Stripes* displayed a disregard for the regulations and common protocol of the Cup. It disappointed the sailing community and baffled the public at large.

But the event succeeded in rallying designers, owners, and sailors around the common cause of avoiding a repeat of the event. Even before the unusual race was over (and long before the winner was determined in the courts) meetings were conducted to give shape to a new America's Cup class yacht.

There were two issues at these meetings: protocol and the boat. The protocol governing the conduct of an America's Cup challenge was straightforward in theory but time consuming in practice as lawyers tried to define what the sailors wanted. The final document covers such necessities as who can challenge, entry fees, mutual consent of the class of boat, format of the challenger selection series, and boat measurement process.

The definition of the new boat was more problematic. The basic intent was clear—the new class rules were to create the fastest, but not necessarily the largest, monohull racing yacht. The 12-Meter class had given up that honor long ago, as its speed on the racecourse was surpassed by the IOR maxi yachts and large IMS racers.

The characteristics that held the Twelve's speed in check were heavy displacement and the Girth Difference portion of the design rule. Factions represented at the meetings presented proposals ranging from multihulls to "new, improved" 12-Meters. The consensus, however, was that the new boat needed to be longer, lighter, and much smaller in the midsection of the hull. With most of the world's brain trust of designers at hand, what was to become the new International America's Cup Class (IACC) Rule was drafted and redrafted over the next year and fine-tuned to the formula that appears at right.

Within the simple formula are heavy penalties if dimensions exceed an acceptable range. For example, if the L dimension (a combination of the length of the hull at 200 millimeters above the waterline and girths measured at the ends of that length) is greater than 21.2 meters, a penalty is applied, which becomes very severe if the length exceeds 22.2 meters. With such "soft" limits, the boats are forced to be within a box of a given width, length, and weight. Although there is freedom of shape within that box, the hope is that the speed changes will not be extreme and therefore the match racing will remain close. Everyone involved in the new rule realized that the success of the class depends on providing close, and therefore entertaining, sailboat racing.

Unlike the earlier 12-Meter rule, which squashed the keel between a deep hull and a maximum draft of about 8.5 feet, the International America's Cup Class permits a draft of 4 meters (more

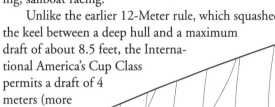

International America's Cup Class Rule

$$\frac{L + (1.25 \times \sqrt{SA}) - (9.8 \times \sqrt[3]{DISP})}{0.679} = 24.00 \text{ meters}$$

FIG. 10.6
Keel innovations under the IACC

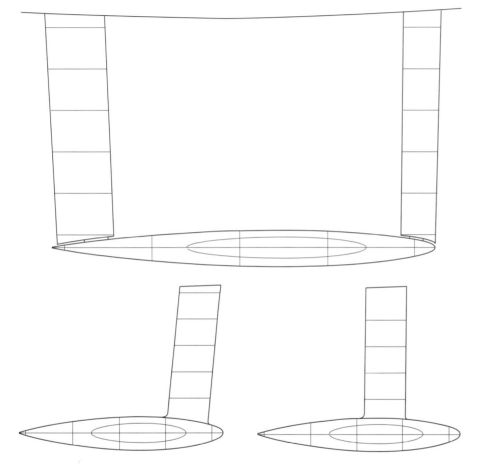

The new International America's Cup Class Rule met with a flurry of keel design innovations in 1992. Top: the tandem keel-rudder of NZL20 of New Zealand, which featured movable foils fore and aft. Above right: the T-shaped keel of 1992 Cup winner *America³*. Above left: the L-shaped keel of 1992 finalist *Il Moro di Venezia* of Italy. All were major engineering as well as design accomplishments.

than 13 feet). Keels designed to the rule have narrow fins, typically less than a meter fore and aft, with heavy lead bulbs hung from the bottom. Structure is as much a design criterion as hydrodynamics—it is not trivial to secure a 45,000-pound lead torpedo to the bottom of a 3-inch-thick keel.

Some interesting keel variations that have been tried with success include the tandem keel-rudder of New Zealand's 1992 entry, the L-shaped keel of the Italian entry in the same year, and the T-shaped configuration of *America³* in 1992 and of Team New Zealand in 1995. (See Fig. 10.6.) The tandem keel-rudder was an intriguing innovation permitted, but not expected, by the rulemakers. Rule 19.4 states that "the total number of moveable surfaces shall not exceed two" and the axis of rotation of those surfaces shall be on centerline and within 45 degrees to the vertical. As Bruce Farr's design office found during the design of the 1992 New Zealand entry, this permits the relocation of the "rudder" to become the aft leg of a twin keel. Although tricky to steer, this arrangement reduces wetted surface and provides two tall, highly efficient lifting surfaces.

Tactically, the tandem keel-rudder was a gold mine. Because both foils could rotate, the boat could be sailed "sideways" with negative leeway for short periods of time to pinch off an unsuspecting opponent. In a close upwind battle, moving to windward half a boatlength is often just what is needed to disturb the wind of the competition.

The successful engineering of this structure was a victory in itself. The lead bulb was supported by two fully rotating foils, requiring the shafts to withstand large bending loads along with the usual torsion. That same year, the Australians and the Americans tried tandem keel-rudders with less success—both had steering problems that appeared to the casual observer to be caused by too much weather helm. In spite of the promising results of the tandem keel-rudder, none were in evidence for the second International America's Cup Class event in 1995.

Initial experimenting with the limits of the new class rule in the first few years of its use produced a definite trend. Hulls began with medium weight and wide flare above the waterline, reaching out to the maximum allowable beam of 5.5 meters. In 1992 the Italian entry *Il Moro di Venezia,* the official challenger, displayed marked flare above the waterline, but was a midweight boat. The New Zealand team, although they also hit the maximum beam, took a different tack and combined their tandem keel-rudder with a much lighter boat with less sail area. It is a credit to the rule that the series between New Zealand and Italy to determine the final challenger was incredibly close, in spite of NZL32's having 6,000 pounds less displacement and 320 square feet less sail area.

As it became apparent that the value of crew sitting on the wide deck did not make up for the extra drag of the asymmetrical hull when heeled, the width of new boats began to shrink. *America³,* the victor in 1992, was the first to climb the learning curve, and that syndicate's final boat was the narrowest, heaviest one of the series. The America's Cup winner from one year becomes the benchmark for the next series, and consequently in 1995 all new boats were slimmed down—some as narrow as 4.25 meters. New Zealand's NZL32 won the Cup easily in 1995 and sailed confidently

After only two matches in the new International America's Cup Class, designers have herded the boats into the extreme limits of length and displacement. The trend leaves one wondering if the class has already reached its full design potential, since such extremes would normally be brought out by heavy-air competition, and the 1992 and 1995 matches in San Diego, which produced this trend, were held in light winds.

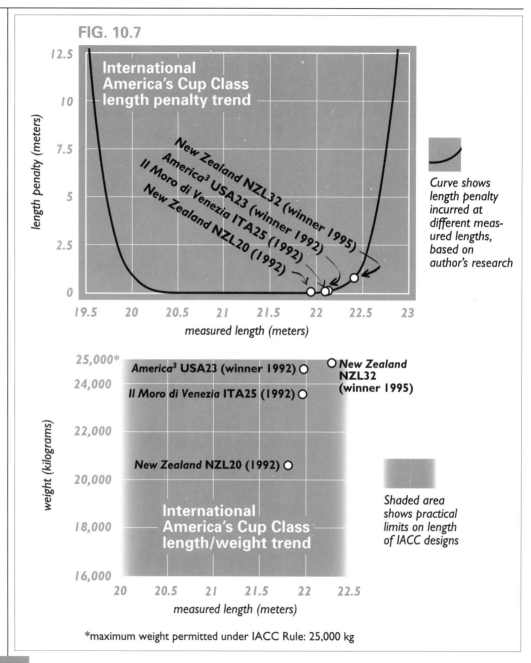

FIG. 10.7

International America's Cup Class length penalty trend

length penalty (meters)

New Zealand NZL32 (winner 1995)
America³ USA23 (winner 1992)
Il Moro di Venezia ITA25 (1992)
New Zealand NZL20 (1992)

measured length (meters)

Curve shows length penalty incurred at different measured lengths, based on author's research

America³ USA23 (winner 1992)
Il Moro di Venezia ITA25 (1992)
New Zealand NZL32 (winner 1995)
New Zealand NZL20 (1992)

weight (kilograms)

International America's Cup Class length/weight trend

measured length (meters)

*maximum weight permitted under IACC Rule: 25,000 kg

Shaded area shows practical limits on length of IACC designs

The new IACC rule has spawned some of the most exciting competition and greatest technological innovations in sailing history.

through the summer with less beam, more weight, and more length than any other boat in the series.

There is not much breathing space left in that corner of the rule's "box"— the imposed penalties are large if the designs continue to lengthen and narrow. (See Fig. 10.7.) The length penalty gets progressively steeper as boats exceed 22.2 meters, and NZL32 is already pushing the limit at around 22.4. The displacement is limited to a maximum of 25,000 kilograms, and many boats, including NZL32, have hit that wall.

The rulemakers, although wise in placing the "soft" limits to keep what would otherwise be increasingly narrow, long, and perhaps unseaworthy designs from being created, I am sure had no idea that the fastest boats would be clumped in one corner of the design space. The first two America's Cup Class events were held in San Diego, a patch of water known for its light (8- to 12-knot) breezes. If these light conditions spawned the longest, heaviest boats the rule will allow, then a venue with heavier winds will only beg for still longer boats, something that the rule will not permit. This means that designs will become increasingly similar, with less experimentation in the overall size of the boat and more effort concentrated on keel and sail details. On the positive side, the match racing will be tight, with smaller differences in speed. The true test of the rule will be whether it continues to provide enough freedom to hold the interest of designers and yet keep the boats within sight of each other on the racecourse.

the learning curve: work-in-progress design

After working with *Canada I* in 1983 and *True North* in 1987, Canada's America's Cup challenges went dormant and I signed on for two challenges with the New Zealand team. Since I do not carry a New

Zealand passport, I could not be part of their design team. You must hold a visa or passport and have principle residence for at least one year before the first race of the event (two years for the 2000 event) in the country of the syndicate for which you design. However, I did put my skills to use as a researcher after the New Zealand challenges' boats were completed. My role was to act as a kind of forensic yacht designer, re-creating the designs of competitors' boats, based on information the New Zealand teams collected.

The contrast in management and design philosophy between the New Zealand and Canadian efforts was quite striking and taught some good lessons that can be applied to syndicate efforts everywhere.

The learning curve during any Cup challenge or defense has hills and plateaus but hopefully few valleys. (See Fig. 10.8.) One of the steepest parts of the curve occurs during the middle to late design phase, when ideas are beginning to gel and solutions are sought for specific problems. The *Canada 1* challenge of 1983 and the *True North* program that followed both fared quite well during that phase—I can find few flaws with the basic parameters determined during the initial design stage. Even our construction, although a bit slow, was second to none.

As our boats arrived at the America's Cup in 1983 or the 12-Meter World Championships in 1986, our spirits were high. The optimism grew to enthusiasm as we entered into the first few encounters, those chance meetings when two teams find themselves drawn together like magnets on the same piece of water. The boats get closer and closer together until finally they are perfectly aligned and sailing upwind. Both teams know the learning curve is just about to make a jump. If one boat is fast they will break off the encounter prematurely, for there is little for them to learn here. I recall our sailors seeking me out after some early skirmishes on *True North I* during the 12-Meter Worlds, exclaim-

ing, "For once we have a 12-Meter with boat speed." Nice praise to get, but we hadn't won the Cup yet.

As the first week progressed and those that would participate in informal races before the 1986 Worlds showed their hand, the Canadians had established themselves as at least one step above the "B" class. Typically an America's Cup fleet can be divided into the "A" fleet, which in 1986/87 was perhaps the top five contenders, all of which have a chance of getting into the finals, and the "B" fleet, the also-rans. We always had the potential to be in that top-five category, but we never had the drive or understood the concept of how to progress further.

One of the harshest realities to grasp in yacht design, construction, and racing is that once the boat has been launched, only the first phase of the design is complete. The final phase is to use on-the-water sailing as a full-size tank test with everyone on the team prepared for long hours of testing and modifying, practicing and modifying, thinking and modifying.

In order to progress in the last three months heading into the America's Cup (and I have to admit that the Canadian team always lagged behind), both designers and management need a more aggressive attitude. The management of the New Zealand challenges in which I participated was always looking 5 or 10 steps ahead of the sailing activity. What do we change if we lose this race? If they protest our bowsprit, how will we defend it? If we lose, should we go to court? If we win, where will we host the defense? With advance thinking like that, 90 percent of the situations that come up have already been dealt with, so

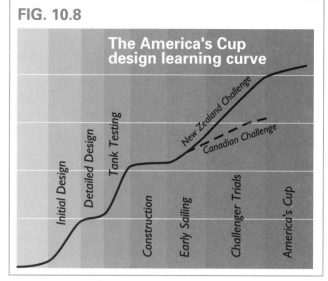

FIG. 10.8

The America's Cup design learning curve

Initial Design
Detailed Design
Tank Testing
Construction
Early Sailing
Challenger Trials
America's Cup
New Zealand Challenge
Canadian Challenge

if there is one occurrence that you haven't considered, then all your energies can be channeled to solve that problem.

Making good use of full-size testing means having some standard to measure yourself against. In the model towing tank the reference was the instruments that measure lift and drag, but those are not available on the water. Even if instrumentation were so accurate that it could be believed, the wind, sea state, sails, and crew change so much that comparisons with a previous day's performance are almost impossible. What is required is known competition. Sometimes your own trial horse, another boat in your own camp, can serve that purpose, but reference with the competition is the real test. However, if the competition is making changes to their boat as well, then you are never sure if you had extra boat speed today because you were going faster or they were going slower.

There is a way to make double use of the competition's performance relative to your own. New Zealand in 1992 spent a lot of time keeping a close eye on the competition. This does not involve aggressive spying, just knowledgeable observers who note that, for example, the Italian crew is carrying their M3 mainsail with the repaired clew today and seem to have moved the mast back about 8 inches overnight. The learning curve can now progress at twice the pace since you can observe your own as well as the competition's experiments.

Designers need to keep an eye on keel and hull changes of other contenders at the same time, for this is where a significant amount of speed development takes place. At the 1986 Worlds, the *True North* Challenge had boat speed early on, but the competitors learned from us and quickly moved ahead, leaving us wondering why we were now so slow. The budget, such an integral part of all America's Cup challenges, must be apportioned to permit new keels, wings, sails,

and instruments at what to the uninitiated must seem like the last minute. Both the *Canada II* and *True North* programs of 1986/87 suffered from not having the budget or the drive to quickly develop new keels and winglets as the competition discovered smaller, high aspect ratio wings really made a difference.

The America's Cup projects have been both the most difficult and stressful and also the most rewarding, exciting, and challenging that I have ever experienced. The excitement is brought about by the chance to perform some leading-edge research and to use or create the latest technology. The grandeur, size, and beauty of the boats add to the challenge—this is, after all, considered by many to be the peak of the sport of sailing and for the designer one of the biggest challenges.

The added stress comes for many of the same reasons. Because the event is so high profile, the eyes of the sailing community and in many cases the nonsailing public are focused on every move. And the press will not hesitate at any point to ask, "Why?" Why is your keel so different? Why did you win today? Why didn't you win either of the last two races? And the most annoying and persistent question repeated at least once a week—Do you really think you can win the America's Cup? Coming up with fresh answers or tolerating the old ones tends to wear on the spirit and detract from the main focus: designing a faster boat.

As with many experiences, the fond memories linger and the bad ones fade. Most designers have had enough by the end of an America's Cup campaign (unless I suppose they have just helped to win the event) and swear that the wear on the body and mind is not worth the rewards. But all it takes is some restful time back in the real world. Six months after the completion of an America's Cup challenge is usually long enough to wait before asking yourself, "Would I do it again?" My answer, like that of most designers, is "Well, of course."

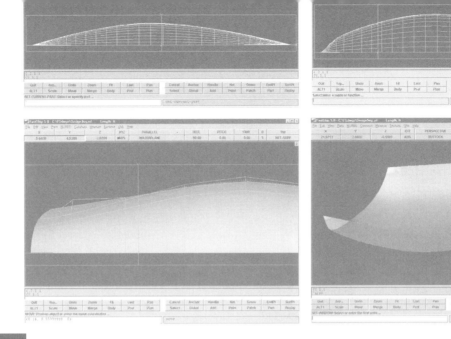

the design process

The tools of the trade have changed, but not the demands on the designer's ingenuity.

opening lines: beginning a design career

I produced my first lines drawing—the three views of a hull that define its shape—during my last year at the University of Western Ontario. The need to draw something that would float arose from my decision to choose sail aerodynamics in turbulent flow as the subject of a compulsory fourth-year engineering project. In order to test sails in the university's Boundary Layer Wind Tunnel, a mast, boom, and hull were required to support them. The only obvious choice to a keen young sailor was a scale model of the boat he sailed himself—the Albacore dinghy. I created a lines drawing of the hull at ⅙ scale so that I could laminate a boat from layers of pine. The kitchen table, some bricks wrapped in dishtowels, and wooden splines allowed me to draw the long curves, while a beginner's set of French curves helped shape the waterlines near the transom.

I still have that model. Looking at it now, I do detect some resemblance to an Albacore. Missing from my repertoire of skills then was the ability to relate the back of the boat to the front, so necessary to ensure that the curves were all of one family. I knew that in the body plan, the bow of the boat was drawn to the right of the centerline and the stern to the left, and perhaps that was my downfall. Since those two sets of curves were not overlaid, it wasn't easy to ensure that the shapes would blend. There is definitely an acquired skill that grows with each hull one draws, whether by hand or with the help of the computer.

Feeble though my first attempt was, that Albacore lines drawing was good enough to land me my first (and I guess my only) job, at the C&C Yachts design office, which introduced me to the tools and processes of professional yacht design.

In 1973, desktop computers were nowhere to be seen. The tools of the trade were the slide rule, the planimeter, the mechanical pencil, ducks (the professional version of my towel-wrapped bricks), splines, and ship's curves. But even then, the slide rule, at which I had become such an expert during university, was about to be phased out. The deluxe model (with its Teflon-coated aluminum edges that I kept lubricated with just a touch of oil) did only half the job. Multiplying and dividing was alright (although my precision was often questioned), but adding and subtracting was simply not possible.

The design process had been somewhat streamlined in the C&C office by the creation of several "cookbook" pages for calculating displacement, righting moment, and keel volume. Just fill in the blanks, add up the columns, and multiply by the station spacing. It took only a few weeks for me to realize the value of the new electronic calculators, swallow my pride, and invest in one of my own. Although the tools we used continued to improve, the design process remained essentially the same—it simply got faster and easier to create the boat that was intended. It would be a long time until the tools themselves began to change the nature of the design process.

The author's first "design": a ⅙-scale wind-tunnel model of an Albacore dinghy.

the desire to draw: creating the hull lines

Designers generally find that the most rewarding drawing for them to create is the lines drawing of the hull, as it represents the essence of the boat. Even in some large design offices, the senior designer will continue to create all the lines drawings, handing the project over to others on the staff only when he is confident the shape is as he wants it. At that point he will have defined the overall look of the boat—a low, sleek racer; a high-freeboard cruiser; fine waterlines; wide transom. Whatever the shape, drawing those first few lines is very exciting. Some designers find it so rewarding that even though they have modern CAD systems that are eventually used to define the shape of the boat, the preliminary lines drawing is still created by hand.

In the precomputer days, the preliminary lines drawing was often created at a smaller scale (½"= 1'0" was typical) than the final drawing to speed the process and prevent the designer from getting caught up in too many fine details. The intent was to define the philosophy of the boat and then, once the shape was close and the client had agreed with the concept, the final lines would be drawn more accurately at a larger scale.

In the traditional design process, the order in which the first few lines of the preliminary hull are drawn vary from designer to designer, but they are sure to be of either the profile shape, the midsection, or the waterline. In order to define those first tentative curves, initial target numbers have to be set. In particular, the overall length, waterline length, displacement, and prismatic coefficient are needed to allow this presoftware design process to proceed in some organized fashion. Overall length is the ballpark size; waterline length indicates potential hull speed; displacement dictates interior volume and performance ambitions; and prismatic coefficient suggests the fineness of the ends and whether the boat's shape is best suited to light, moderate, or heavy winds.

The combination of waterline length and prismatic coefficient gives the first target for the boat's shape. Knowing that the prismatic coefficient (Cp) is the displacement $(Displ)$ of the boat divided by the immersed maximum section (MS) area times the design waterline length (DWL) allows the required immersed maximum midsection area to be calculated. (See Fig. 11.1.)

Obviously, an infinite number of shapes can be drawn that contain a given area under the waterline—some wide and shallow, others deep and narrow. Drawing shapes that have the required area but also match the desired profile or waterline shape soon limits the options.

Calculating the area under the waterline of each section can be estimated by dividing the shape into a number of small squares, or determined with more accuracy using a clever mechanical device called a *planimeter*. It consists of a small metal wheel that rolls and slides across the drawing on the end of an articulated arm. The wheel is directly connected to a units scale and further connected through a worm gear to a tens scale. By outlining a section of the drawing with its pointer and subtracting the readings before and after the tracing, a direct measure of its area is made in square inches. Two or three readings are generally taken for each section and the results are averaged. My planimeter is still in good working order, although it was last used about 1985 and now occupies a place of

Before the arrival of computer design programs, calculating the area under the waterline of each hull section was done most accurately with a clever mechanical device called a planimeter.

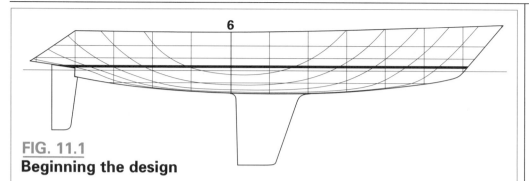

FIG. 11.1
Beginning the design

A yacht's lines drawing usually begins by establishing the maximum section (MS) shape, found at or very near station 6. Shown here in lines plan and 3D computer modeling is the author's 40-foot IOR racer *Chariot,* with station 6 highlighted. This cross-sectional shape is indicative of the general character of the boat, reflecting such key measurements as maximum beam, waterline beam, and freeboard. It is also critical to the yacht's overall performance, as the immersed area of the maximum section shape is central to the calculation of prismatic coefficient, which contains the fundamental dimensions of displacement and waterline length. By selecting target values for prismatic coefficient (Cp), displacement, and design waterline length (DWL), the designer "rearranges" the prismatic coefficient calculation (see page 34) so that the immersed MS area becomes its output. (Displacement is expressed as volume for the calculation.) With the immersed MS area determined, station 6 can serve as the starting point of the hull shape.

$$\text{Immersed } \textit{MS} \text{ Area} = \frac{\text{Volume}}{\textit{Cp} \times \textit{DWL}}$$

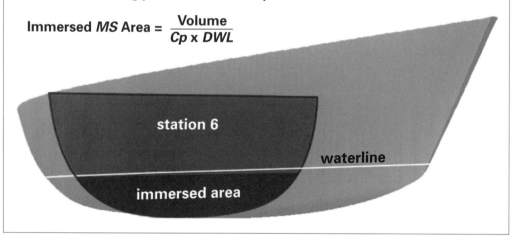

honor in my "history" department next to the slide rule.

A more sophisticated development of the planimeter, but still a mechanical device, was the *integrator.* This heavyweight was based on the same principles (somewhat magical to me) of sliding and turning wheels, but the entire unit traveled on a rail across the top of the drafting board. The additional information provided by the integrator was the center of gravity of a measured area. This valuable piece of information permitted the calculation of heeled stability, which was determined by multiplying each sectional area of the heeled hull by its distance from the centerline of the boat. In reality, the difficulty of using the machine with a consistent repeatability of results led me, and others with similar frustrations, to leave the calculation to other techniques and the integrator on the shelf.

The design process, and in particular the drawing of the hull lines plan, is an interesting combination of accurate draftsmanship and creative design. Although the designer may have his mind set on particular midsection and waterline shapes for a new boat, it may not be possible for them to coexist in the same hull—the three views of the boat that form its lines (front, back, and side) are not independent. Changing the midsection to please the designer may result in a waterline shape that displeases him. Creating the drawing sometimes seems incredibly easy, with the desired shapes just falling into place and resulting in a beautiful and fair boat. But at other times, the process can be a great wrestling match: the three views of the boat do not want to live together. Achieving the desired section shape at station 8, for example, may require a local hollow in the buttock line, but then smoothing out the buttock line requires an undesirable shape change in station 8. A fresh look with a few compromises on the following day is often the answer.

Once the shape has been defined by 10 stations

along the waterline, and by 2 buttocks and perhaps 4 waterlines, finishing the drawing is simply a drafting exercise. Final half stations, diagonals, and buttocks are added to give the builder enough shape definition. It continues to be a matter of pride when a designer produces a lines drawing by hand, to have all the views match within a pencil-width tolerance at drawing scale, which translates into about 1/16 of an inch at full size. For drawings that merit extra effort, and when the designer has the luxury of time, the final touch is to ink the drawing, so that clear, crisp blueprints can be made.

The taking of offsets from the drawing is the ultimate test. *Offsets* are the dimensions taken from centerline or baseline to the various crossings of stations and waterlines, so that the builder has enough measurements to create a full-size version of the lines drawing. The distance measured on the body plan from the centerline to the design waterline at station 4, for example, must agree with the distance shown on the plan view for the same waterline at station 4. When the shop is reproducing the lines drawing on several sheets of plywood on the shop floor, inaccurate offsets will prevent the builder from confidently reproducing the true shape of the boat.

The loftsman—the designer's counterpart at the shop—needs to have talents similar to those of the designer. The worse the drawing, the more talent the loftsman needs. The plotted offsets indicate to him where to place nails in the loft floor to control the shape of a wooden batten fitted around each curve. Pencils (or colored pens) are then used to draw the final shape. If the plan view and the body plan do not both "fair through" with the wooden battens, adjustments similar to those the designer has to make on the drafting table must be confronted.

During this process the designer needs to work quite closely with the loftsman, for if the offsets do not produce a fair line, who better to resolve the conflict

than the designer. I know of a few cases in which the designer arrived at the builder's shop early in the project to discover that the shape being drawn on the loft floor had only a slight resemblance to the designer's drawing. Decisions made by the loftsman to "fair" the boat were creating quite a different shape from the one the designer had in mind.

By the time the lines have reached the loft floor, the design of the keel and rudder must be completed as well, for they contribute significantly to the displacement of the vessel. The keel in particular displaces a large amount of water, and despite the paradox, the extremely heavy foil provides buoyancy through its volume. For example, the old C&C 27, a popular racer-cruiser designed in 1970, had a final displacement of 5,180 pounds, which meant the total underwater portion of the boat displaced 80.9 cubic feet of salt water (5,180 lbs/64 lbs per cubic foot). Of that volume, about 4 cubic feet— 5 percent of the total—was contributed by the keel. Forgetting to include the keel in the displacement, which happens on occasion, would have resulted in a boat that floated higher than expected.

In traditional practice, curves are drawn using ducks and splines—"ducks" being the weights that hold the spline to a particular shape that a pen or pencil can follow.

bit by bit:
the computer's ascent

The latest design tool, the computer, started to change the standard design process about 1979, just when I was launching my own yacht design business. The first personal computers were making their presence felt, and I entered the market by purchasing a TRS 80 from Radio Shack with a whopping 8K of RAM (for comparison, my current machine has 8,000 times that amount of RAM—64 MB) and a cassette recorder for data and program storage. It was an ideal opportunity to get the machine to do some of those repetitive calculations, such as the ones required to design the keel. This task was more than somewhat tedious, and although keel shapes varied from boat to boat, the calculation procedure was exactly the same. The area and volume of the keel had to be determined for each one. The volume of a tapered foil shape is not a simple thing to resolve by hand. But determining the appropriate formulas manually and then incorporating them into a computer program was an acceptable job.

Each calculation sheet for routine tasks made its way into the computer. It was simplistic, but effective. Data sheets were now neat and tidy, calculation time was greatly reduced, and particularly valuable was the fact that the calculations were so much less tedious that they would get done, and not be left aside until it was too late to make corrective changes. More up-to-the-minute calculations meant that boats were being designed that more closely matched the original goals. When drawing and calculating by hand, the elapsed time between the start of drawing and the end of calculations on a hull could easily be two weeks, one week if things flowed perfectly. If at the end of that

period the displacement turned out to be 10 percent high, there was great reluctance to go through the entire process again to get it right. With faster calculations and better estimates of stability and displacement before pencil ever touched paper (or Mylar), the hesitation to go through another iteration of design was almost eliminated.

But it wasn't until hull generation itself moved to three-dimensional shaping on the computer screen that a fundamental change was made in the way boats are designed. The FastShip surface design program, created by C&C alumnus George Hazen (with a modest amount of help from the author) was the first of many commercial software programs used to model boat hulls and appendages. In its infancy in 1979, the package included a suite of programs, some based on the old "cookbook" procedures and others, like the surface modeling software, written from scratch. As computers gained speed and graphic display quality grew, the software's usefulness leapt forward. In 1981 the software ran only on Hewlett Packard products and, typically, small monochrome screens. Now the program, in its fifth generation, will shade hulls in full color, and slice hundreds of stations through the hull without hesitation on any PC-compatible computer.

Many traditional designers have resisted embracing the new technology. Boats designed with one of the many ship or yacht CAD programs are created as three-dimensional shapes, and the precision drafting job, so crucial to the designer in the past, is gone, a change some practitioners cannot abide. The decisions to be made during the design process, however, are the same—how wide should the transom be, how much flare in the topsides. Gone are the inaccuracies in drafting. Since the shape is mathematically defined, at any time slices can be taken through the hull in any direction to help visualize or analyze the shape. Many designers, including myself, stick to standard station,

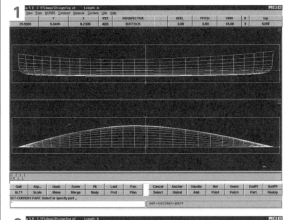

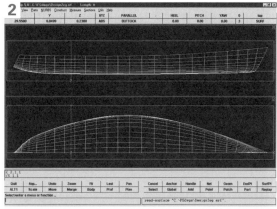

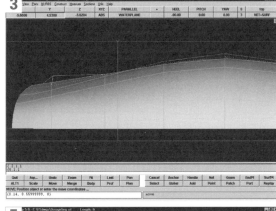

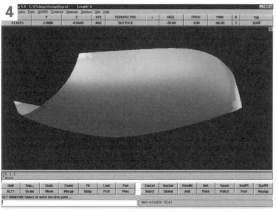

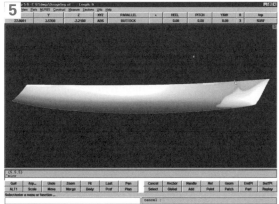

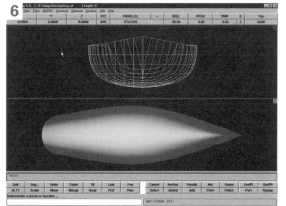

FIG. 11.2
The computer design process

The process of creating a yacht in a computer design program (in this case FastShip) can begin with any existing hull. A 17-foot canoe (1) has begun a transformation into a 35-foot keelboat (2). The early stages of transom and bow modification can be seen.

Modeled in solid color, the hull undergoes finer shaping just forward of the transom (3). Moving to a perspective view, the program allows the designer to view the sheerline from any angle (4). The hull shading is a curvature plot, and reveals poorly faired areas in light shades, around the bow and at the stern near the deck.

A profile view of the almost completed hull (5) illuminates the areas requiring attention. The final faired hull (6) can be viewed as a lines drawing or rendered three-dimensionally.

This design sequence took about 1 hour to complete—about 40 hours less than if done by hand.

buttock, and waterline slices, but diagonals, cants, and inclines are also available. These can be viewed from any direction so that the conflicts between desired waterline and section shapes can be resolved.

Also gone with this new technology is the blank sheet of paper. Every boat I have drawn in the last 10 years has started with another boat as a base boat, if for no other reason than to have a three-dimensional shape as the "raw lump of clay." Some of the parent models for the new boats are surprising—there does not have to be a great similarity in the hull shapes to make the starting point sensible. I have started new canoe designs by scaling a 35-foot sailboat hull to 17 feet, and then refined it to the desired sheerline and profile. Within an hour, the shape is close to final. The process works just as well in the opposite direction. (See Fig. 11.2.) Designing a rudder often begins with an existing keel: shorten it, narrow it, and alter the foil shape to get a good starting point. Of course, once a given genre of boat has been completed, it is the logical choice for other boats of the type—a 40-foot racer would begin life as an enlarged version of a successful 35-footer, or a 30-foot cruiser might have a similar 45-foot cruiser as a parent.

Some of the thought processes are exactly the same for the designer, even when using the computer as a tool. Making a change in the midsection shape will alter sections, waterlines, and buttocks at the same time—something that the designer was always aware of, but it now happens instantaneously and automatically. When the hull is tweaked a little in the midsection, the designer can see the effect in real time as the nearby hull sections are altered. This process is perhaps a little more intuitive now than it was before.

However, gone is the physical feel of a batten bending under the force of the designer's hand and the carefully positioned spline weights. It is more difficult to get a feel for the fairness of a curve on the screen, for it cannot be sighted as it can with a batten on the drafting table. In the early days of the transition to the computer, I spent many hours plotting out my computer-designed boats so that I could place a batten on the curves to check their fairness. Now there are new measures of fairness that can be displayed on the screen that are every bit as good (and often better) than the designer's spline. For individual curves, a curvature plot can be made, which can be thought of as an amplified version of the fairness of the line. A straight line would have zero curvature; a circular arc, constant curvature; a hollow, negative curvature; and a convex curve, positive curvature. If the curvature plot has some semblance of a smooth curve, then the line itself is guaranteed to be quite fair. For overall surface fairness, many software programs can produce a surface plot of curvature. The hull is shaded solid, with colors representing the curvature. Hot spots will indicate small bumps or hollows, which may have been inadvertently designed into the hull.

Designing on the computer gives instant results for displacement, areas, center of buoyancy, prismatic coefficient, righting moment, and in some cases sailing performance. The calculations are a simple matter for the program, and in the case of heeled parameters, like righting moment, they include calculations that were simply not practical by hand. To find out how a boat floats when heeled at 20 degrees is not at all trivial. Even the computer will iterate several times before it gets the correct answer—matching the displacement by lifting and dropping the waterline, and determining the trim by matching the longitudinal center of buoyancy.

The ease of design and instantaneous calculations can also be one of the designer's pitfalls. It is so simple to create a hull that looks smooth, with detailed, precise calculations, that it can convince the onlooker that the hull behind the data is superb, when it may be the result of little design skill. Software is a tool, not a substitute for critical thought. Just as a word processor with spellcheck will not make you a writer, or a spreadsheet program will not turn you into a tax professional, a yacht design program does not transform people into yacht designers. Even so, software marketers sometimes claim that "anyone can design a boat with our software." I suppose it depends on how one defines "boat." Indeed one can create a three-dimensional shape that will float, but without proper care and knowledge of what is an appropriate stability, center of buoyancy, and more, the boat will not meet anyone's needs. But perhaps I should temper that caution with the knowledge that just as a many bad boats have be designed by hand as by computer. I have seen examples of both.

The design loop, from preliminary ideas to completed hull definition, is now a longer but faster trip. Longer, because included in the process is more analysis and a better understanding of the design's potential. When the designer had only his pencil and splines and a modest budget, the prediction of performance was at best an educated guess. Now, still within a small budget, performance prediction programs can project with high confidence the speed potential of new designs. If the initial target stability or speed prediction falls short of the mark, then on the next design iteration 50 square feet of sail or 200 pounds of lead can be added

to rectify the problem. For a typical project I spend no less time creating the hull, keel, rudder, and sail plan than I did when everything was done by hand, but during that time I now may have iterated through 10 different hulls and ended up with a combination that is closer to "perfect" than I could have managed before. The computer has truly increased the chances of success for a new design.

Aesthetics are not left aside by the switch to digital information. Many scoff at the use of computers in yacht design, dismissing them as inhuman, permitting none of the art required by the truly talented designer. There is, however, more opportunity for the designer to perfect the look of a boat on the screen than there ever was on paper. There is the obvious benefit of rendering the hull, keel, rudder, cabinhouse, and anything else that has been modeled in true color, with lights and shading. You can actually *see* the hull shape.

The benefit is realized most when shaping the sheerline, the most prominent and significant line on a

Traditionally, ship's curves provided the designer with the means to draw fair lines. Computer software can now assist in complex hull fairing tasks, but the designer must still make personal decisions about what constitutes "fair."

hull. It not only defines the character of the boat, but if done well will be (in truth, must be) beautiful at any angle. When drawing three separate views by hand to represent the sheerline, it is next to impossible to guarantee how this complex curve, which arcs through three dimensions and is modified in the eye by perspective, will appear from all angles. Through experience one gains the knowledge of what defines a "goodlooking" sheer, but even seasoned designers are occasionally surprised. Sheers that look fine in each individual view can end up having some harsh curves when viewed in three dimensions. In particular, when viewed from the starboard bow, the sheer can have a hump that appears seemingly out of nowhere, about one-quarter of the way back from the stem. Conversely, when viewed from the same vantage point, the sheer near the transom can appear much too straight. The computer screen helps to avoid these problems by permitting the designer to view the completed hull with its accurately portrayed perspective view of the sheerline. A "walk around" on the screen with particular attention to those problem spots can eliminate surprises on the shop floor.

Much of my time in the final days of a new design is spent refining the hull shape to make it fair, pushing the hull in and out small amounts to

Once the primary calculating device of engineers, the slide rule has been rendered all but obsolete by electronic calculators and computers.

ensure that the curvatures are gradually changing and there are no flat spots or small humps. It would seem natural to leave this to the computer. Since it has the ability to calculate curvature and also the capability to move points in and out to change the hull shape, why not have it perform both interactively and do the final fairing itself, in a process akin to sanding the hull with a long fairing board?

Thinking about such a fairing program (and a number of them exist) brings forward some interesting discussion about the meaning of the word "fair." To some, it simply means that the surface is smooth like glass, but that doesn't go far enough. Usually it implies something about how a long strip of wood would follow the contours of a hull surface. If it had to be straight at the forward end of the waterline, then dipped into a hollow, but soon after became convex near the maximum beam, it would not be fair because the wooden batten would not naturally fall into the hollow aft of the straight section.

Each designer has his own set of mental rules about what "fair" means. My own rules change with the boat. For a clean, modern hull, curvatures are greatest in the middle of the boat, but must decrease toward the bow—the only exception being the forefoot at the bottom of the stem, where curvature in the profile must increase. In plan view, increasing the curvature of the sheer near the bow would not be appropriate. In the aft end of the boat, curvature in the sheerline must continue to decrease, while curvature in the profile may or may not increase. The hull surface will blend between the two rules of the sheer and profile. These rules for fairing change when re-creating historic sailing ships, which often had a sheerline that was very full (high curvature) forward. In these boats, the maximum curvature may indeed be near the bow. The contradictory "modern" and "historic" rules point out the difficulty in writing an all-purpose fairing program. What may work for one designer—no hollows permitted, for example—may not be appropriate for another.

Once the three-dimensional shaping of the hull, keel, rudder, and deck is complete, details need to be added. Still missing is the interior, the deck fittings, and the construction details. These will be done either in conjunction with the marketing department of the client company, or with the customer if the boat is for an individual.

Here is where much of the give and take of a design commission comes to the fore. Typically, clients will have fewer of their own ideas about hull shape and ballast weight than they will about the accommodations. They assume most times that the designer knows the trade and can produce a hull shape that matches the requirements of the client. However, from then on the layout becomes more personal and the designer has to be more flexible with his own desires to permit the owner more control of the discussion. It is not unlike taking a dog for a walk (no offense to my clients), with the designer being the one holding the leash. The dog takes many side excursions and perhaps travels a slightly different route, but the designer is always there to pull the client closer to the safe path, or to stop him from barking up the wrong tree. With a moderate length of leash, the client can end up at a slightly different destination, but it should be one that is not far from the designer's own.

The designer's job is to give the client what he wants with the added proviso that the boat must remain safe and meet the initial goals. Sometimes this means the designer must limit a specific request of the owner, for example if he wants to add an extra head or air conditioning—it may be that the performance requirement of the boat won't allow it, or freeboard

must be held to a given height to keep the boat attractive. Probably the most difficult job for the designer is to give up his personal preferences, when the owner's preferences are just as legitimate. Counter and seat heights can easily be tuned to the owner's desires, although many designers have trouble tolerating deviations from their own standards.

As stated in the introduction, this book has not addressed interior design, as it does not fall within the purview of performance fundamentals that I set out to address. However, arriving at an interior does crop up during the design process for all boats. Discussions with the client will lead to a general feeling for the type of interior, with some specific requests based on their recent experience with other boats. A typical project

A skeleton of aluminum frames begins to breathe life into the author's 12-Meter design True North I. *Transforming a design into a finished yacht requires close cooperation between the designer, loftsman, and builder.*

will have the designer presenting an interior layout based on his interpretation of the client's requests, which is meant to be a starting point only. Once client and designer sit down in front of the same drawing, then the partitioning of the interior space begins to change—less space in the head perhaps, and more in the galley; give up the luxury of an extra berth and have more storage and a larger navigation station. Drawing revisions are inevitable, and the erasers and tracing paper overlays should always be at hand.

With advancing technologies, there comes another decision for the designer: how to create the construction drawings for the boat. Unless the boat is being milled from a solid plug, the three-dimensional hull shape in the computer must be converted to two-dimensional drawings. The builder likes to receive either a traditional three-view drawing that accurately represents the hull shape, or a full-size version of same that eliminates the lofting process for the shop. The added benefit of providing full-size body plan drawings to the builder is the elimination of the refairing of the boat in the lofting process. The inevitable inaccuracies involved in transferring offsets to the floor and re-drawing the curves makes the process one to avoid. The numerical accuracy in the shape created in the machine is whatever the designer wants—often .001 inch, well beyond what the builder needs. Therefore, expanding that shape to full size and maintaining accuracy is not a problem.

Creating other drawings from the hull surface file is an exact process. That well-defined shape can be

The eraser and erasing shield, whether real or wielded as a keyboard stroke in a design program, should always be used liberally in the course of creating a design.

used to create sections for accommodation drawings, outlines, and foil shapes for ballast drawings. This is often done by having the software slice up the hull into stations, buttocks, and waterlines and then exporting those curves to a two-dimensional drafting program. AutoCAD, Generic CADD, CADKey and CorelDraw are a few popular programs. The two-dimensional drawings of my designs in this book were done by exporting from FastShip (three-dimensional) to CorelDraw (two-dimensional). No doubt as the years pass the software will change and with it my preferences, but for the last five years my 2-D program of choice has been CorelDraw. All programs can draw the curves required; the differences lie in the ease of use and specific limitations.

Just as there are good and bad boats designed by hand or with the aid of a computer, so there are good and bad, neat and sloppy, accurate and inaccurate drawings. The computer does nothing to guarantee any of these. The computer does have consistent line quality and good precision—it will place a line exactly where requested (even if the request is wrong), and the line will be a consistent, specified line weight. Compare that to a hand-drawn detail in which the precision is not quite so high, nor the line weight so finely controlled, and yet ironically it can be easier for a craftsman to read the drawing created by hand. Perhaps it is easier for him because the line weight does vary more—the outline is heavier, the end of the line is stronger than the middle, the dimensioning arrows have a little more character. All these features of a hand-drawn detail are well worth remembering when drawing on the machine. Variations in line weight are important, including heavy outlines, lighter dimension lines, curved lines that point to specific areas, and heavier line weight on titles. A computer-aided drawing should be indistinguishable from a hand-drawn detail and vice-versa. I have seen inspiring examples of both.

character studies: the yacht designer

Discussions of yacht design must include discussions of yacht designers, for their nature and idiosyncrasies shape the boats we use for racing and cruising. It is also their knowledge of design science and engineering that keeps sailors safe and (if the design requirements have been met) happy on the water.

The yacht designer in a small design office (as most of us are) works by himself or perhaps with one or two others, and must have a broad understanding of all aspects of a boat, from the type of lead to use in the keel, to the engine specification, to the order of laying up the layers of the fiberglass hull laminate. It is this broad general knowledge, seldom required in other professions, that lets him succeed in the task, but that also requires him sometimes to lean upon others. Perhaps it is because the industry itself is so small—diminutive compared to, say, the aerospace industry—that this requirement of versatility is set upon the yacht designer. Most do not have the luxury of calling upon a host of backup engineers to fine-tune a carbon laminate to hold the keel structure or detail the sheaves at the top of the mast. Instead, designers pull their knowledge from a host of sources, including research conducted by other designers on "special" projects and papers published by members of parallel scientific industries.

There is seldom the time or resources in a normal design project to delve into new keel theories or construction processes, but when a high profile event like the America's Cup or a round-the-world race comes along, budgets loosen up, and those who are involved get the rare treat of conducting some pure research. The "trickle-down" effect, which many argue never happens, does take place and the entire industry benefits. The winged keel started life in the America's Cup and ended up bolted to cruising boats around the world. Mylar sail construction started on the racecourse and found acceptance in the weekend boater's sailbag. Carbon fiber masts, unheard of 10 years ago, stand strong in the open ocean and quiet harbors.

Paradoxically, the small marine industry has one of the most difficult scientific tasks. Since hydrodynamics and aerodynamics have so much in common—both involve bodies travelling through a fluid—we

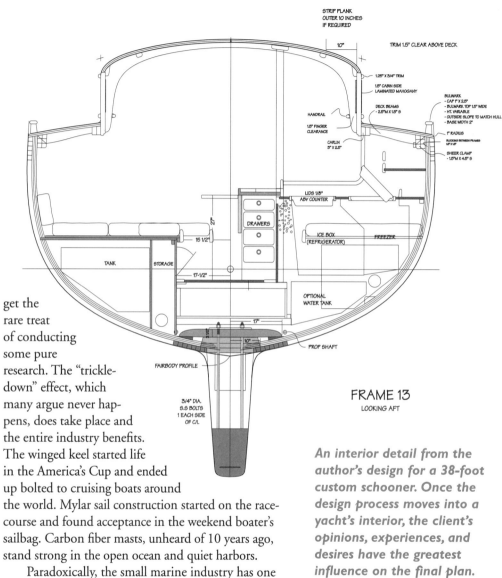

FRAME 13
LOOKING AFT

An interior detail from the author's design for a 38-foot custom schooner. Once the design process moves into a yacht's interior, the client's opinions, experiences, and desires have the greatest influence on the final plan.

The author in his studio: most yacht designers work alone, and must have a broad understanding of all aspects of a boat, from the type of lead to use in the keel, to the engine specification, to the order of laying up the layers of the fiberglass hull laminate. The drafting board, once the heart of the design process, has given way to the more versatile (and more accurate) computer.

But that example, analyzing the drag associated with waves made by a sailboat traveling through water is only one of many complex situations that wait to be solved. We don't know everything about sailboats and we never will. What are the slamming loads on the bottom of a hull when sailing through steep ocean waves? Do winglets on rudders actually work—what kind of motion do they actually see?

Part of the romance of the yacht has always been the unknown. The discussion of the art of yacht design has traditionally referred to the seat-of-the-pants aspect of the task, not the beauty of the boats as in a "work of art." As the industry moves closer to being able to design the entire boat by science, the art or quasi-science portion of the process diminishes. As this guesswork segment is reduced (I am confident it will never be eliminated), the guarantee of a successful design grows. In the eighteenth century there wasn't much hope that the latest warship would perform exactly as predicted, if there even was a prediction. Now one hopes that diligent designers, using better tools, will have a good chance of drawing a boat that will do the job.

Where does that leave the sailor and the owner? With sources of knowledge (including this book) growing in number, sailors will learn about not just the tools that designers have at their disposal, but the theory of the tools and practical examples of the solutions they have provided.

We don't expect that every sailor will either obtain all the knowledge, software, or hardware mentioned here and leap out of the cockpit to become a practicing yacht designer. There is, however, more joy to be gained in any endeavor, whether walking, bicycling, cooking, or even sailing, if one understands the underlying principles of the activity. And looking back more than 25 years, I can honestly say I have a better idea today of what an Albacore looks like, and why.

tend to lean on the wealthier "aero" industries for some of our basic research material. *Theory of Wing Sections* by Abbott and Von Doenhoff, originally published in 1949, is one such document. The behavior of foils in water is directly paralleled by foils in air. But when the entire boat begins to be considered, with its complex motion in waves and its top and bottom in different fluids, the scientific problems blossom. Because sailboats operate in air and water, their analysis when put in purely aeronautical terms becomes inadequate. The software that calculates the flow of air around a plane's fuselage can do likewise for a keel, but bring those theories near the surface of the water and watch the computer programs scratch their electronic heads. The waves that boats make in that confusing interface between air and water are unique to the boat world—planes don't make waves. So we get no help from our airplane designers, and it is left to the yacht designers to solve these particular problems with their own practical solutions.

glossary

angle of attack: the angle between a foil's centerline and its direction of motion. Also called the *angle of incidence* or (in yachting) *leeway angle*. (See Figs. 2.1, 2.2.)

aspect ratio: the ratio of an object's span (or height) to its average length. For odd-shaped objects the aspect ratio can be calculated by dividing the span squared by the area. Keels, rudders, and sails are often described as being "high aspect" or "low aspect." In keel design, a foil's *aerodynamic aspect ratio* is critical when determining its efficiency. (See Figs. 2.4, 2.5, 2.6.)

beam: the width of the boat. Informally, it usually denotes the maximum width, not necessarily at the deck level. Formally, this is referred to as *maximum beam (Bmax). Waterline beam* may also be referred to, with maximum value either implied by the term or specified.

body plan: the fore-and-aft view of the hull in the lines drawing, which shows the hull "split" down the middle, with the stern view on the left and the bow view on the right. Also called the *section* or *station view*. (See page 18.)

bustle: an enlargement of the hull in front of the rudder that increases hull volume aft and with it the effective sailing length. (See Fig. 1.3.)

buttock lines: vertical fore-and-aft slices through the hull lines used to describe the hull shape. Each buttock line is labeled according to its distance from the centerline. (See page 21.)

center of buoyancy: the center of water's supporting force of the hull, which shifts away from the centerline as the boat heels. The force always acts directly upward. It is used in calculating righting moment and trim. (See Fig. 3.2.)

center of gravity: the center of gravitational force acting on the boat. The force always acts directly downward. It is used in calculating righting moment. *Ballast center of gravity* may also be referred to; its location affects the overall center of gravity. (See Fig. 3.2.)

center of lift: The position of the center of lift force generated by a foil. Sometimes called the *center of effort.* This book uses the term in conjunction with the keel and rudder, but it can also be applied to sails or wings.

center of sail force: The center of total lift forces generated by the sails. It may also be called the *center of effort,* and can be defined as either *geometric* or *aerodynamic.* (See Fig. 6.4.)

chine: a sharply delineated edge in the sectional shape of a hull, sometimes the result of simplified construction techniques, but often used to promote planing in high-speed designs. (See Fig. 1.16.)

chord: the length of a keel, rudder, or sail foil, measured in the direction of flow. It is typically defined at a foil's root, tip, and midspan.

coefficient: in yacht design, a mathematical expression used to compare different shapes or performance

chine, body plan

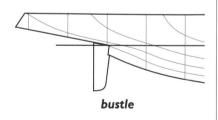

bustle

criteria, such as lift and drag. Many coefficients are dimensionless to permit direct comparisons of different-size objects. *See also: prismatic coefficient.*

displacement: the amount of water displaced by a floating hull. It is equal to the hull volume below the waterline. Displacement may be expressed in cubic feet or meters (e.g., salt water, 128 cu ft), or as the weight of the displaced fluid (e.g., 8,200 lbs). If volume is used, then the fluid type, salt water or fresh water, must be specified. (See page 55.)

draft: the vertical distance from the waterline to the yacht's deepest point, usually the bottom of the keel.

drag: a measurement of impediment to a yacht's progress or to a lift-generating object's efficiency. There are three kinds of drag in yacht design: *parasitic, induced,* and *wavemaking.* Parasitic drag has two components: *frictional* and *form. Frictional drag* results from the interaction between air or water and the surface of an object, and is directly related to total surface area and its smoothness. *Form drag* refers to the difficulty a particular object has moving through air or water and is the product of an object's overall bulk and bluntness. *Induced drag* is a by-product of the lift force generated by a foil, such as a sail, rudder, or keel, and is influenced by the foil's aspect ratio. (See Fig. 2.3.) *Wavemaking drag* is directly related to the energy used by the hull in generating waves on the surface of the water. (See Figs. 1.2, 1.7.)

effective sailing length: sometimes referred to simply as *sailing length* or *effective length,* it is the actual length of the waterline plane, adjusted by factors that account for the fullness of the ends of the boat. The effective sailing length is used in estimating a boat's potential speed.

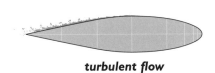

turbulent flow

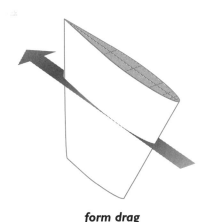

form drag

flow, laminar and turbulent: refers to the behavior of air or water as it moves along an object. *Laminar flow* is smooth, with minimum frictional drag. *Turbulent flow* is confused and greatly increases frictional drag. (See Fig. 2.10.)

flow separation: occurs at the aft end of a bluff sailing hull, or behind a foil at a large angle of attack (incidence). Refers to either air or water that does not remain attached to the surface but separates, usually in vortices.

fluid: a substance that can flow. Applies equally to air and water.

foil: a curved surface that is designed primarily to produce lift. Sails are thin foils that change their shape from tack to tack, while keels and rudders are thicker and are fixed in shape.

form stability: the stability imparted to a yacht by the sectional shape of the hull. (See Fig. 1.13.)

freeboard: the vertical distance from the waterline to the deck.

Froude number: a value used to calculate the "corresponding speeds" of a full-size design and a scale towing model so that their wavemaking patterns are identical. (See Chapter 9.)

heeling moment: also called *overturning moment.* This product of the sail force times a lever arm causes a yacht to heel. (See Fig. 1.11.)

hull speed: the theoretical maximum speed of a hull, as determined by its waterline length. (See Fig. 1.2.)

IACC: International America's Cup Class. Current America's Cup design rule, introduced for the 1992 match.

IMS: International Measurement System. A rating system based on a detailed computer performance prediction of the hull, sails, keel, and rudder, rather than point measurements.

IOR: International Offshore Rule. The prevailing rating system for keelboat racing in the 1970s. Used for both handicapping and level rating. Based on point measurements, it encouraged distortions in hull shapes to improve ratings.

International Rule: Measurement rule, initially Europe-based, introduced in 1906. Divided yachts into level rating classes according to a constant expressed in meters. Most popular designs were 5.5-, 6-, 8-, and 12-Meters. (See page 204.)

iterative: an analytical process employing repetition, each repetition being an *iteration*.

lateral plane: the two-dimensional underwater profile of the yacht, sometimes called the lateral plane area. (See page 108.)

length: a hull's length along the centerline is normally defined as *length overall (LOA)*. This generally refers only to the hull form, and does not incorporate such "add ons" as bowsprits or bow or stern platforms. *Length on deck (LOD)* is a measure of the horizontal surface negotiable by the crew; it too may or may not include "add ons." With a reverse-transom design, LOD is generally shorter than LOA. *See also: waterline, chord, effective sailing length.*

lever arm: the distance component of a *moment*. The longer a lever arm is, the less force is required to produce a particular moment.

lift: a force generated by a fluid flowing past an object, following the law known as Bernoulli's principle. (See Fig. 2.1.)

lines drawing: a drawing incorporating three views of a hull that provides the three-dimensional information necessary for its shape to be lofted for construction. The information is contained in the stations, buttock lines, and waterlines. The lines drawing consists of the *profile (side) view, plan view,* and the *body plan.* (See page 18.)

lofting: the process of transferring a design's lines to the builder's floor at the beginning of construction.

MORC: Midget Ocean Racing Club. A rating rule used for keelboats of 30 feet or less.

metacenter: the imaginary point about which a yacht rotates as it heels. (See Figs. 1.11, 3.2.)

moment: a force times a distance, expressed accordingly, i.e., as foot-pounds. Examples: *righting moment, heeling moment, turning moment.*

prismatic coefficient: a mathematical expression used to judge the fineness of a yacht's ends. It is calculated using the immersed hull volume, waterline length, and maximum section's immersed area. (See Fig. 1.6.)

Reynolds number: numerical value used to properly scale the frictional drag experienced by a scale model. (See Chapter 9.)

prismatic coefficient

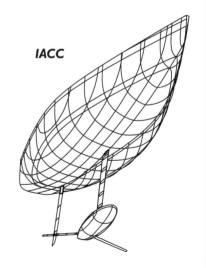

IACC

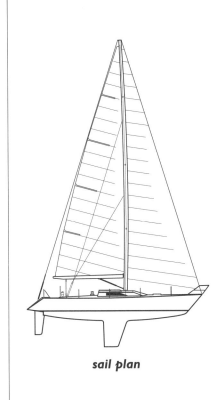

sail plan

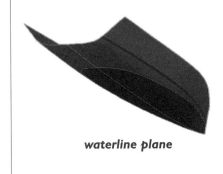

waterline plane

righting moment: a measure of the tendency of a yacht to return to upright when heeled. It is a product of the distance between the centers of gravity and buoyancy and the total weight of the yacht. (See Figs. 1.11, 3.3.)

root: the structural base of a foil—in yacht design the portion of the keel or rudder next to the hull. The *root chord* is the chord length of the keel or rudder at the root.

sailing length: *see effective sailing length*

sail plan: the profile view of a yacht's sail configuration. For purposes of calculating sail force and stability, it often does not include downwind sails such as the spinnaker. The term also refers to the profile drawing, which shows the hull (not necessarily below the waterline), rig, and sails.

Seawanhaka Rule: an extremely simple late-nineteenth-century measurement rule that took into account only sail area and waterline length, making it easy for designers to exploit. (See Fig. 1.13.)

section: a cross-sectional shape of an object; in hulls, called a *station*.

station: one of a series of equally spaced transverse "slices" of the hull shape, as specified in the lines drawing. (See page 19.)

Thames Rule: an English measurement rule in use from 1855 to 1887, which produced the classic narrow shape of racing cutters of the day. The rule's method of rating yachts by their cargo-carrying capacity encouraged blunt bows, long stern overhangs, and poor stability. (See Fig. 1.9.)

tip: the portion of a wing, rudder, or keel not bounded by the hull or fuselage. In the case of a keel, it is the bottom of the keel.

Universal Rule: measurement rule initially devised by N. G. Herreshoff in 1903, incorporating length, sail area, and displacement; used in North America. It produced yachts similar in concept to the International Rule, with alphabetical level rating classes such as P, R, and J. (See page 204.)

VPP: Velocity Prediction Program. Computer software that generates performance data from its analysis of a particular design. The results can be presented numerically or graphically. (See Chapter 8.)

vortex: a spiraling shaft of fluid often attached to the tip of a keel or rudder as it produces lift. Vortices cause drag, and their elimination is one of the reasons for installing wings on the bottom of keels. (See pages 67, 69.)

waterline: in the lines drawing, the *design waterline (DWL)* is measured from station 0 to 10. The *load waterline (LWL)* is the length along the centerline of the hull at the level of the water and often includes the skeg and sometimes the rudder. (See pages 20, 27.)

waterline plane: the two-dimensional shape of the hull where it is "sliced" along the load waterline. This plane changes with heel and fore-and-aft trim. (See Fig. 1.4.)

wetted surface: the total surface area of the immersed hull. Wetted surface of the rudder and the lift-generating foil (keel, centerboard, or daggerboard) may also be included, or considered separately. (See Figs. 1.4, 1.17.)

conversion factors and values

Weight
1 kilogram = 2.2046 pounds; 9.80 newtons
1 pound = 0.4536 kilogram; 4.448 newtons
1 ton (short) = 2,000 pounds; 907.18 kilograms
1 ton (long) = 2,240 pounds; 35 cubic feet seawater
1 tonne (metric) = 1,000 kilograms; 2,204.6 pounds

Length
1 mile (statute or land) = 0.8685 nautical mile; 5,280 feet; 1.6093 kilometers; 1,609.3 meters
1 mile (nautical) = 1.1515 statute miles; 6,080 feet; 1,853.1 meters; 1.8531 kilometers
1 kilometer = 0.6214 mile; 0.5397 nautical mile
1 centimeter = 0.0328 foot; 0.3937 inch
1 meter = 3.2808 feet
1 inch = 2.54 centimeters
1 foot = 0.3048 meter

Velocity
1 knot (1 nautical mile/hour) = 1.6888 feet/second; 1.1515 miles/hour; 1.8531 kilometers/hour; 0.5148 meter/second
1 mile/hour = 0.8684 knot; 1.4666 feet/second; 1.6093 kilometers/hour; 0.4471 meter/second
1 kilometer/hour = 0.5396 knot; 0.9113 foot/second; 0.6214 mile/hour; 0.2778 meter/second
1 meter/second = 1.9425 knots; 3.2808 feet/second; 2.2368 miles/hour; 3.6 kilometers/hour
1 foot/second = 0.5921 knot; 0.6818 mile/hour; 1.0973 kilometers/hour; 0.3048 meter/second

Volume
1 cubic foot = 7.4805 US gallons; 6.2305 Imp. gallons; 28.3161 liters
1 liter = 0.2642 US gallon, 0.2200 Imp. gallon; 0.0353 cubic foot
1 cubic meter = 35.3147 cubic feet; 264.17 US gallons; 219.65 Imp. gallons
1 gallon (US) = 0.1337 cubic foot; 0.8327 Imp. gallon; 0.003785 cubic meter; 3.785306 liters; (3.78 kilograms/8.34 pounds fresh water)
1 gallon (Imperial) = 0.1605 cubic foot; 1.2009 US gallons; 0.004546 cubic meter; 4.546 liters; 4.55 kilograms/10.02 pounds fresh water; 3.06 kilograms/6.74 pounds gasoline)

Density
Air (@15°C) = 0.0766 pound/cubic foot; 1.227 kilograms/cubic meter
Water (fresh) = 62.4 pounds/cubic foot; 1,000 kilograms/cubic meter; 1 gram/cubic centimeter
Water (salt) = 64 pounds/cubic foot; 1,025 kilograms/cubic meter

Sample values
For a 30-foot object traveling at 6 knots in fresh water
Speed-length ratio: 1.10
Reynolds number: 2.47×10^7
Froude number: 0.33

Viscosity (at 15°C)
Fresh water = 1.23×10^{-5} ft^2/sec
Air = 1.57×10^{-4} ft^2/sec

bibliography

The following titles are from the authors' personal libraries and were used as references during the creation of this book.

Aero-Hydrodynamics of Sailing, by C. A. Marchaj. Dodd, Mead & Co., 1979

Against the Odds: The Incredible Story of Evergreen *and the Canada's Cup,* by Douglas Hunter. Personal Library, 1981

American Small Sailing Craft, by Howard I. Chapelle. W.W. Norton & Co., 1951

The America's Cup 1987: The Official Record, by Bob Fisher and Bob Ross. Henry Holt and Co., 1987

America's Cup 1851–1983, by John Rousmaniere. Taylor Publishing Co., 1983

America's Cup Fever, by Bob Bavier. Ziff-Davis Publishing Co., 1981

Annals of the Royal Canadian Yacht Club 1852–1937, by C. H. J. Snider. Rous & Mann Ltd., 1937

"Antiope": *Full Scale Tank Tests of the 5.5 Meter,* by H.C. Herreshoff and J.N. Newman. Society of Naval Architects and Marine Engineers, 1967

Australia II: The Official Record, Bruce Stannard and Andy Park, Editors. Joyce Childress Management Pty. Ltd., 1984

Ben Lexcen: The Man, the Keel and the Cup, by Bruce Stannard. Faber and Faber, 1984

Best of Uffa: Immortal Designs from Uffa Fox's Five Famous Volumes, Guy Cole, Editor. Nautical Publishing Co., 1978

Bluenose and Bluenose II, by R. Keith McLaren. Hounslow Press, 1981

Bluenose II, by L. B. Jensen. Nimbus Publishing Ltd., 1994

Building Classic Small Craft, by John Gardner. International Marine Publishing Co., 1984

F. H. Chapman: The First Naval Architect and His Work, by Daniel G. Harris. Naval Institute Press, 1989

Chesapeake Sailing Yacht Symposium, by various authors. Society of Naval Architects and Marine Engineers, Proceedings 2 through 13, 1975–1997

Defending the America's Cup, by R. W. Carrick and Stanley Rosenfeld. Alfred Knopf Inc., 1969

The Encyclopedia of Ships, Chris Marshall, General Editor. Blitz Editions, 1995

The Evolving Role of the Towing Tank, by Karl L. Kirkman, Chesapeake Sailing Yacht Symposium, 1979

The Gougeon Brothers on Boat Construction, by Gougeon Brothers. Gougeon Brothers, 1985

The Grand Gesture: Ted Turner, Mariner and the America's Cup, by Roger Vaughan. Little, Brown and Co., 1975

A History of the America's Cup, by Halsey C. Herreshoff, Marine Technology, 1992

An L. Francis Herreshoff Reader, by L. Francis Herreshoff. International Marine Publishing Co., 1978

Merchant Sailing Ships 1850–1875, by David R. MacGregor. Naval Institute Press, 1984

One Hundred Years and Still Sailing, by Harry L. Penny. Royal Hamilton Yacht Club, 1988

Piloting, Seamanship and Small Boat Handling (52nd Edition), by Charles F. Chapman. The Hearst Corporation, 1976

Principles of Naval Architecture, John. P. Comstock, Editor. Society of Naval Architects and Marine Engineers, 1967

Racing for the America's Cup 1974, by Theodore A. Jones. The New York Times Book Co., 1975

Sailing Alone Around the World, by Capt. Joshua Slocum. Sheridan House, 1972 reprint

The Sailing Spirit: Meeting the BOC Challenge, by John Hughes. Seal Books, 1988

Sailing Theory and Practice, by C. A. Marchaj. Dodd, Mead & Co., 1964

Sailing Yacht Performance with Optimization, by George S. Hazen. MScNA thesis, Princeton University, 1973

Sails, by Jeremy Howard-Williams. Adlard Coles Ltd, 1967

The Search for Speed Under Sail, by Howard I. Chapelle. W.W. Norton & Co., 1967

Skene's Elements of Yacht Design (8th Edition), by Francis S. Kinney. Dodd, Mead & Co., 1973

The Southern Cross, by Hugh D. Whall. Admiralty Publishing House Ltd., 1974

Standard Mathematical Tables, Samuel M. Selby, Editor. The Chemical Rubber Co., 1969

Theory of Wing Sections, by I. H. Abbott and A. E. Von Doenhoff. Dover Publications, 1949

Traditions and Memories of American Yachting, by William P. Stephens. International Marine Publishing Co., 1981

Trials: Canada 1 and the 1983 America's Cup, by Jeff Boyd and Douglas Hunter. Macmillan of Canada, 1984

Uffa Fox, by June Dixon. Angus and Robertson Ltd., 1978

Wooden Ship, by Peter Spectre and David Larkin. Houghton Mifflin Co., 1991

You Are First: The Story of Olin and Rod Stephens, by Francis. S. Kinney. Dodd, Mead and Co.,1978

index

Reference appearances are cited in text as page numbers, in Figures as Figure numbers, and in photos and illustrations with italicized page numbers. For individual yachts and classes, see the Yacht Index on pages 255–56. References listed in the Glossary have the page number noted with *def.*

yacht index

yacht index

credits

PHOTOGRAPHY

Sharon Green, 15, 22, 32, 47, 57, 62, 89, 90, 93, 101, 107, 118, 128, 131, 134, 141, 142, 144, 146, 150, 160, 174, 176, 179, 204, 212, 217, 225, 230
Steve Killing, 12, 23, 49, 54, 126, 155, 183, 184, 188, 191, 192, 194, 199, 201, 208 (bottom), 214, 219, 220, 222, 234, 235, 237, 238, 240, 241, 242, 243, 244
Margaret Killing, 246
Douglas Hunter, 152, 157, 158, 208 (top)
The Royal Canadian Yacht Club, 38, 43, 161
PDQ Yachts, 168
Center for Marine Dynamics, St. John's, Newfoundland, 197
Margherita Bottini for The Hinckley Company, 46

ILLUSTRATIONS

• All illustrations unless otherwise credited are the work of the authors.
• Lines drawings and other illustrations of yachts have been developed from Steve Killing's own designs, and in the cases of the Mazza III International 14, C&C 35, and PDQ 36, from plans provided to him by their designers. Illustrations of other yachts have been developed with the aid of published drawings, photographic evidence, and a trained eye.
• Drawings of the Star, Lightning, and Thunderbird classes are based on official plans. The Albacore lines on page 159 were created with input from licensed builder Ontario Yachts.
• The Fredrik Chapman portrait on page 186 was graciously provided by Daniel G. Harris.

PRODUCTION NOTES

• Interior design and assembly by Douglas Hunter
• Image scanning by the authors
• All illustrations produced by the authors were the end result of a battery of computer design tools. Steve Killing employed the programs FastShip and Corel Draw; Douglas Hunter used the programs Adobe Illustrator and PhotoShop. Many illustrations are a compendium of creative work in all four programs.
• Page layout was executed in Quark XPress, employing the fonts Adobe Garamond for body text, and Univers and Gill San for display text.